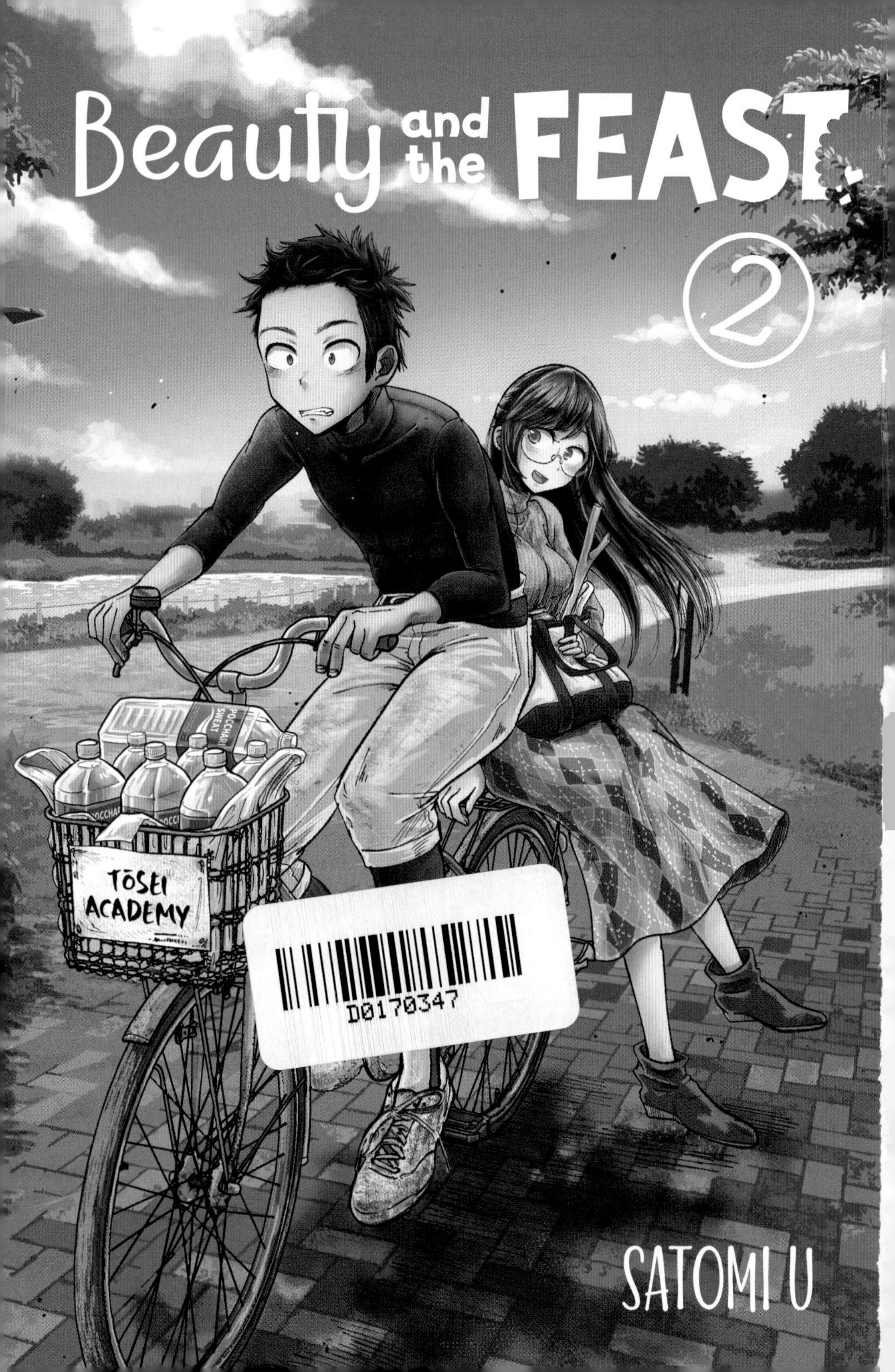
Beauty and the FEAST
2
POCCHARI SWEAT
TŌSEI ACADEMY
SATOMI U

contents & characters

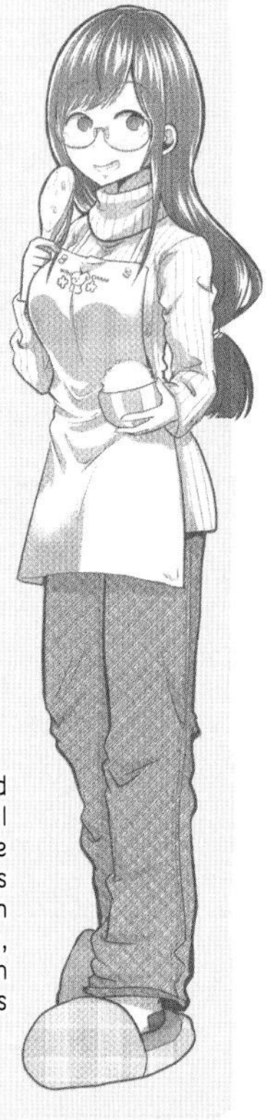

SHUKO YAKUMO

Shuko is 28 years old. Her hobby is cooking. Every night, she secretly feeds Yamato, the high school boy next door. Her husband passed away some years ago.

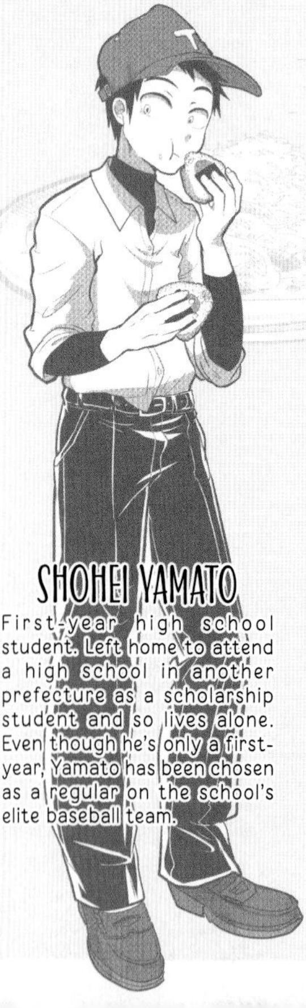

SHOHEI YAMATO

First-year high school student. Left home to attend a high school in another prefecture as a scholarship student and so lives alone. Even though he's only a first-year, Yamato has been chosen as a regular on the school's elite baseball team.

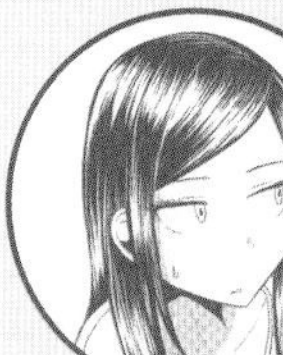

RITSUKO NAGAI

Rui's friend. She doesn't especially like baseball but always hangs out with Rui and is thus recruited to help cheer on their high school baseball team.

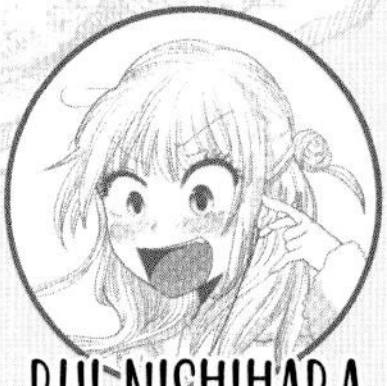

RUI NISHIHARA

Yamato's childhood friend and classmate. Baseball fanatic. She has a huge crush on Yamato, who was a player of some renown back in their hometown, but he has turned down her romantic overtures every time.

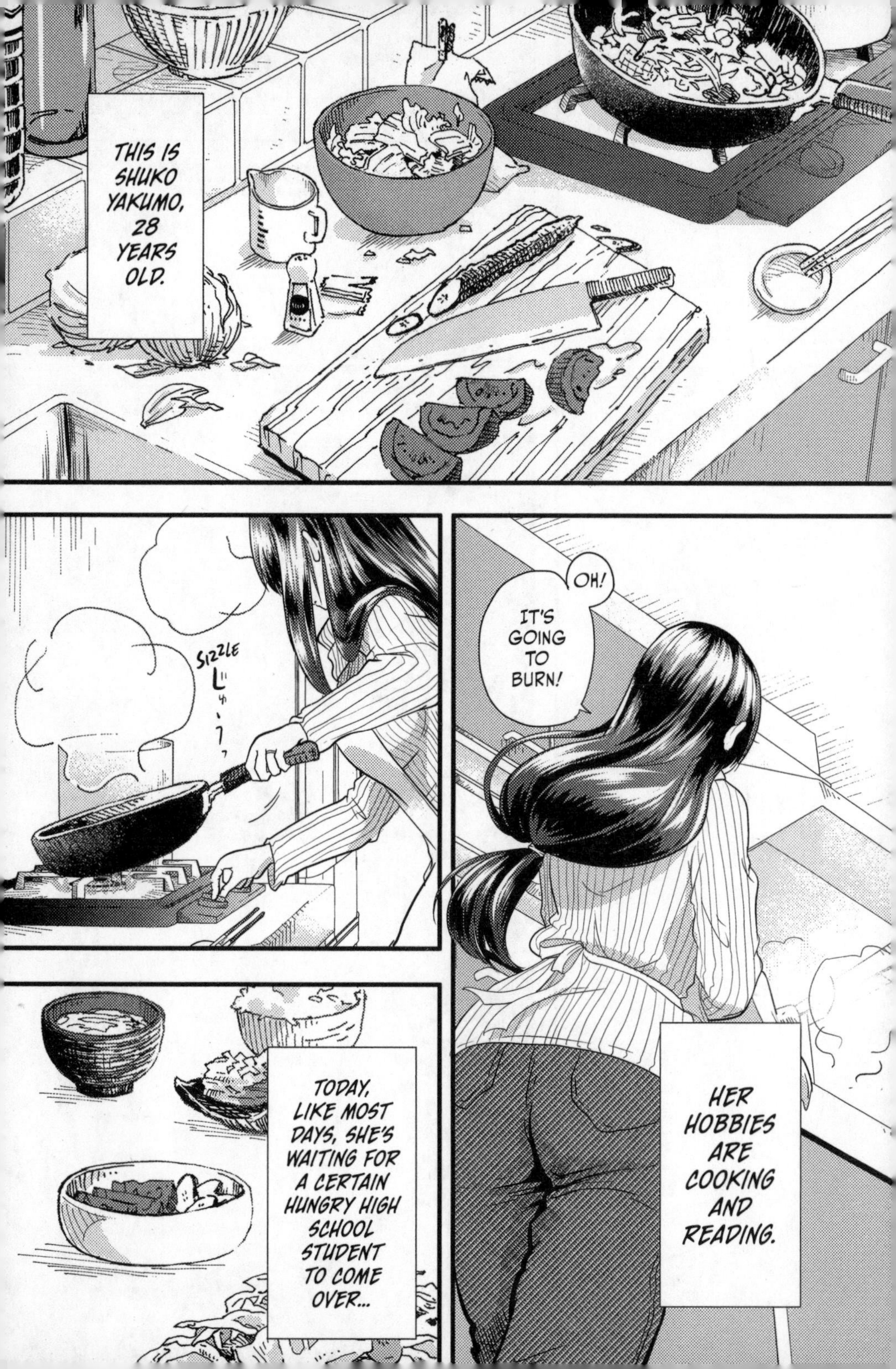
THIS IS SHUKO YAKUMO, 28 YEARS OLD.
OH!
IT'S GOING TO BURN!
HER HOBBIES ARE COOKING AND READING.
SIZZLE
TODAY, LIKE MOST DAYS, SHE'S WAITING FOR A CERTAIN HUNGRY HIGH SCHOOL STUDENT TO COME OVER...

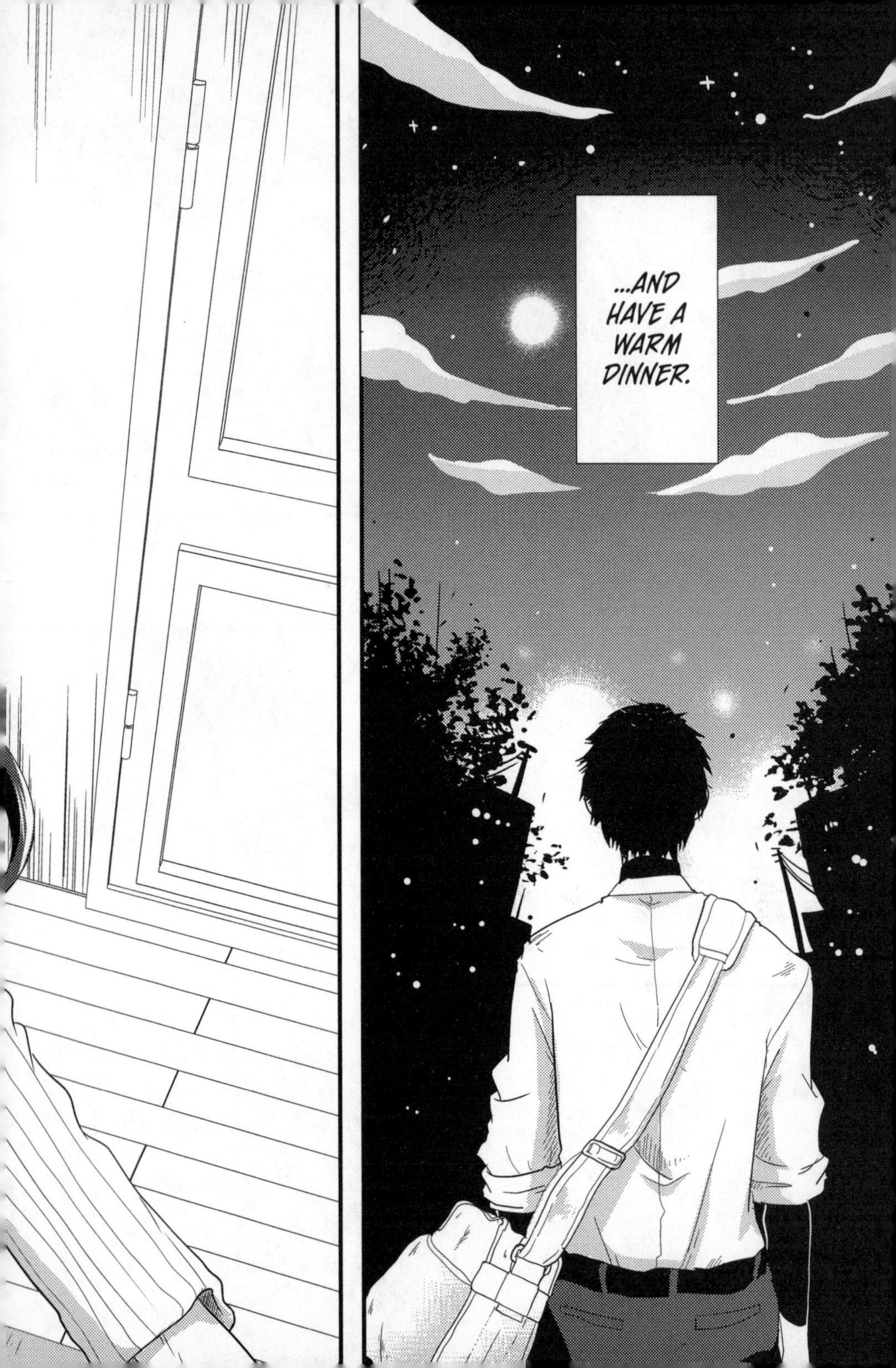
...AND HAVE A WARM DINNER.

Meal 8: The Supreme Side Dish

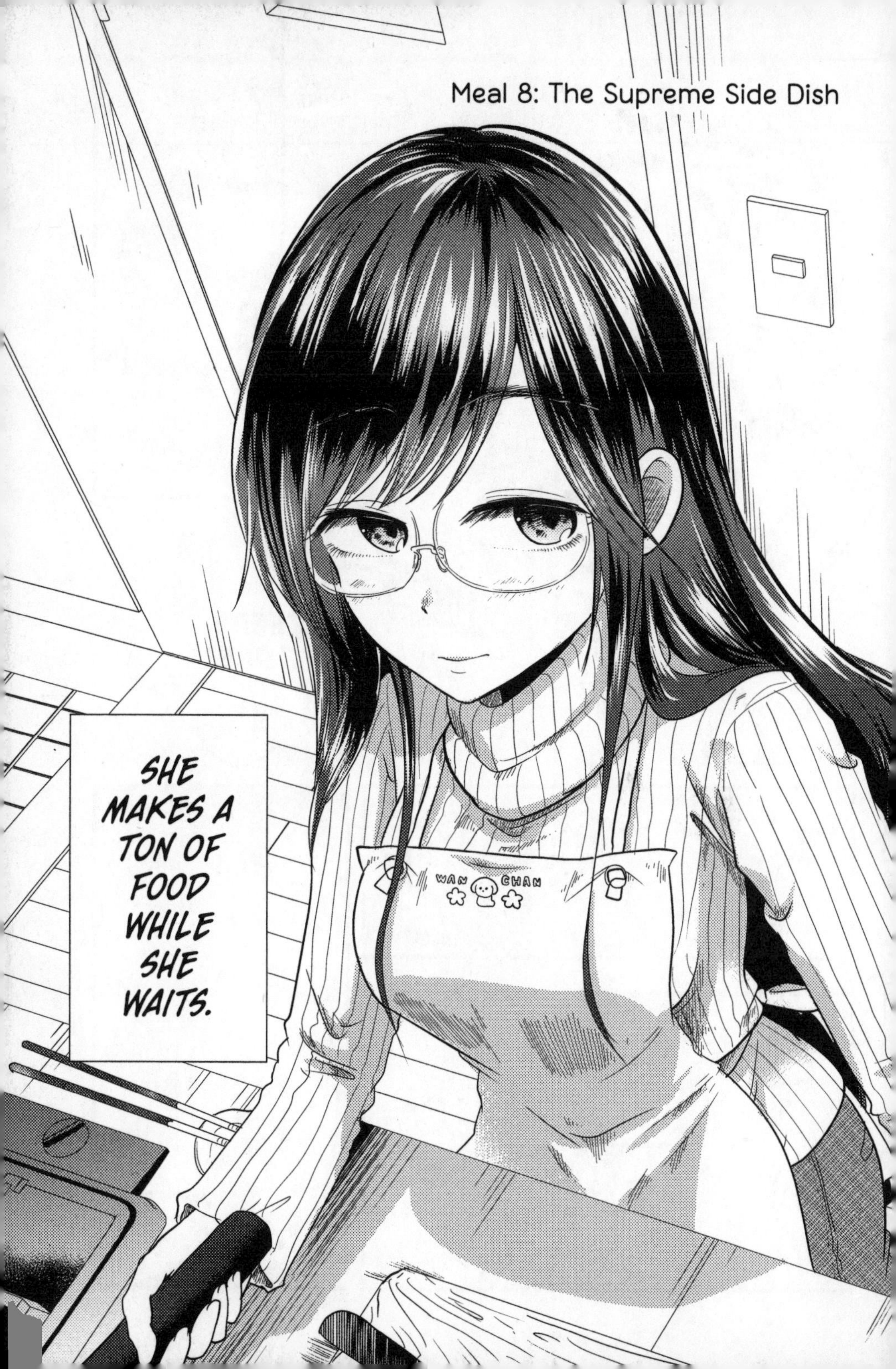
SHE MAKES A TON OF FOOD WHILE SHE WAITS.
WAN CHAN

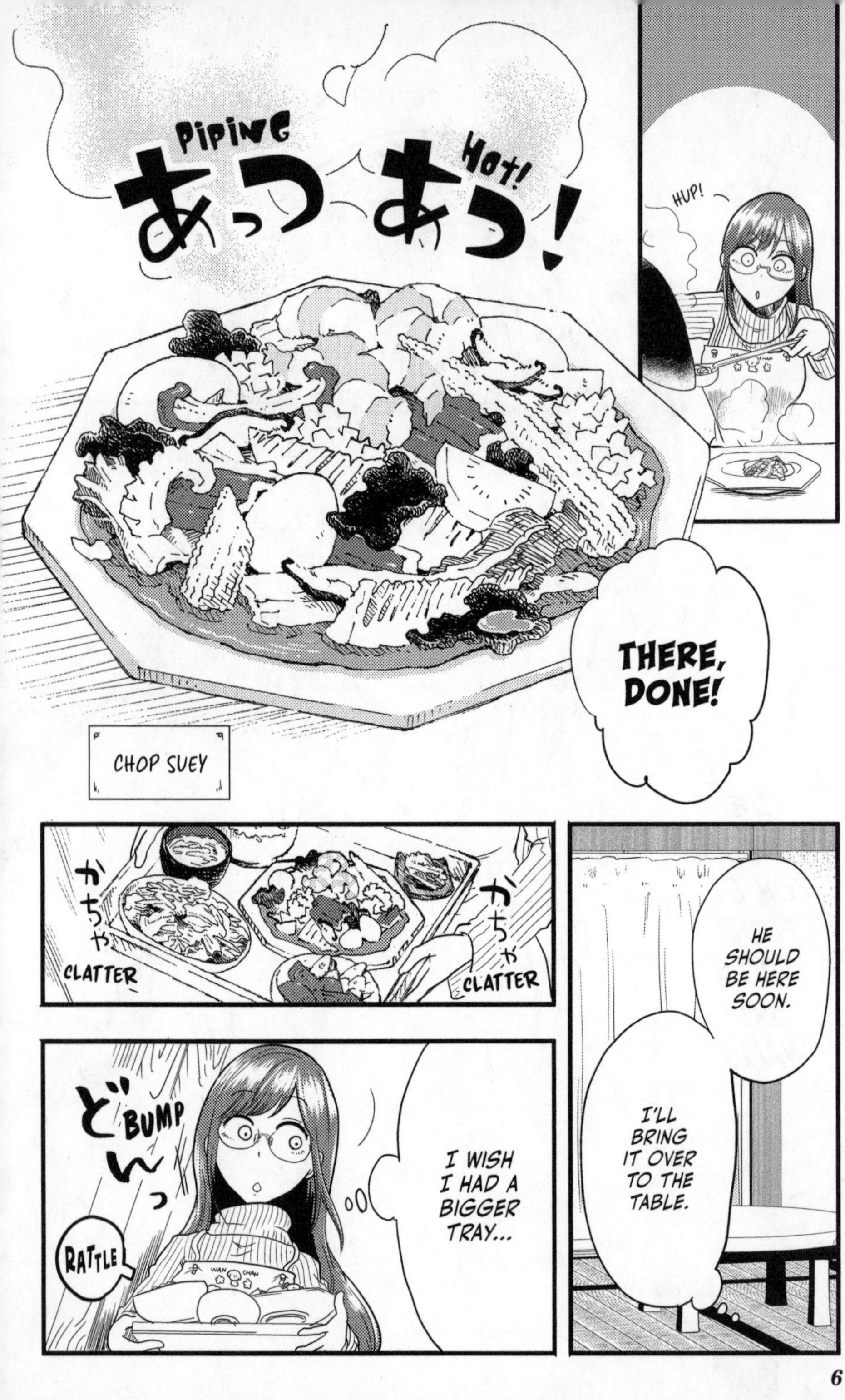
HUP!
PIPING HOT!
あつあつ!
THERE, DONE!
CHOP SUEY
HE SHOULD BE HERE SOON.
I'LL BRING IT OVER TO THE TABLE.
かちゃ
CLATTER
かちゃ
CLATTER
どんっ
BUMP
RATTLE
I WISH I HAD A BIGGER TRAY...

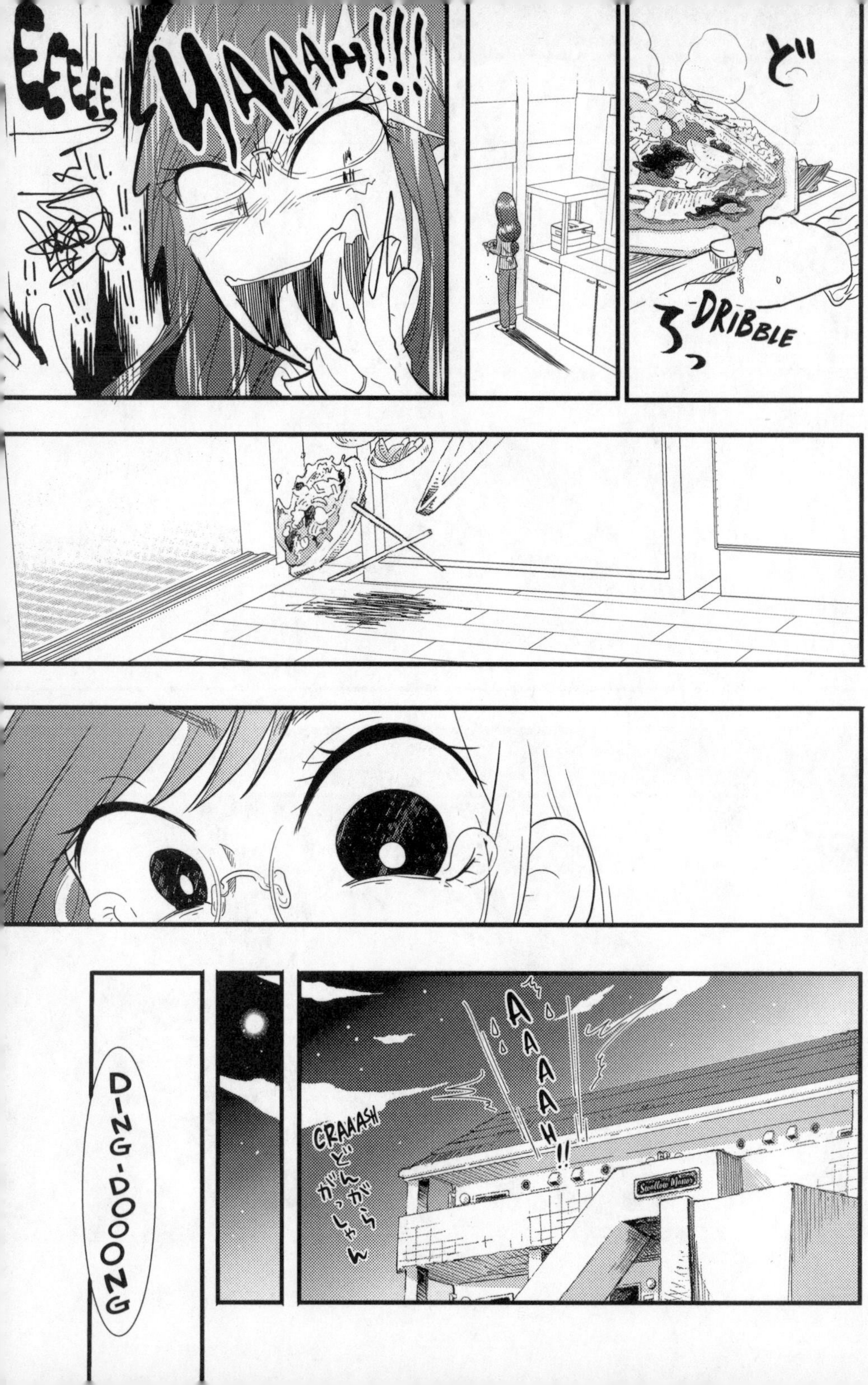
ど
DRIBBLE
EEEEEE
YAAAH!!!
AAAAAH!!
CRAAASH
どんがらがっしゃん
DING-DOOOONG

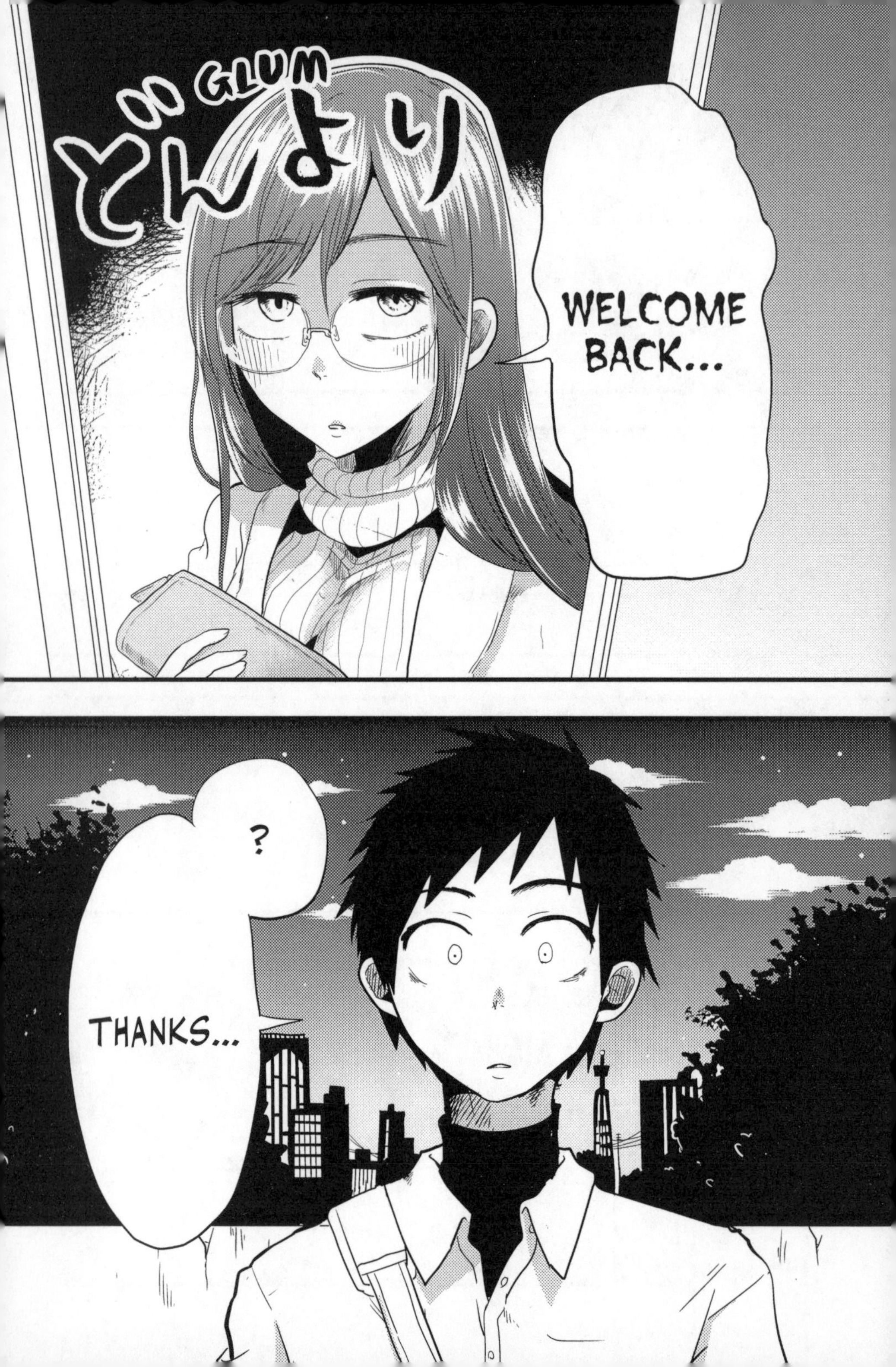
GLUM
どんより
WELCOME BACK...
?
THANKS...

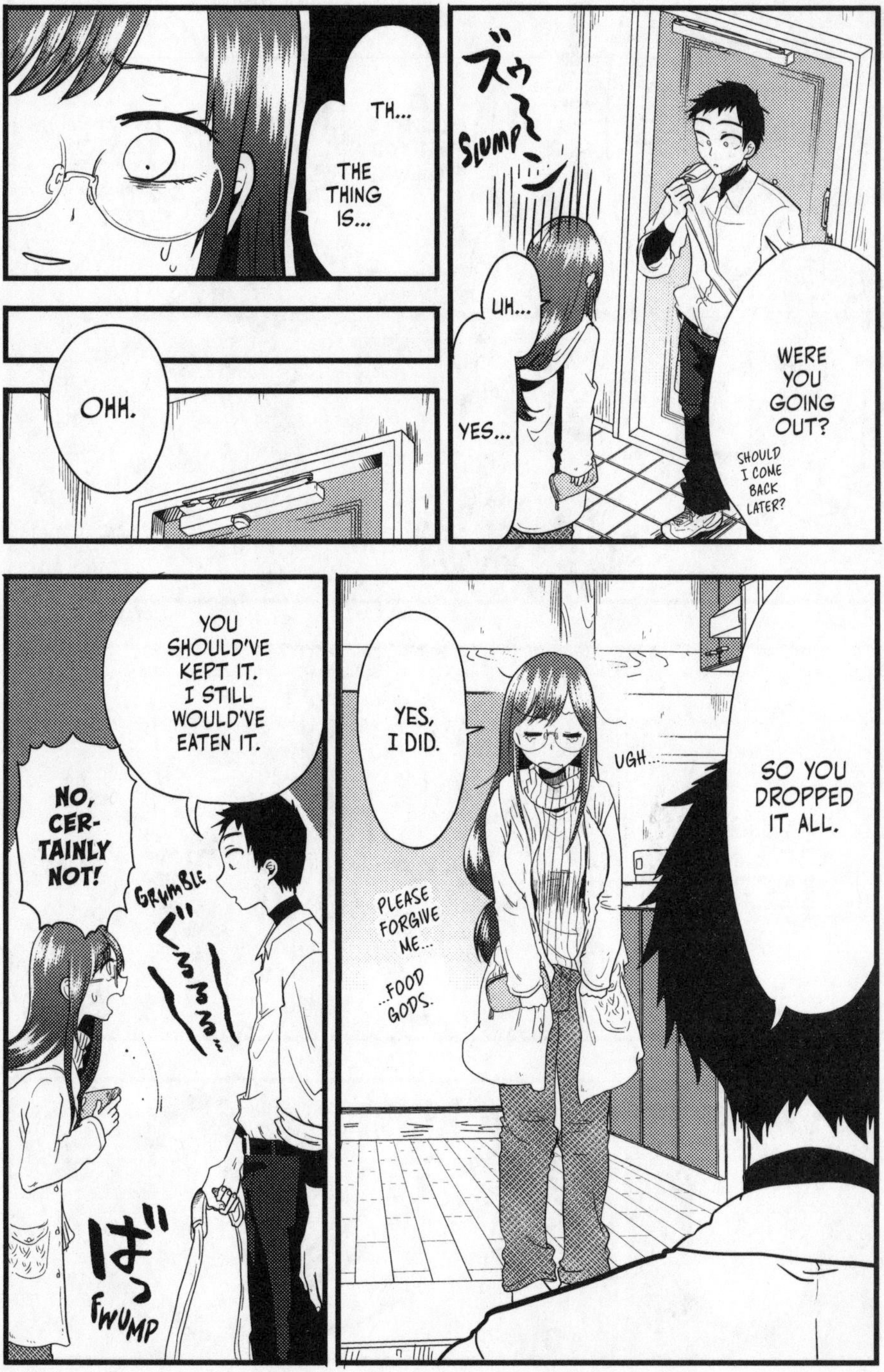
ズゥ～
SLUMP
WERE YOU GOING OUT?
SHOULD I COME BACK LATER?
UH...
YES...
TH...
THE THING IS...
OHH.
SO YOU DROPPED IT ALL.
UGH...
YES, I DID.
PLEASE FORGIVE ME...
...FOOD GODS.
YOU SHOULD'VE KEPT IT. I STILL WOULD'VE EATEN IT.
NO, CER-TAINLY NOT!
ぐるるる
GRUMBLE
ばっ
FWUMP

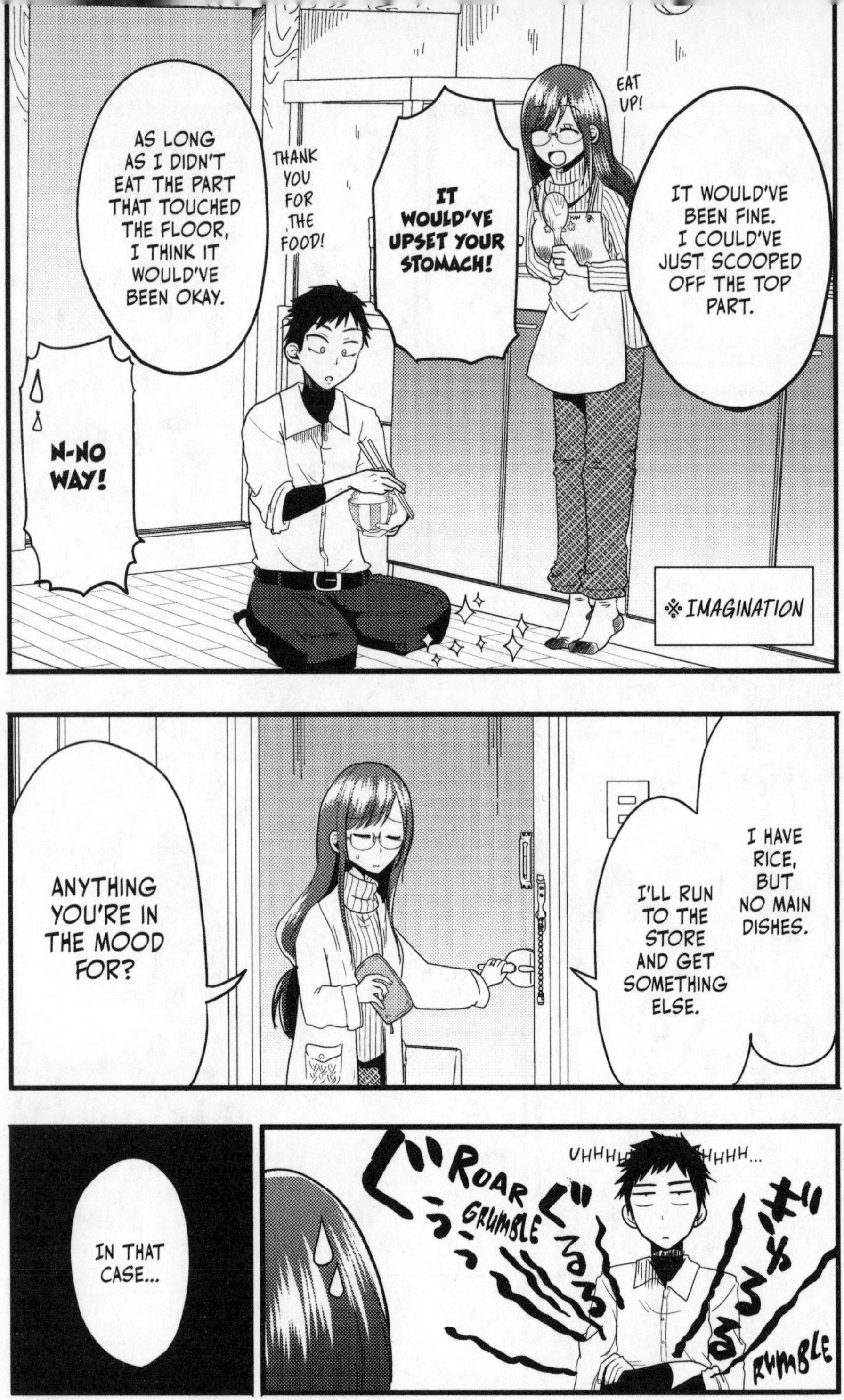
EAT UP!
IT WOULD'VE BEEN FINE. I COULD'VE JUST SCOOPED OFF THE TOP PART.
IT WOULD'VE UPSET YOUR STOMACH!
THANK YOU FOR THE FOOD!
AS LONG AS I DIDN'T EAT THE PART THAT TOUCHED THE FLOOR, I THINK IT WOULD'VE BEEN OKAY.
N-NO WAY!
※IMAGINATION
I HAVE RICE, BUT NO MAIN DISHES.
I'LL RUN TO THE STORE AND GET SOMETHING ELSE.
ANYTHING YOU'RE IN THE MOOD FOR?
HHHH...
RUMBLE
ROAR
GRUMBLE
IN THAT CASE...

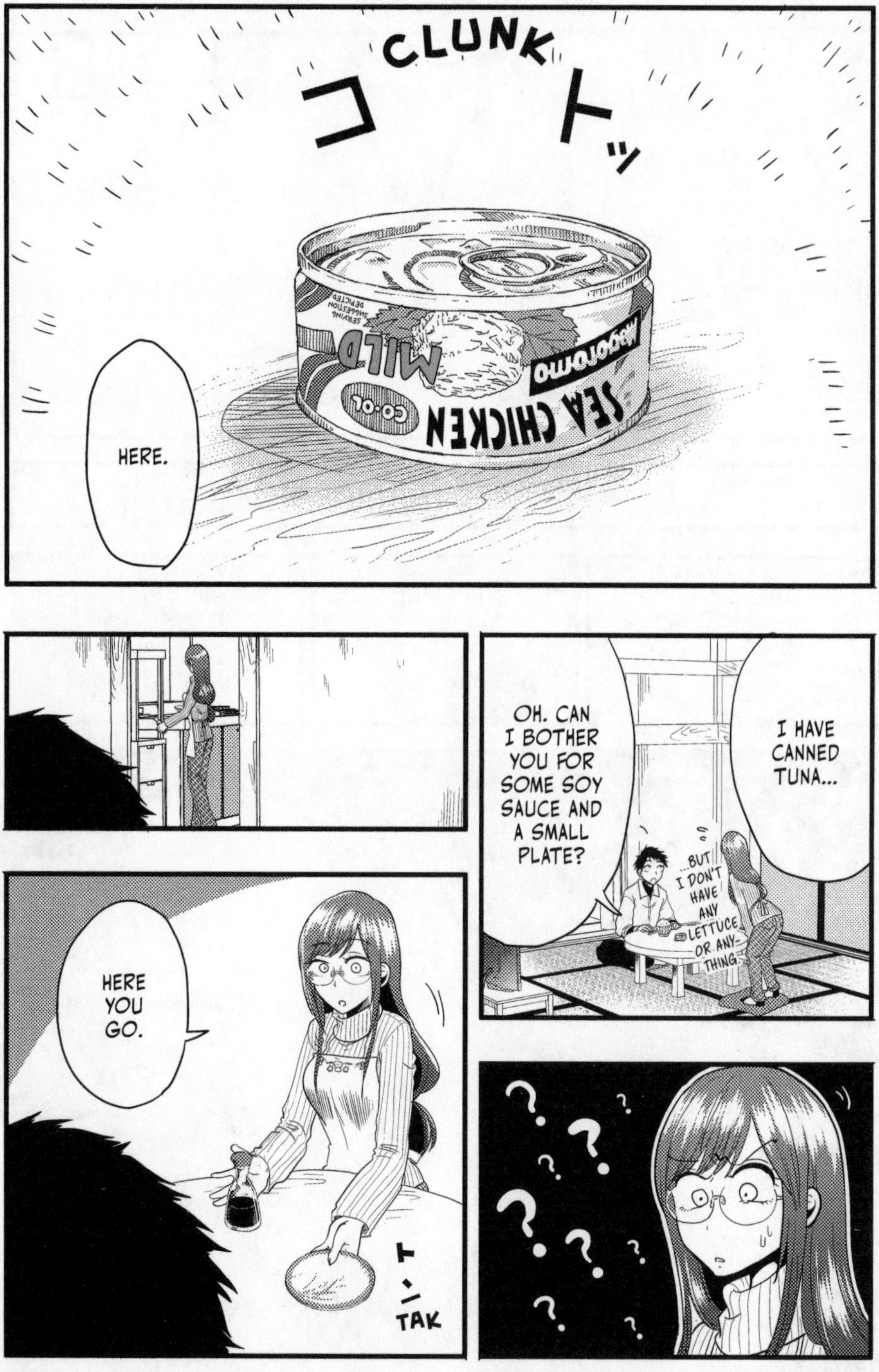
CLUNK
コトッ
SEA CHICKEN
MILD
HERE.
I HAVE CANNED TUNA...
...BUT I DON'T HAVE ANY LETTUCE OR ANYTHING.
OH. CAN I BOTHER YOU FOR SOME SOY SAUCE AND A SMALL PLATE?
HERE YOU GO.
トン
TAK

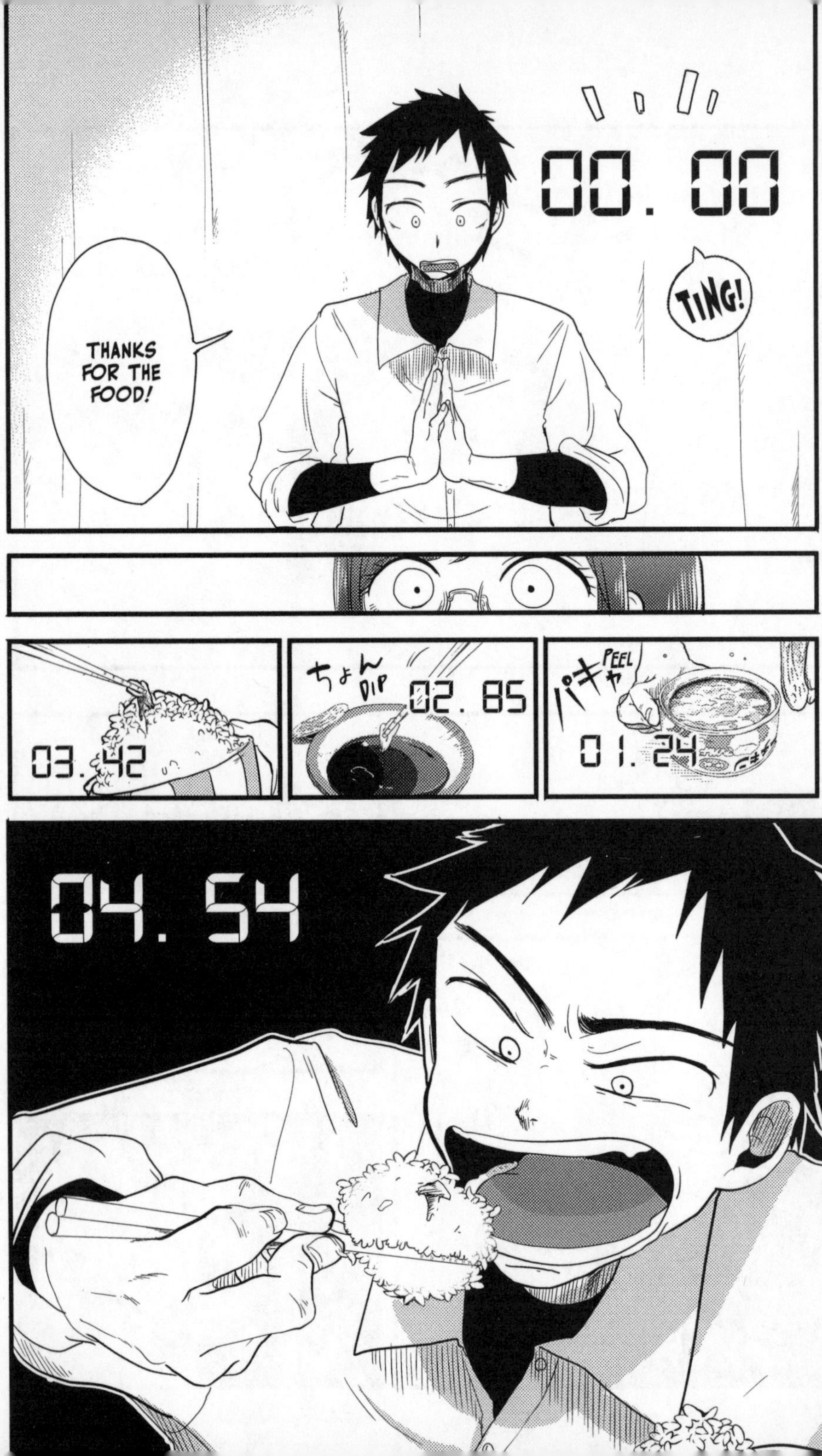
00.00
TING!
THANKS FOR THE FOOD!
パキャ
PEEL
01.24
ちょん
DIP
02.85
03.42
04.54

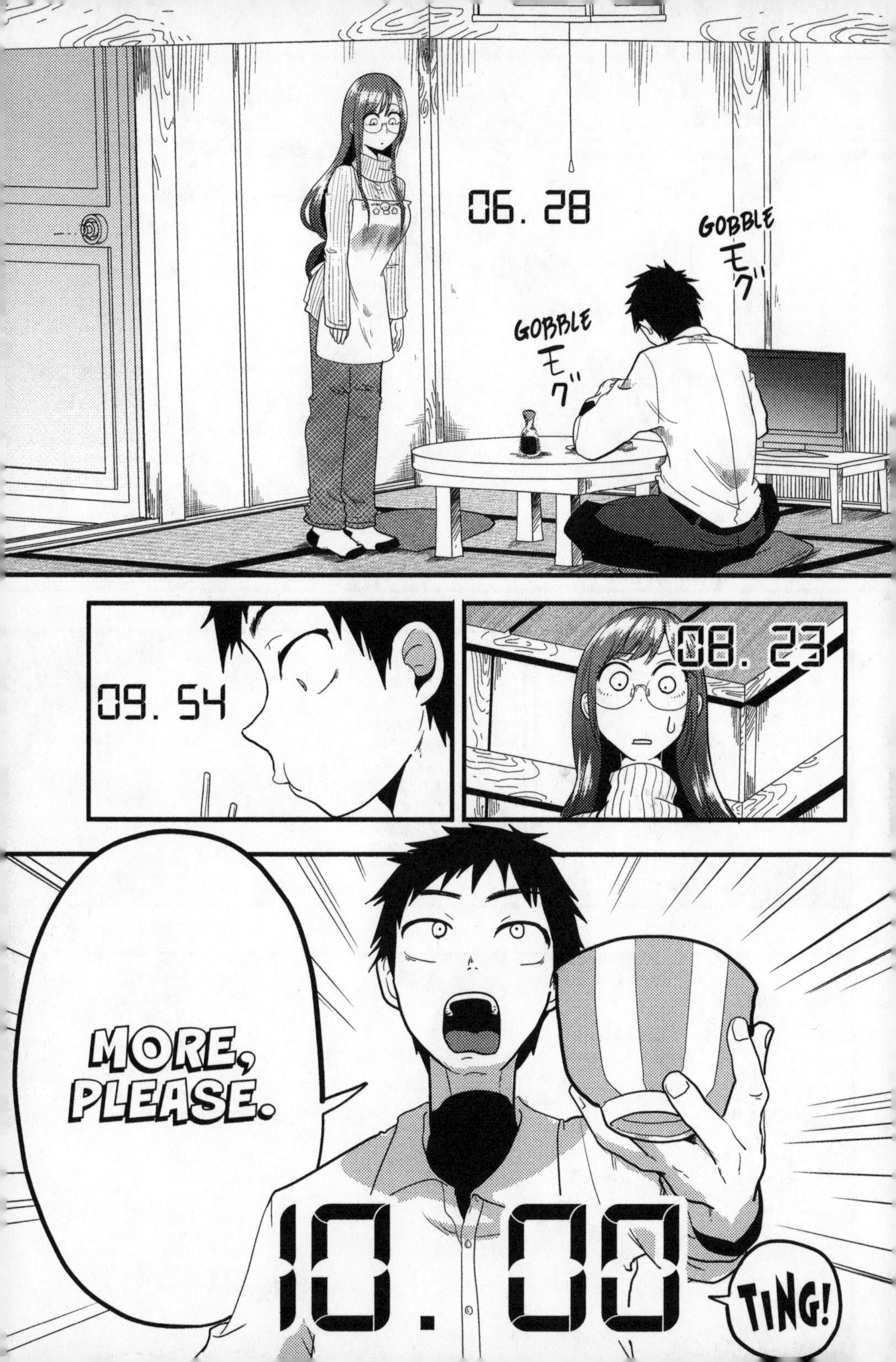
GOBBLE
モグ
06. 28
GOBBLE
モグ
08. 23
09. 54
MORE, PLEASE.
10. 00
TING!

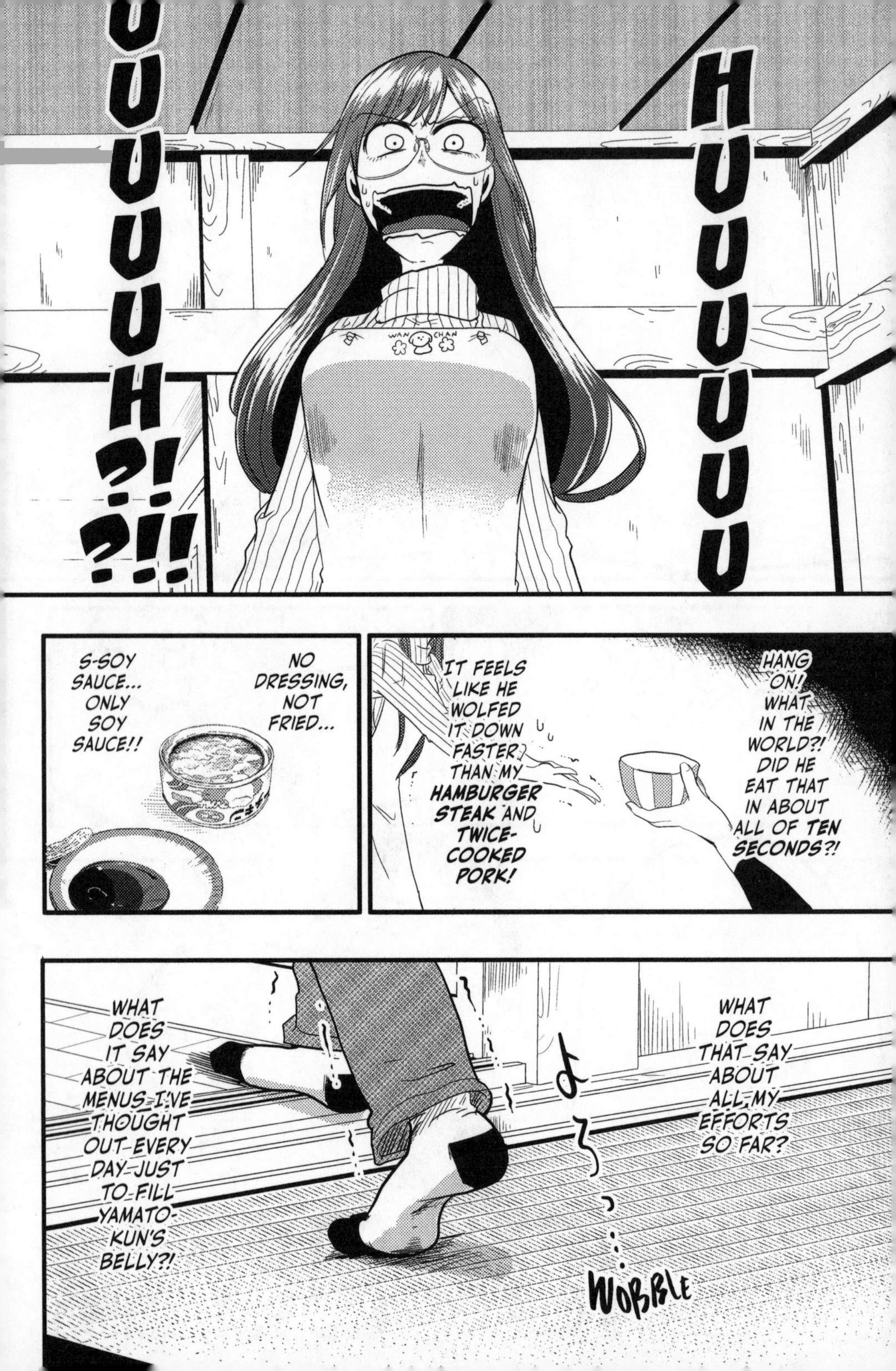
HUUUUUUUUU
UUUUUUUH?!?!!
WAN CHAN
HANG ON! WHAT IN THE WORLD?! DID HE EAT THAT IN ABOUT ALL OF TEN SECONDS?!
IT FEELS LIKE HE WOLFED IT DOWN FASTER THAN MY HAMBURGER STEAK AND TWICE-COOKED PORK!
NO DRESSING, NOT FRIED...
S-SOY SAUCE... ONLY SOY SAUCE!!
WHAT DOES THAT SAY ABOUT ALL MY EFFORTS SO FAR?
WOBBLE
WHAT DOES IT SAY ABOUT THE MENUS I'VE THOUGHT OUT EVERY DAY JUST TO FILL YAMATO-KUN'S BELLY?!

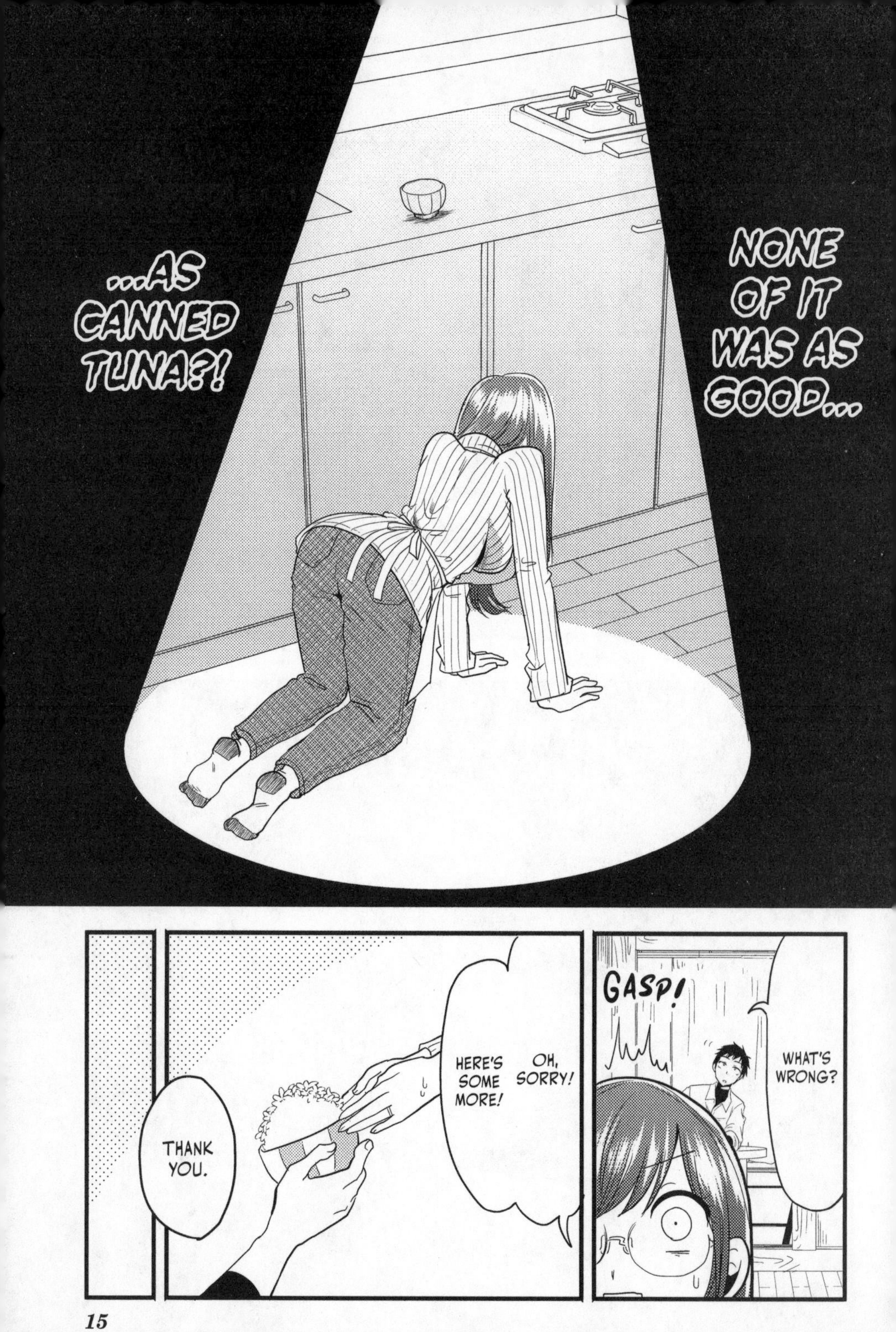
NONE OF IT WAS AS GOOD...
...AS CANNED TUNA?!
WHAT'S WRONG?
GASP!
OH, SORRY!
HERE'S SOME MORE!
THANK YOU.

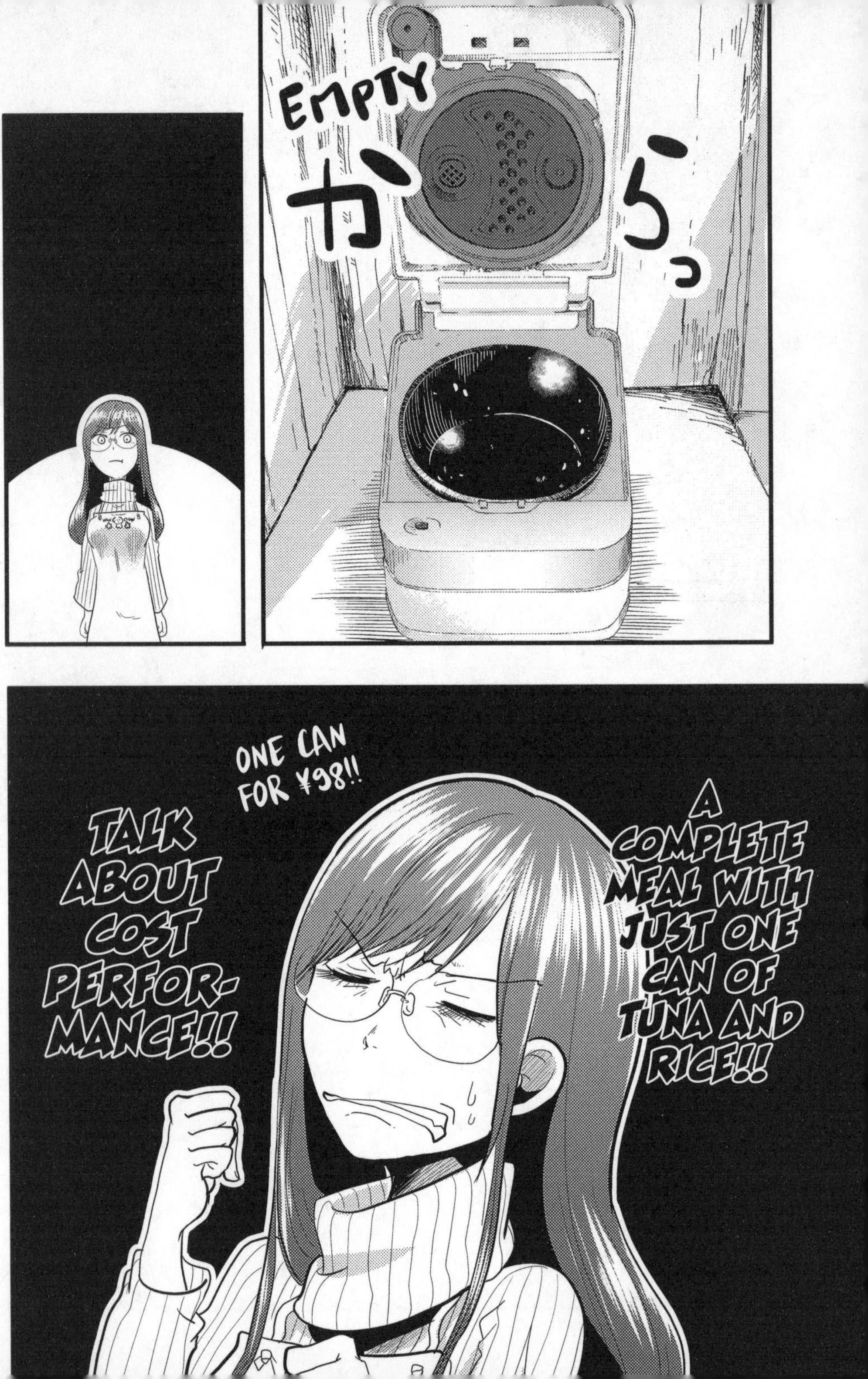
EMPTY
からっ
A COMPLETE MEAL WITH JUST ONE CAN OF TUNA AND RICE!!
ONE CAN FOR ¥98!!
TALK ABOUT COST PERFORMANCE!!

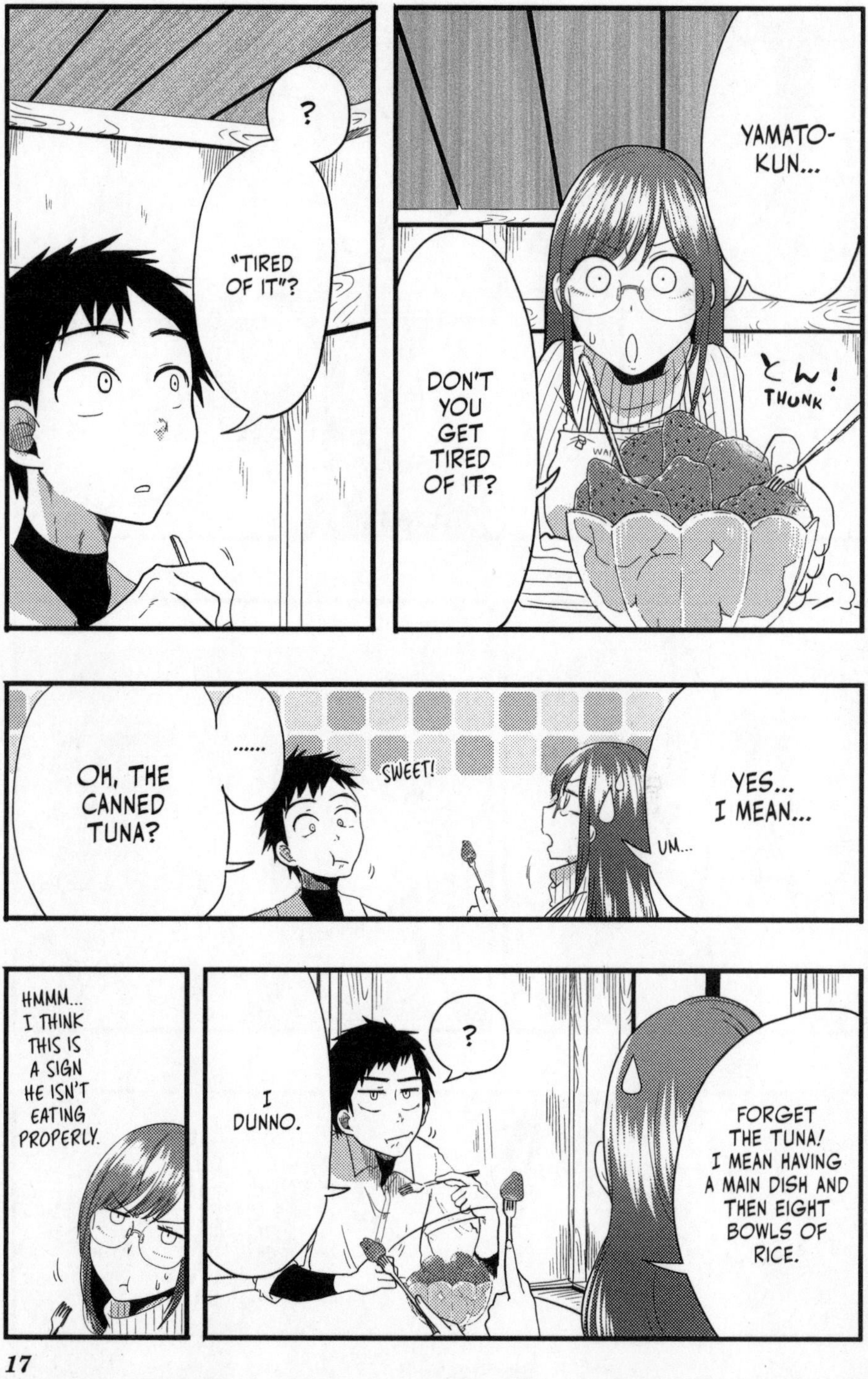
YAMATO-KUN...
とん! THUNK
DON'T YOU GET TIRED OF IT?
?
"TIRED OF IT"?
YES... I MEAN...
UM...
SWEET!
......
OH, THE CANNED TUNA?
FORGET THE TUNA! I MEAN HAVING A MAIN DISH AND THEN EIGHT BOWLS OF RICE.
?
I DUNNO.
HMMM... I THINK THIS IS A SIGN HE ISN'T EATING PROPERLY.

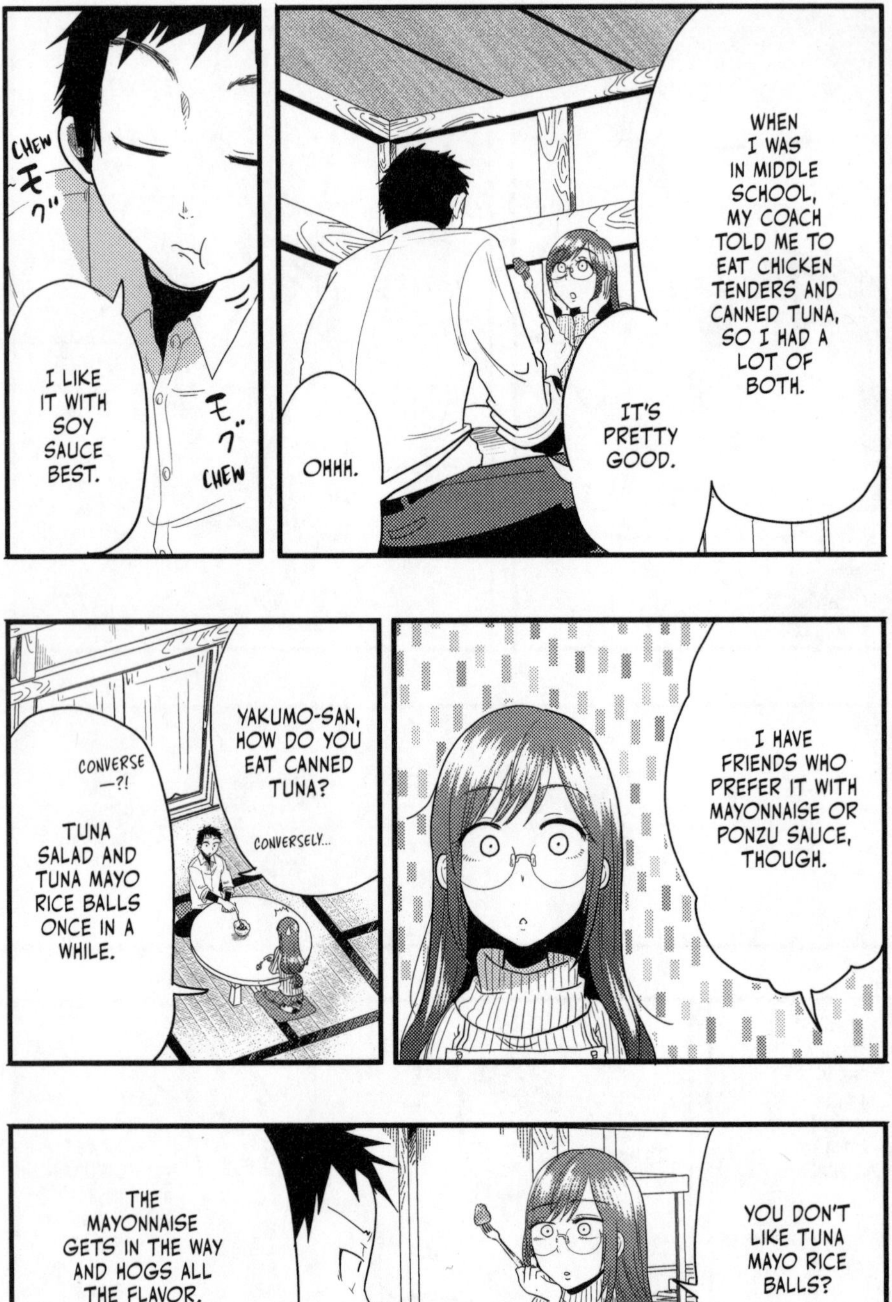
WHEN I WAS IN MIDDLE SCHOOL, MY COACH TOLD ME TO EAT CHICKEN TENDERS AND CANNED TUNA, SO I HAD A LOT OF BOTH.
IT'S PRETTY GOOD.
OHHH.
CHEW モグ
I LIKE IT WITH SOY SAUCE BEST.
モグ CHEW
I HAVE FRIENDS WHO PREFER IT WITH MAYONNAISE OR PONZU SAUCE, THOUGH.
YAKUMO-SAN, HOW DO YOU EAT CANNED TUNA?
CONVERSELY...
CONVERSE—?!
TUNA SALAD AND TUNA MAYO RICE BALLS ONCE IN A WHILE.
YOU DON'T LIKE TUNA MAYO RICE BALLS?
THE MAYONNAISE GETS IN THE WAY AND HOGS ALL THE FLAVOR.

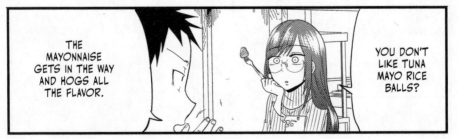

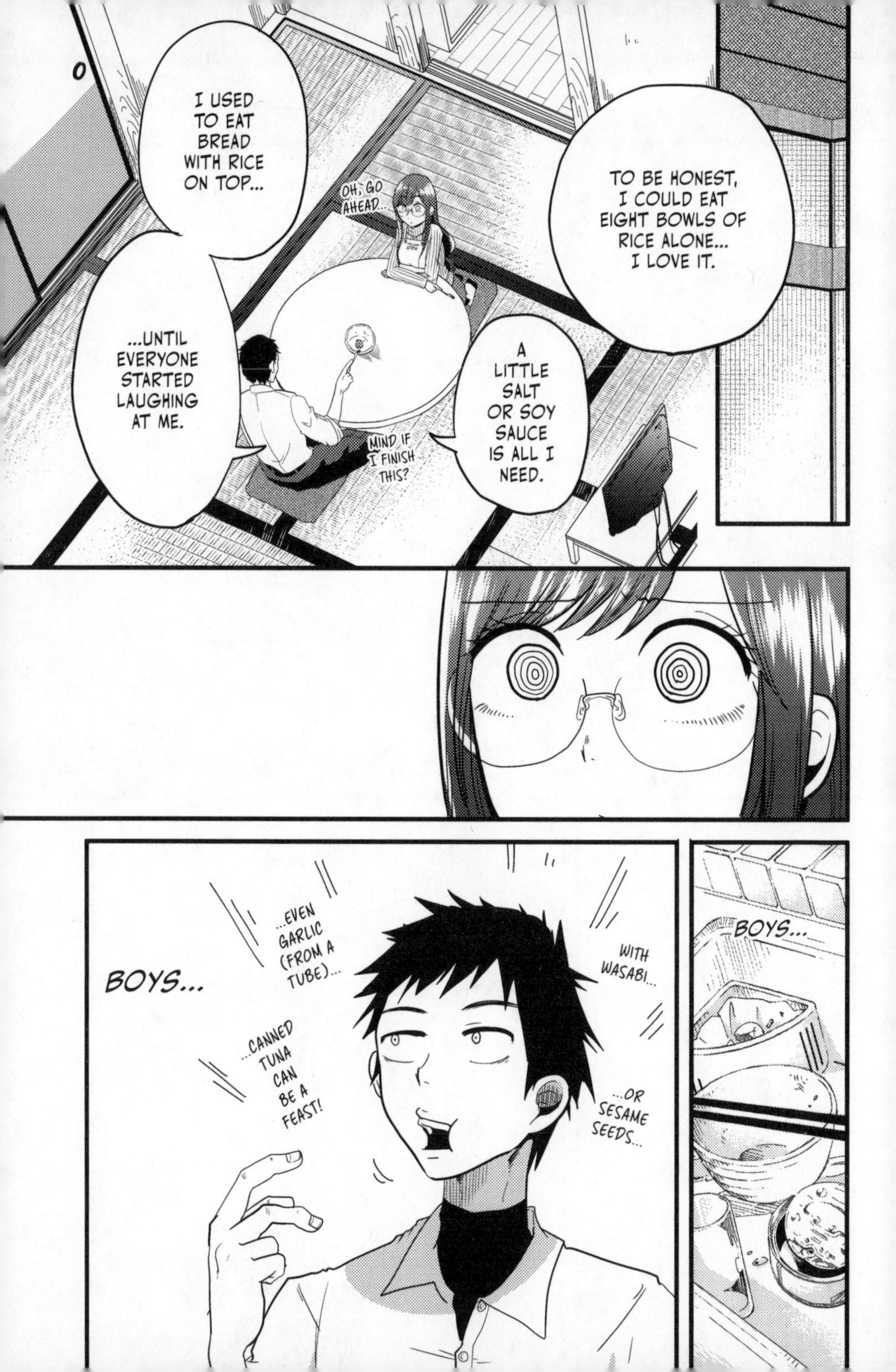
TO BE HONEST, I COULD EAT EIGHT BOWLS OF RICE ALONE... I LOVE IT.
A LITTLE SALT OR SOY SAUCE IS ALL I NEED.
MIND IF I FINISH THIS?
OH, GO AHEAD...
I USED TO EAT BREAD WITH RICE ON TOP...
...UNTIL EVERYONE STARTED LAUGHING AT ME.
BOYS...
WITH WASABI...
...OR SESAME SEEDS...
...EVEN GARLIC (FROM A TUBE)...
...CANNED TUNA CAN BE A FEAST!
BOYS...

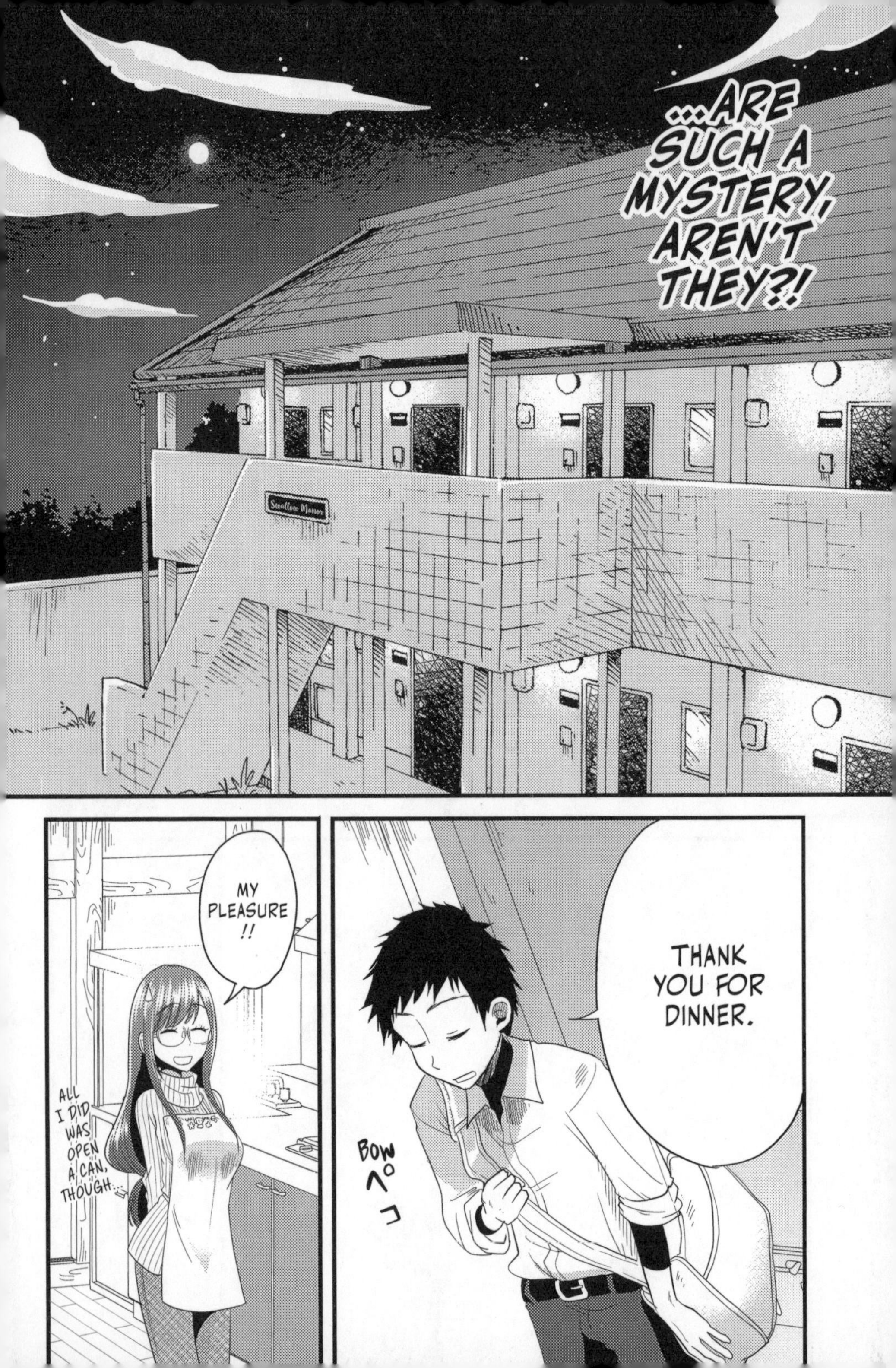
...ARE SUCH A MYSTERY, AREN'T THEY?!
Swallow Manor
THANK YOU FOR DINNER.
BOW ペコ
MY PLEASURE!!
ALL I DID WAS OPEN A CAN, THOUGH...

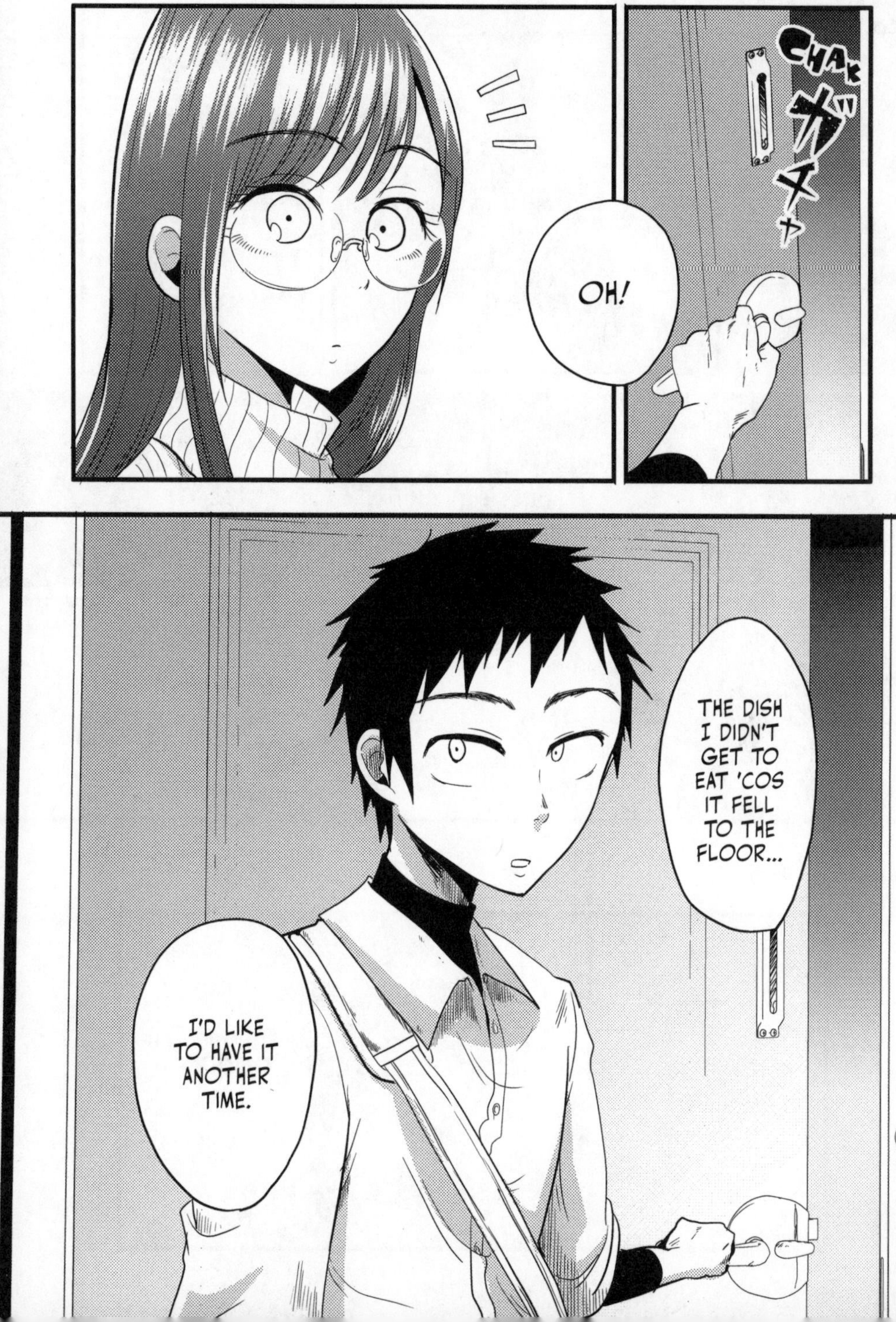
CHAK
ガチャ
OH!
THE DISH I DIDN'T GET TO EAT 'COS IT FELL TO THE FLOOR...
I'D LIKE TO HAVE IT ANOTHER TIME.

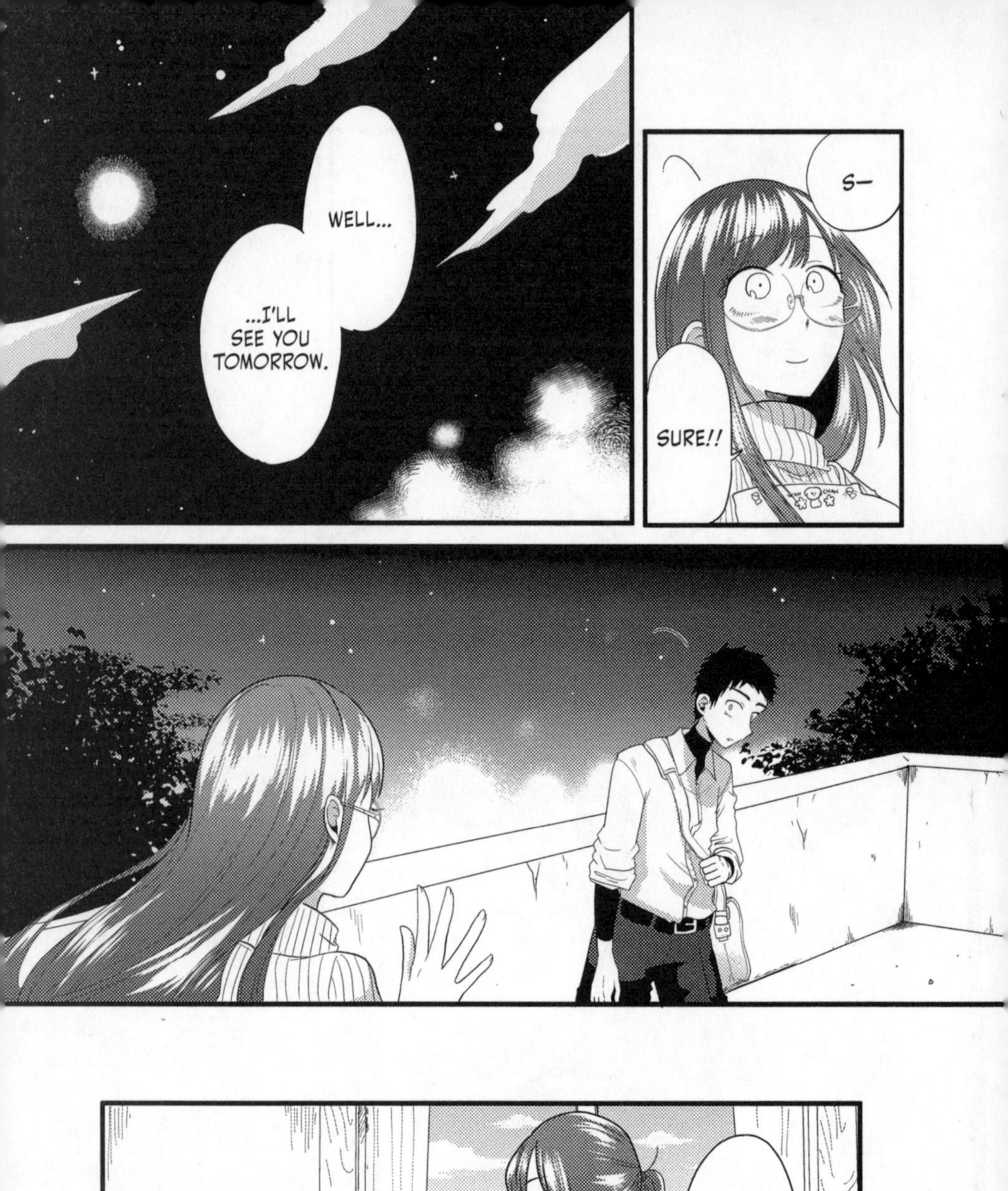
S—
SURE!!
WELL...
...I'LL SEE YOU TOMORROW.
THIS IS GOOD!
MUNCH
モグ…
SHE GOT HOOKED.

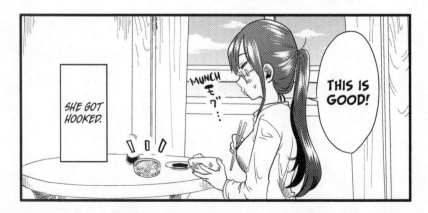

Beauty and the FEAST.

Beauty and the FEAST

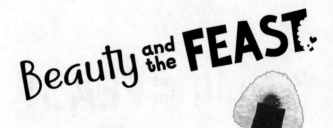

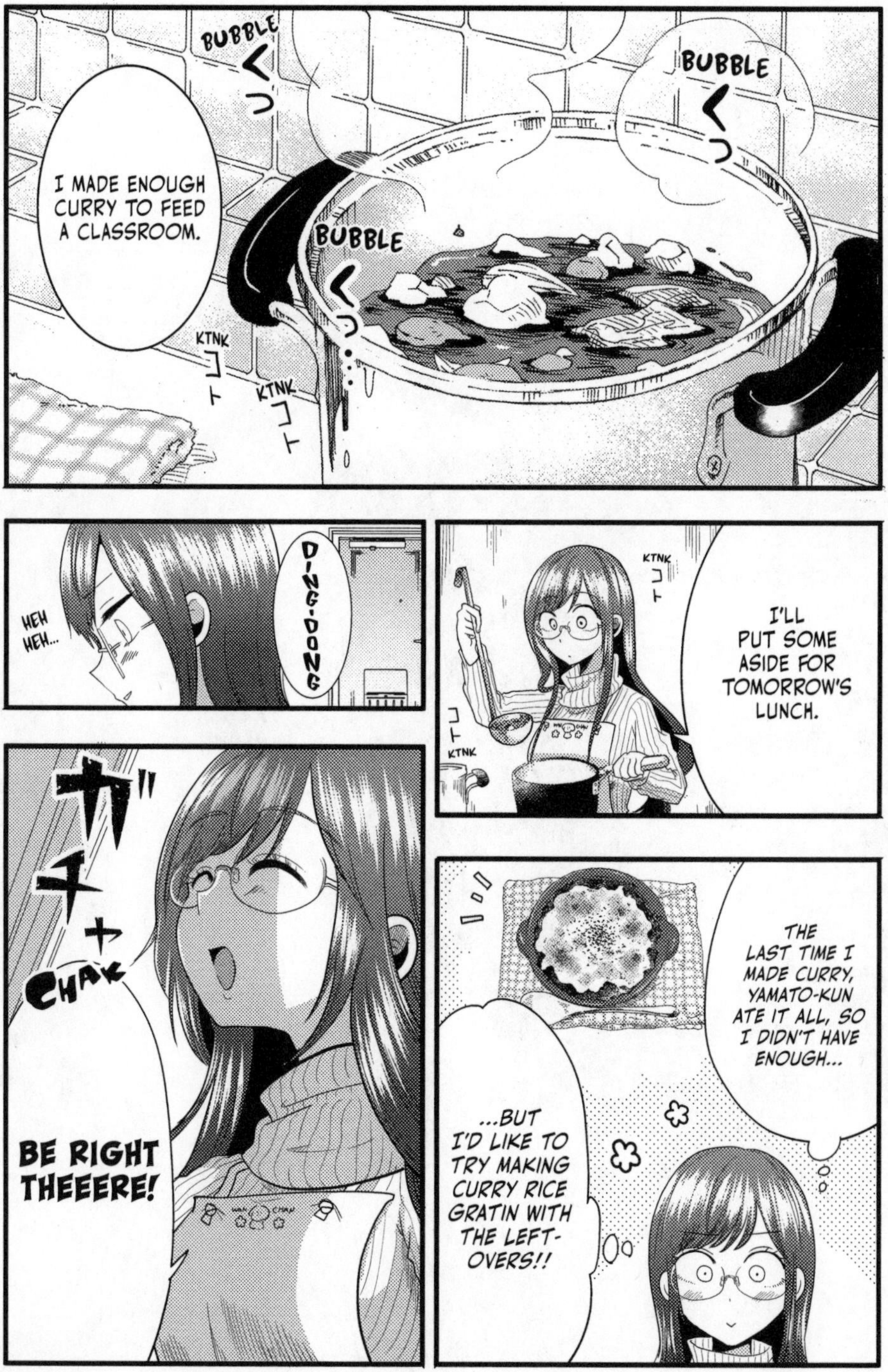
BUBBLE
BUBBLE
I MADE ENOUGH CURRY TO FEED A CLASSROOM.
BUBBLE
KTNK
KTNK
KTNK
I'LL PUT SOME ASIDE FOR TOMORROW'S LUNCH.
KTNK
THE LAST TIME I MADE CURRY, YAMATO-KUN ATE IT ALL, SO I DIDN'T HAVE ENOUGH...
...BUT I'D LIKE TO TRY MAKING CURRY RICE GRATIN WITH THE LEFT-OVERS!!
DING-DONG
HEH HEH...
CHAK
BE RIGHT THEEERE!

Meal 9: What I Can Do

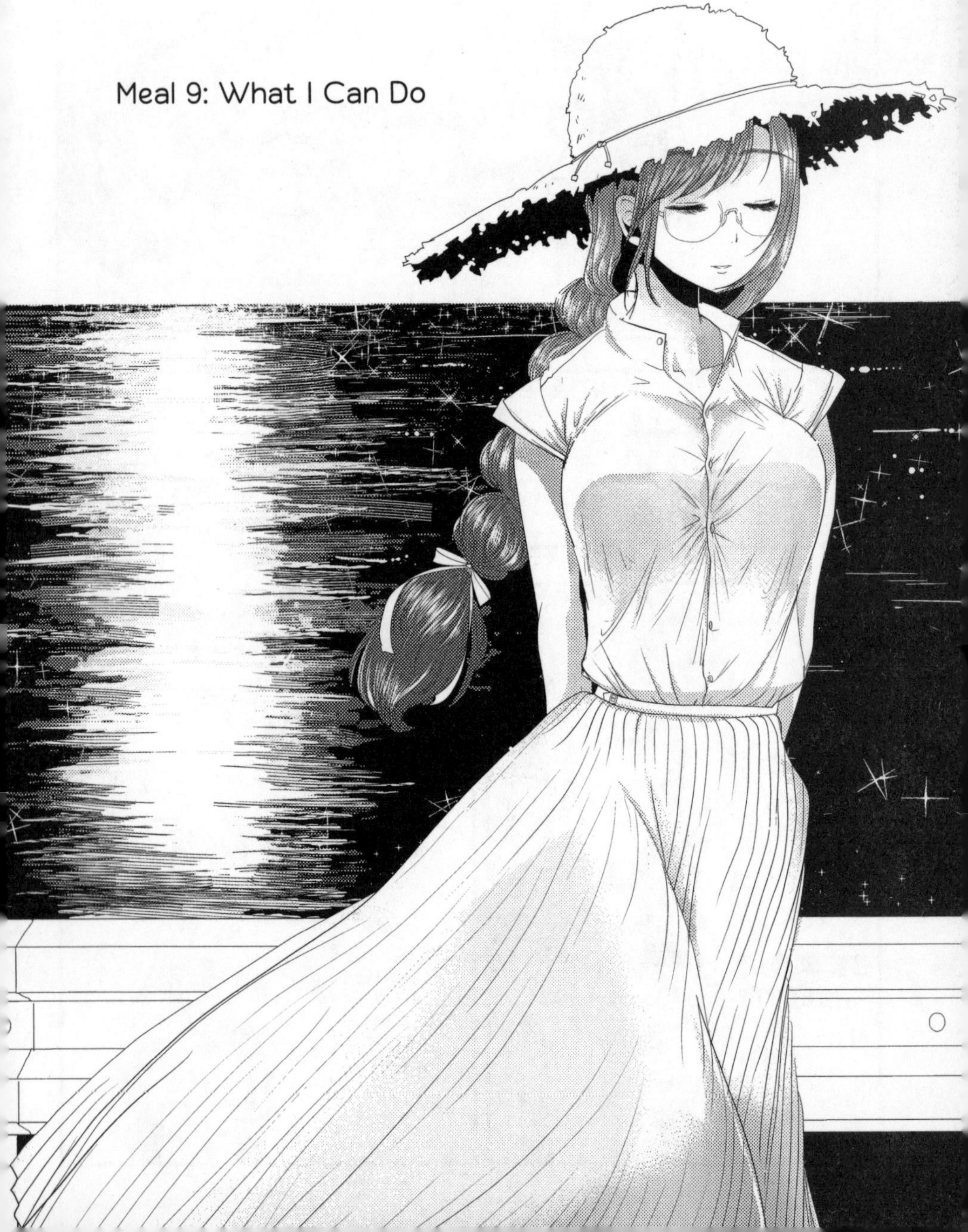

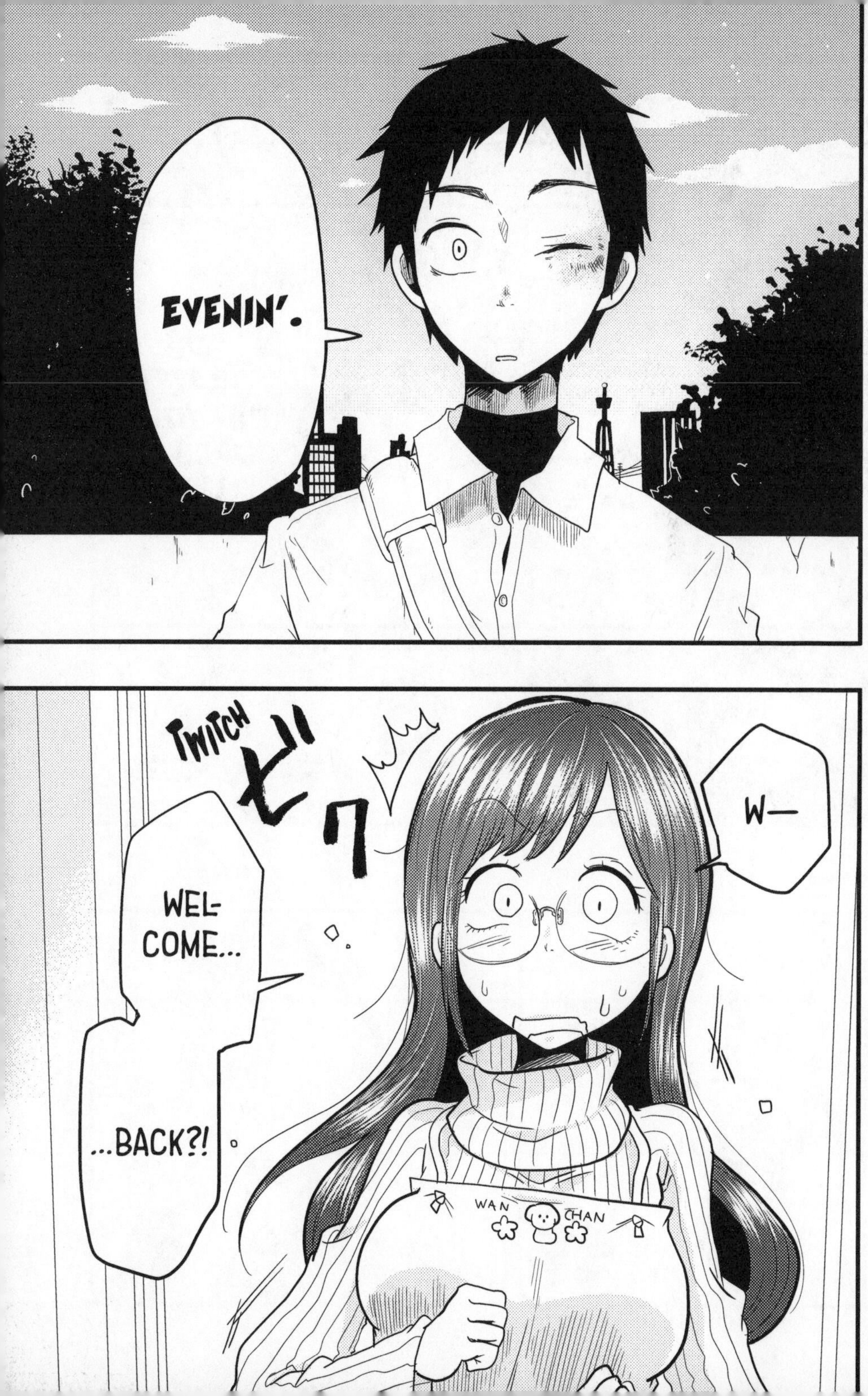
EVENIN'.
W—
TWITCH
WEL-COME...
...BACK?!
WAN CHAN

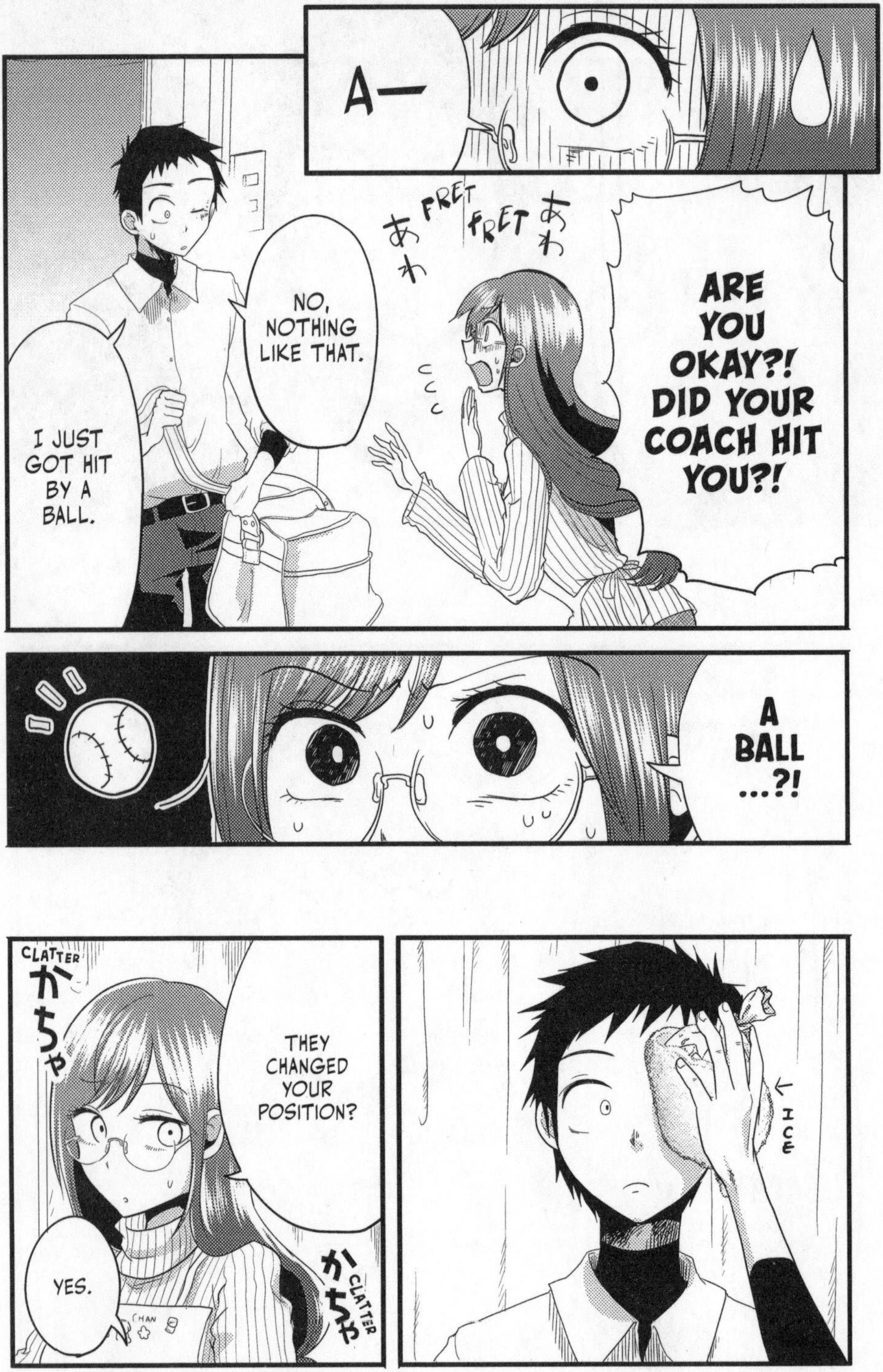
A—
ARE YOU OKAY?! DID YOUR COACH HIT YOU?!
あわ FRET FRET あわ
NO, NOTHING LIKE THAT.
I JUST GOT HIT BY A BALL.
A BALL ...?!
← ICE
かちゃ CLATTER
THEY CHANGED YOUR POSITION?
YES.
かちゃ CLATTER

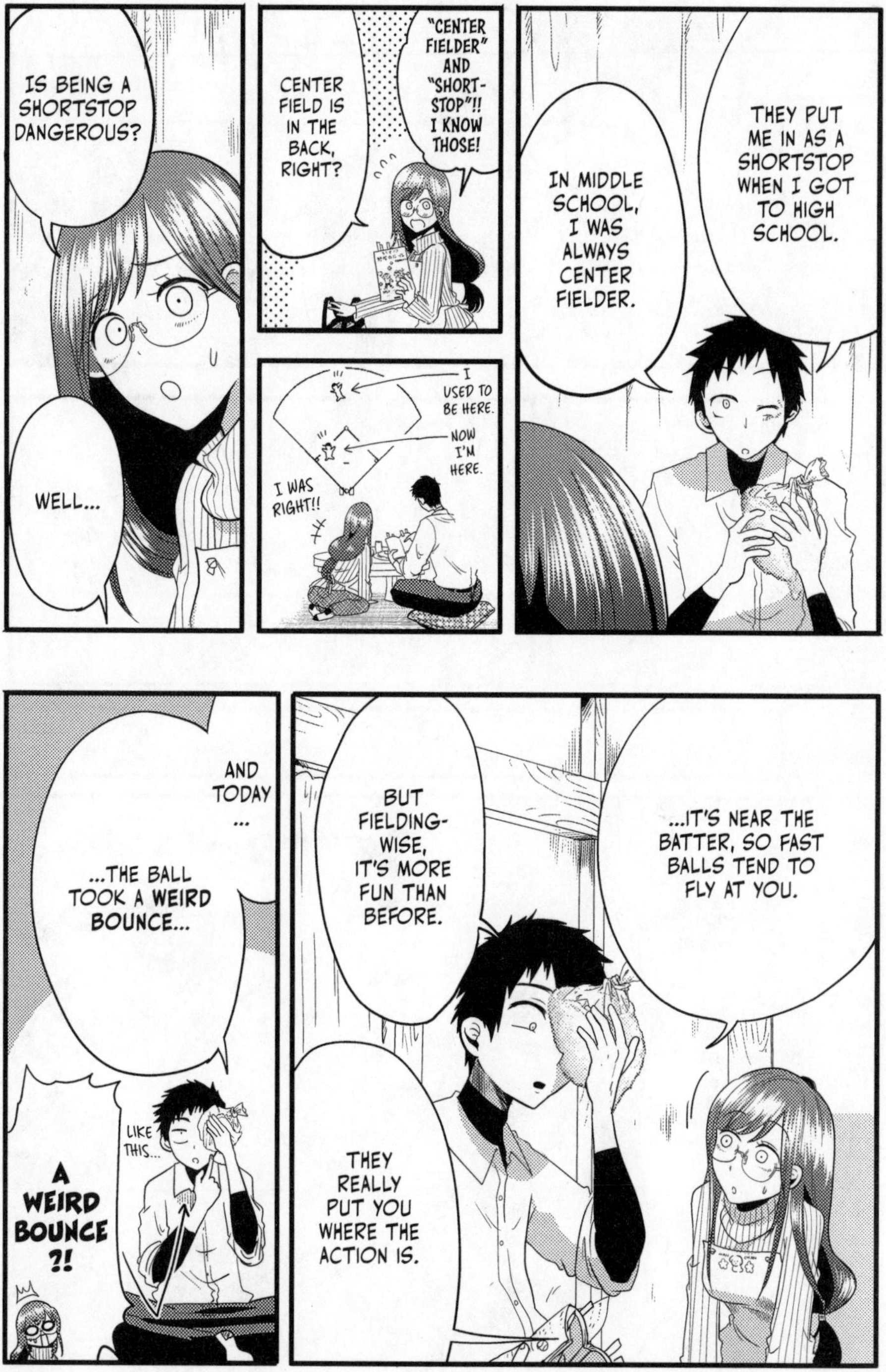
THEY PUT ME IN AS A SHORTSTOP WHEN I GOT TO HIGH SCHOOL.
IN MIDDLE SCHOOL, I WAS ALWAYS CENTER FIELDER.
"CENTER FIELDER" AND "SHORT-STOP"!! I KNOW THOSE!
CENTER FIELD IS IN THE BACK, RIGHT?
I USED TO BE HERE.
NOW I'M HERE.
I WAS RIGHT!!
IS BEING A SHORTSTOP DANGEROUS?
WELL...
...IT'S NEAR THE BATTER, SO FAST BALLS TEND TO FLY AT YOU.
BUT FIELDING-WISE, IT'S MORE FUN THAN BEFORE.
THEY REALLY PUT YOU WHERE THE ACTION IS.
AND TODAY...
...THE BALL TOOK A WEIRD BOUNCE...
LIKE THIS...
A WEIRD BOUNCE?!

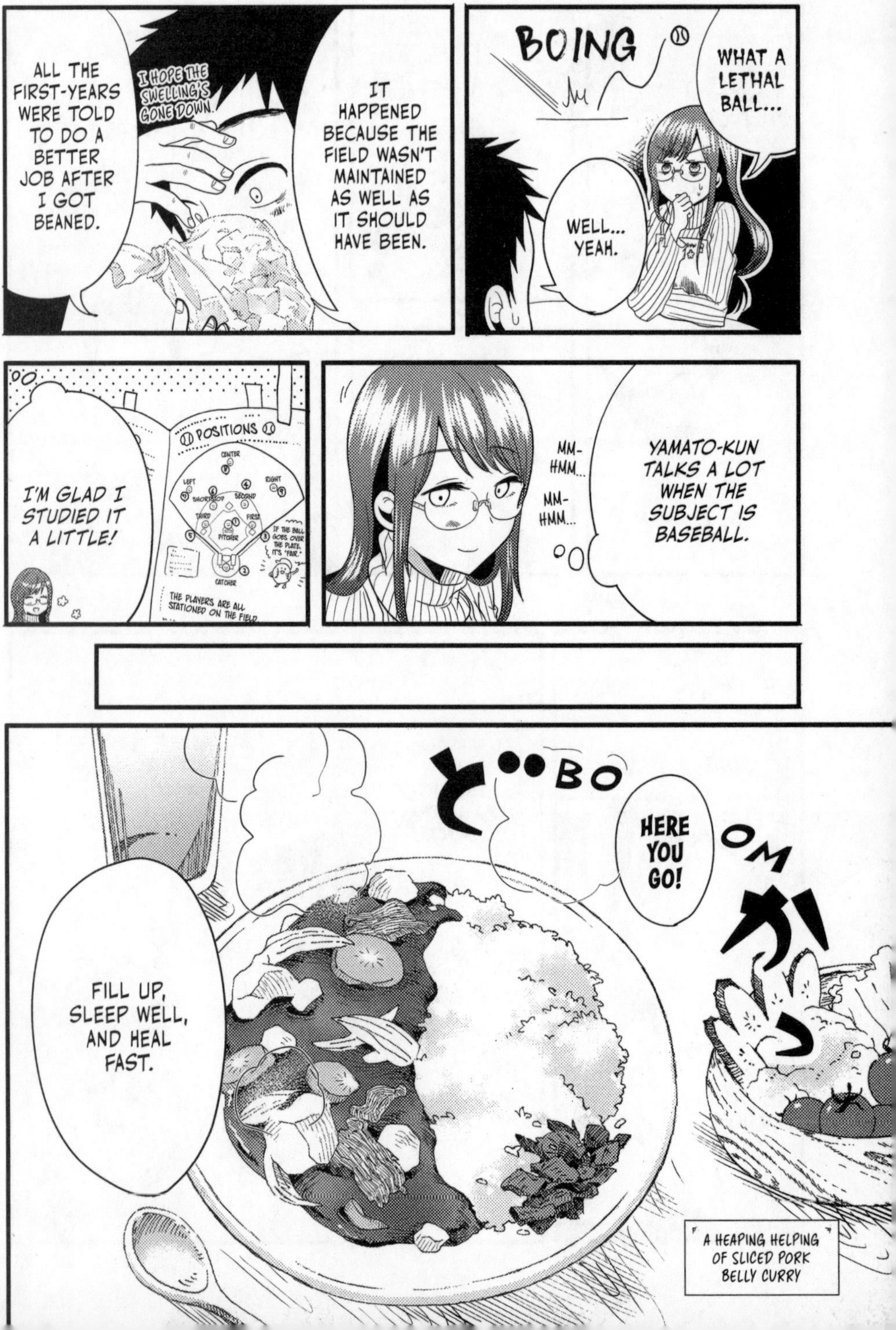
BOING
WHAT A LETHAL BALL...
WELL... YEAH.
IT HAPPENED BECAUSE THE FIELD WASN'T MAINTAINED AS WELL AS IT SHOULD HAVE BEEN.
I HOPE THE SWELLING'S GONE DOWN.
ALL THE FIRST-YEARS WERE TOLD TO DO A BETTER JOB AFTER I GOT BEANED.
YAMATO-KUN TALKS A LOT WHEN THE SUBJECT IS BASEBALL.
MM-HMM...
MM-HMM...
POSITIONS
CENTER
LEFT
RIGHT
SHORTSTOP
SECOND
THIRD
FIRST
PITCHER
IF THE BALL GOES OVER THE PLATE, IT'S "FAIR."
CATCHER
THE PLAYERS ARE ALL STATIONED ON THE FIELD.
I'M GLAD I STUDIED IT A LITTLE!
BO
HERE YOU GO!
OM
FILL UP, SLEEP WELL, AND HEAL FAST.
A HEAPING HELPING OF SLICED PORK BELLY CURRY

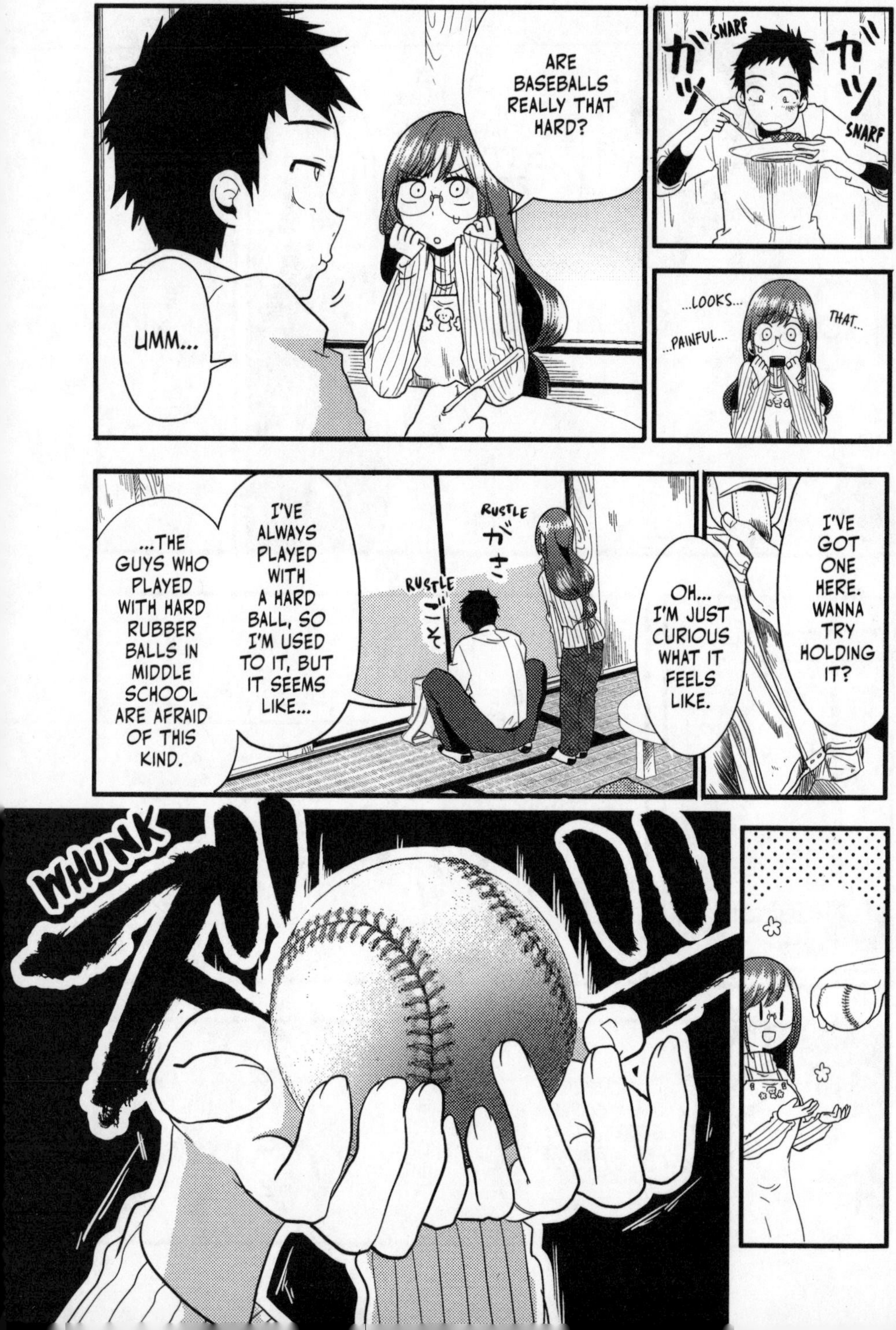
ガツ
SNARF
ガツ
SNARF
THAT...
...LOOKS...
...PAINFUL...
ARE BASEBALLS REALLY THAT HARD?
UMM...
I'VE GOT ONE HERE. WANNA TRY HOLDING IT?
OH... I'M JUST CURIOUS WHAT IT FEELS LIKE.
RUSTLE
がさ
RUSTLE
ごそ
I'VE ALWAYS PLAYED WITH A HARD BALL, SO I'M USED TO IT, BUT IT SEEMS LIKE...
...THE GUYS WHO PLAYED WITH HARD RUBBER BALLS IN MIDDLE SCHOOL ARE AFRAID OF THIS KIND.
WHUNK

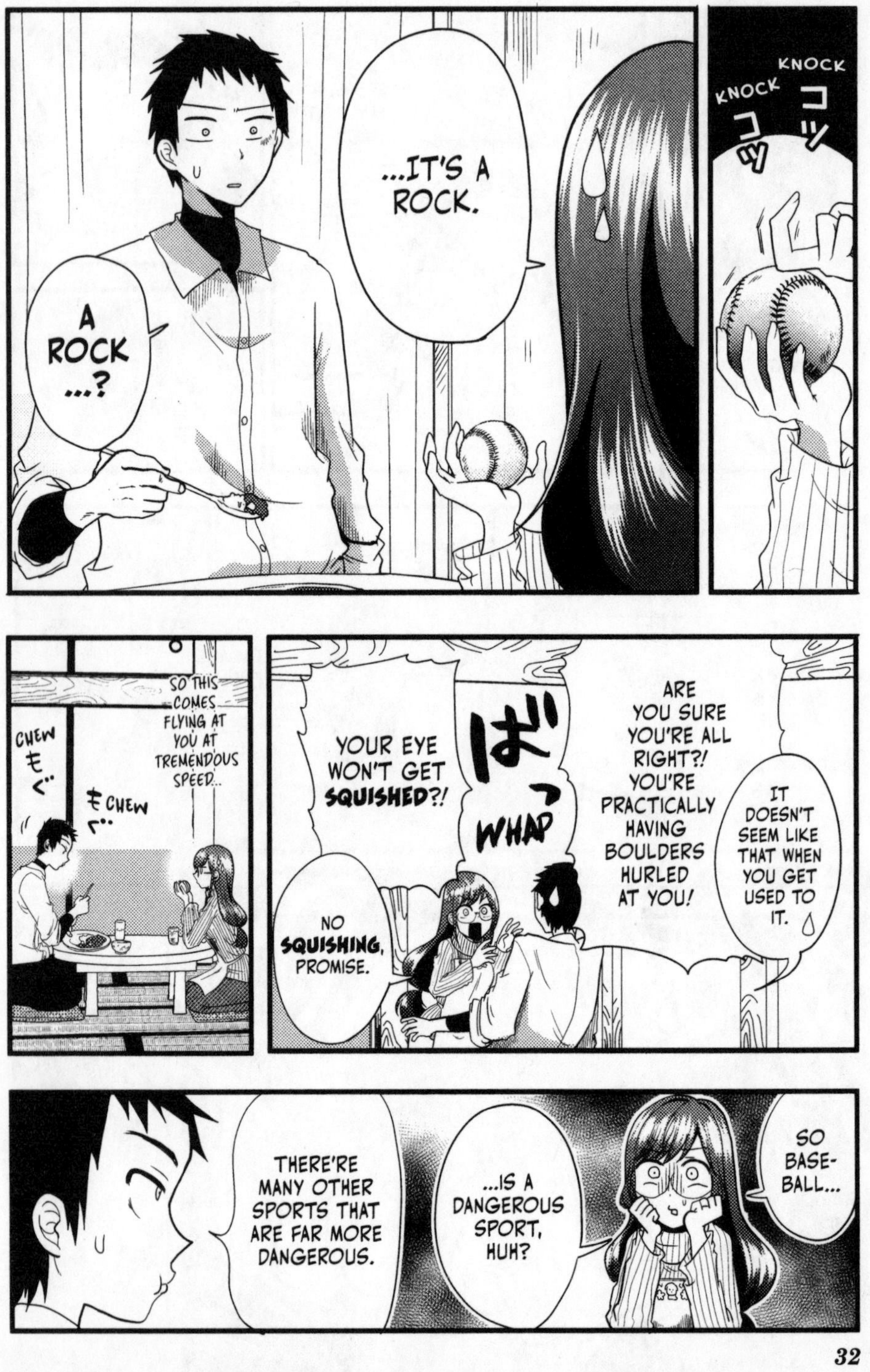
KNOCK
コツ
KNOCK
コツ
...IT'S A ROCK.
A ROCK ...?
ARE YOU SURE YOU'RE ALL RIGHT?! YOU'RE PRACTICALLY HAVING BOULDERS HURLED AT YOU!
IT DOESN'T SEEM LIKE THAT WHEN YOU GET USED TO IT.
ばっ
WHAP
YOUR EYE WON'T GET SQUISHED?!
NO SQUISHING, PROMISE.
SO THIS COMES FLYING AT YOU AT TREMENDOUS SPEED...
CHEW
もぐ
もぐ
CHEW
SO BASE-BALL...
...IS A DANGEROUS SPORT, HUH?
THERE'RE MANY OTHER SPORTS THAT ARE FAR MORE DANGEROUS.

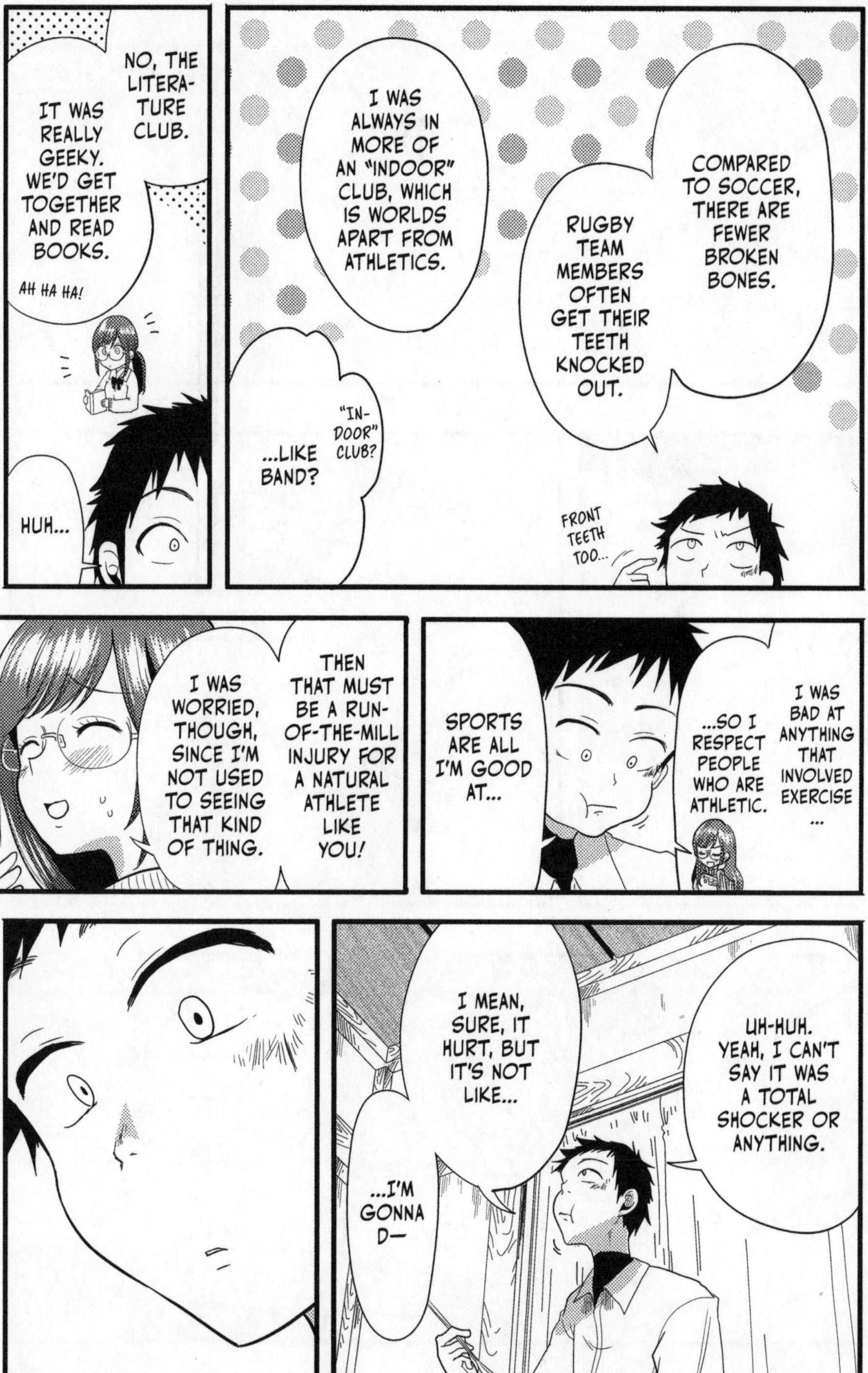
COMPARED TO SOCCER, THERE ARE FEWER BROKEN BONES.
RUGBY TEAM MEMBERS OFTEN GET THEIR TEETH KNOCKED OUT.
FRONT TEETH TOO...
I WAS ALWAYS IN MORE OF AN "INDOOR" CLUB, WHICH IS WORLDS APART FROM ATHLETICS.
"IN-DOOR" CLUB?
...LIKE BAND?
NO, THE LITERA-TURE CLUB.
IT WAS REALLY GEEKY. WE'D GET TOGETHER AND READ BOOKS.
AH HA HA!
HUH...
I WAS BAD AT ANYTHING THAT INVOLVED EXERCISE...
...SO I RESPECT PEOPLE WHO ARE ATHLETIC.
SPORTS ARE ALL I'M GOOD AT...
THEN THAT MUST BE A RUN-OF-THE-MILL INJURY FOR A NATURAL ATHLETE LIKE YOU!
I WAS WORRIED, THOUGH, SINCE I'M NOT USED TO SEEING THAT KIND OF THING.
UH-HUH. YEAH, I CAN'T SAY IT WAS A TOTAL SHOCKER OR ANYTHING.
I MEAN, SURE, IT HURT, BUT IT'S NOT LIKE...
...I'M GONNA D—

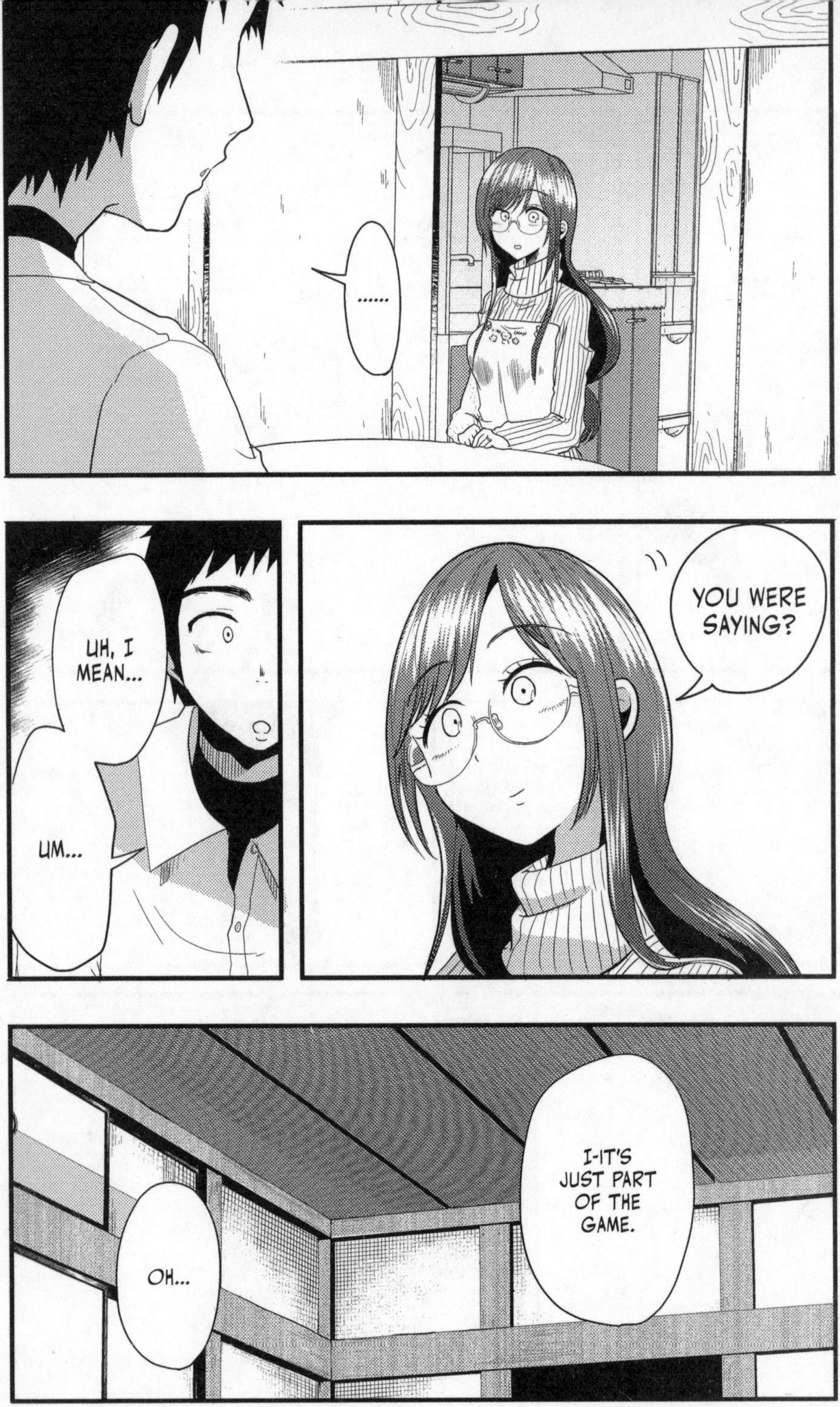
......
YOU WERE SAYING?
UH, I MEAN...
UM...
I-IT'S JUST PART OF THE GAME.
OH...

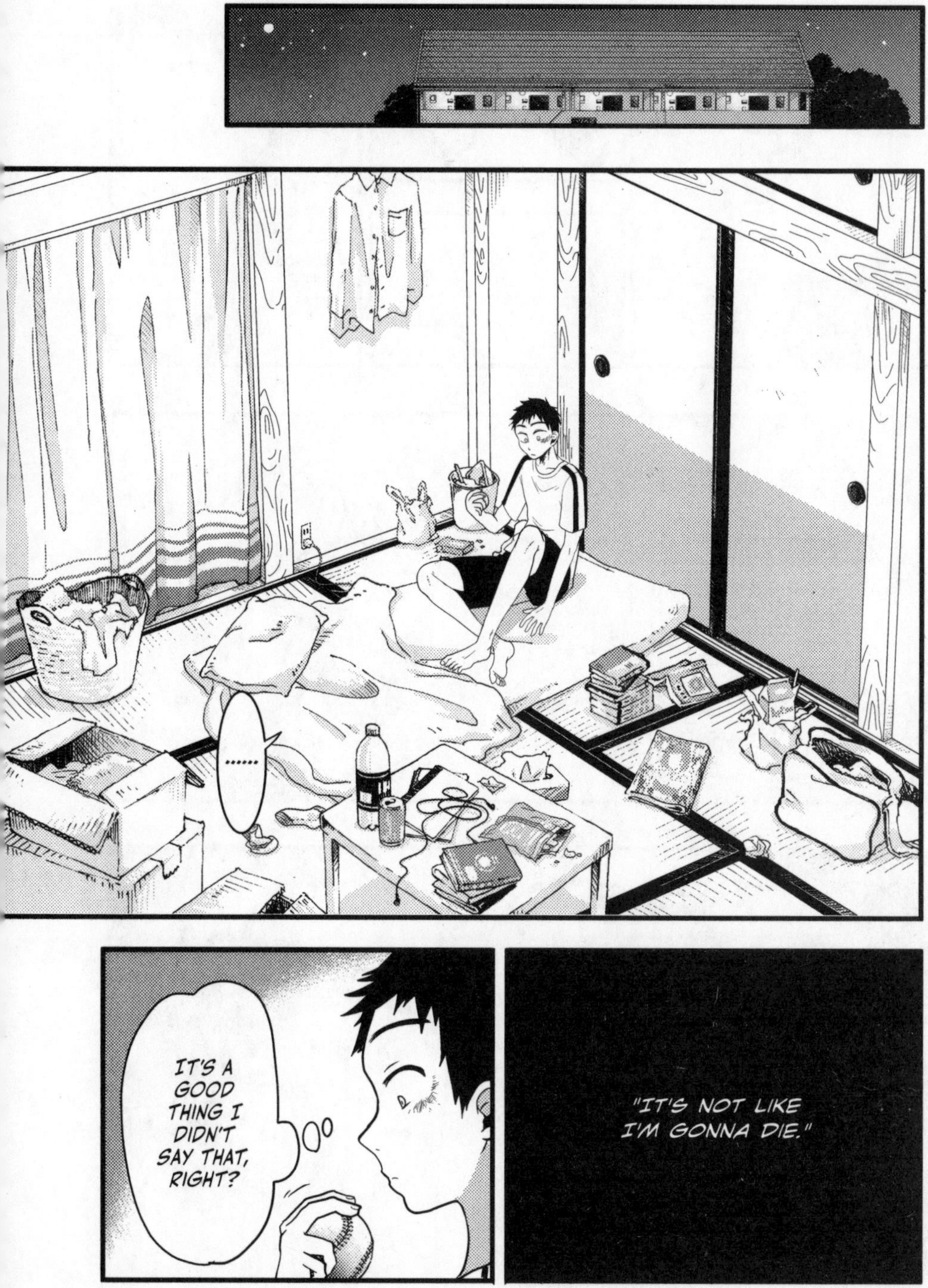
......
"IT'S NOT LIKE I'M GONNA DIE."
IT'S A GOOD THING I DIDN'T SAY THAT, RIGHT?

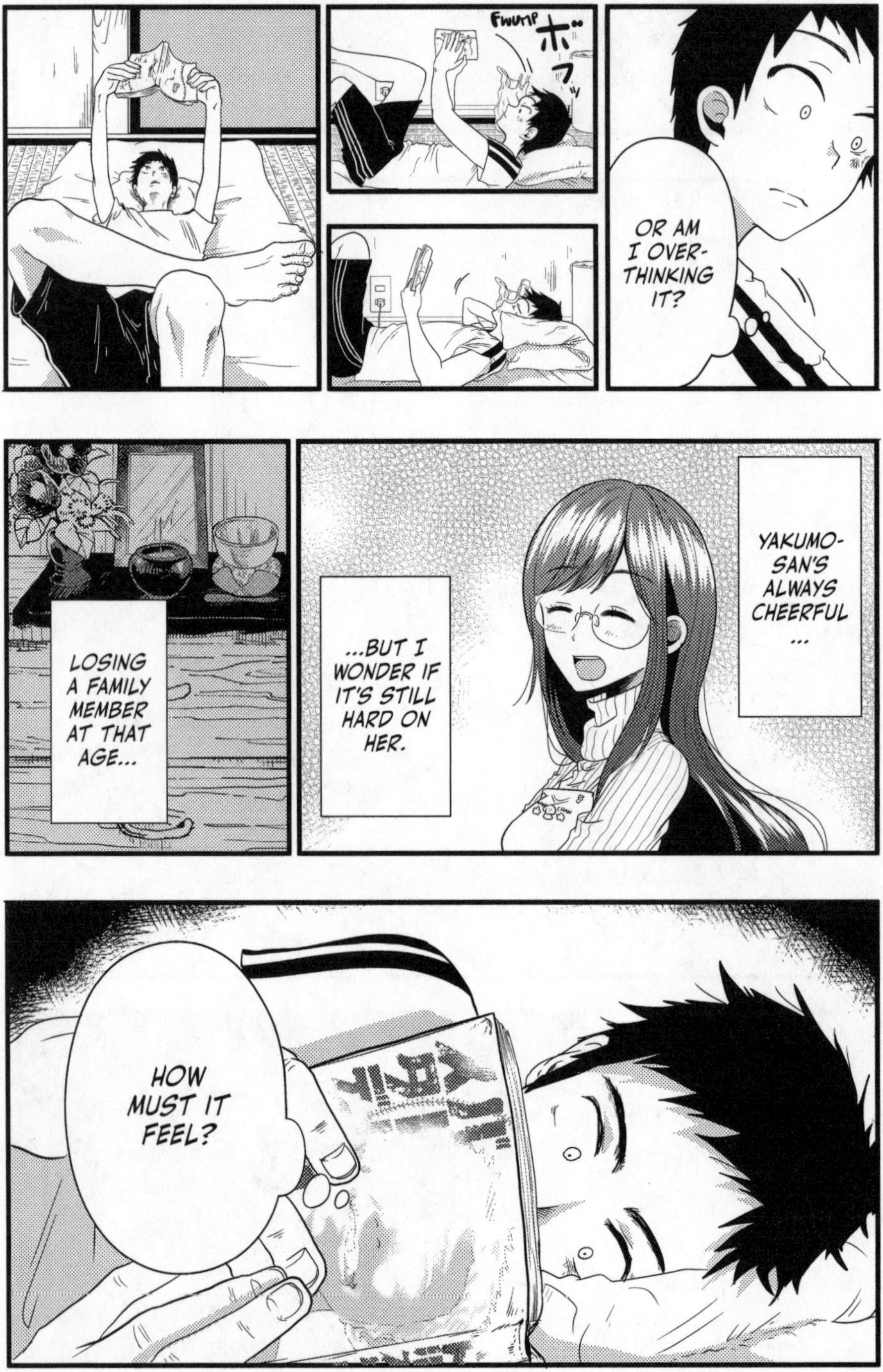
OR AM I OVER-THINKING IT?
FWUMP
ボフッ
YAKUMO-SAN'S ALWAYS CHEERFUL ...
...BUT I WONDER IF IT'S STILL HARD ON HER.
LOSING A FAMILY MEMBER AT THAT AGE...
HOW MUST IT FEEL?

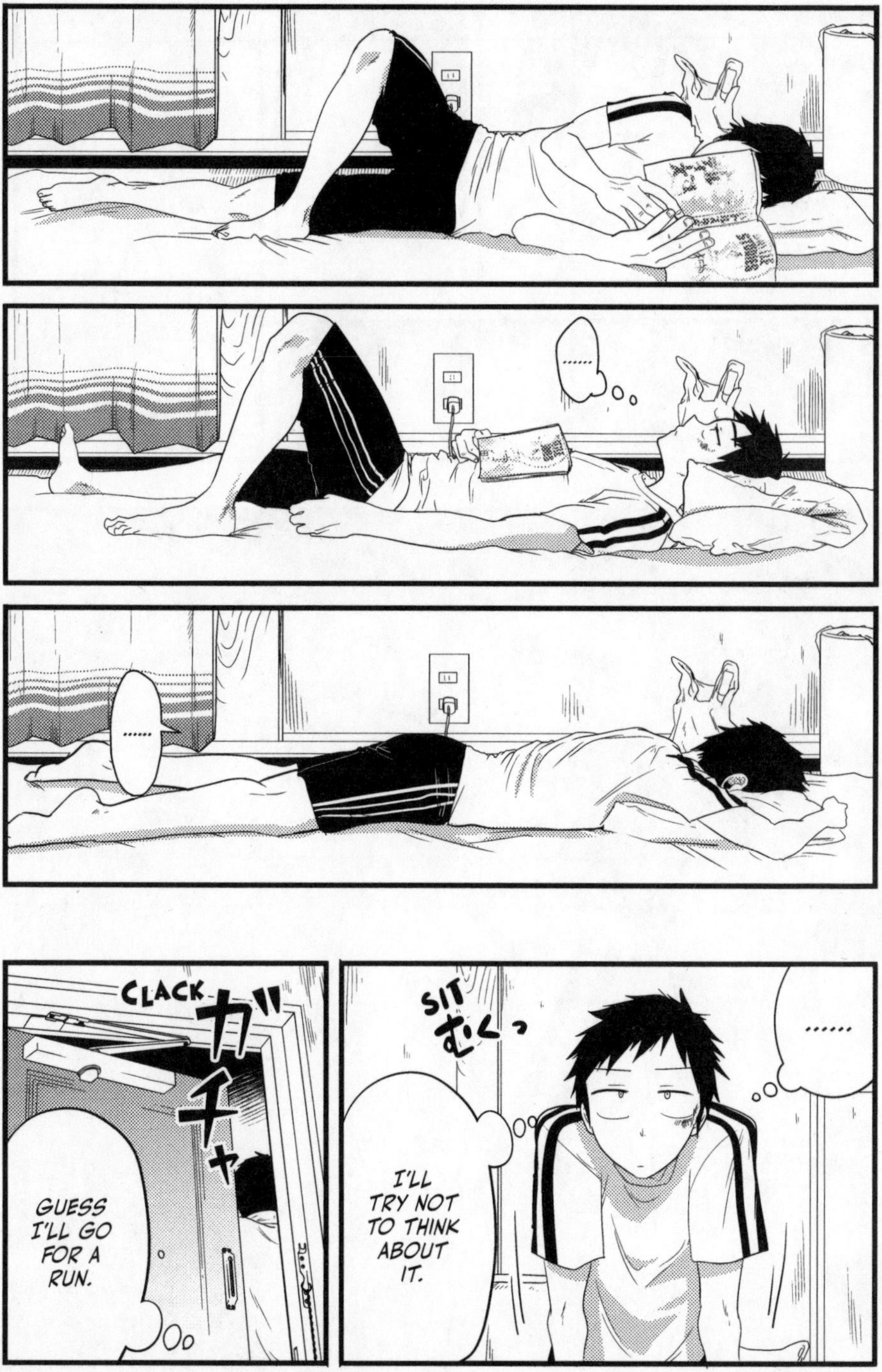
……
……
……
SIT むくっ
I'LL TRY NOT TO THINK ABOUT IT.
CLACK ガチャ
GUESS I'LL GO FOR A RUN.

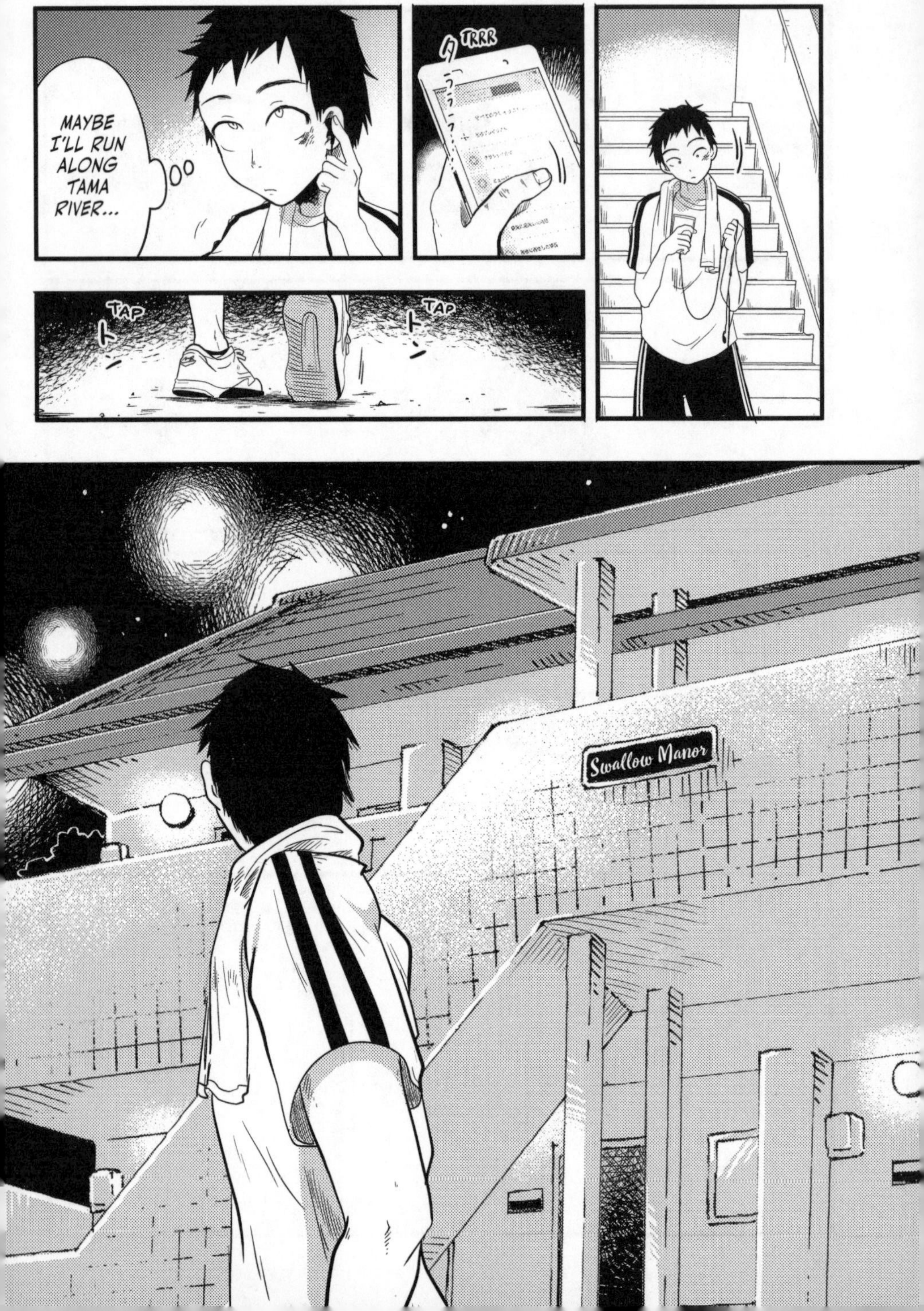
TRRR
MAYBE I'LL RUN ALONG TAMA RIVER...
TAP
TAP
Swallow Manor

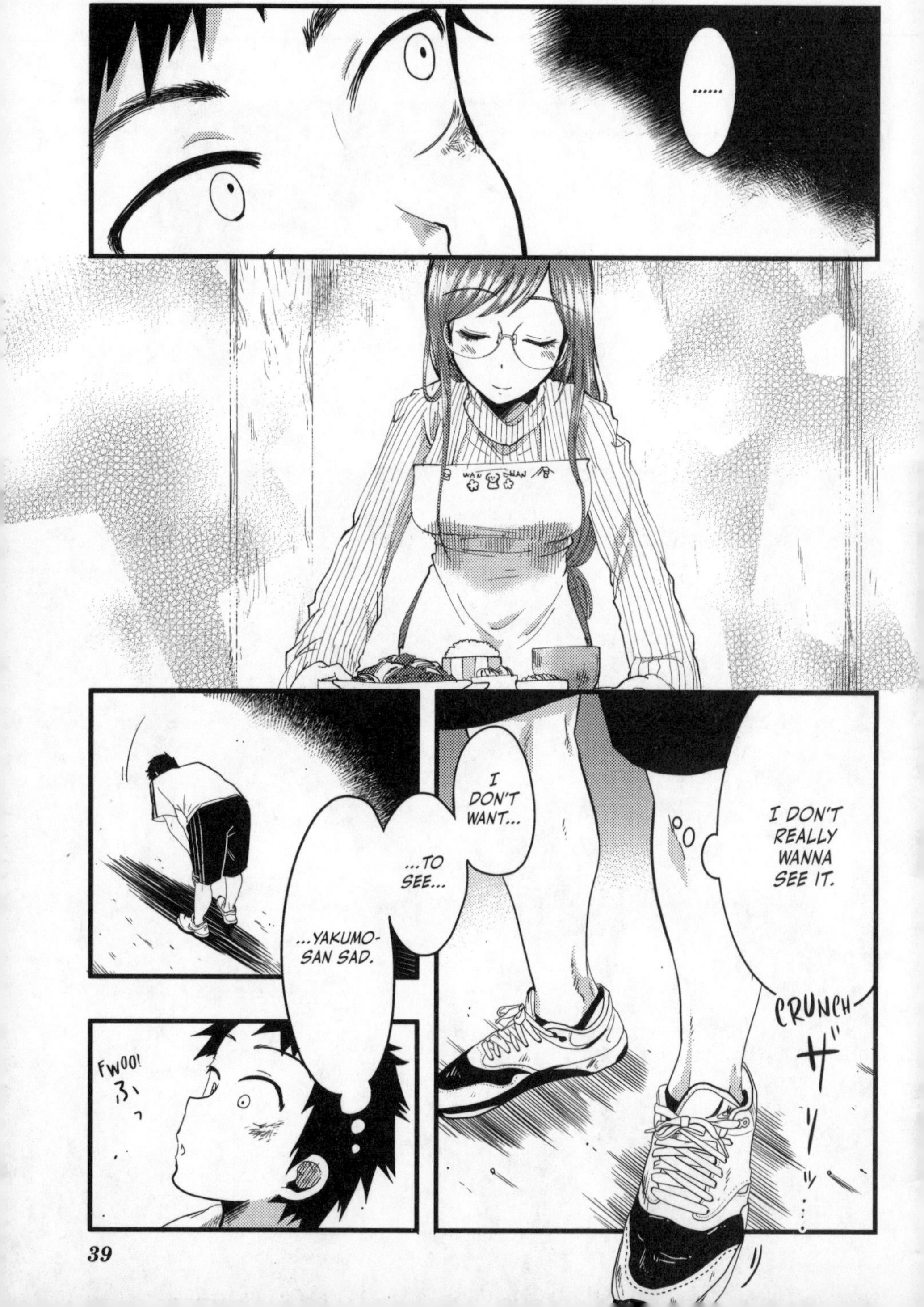
......
I DON'T REALLY WANNA SEE IT.
CRUNCH
ザリッ…
FWOO!
ふっ
I DON'T WANT...
...TO SEE...
...YAKUMO-SAN SAD.

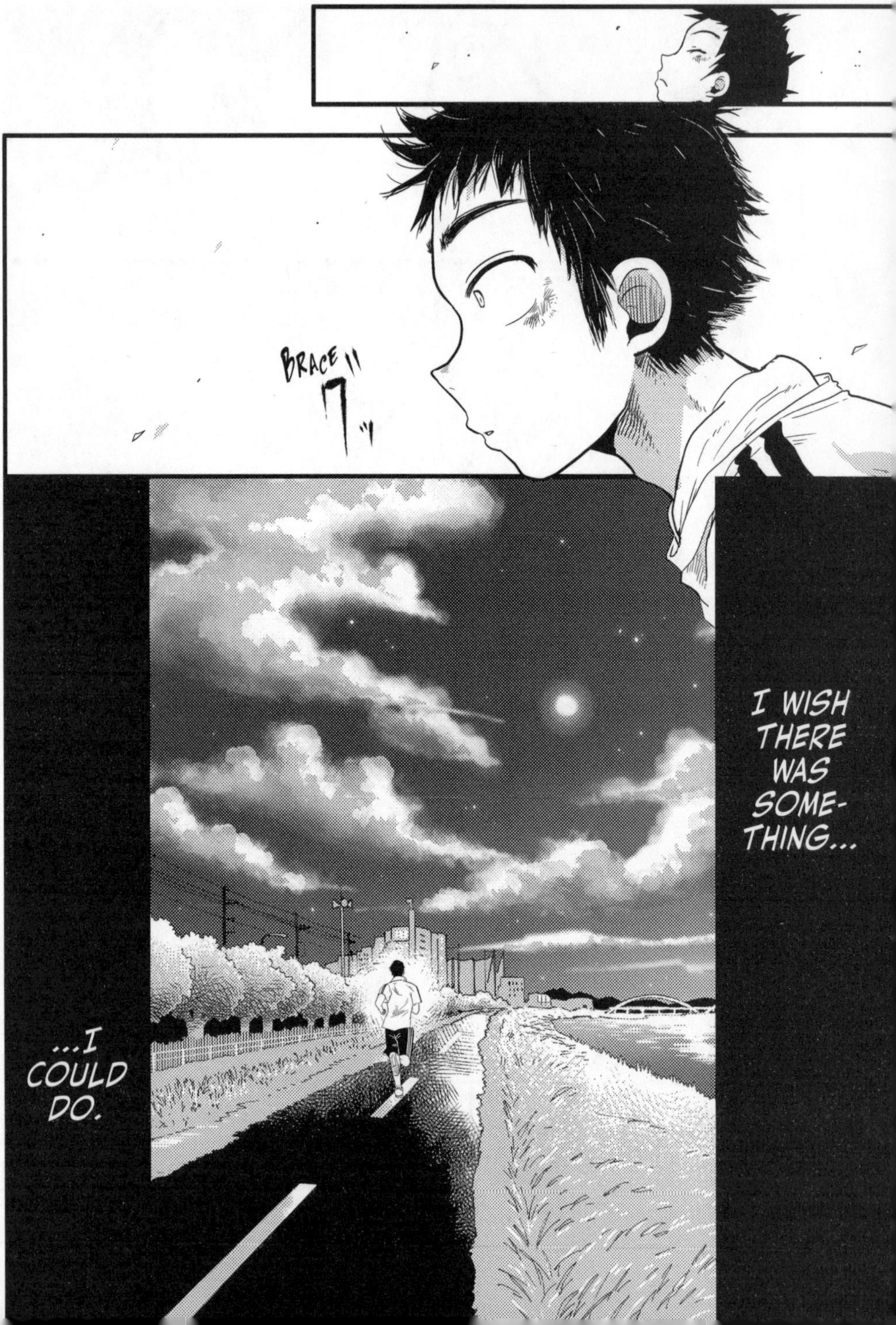
BRACE
I WISH THERE WAS SOME-THING...
...I COULD DO.

Beauty and the **FEAST**.

Beauty and the FEAST.

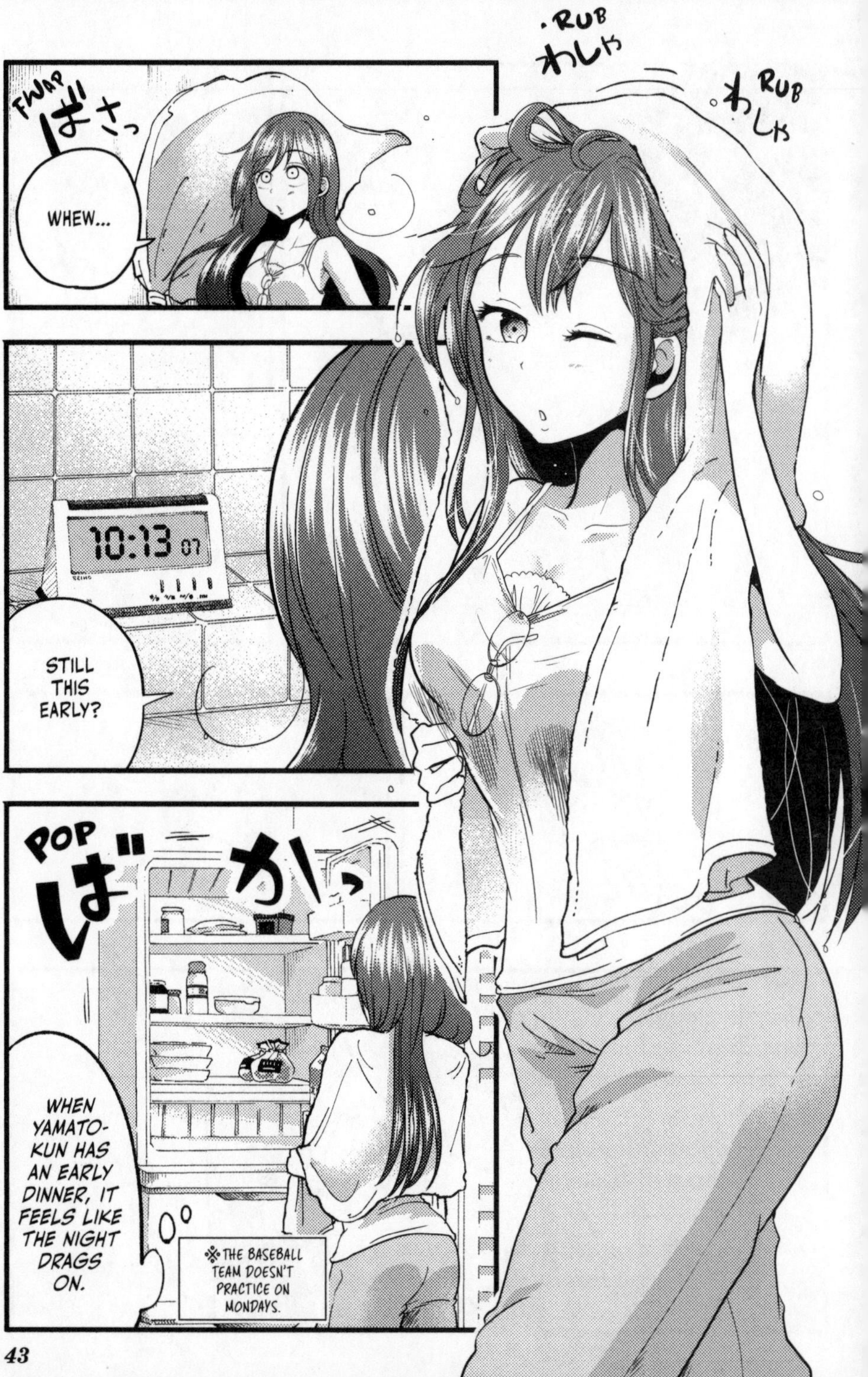
RUB
わしゃ
RUB
わしゃ
FWAP
ばさっ
WHEW...
10:13 07
STILL THIS EARLY?
POP
ばかっ
WHEN YAMATO-KUN HAS AN EARLY DINNER, IT FEELS LIKE THE NIGHT DRAGS ON.
※THE BASEBALL TEAM DOESN'T PRACTICE ON MONDAYS.

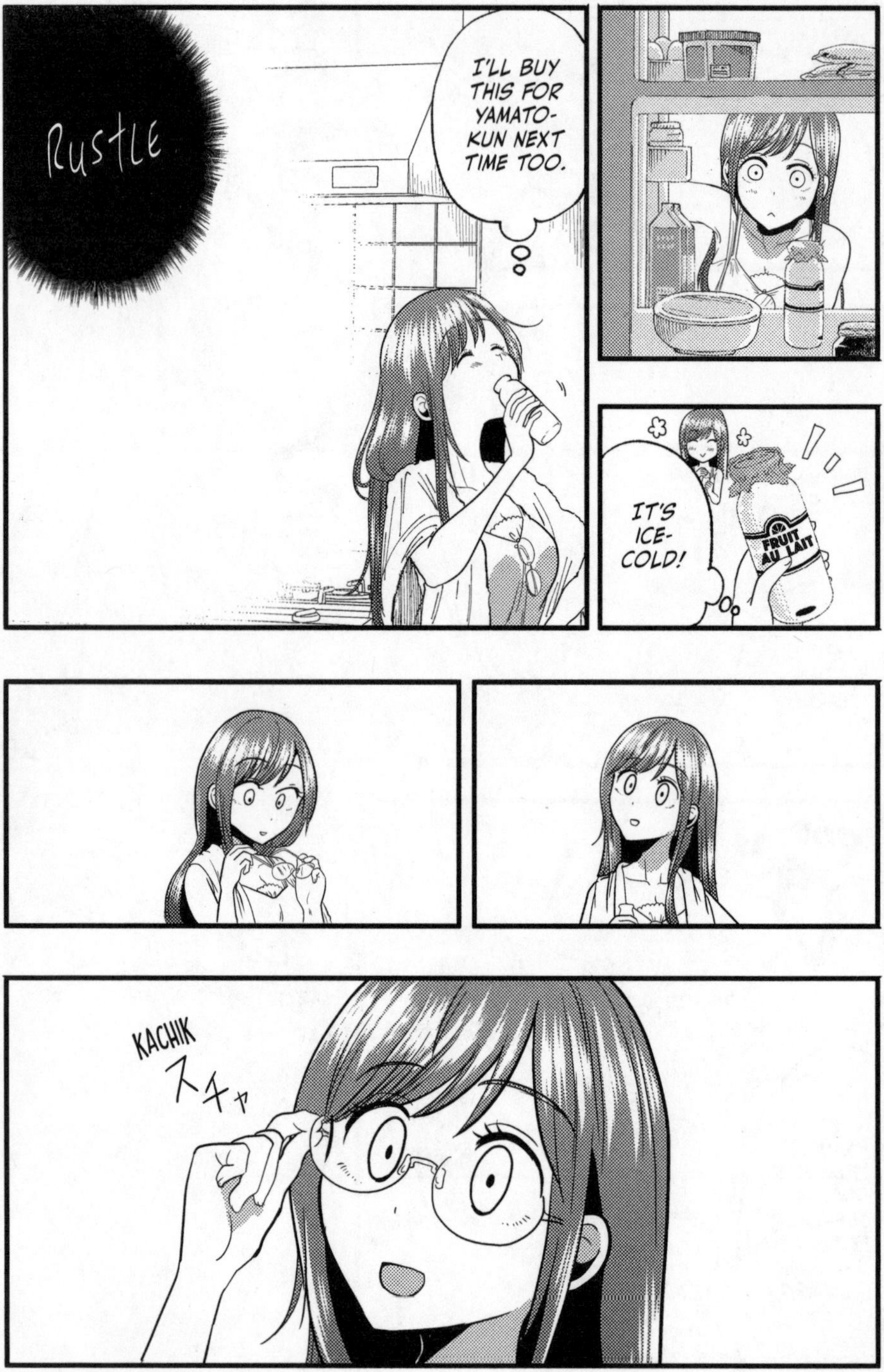
IT'S ICE-COLD!
FRUIT AU LAIT
I'LL BUY THIS FOR YAMATO-KUN NEXT TIME TOO.
RUSTLE
KACHIK
スチャ

Meal 10: The Terrifying C

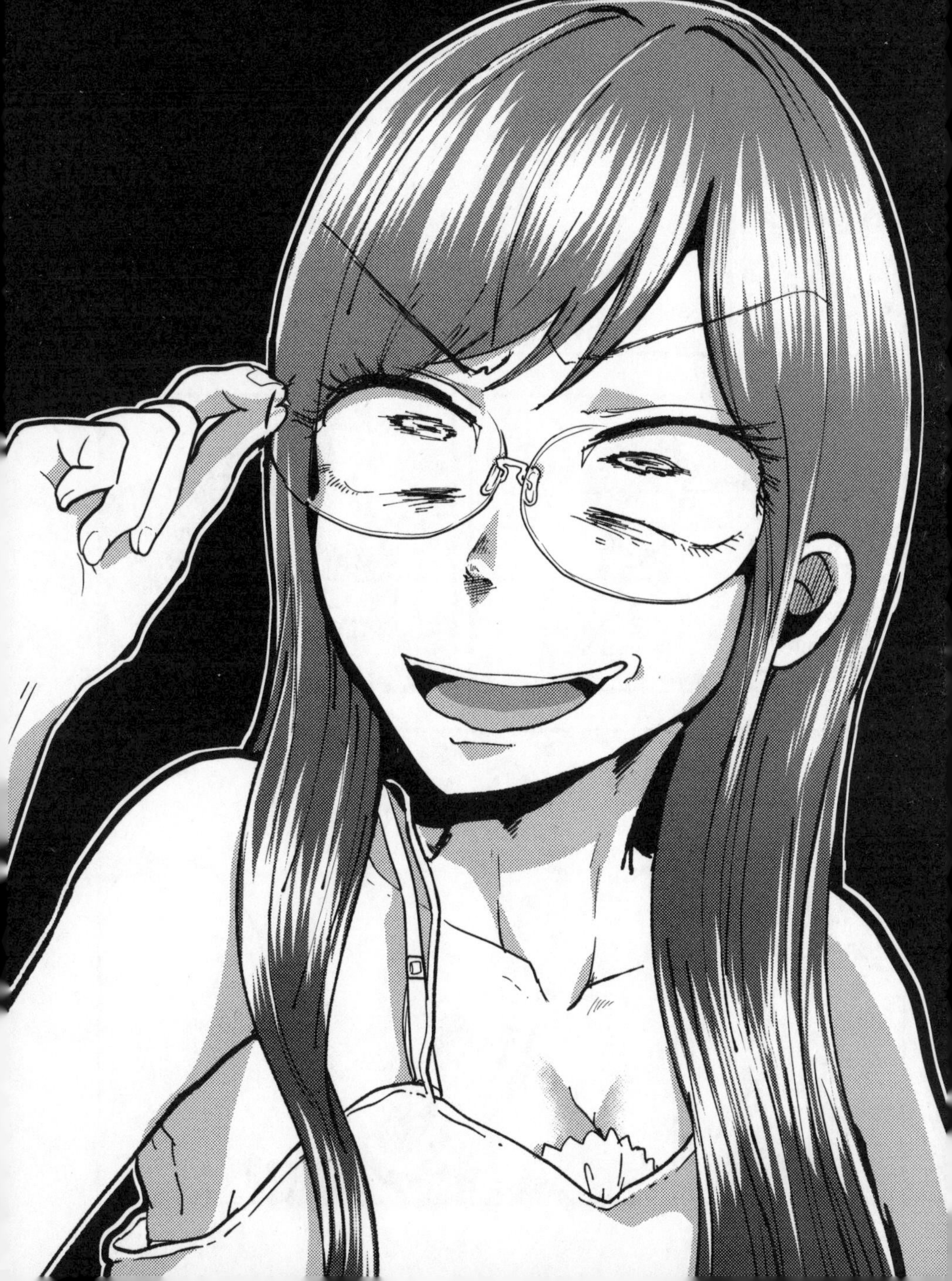

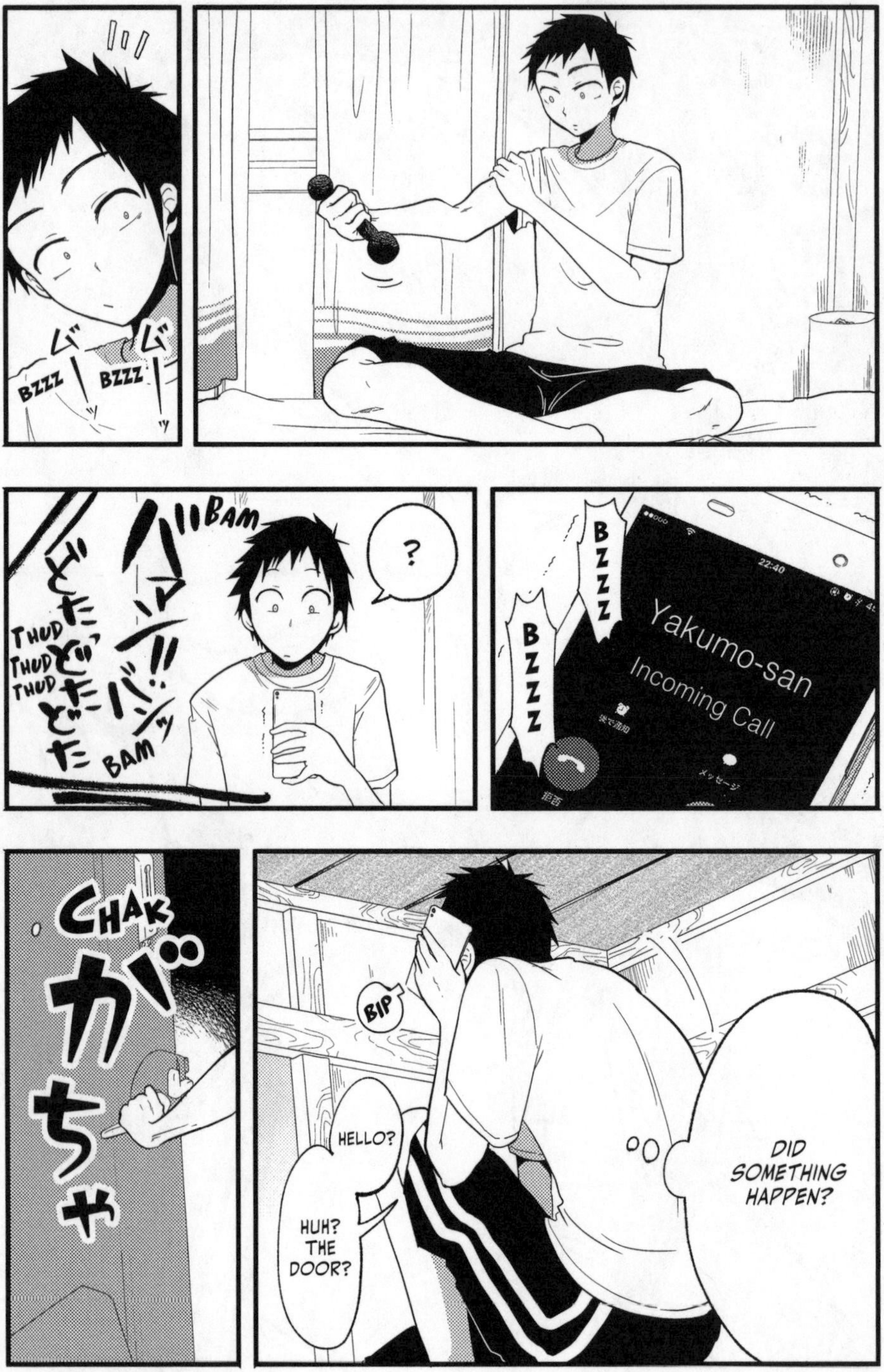

BZZZ
BZZZ
B Z Z Z
B Z Z Z
22:40
Yakumo-san
Incoming Call
?
BAM
THUD THUD THUD
BAM
BIP
HELLO?
DID SOMETHING HAPPEN?
HUH? THE DOOR?
CHAK

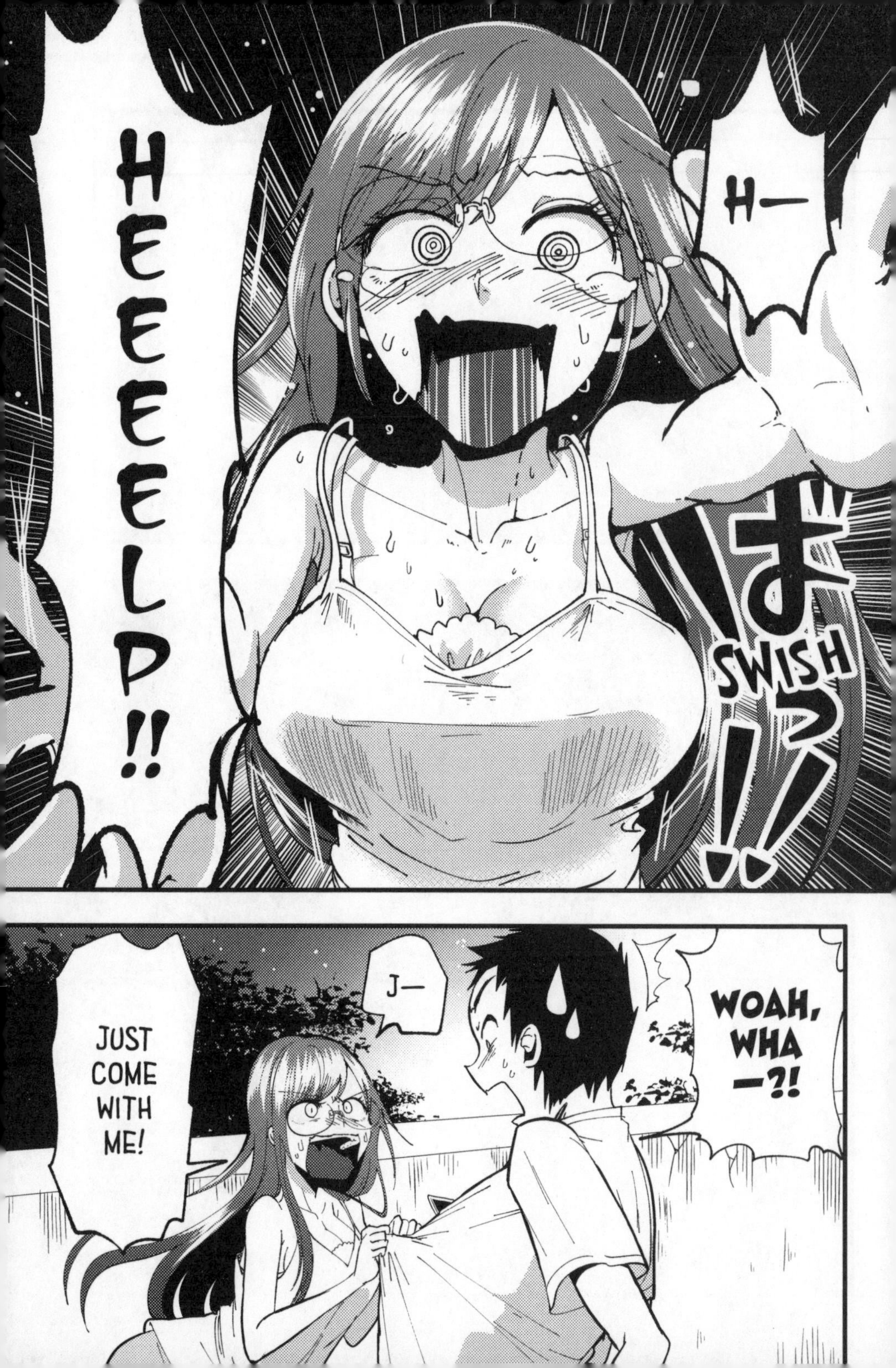
H—
HEEEELP!!
ばっ!!
SWISH
WOAH, WHA—?!
J—
JUST COME WITH ME!

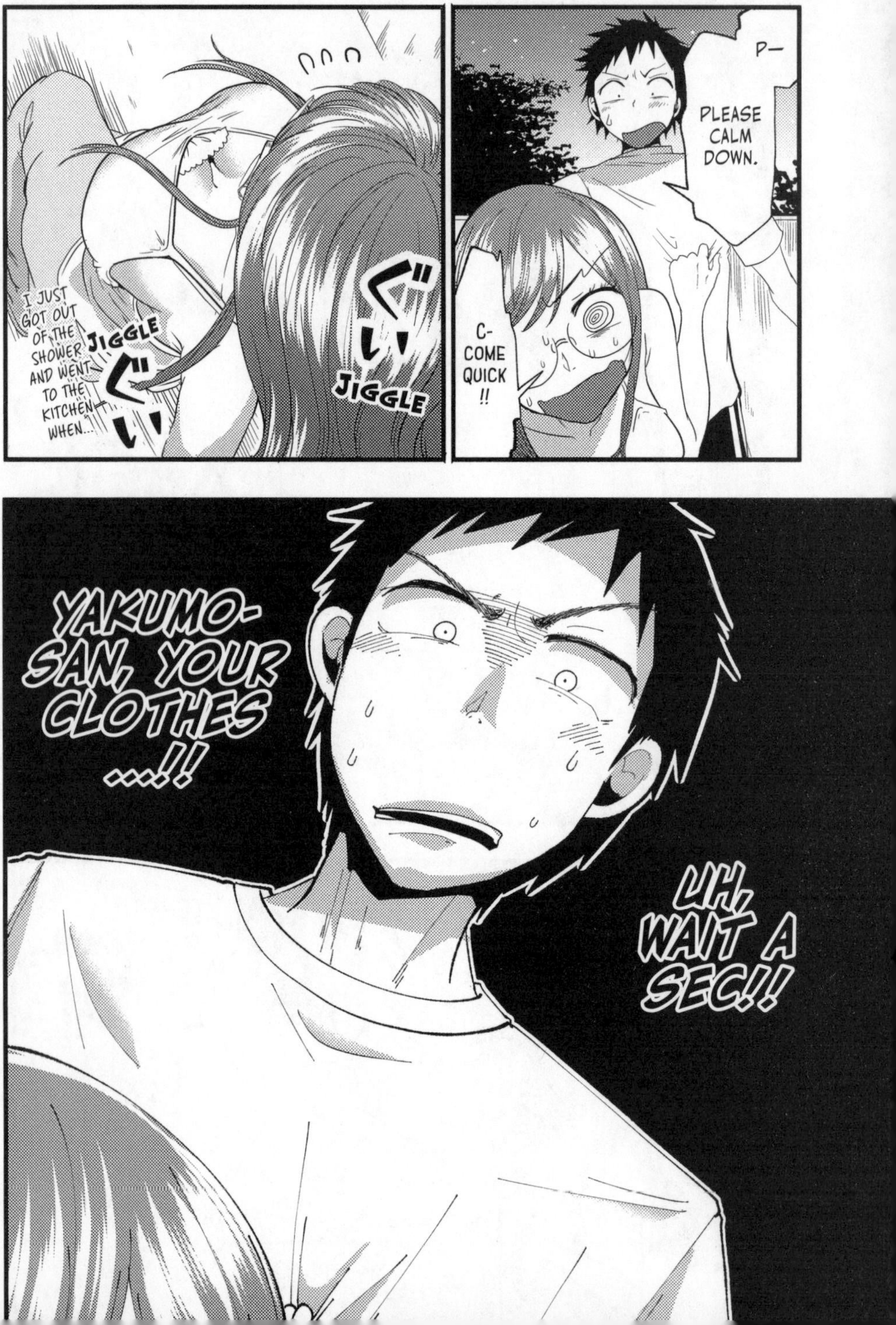
P—
PLEASE CALM DOWN.
C- COME QUICK !!
JIGGLE
I JUST GOT OUT OF THE SHOWER AND WENT TO THE KITCHEN WHEN...
JIGGLE
YAKUMO-SAN, YOUR CLOTHES ...!!
UH, WAIT A SEC!!

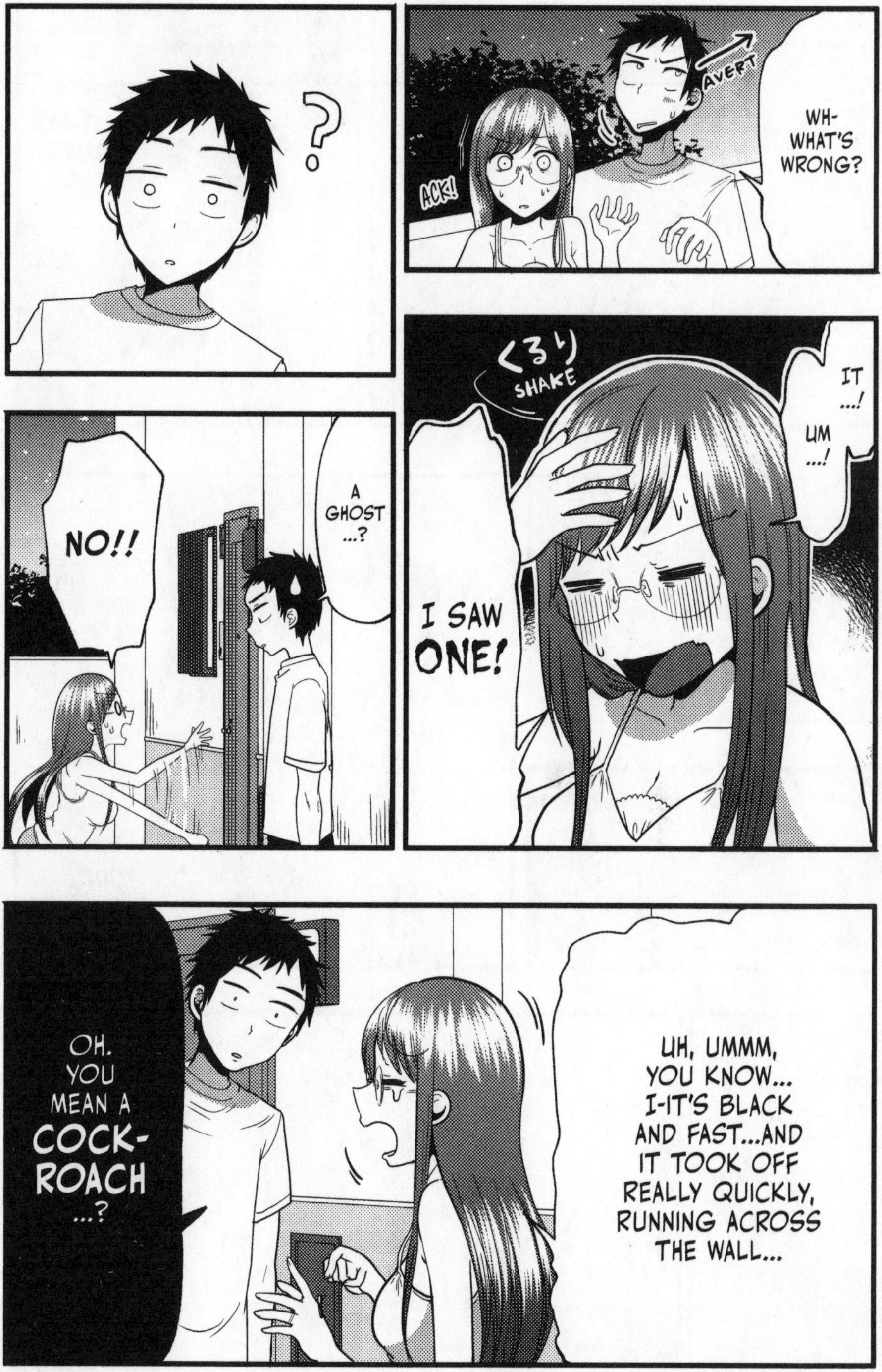
WH- WHAT'S WRONG?
AVERT
ACK!
?
IT ...!
UM ...!
くるり
SHAKE
I SAW ONE!
A GHOST ...?
NO!!
UH, UMMM, YOU KNOW... I-IT'S BLACK AND FAST...AND IT TOOK OFF REALLY QUICKLY, RUNNING ACROSS THE WALL...
OH. YOU MEAN A COCK-ROACH ...?

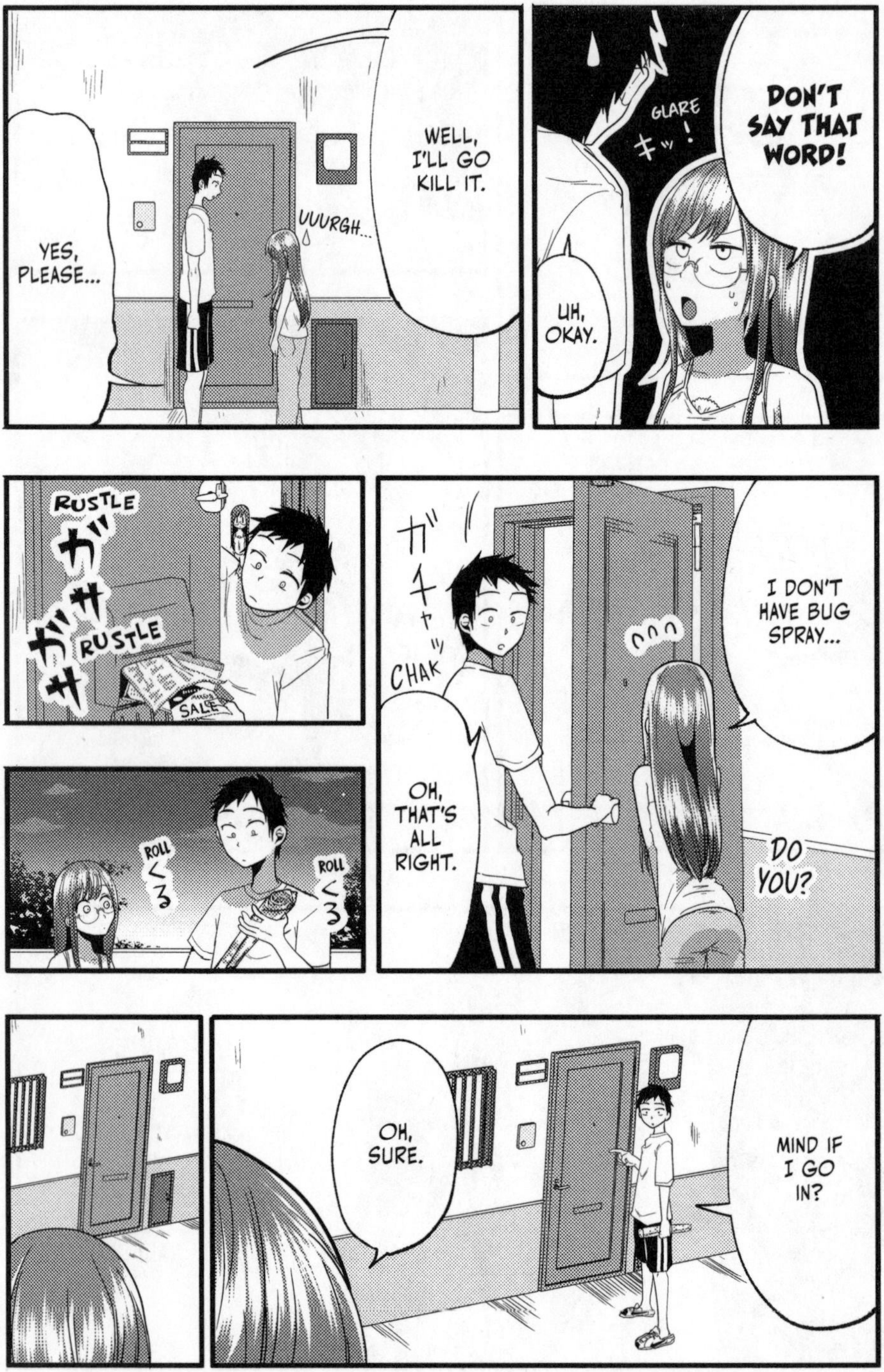
GLARE
キッ！
DON'T SAY THAT WORD!
UH, OKAY.
WELL, I'LL GO KILL IT.
UUURGH...
YES, PLEASE...
ガチャッ
CHAK
I DON'T HAVE BUG SPRAY...
DO YOU?
OH, THAT'S ALL RIGHT.
RUSTLE
ガサ
ガサ
RUSTLE
SALE
ROLL
くる
ROLL
くる
MIND IF I GO IN?
OH, SURE.

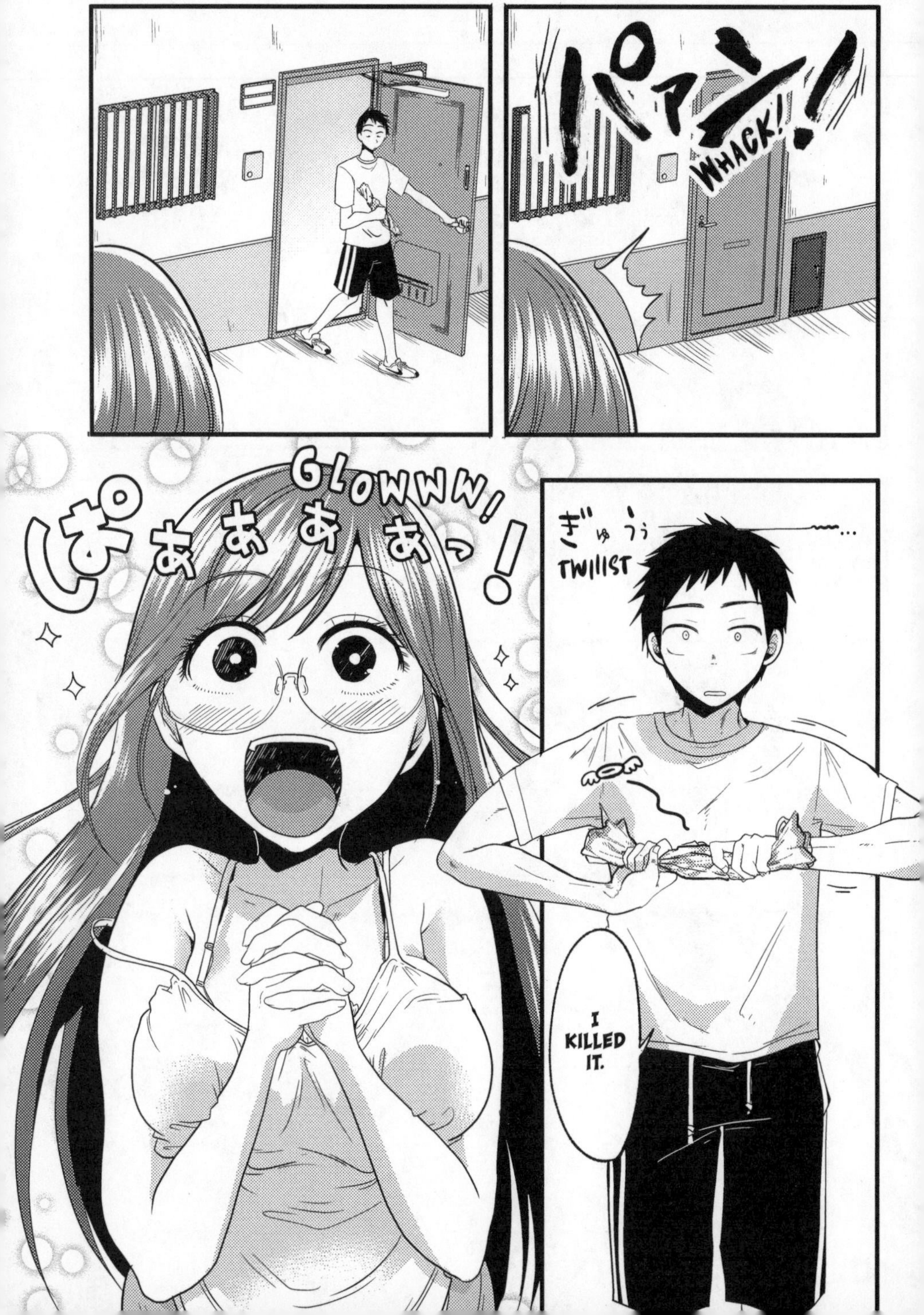
パァン!
WHACK!!
ぎゅうう
TWIIIST
I KILLED IT.
ぱああああっ!
GLOWWW!

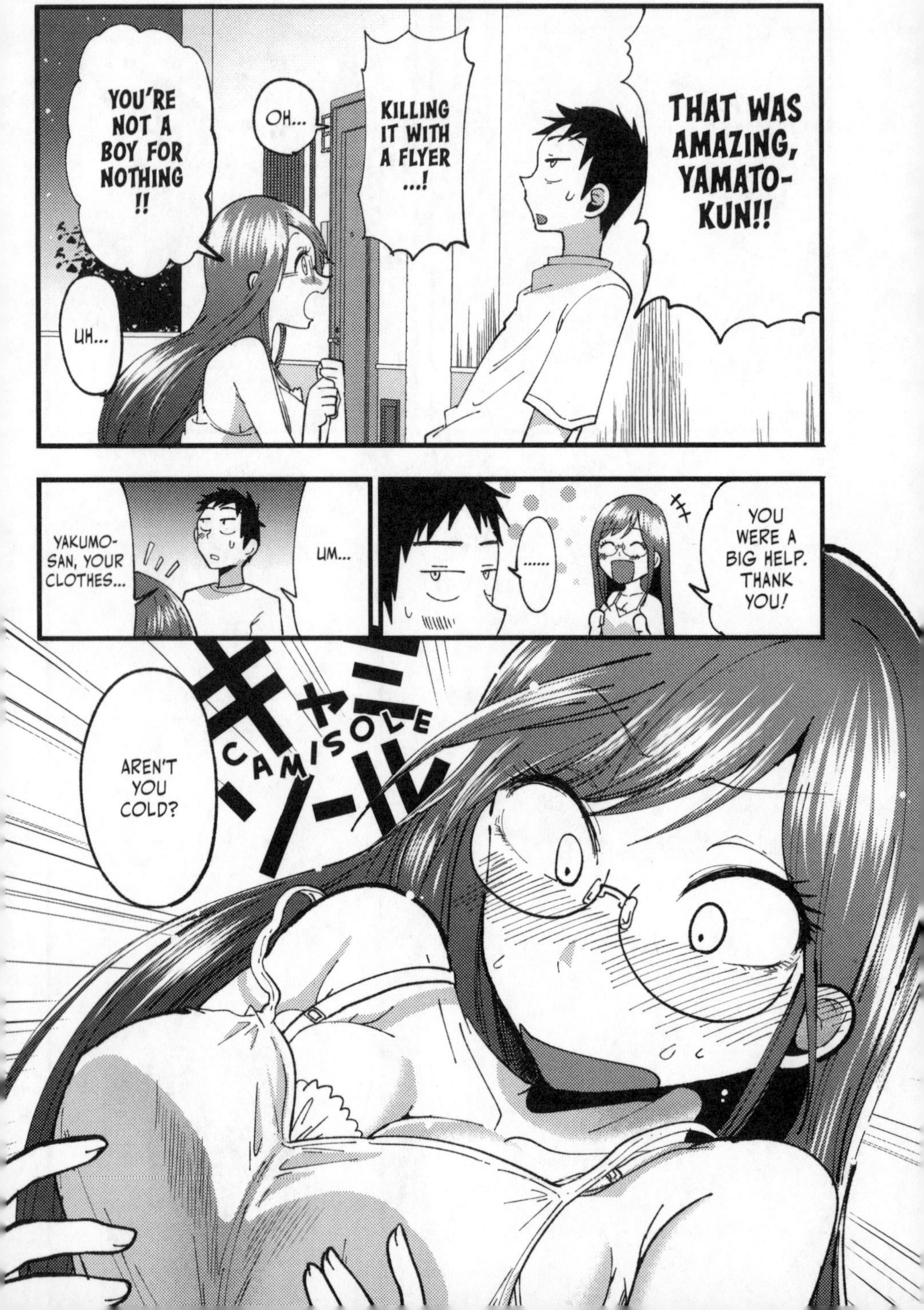
THAT WAS AMAZING, YAMATO-KUN!!
KILLING IT WITH A FLYER ...!
OH...
YOU'RE NOT A BOY FOR NOTHING !!
UH...
YOU WERE A BIG HELP. THANK YOU!
......
UM...
YAKUMO-SAN, YOUR CLOTHES...
キャミソール
CAMISOLE
AREN'T YOU COLD?

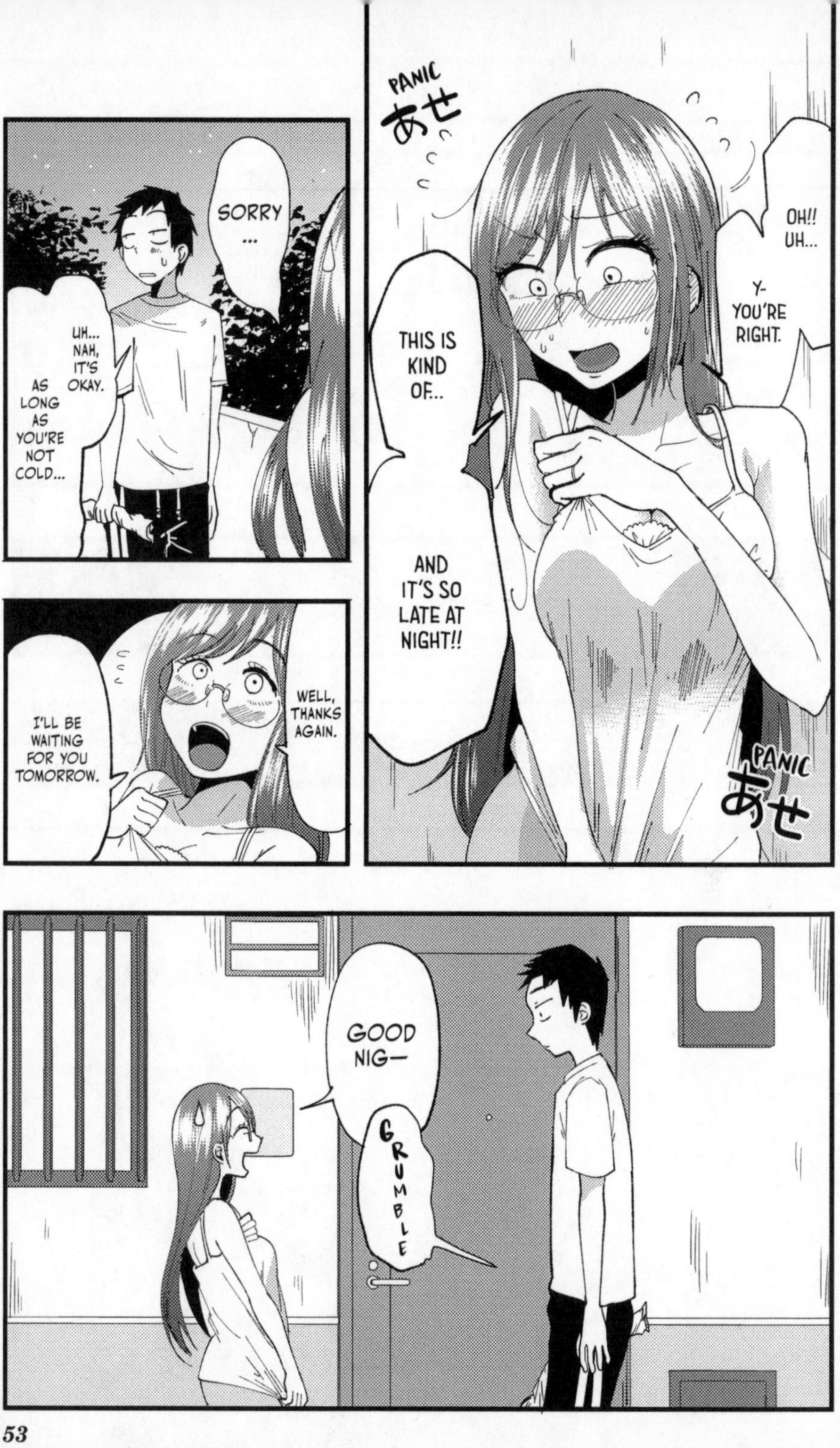
PANIC
あせ
OH!! UH...
Y- YOU'RE RIGHT.
THIS IS KIND OF...
AND IT'S SO LATE AT NIGHT!!
PANIC
あせ
SORRY ...
UH... NAH, IT'S OKAY.
AS LONG AS YOU'RE NOT COLD...
WELL, THANKS AGAIN.
I'LL BE WAITING FOR YOU TOMORROW.
GOOD NIG—
GRUMBLE

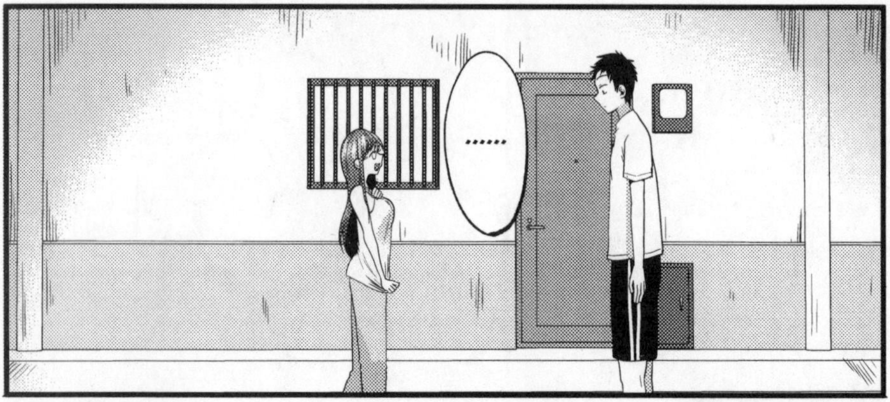
......

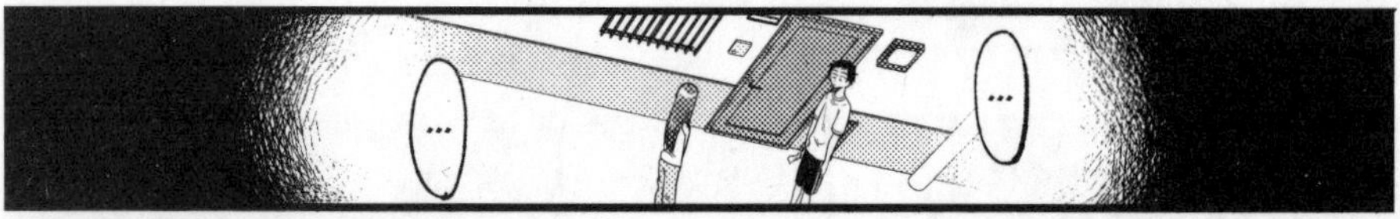
...
...

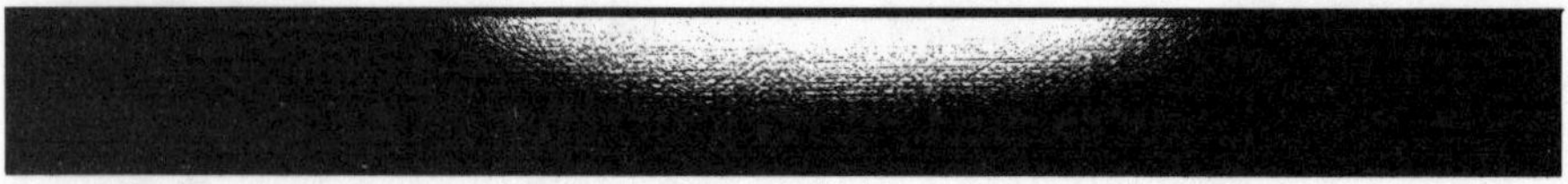

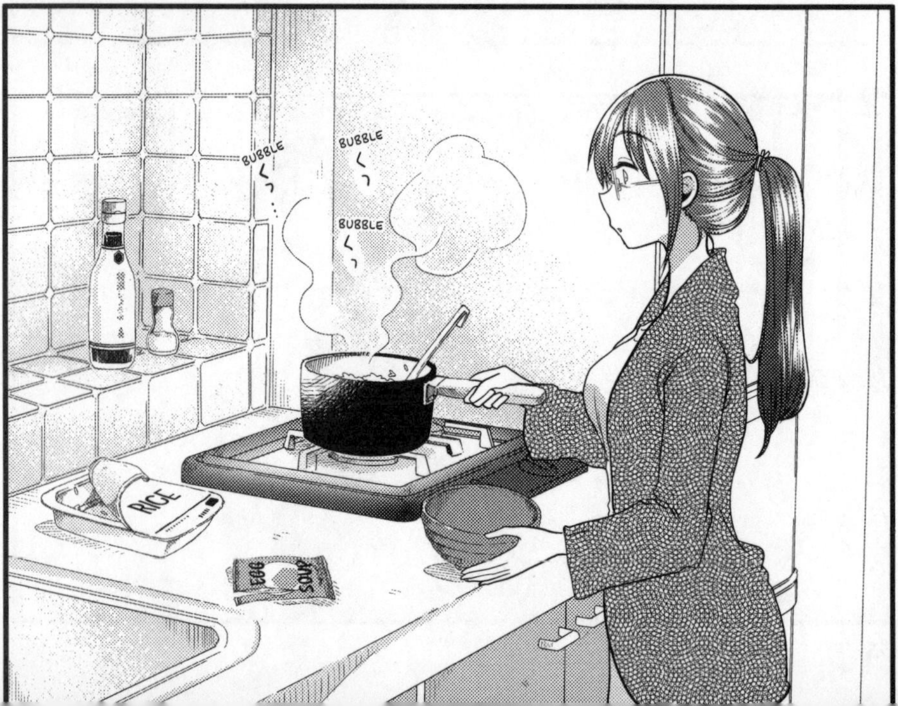
BUBBLE
くつ
BUBBLE
くつ...
BUBBLE
くつ
RICE
EGG SOUP

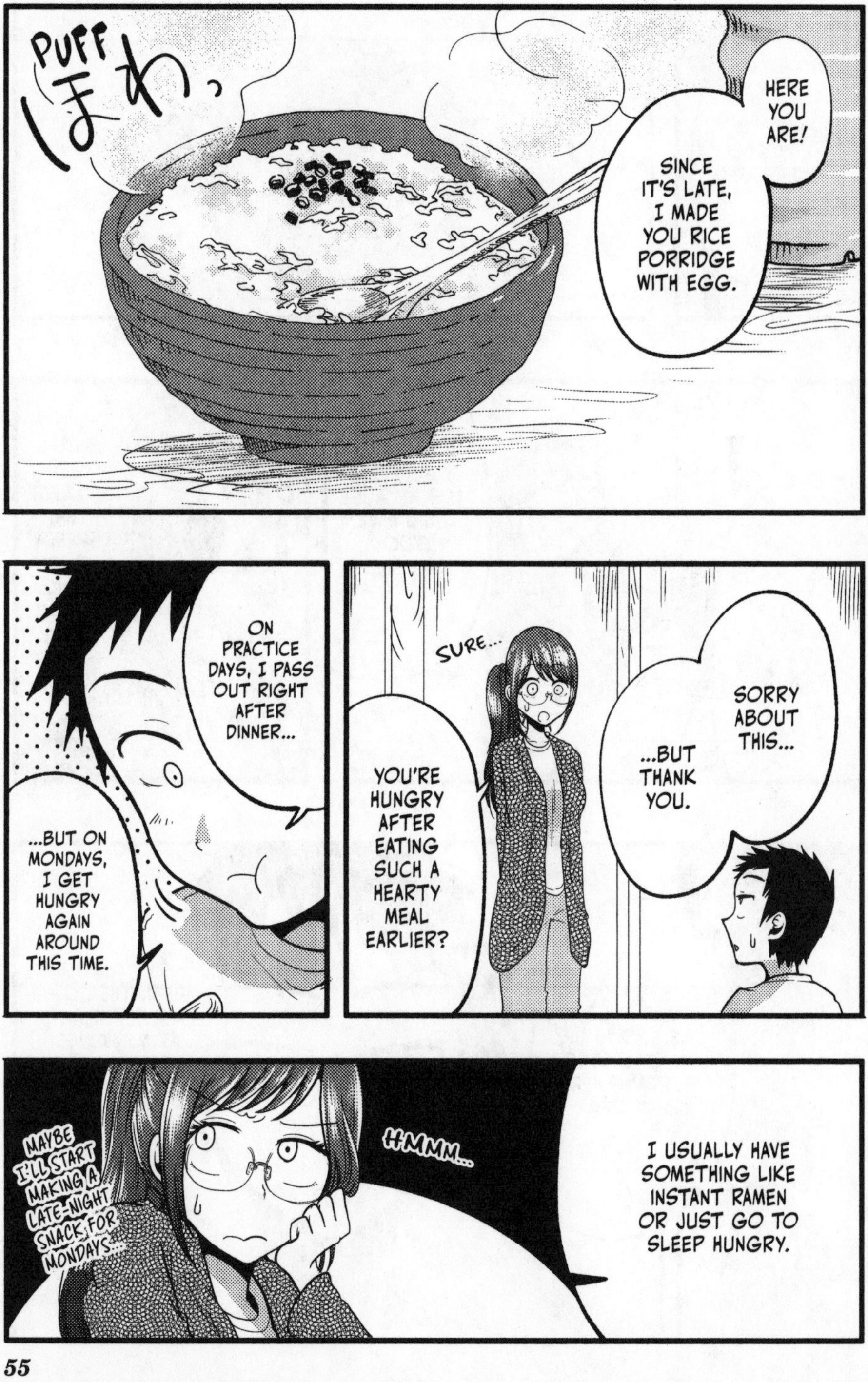
HERE YOU ARE!
SINCE IT'S LATE, I MADE YOU RICE PORRIDGE WITH EGG.
PUFF ほわっ
SORRY ABOUT THIS...
...BUT THANK YOU.
SURE...
YOU'RE HUNGRY AFTER EATING SUCH A HEARTY MEAL EARLIER?
ON PRACTICE DAYS, I PASS OUT RIGHT AFTER DINNER...
...BUT ON MONDAYS, I GET HUNGRY AGAIN AROUND THIS TIME.
I USUALLY HAVE SOMETHING LIKE INSTANT RAMEN OR JUST GO TO SLEEP HUNGRY.
HMMM...
MAYBE I'LL START MAKING A LATE-NIGHT SNACK FOR MONDAYS...

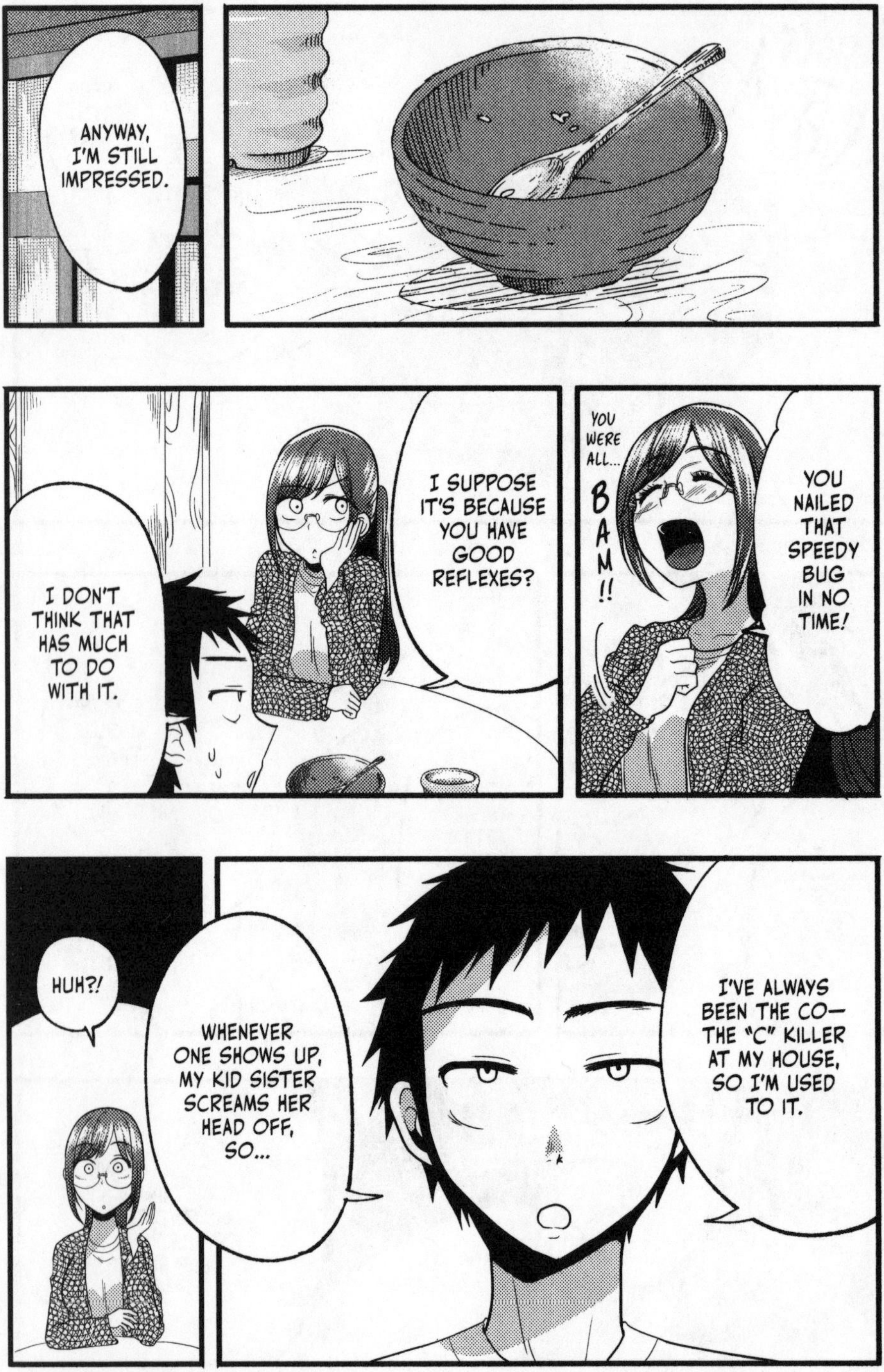
ANYWAY, I'M STILL IMPRESSED.
YOU NAILED THAT SPEEDY BUG IN NO TIME!
YOU WERE ALL...
BAM!!
I SUPPOSE IT'S BECAUSE YOU HAVE GOOD REFLEXES?
I DON'T THINK THAT HAS MUCH TO DO WITH IT.
I'VE ALWAYS BEEN THE CO— THE "C" KILLER AT MY HOUSE, SO I'M USED TO IT.
WHENEVER ONE SHOWS UP, MY KID SISTER SCREAMS HER HEAD OFF, SO...
HUH?!

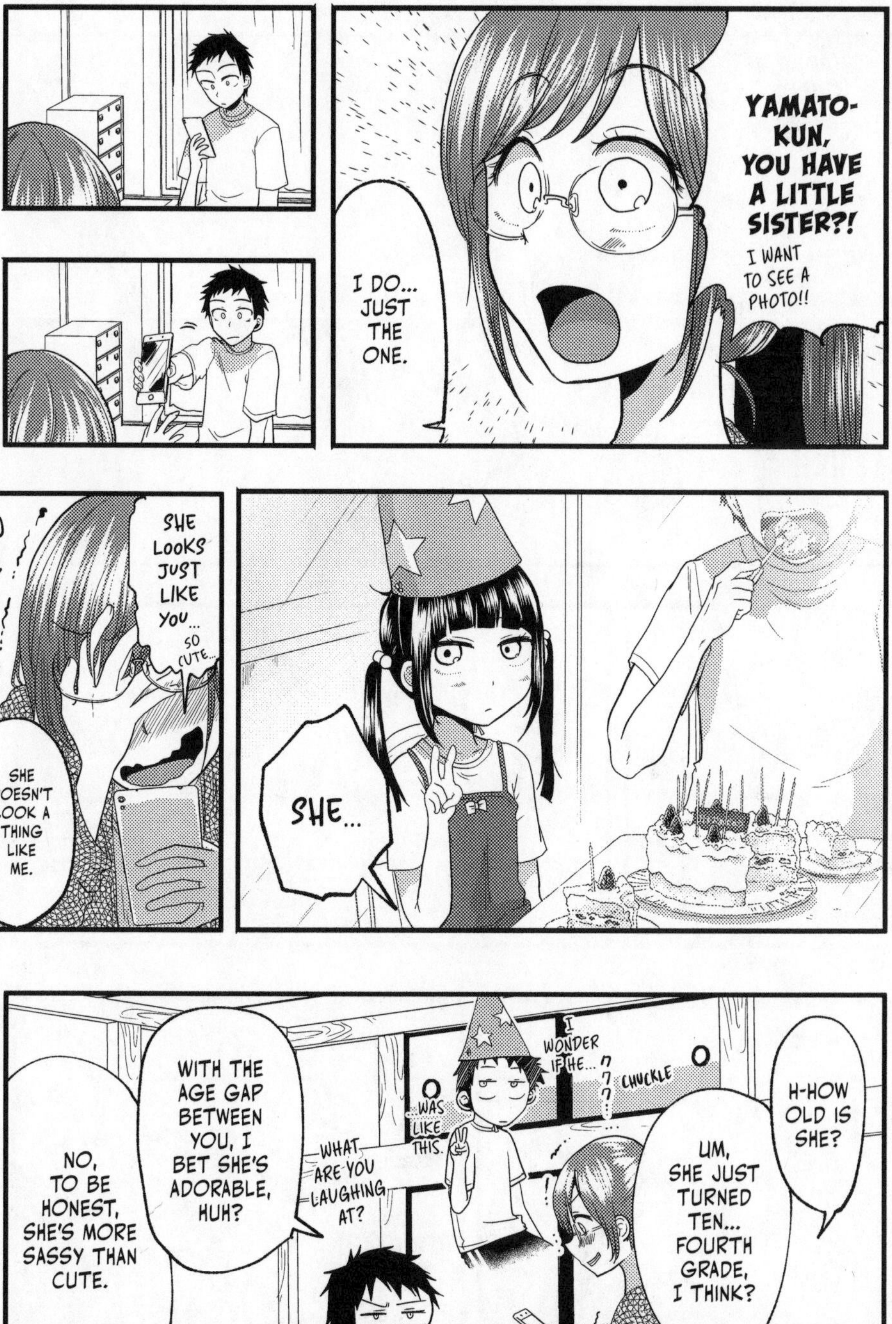
YAMATO-KUN, YOU HAVE A LITTLE SISTER?!
I WANT TO SEE A PHOTO!!
I DO... JUST THE ONE.
SHE...
SHE LOOKS JUST LIKE YOU...
SO CUTE...
QUIVER
QUIVER
SHE DOESN'T LOOK A THING LIKE ME.
H-HOW OLD IS SHE?
UM, SHE JUST TURNED TEN... FOURTH GRADE, I THINK?
I WONDER IF HE...
...WAS LIKE THIS.
CHUCKLE
WHAT ARE YOU LAUGHING AT?
WITH THE AGE GAP BETWEEN YOU, I BET SHE'S ADORABLE, HUH?
NO, TO BE HONEST, SHE'S MORE SASSY THAN CUTE.

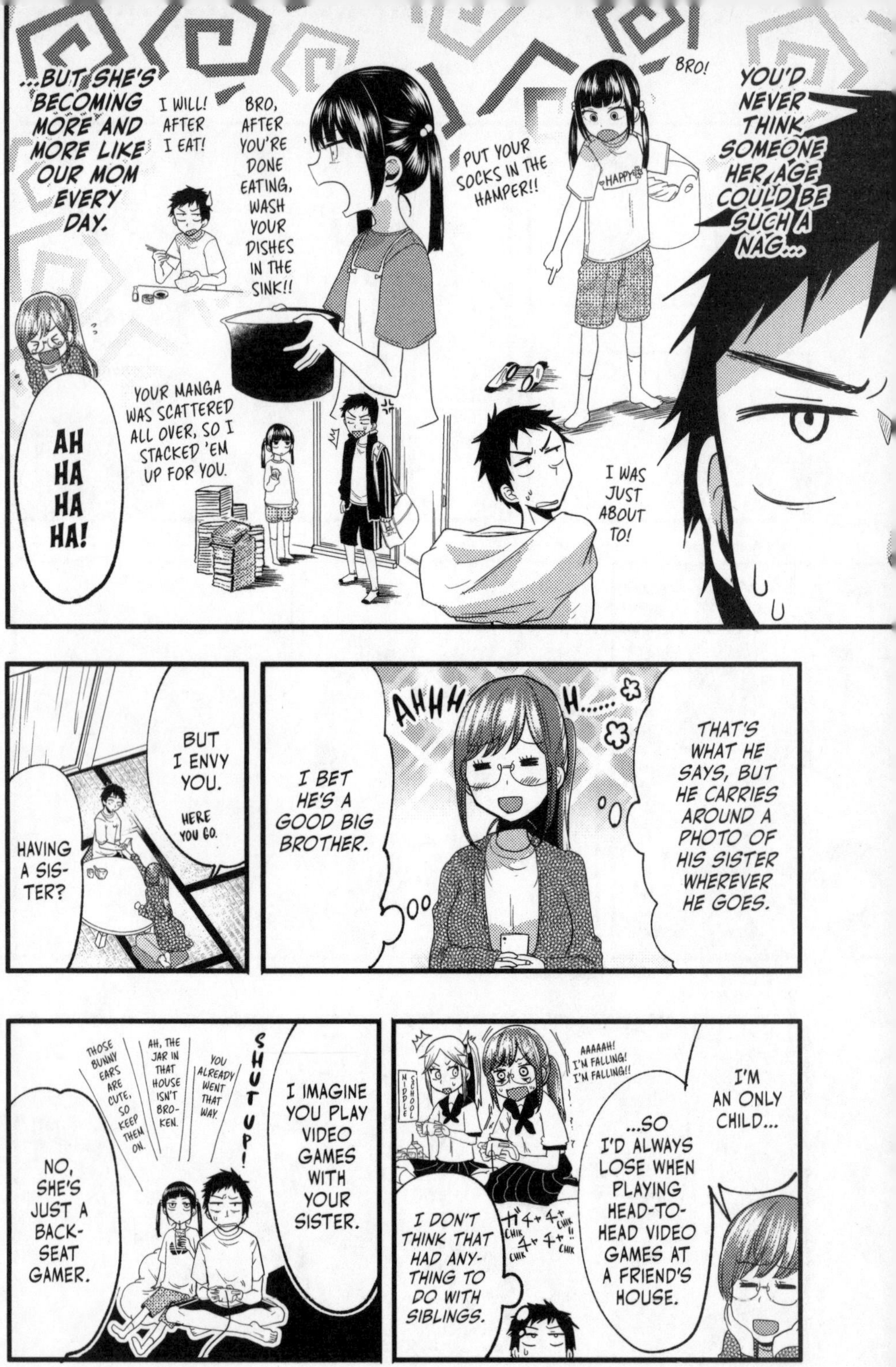
YOU'D NEVER THINK SOMEONE HER AGE COULD BE SUCH A NAG...
BRO!
PUT YOUR SOCKS IN THE HAMPER!!
BRO, AFTER YOU'RE DONE EATING, WASH YOUR DISHES IN THE SINK!!
I WILL! AFTER I EAT!
...BUT SHE'S BECOMING MORE AND MORE LIKE OUR MOM EVERY DAY.
I WAS JUST ABOUT TO!
YOUR MANGA WAS SCATTERED ALL OVER, SO I STACKED 'EM UP FOR YOU.
AH HA HA HA!
AHHHH......
THAT'S WHAT HE SAYS, BUT HE CARRIES AROUND A PHOTO OF HIS SISTER WHEREVER HE GOES.
I BET HE'S A GOOD BIG BROTHER.
BUT I ENVY YOU.
HERE YOU GO.
HAVING A SISTER?
I'M AN ONLY CHILD...
...SO I'D ALWAYS LOSE WHEN PLAYING HEAD-TO-HEAD VIDEO GAMES AT A FRIEND'S HOUSE.
AAAAAH! I'M FALLING! I'M FALLING!!
MIDDLE SCHOOL
CHIK CHIK CHIK CHIK
I DON'T THINK THAT HAD ANYTHING TO DO WITH SIBLINGS.
SHUT UP!
I IMAGINE YOU PLAY VIDEO GAMES WITH YOUR SISTER.
YOU ALREADY WENT THAT WAY.
AH, THE JAR IN THAT HOUSE ISN'T BROKEN.
THOSE BUNNY EARS ARE CUTE, SO KEEP THEM ON.
NO, SHE'S JUST A BACKSEAT GAMER.

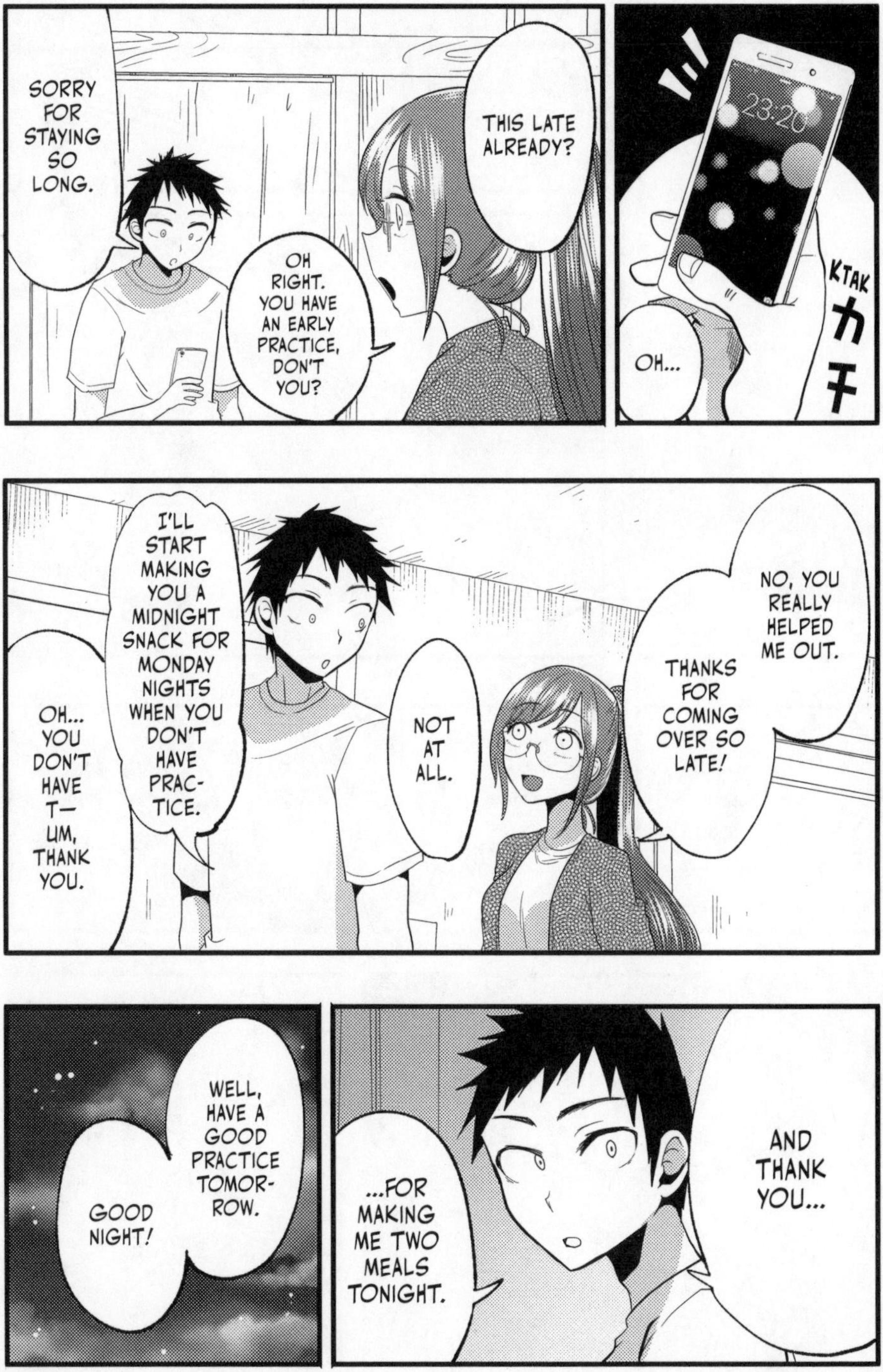
23:20
KTAK
カチ
OH...
THIS LATE ALREADY?
OH RIGHT. YOU HAVE AN EARLY PRACTICE, DON'T YOU?
SORRY FOR STAYING SO LONG.
NO, YOU REALLY HELPED ME OUT.
THANKS FOR COMING OVER SO LATE!
NOT AT ALL.
I'LL START MAKING YOU A MIDNIGHT SNACK FOR MONDAY NIGHTS WHEN YOU DON'T HAVE PRAC-TICE.
OH... YOU DON'T HAVE T— UM, THANK YOU.
AND THANK YOU...
...FOR MAKING ME TWO MEALS TONIGHT.
WELL, HAVE A GOOD PRACTICE TOMOR-ROW.
GOOD NIGHT!

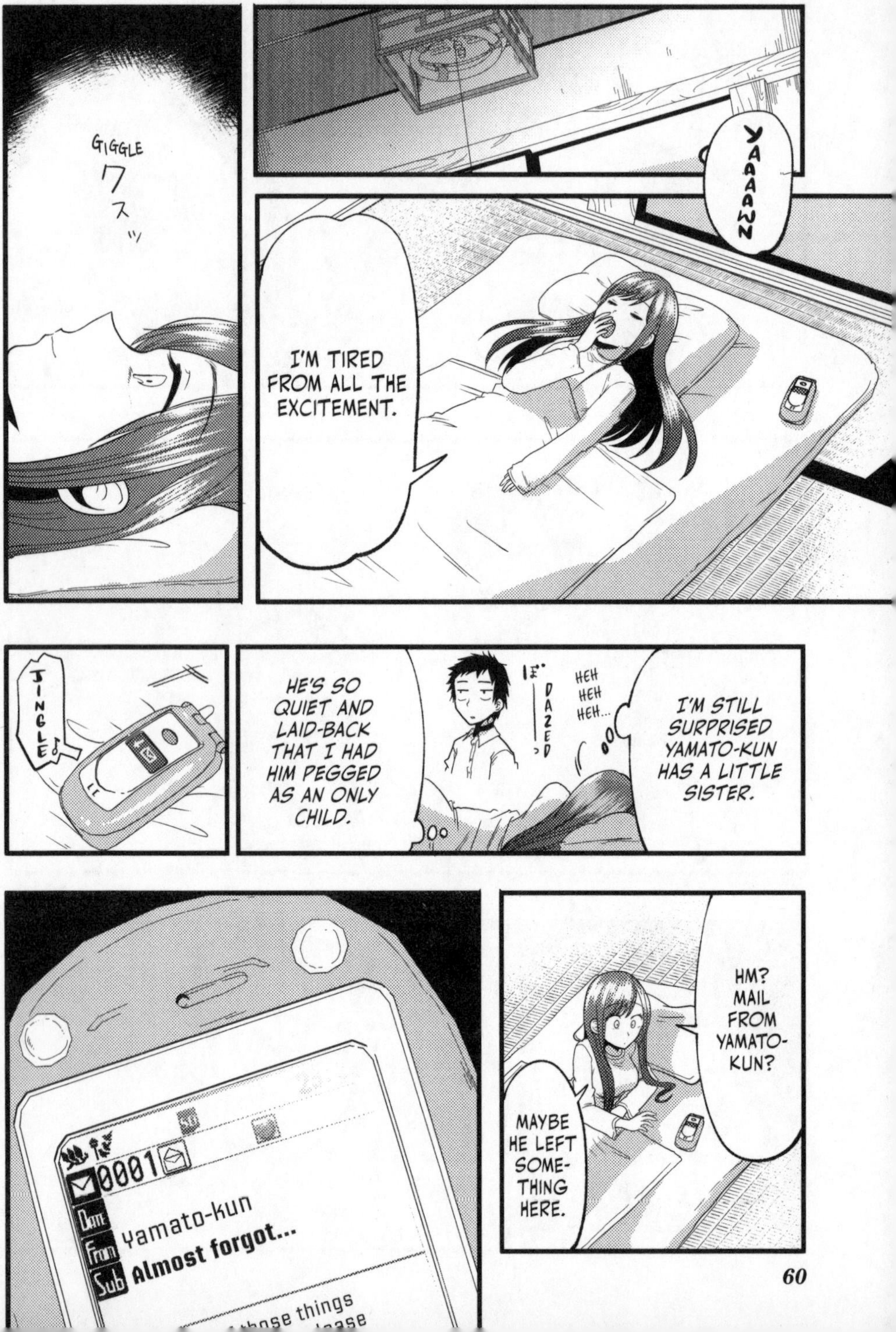

YAAAAWN
I'M TIRED FROM ALL THE EXCITEMENT.
GIGGLE
クスッ
I'M STILL SURPRISED YAMATO-KUN HAS A LITTLE SISTER.
HEH HEH HEH...
ぼー
DAZED
HE'S SO QUIET AND LAID-BACK THAT I HAD HIM PEGGED AS AN ONLY CHILD.
JINGLE♪
HM? MAIL FROM YAMATO-KUN?
MAYBE HE LEFT SOME-THING HERE.
0001
Date
From yamato-kun
Sub Almost forgot...

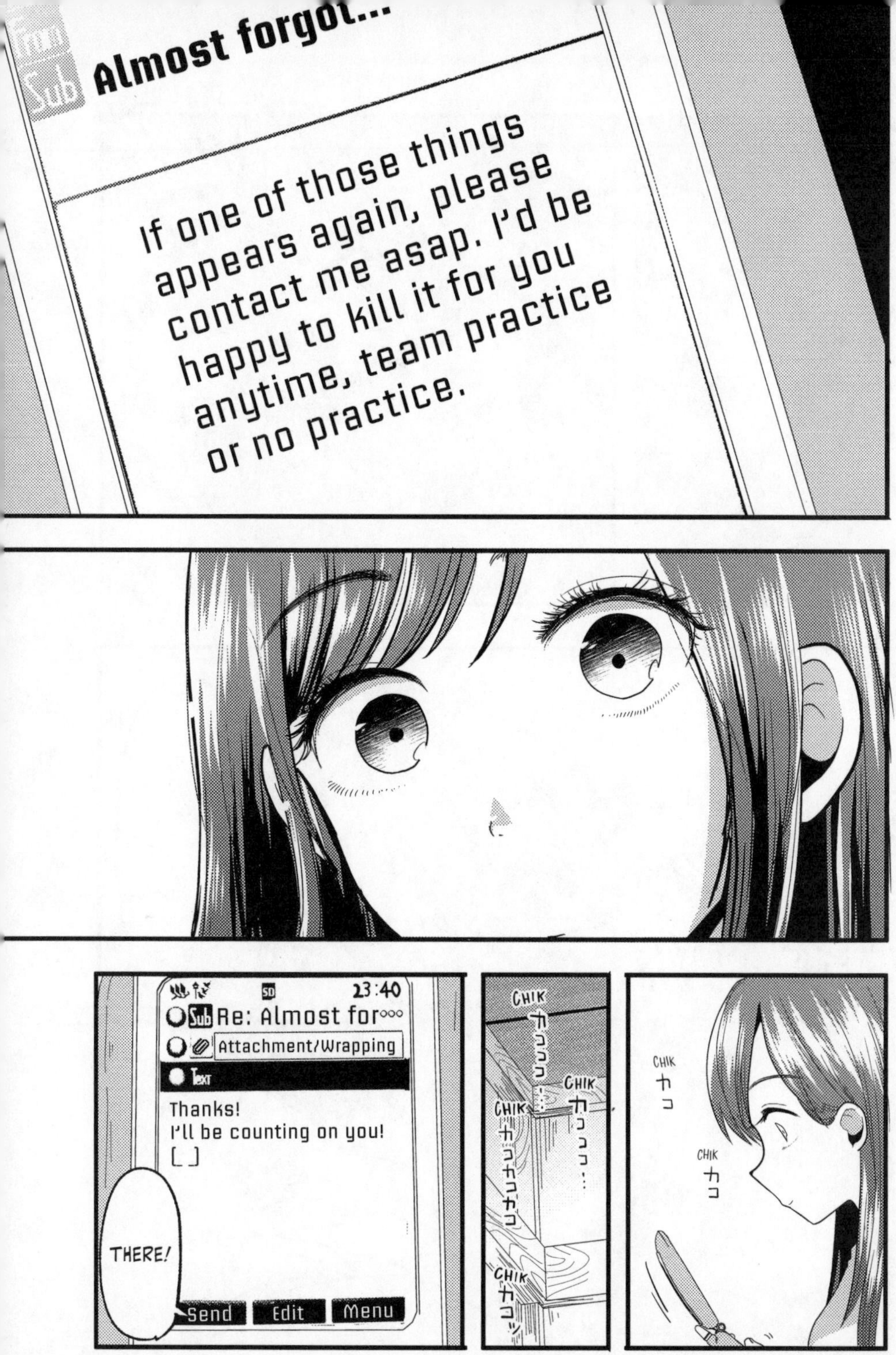
From
Sub
Almost forgot...
If one of those things appears again, please contact me asap. I'd be happy to kill it for you anytime, team practice or no practice.
CHIK
CHIK
CHIK
CHIK
CHIK
CHIK
23:40
Sub Re: Almost for...
Attachment/Wrapping
Text
Thanks!
I'll be counting on you!
[ ]
THERE!
Send
Edit
Menu

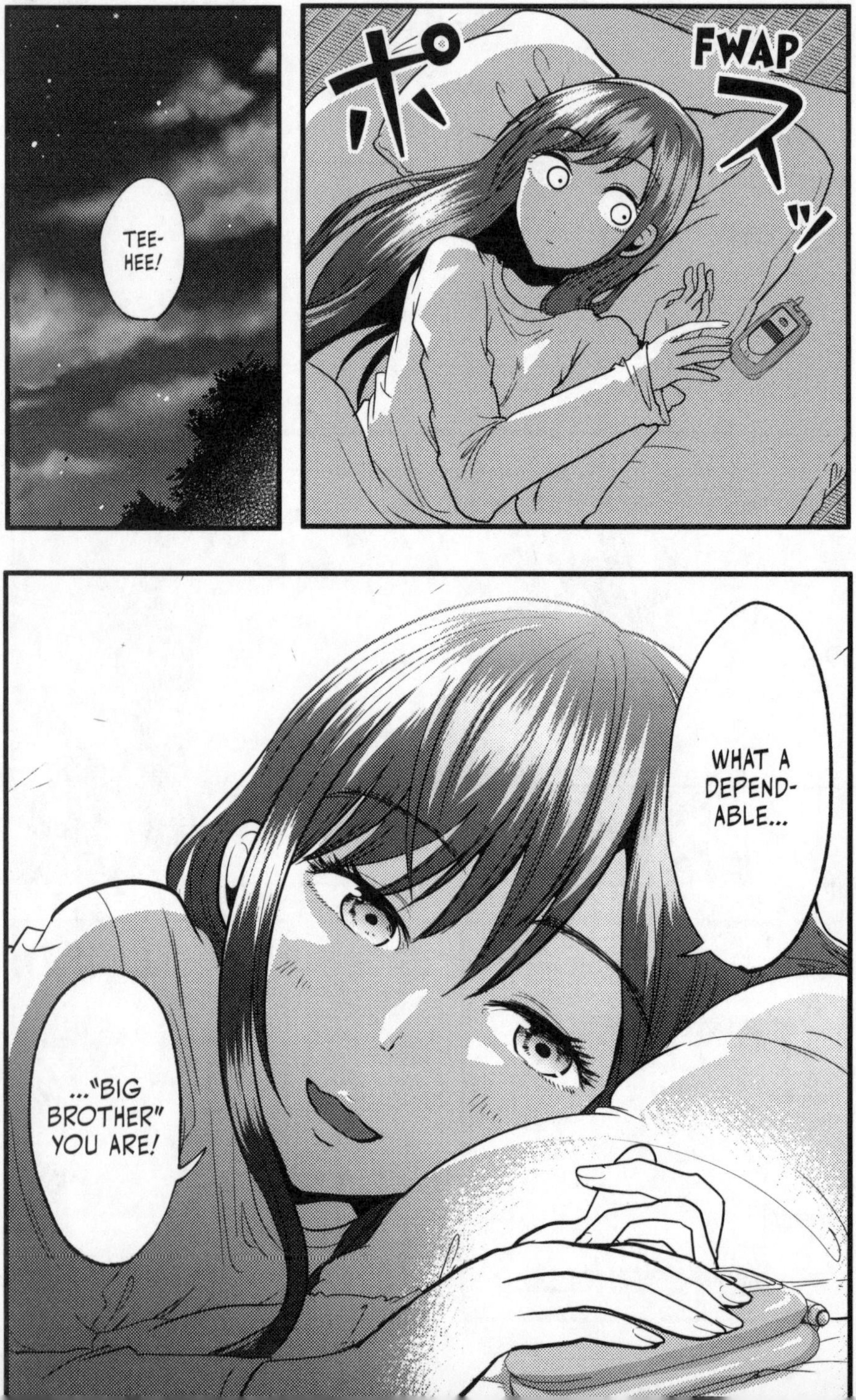
ポスッ
FWAP
TEE-HEE!
WHAT A DEPENDABLE...
..."BIG BROTHER" YOU ARE!

Beauty and the FEAST.

Beauty and the FEAST

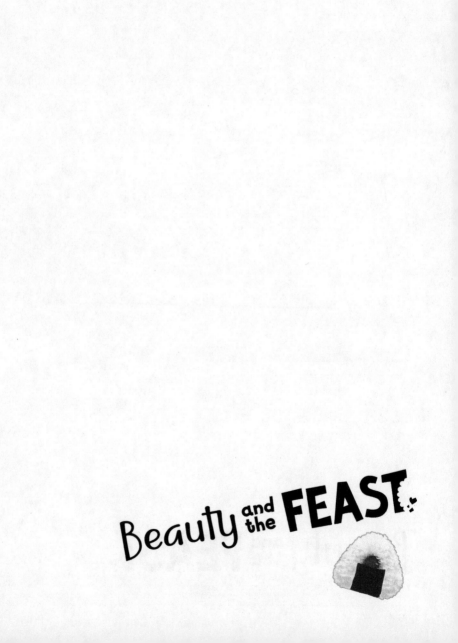

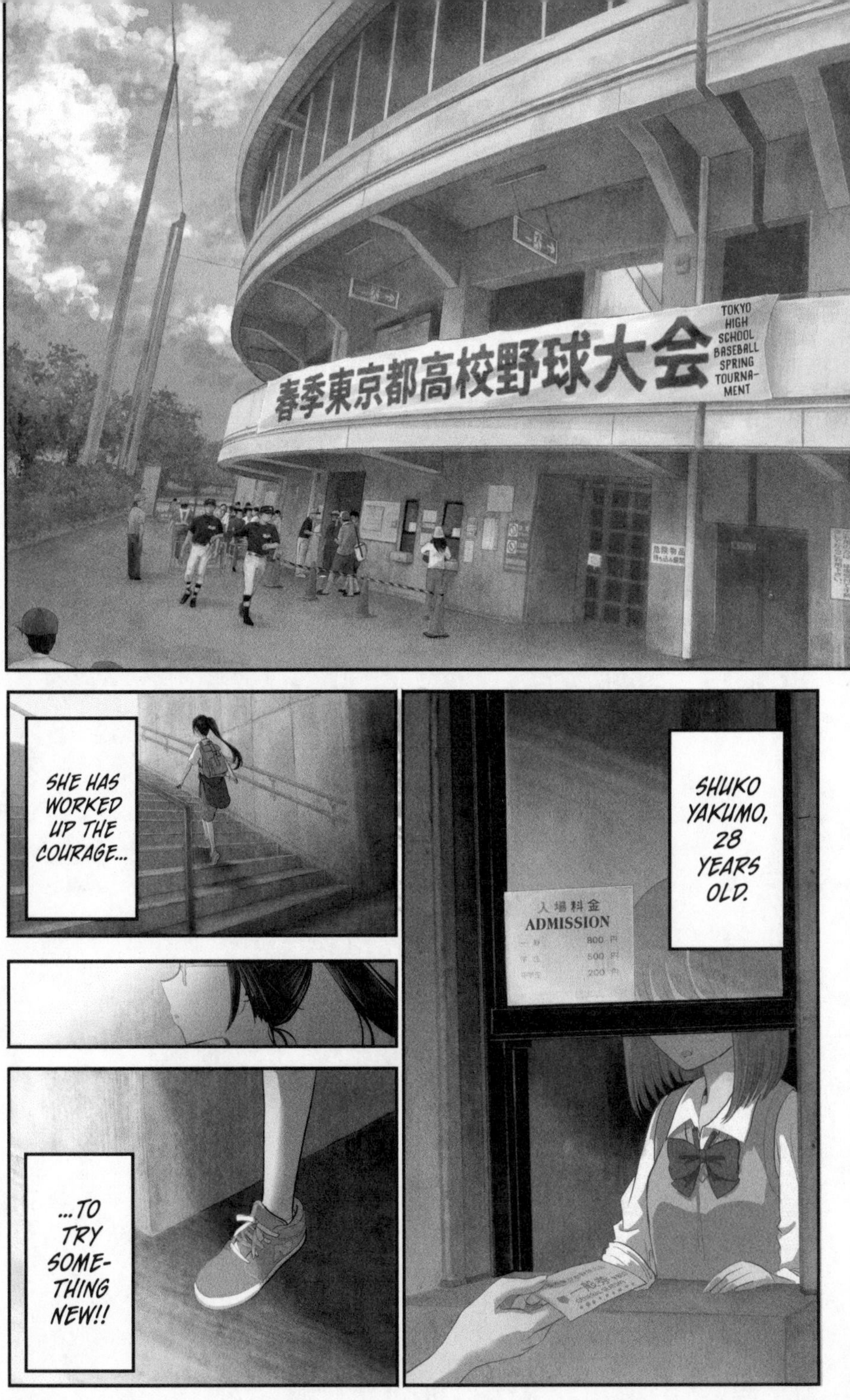
春季東京都高校野球大会
TOKYO HIGH SCHOOL BASEBALL SPRING TOURNAMENT
SHUKO YAKUMO, 28 YEARS OLD.
入場料金
ADMISSION
SHE HAS WORKED UP THE COURAGE...
...TO TRY SOMETHING NEW!!

Meal 11: Take Me Out to the Ball Game

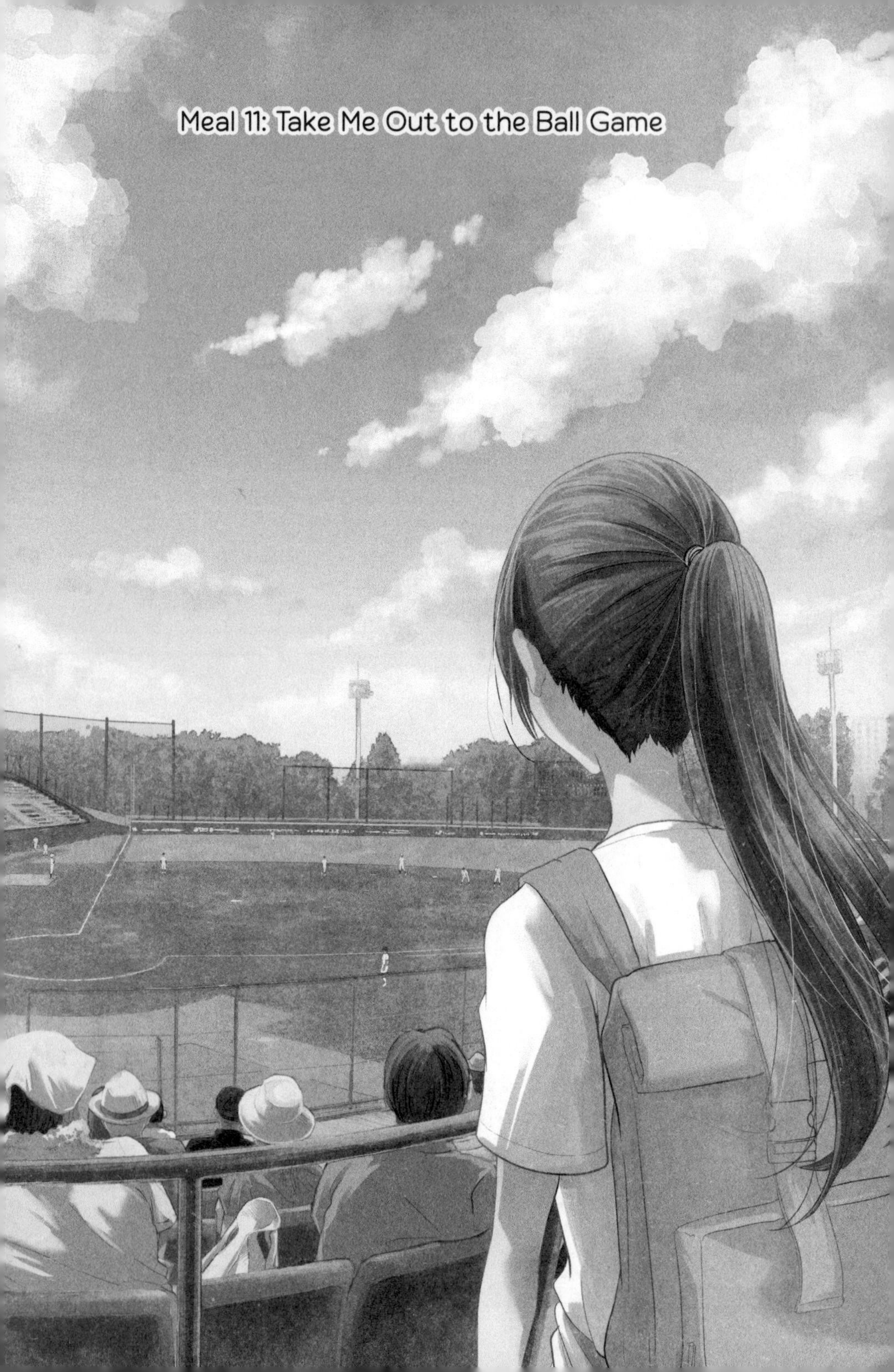

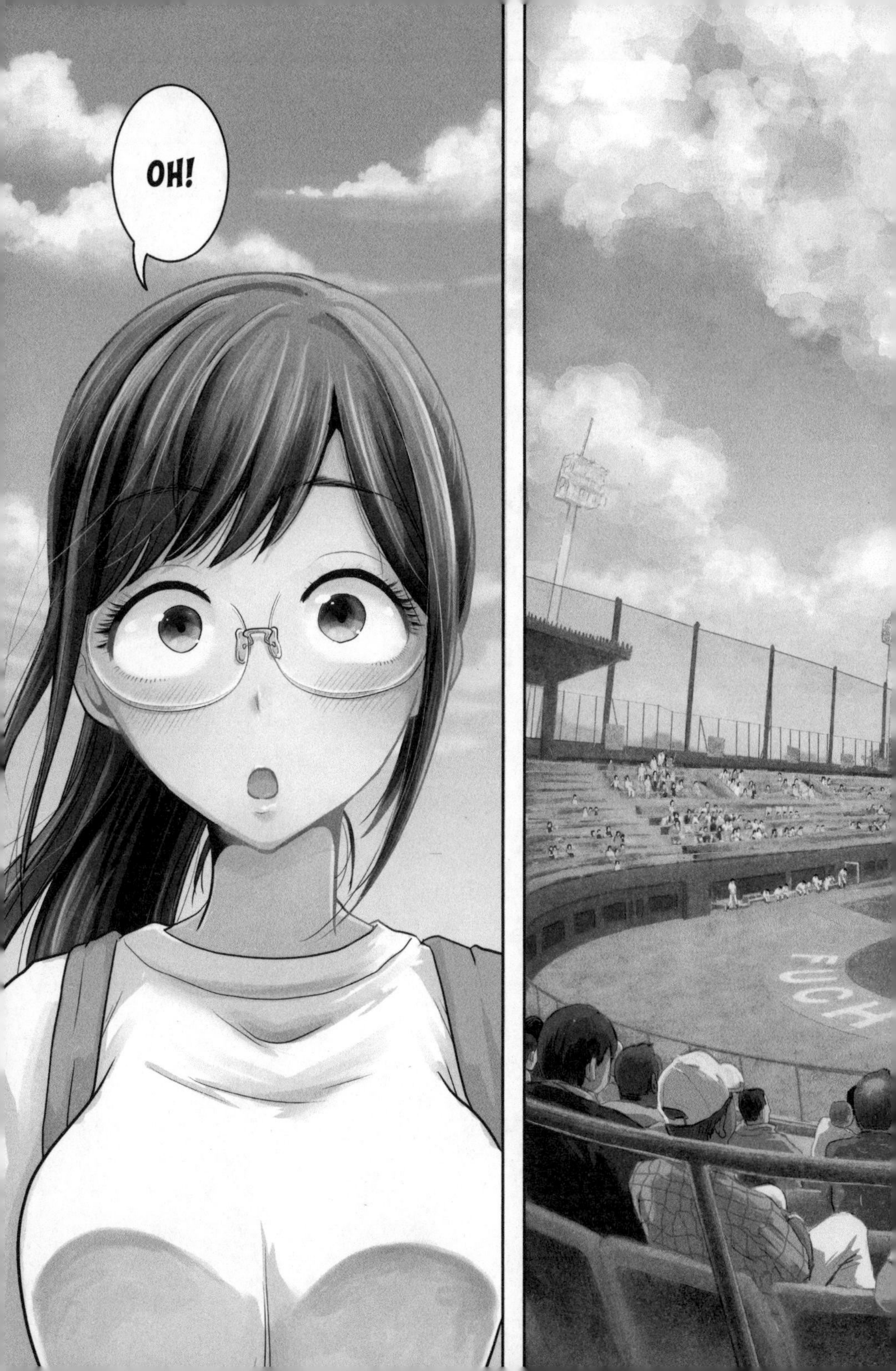
OH!

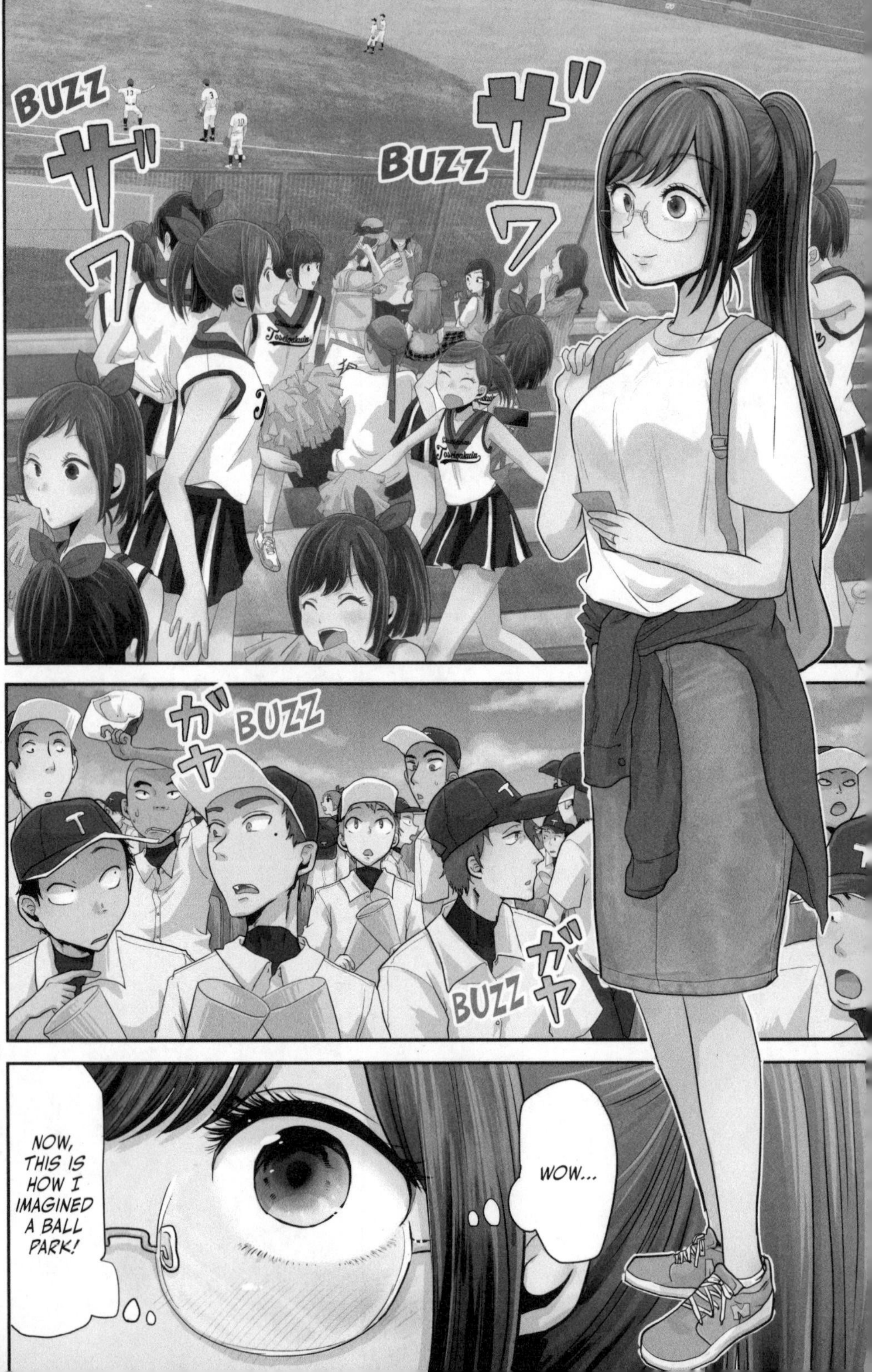
ザワ
BUZZ
BUZZ
ザワ
ガヤ
BUZZ
ガヤ
BUZZ
WOW...
NOW, THIS IS HOW I IMAGINED A BALL PARK!

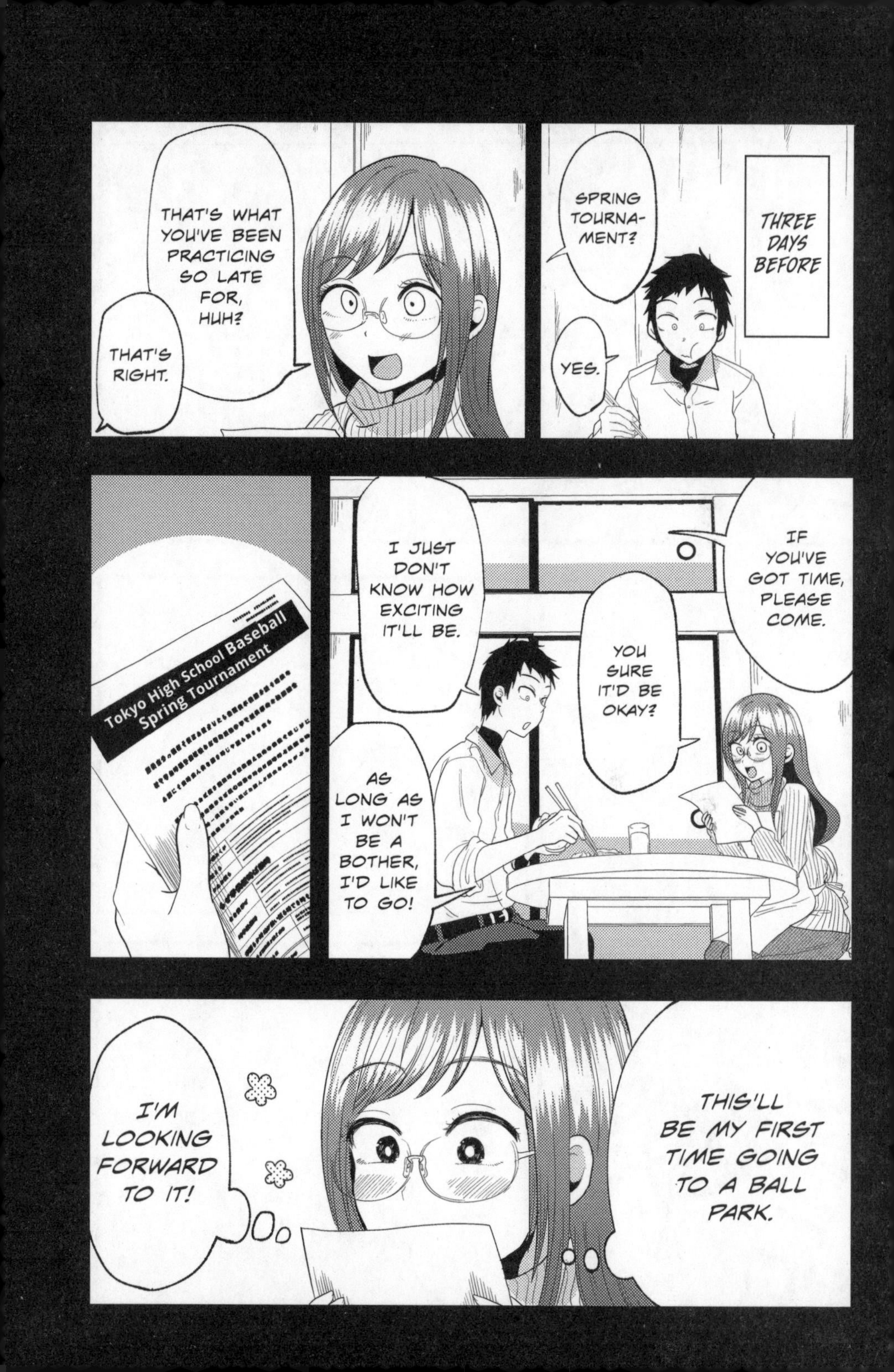
THREE DAYS BEFORE
SPRING TOURNAMENT?
YES.
THAT'S WHAT YOU'VE BEEN PRACTICING SO LATE FOR, HUH?
THAT'S RIGHT.
IF YOU'VE GOT TIME, PLEASE COME.
I JUST DON'T KNOW HOW EXCITING IT'LL BE.
YOU SURE IT'D BE OKAY?
AS LONG AS I WON'T BE A BOTHER, I'D LIKE TO GO!
Tokyo High School Baseball Spring Tournament
THIS'LL BE MY FIRST TIME GOING TO A BALL PARK.
I'M LOOKING FORWARD TO IT!

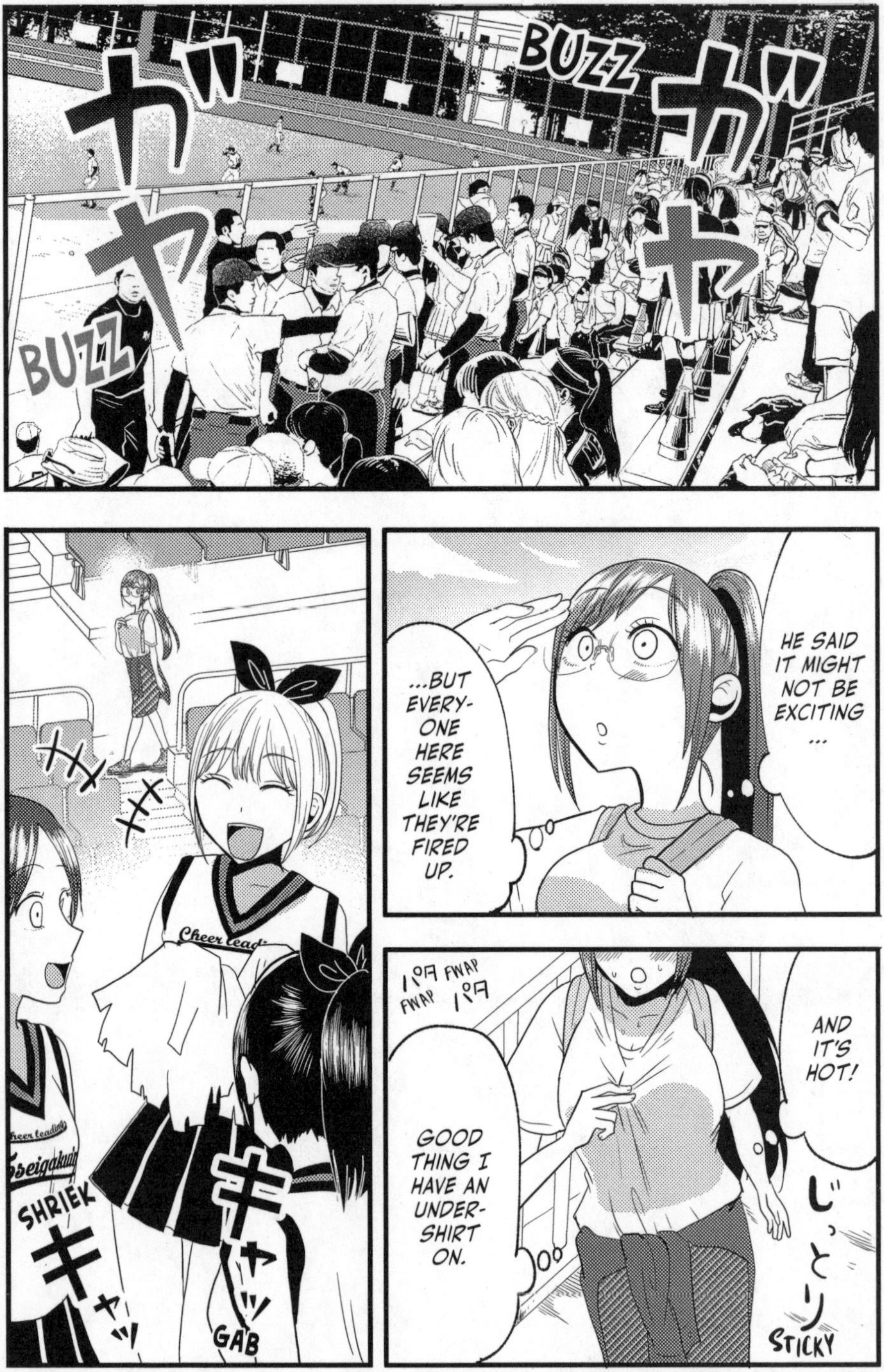
ガヤ
BUZZ
BUZZ
HE SAID IT MIGHT NOT BE EXCITING ...
...BUT EVERY-ONE HERE SEEMS LIKE THEY'RE FIRED UP.
パフ FWAP
パフ FWAP
AND IT'S HOT!
GOOD THING I HAVE AN UNDER-SHIRT ON.
じっとり
STICKY
キャッ
SHRIEK
キャッ
GAB
Cheer leading
Seigakuin

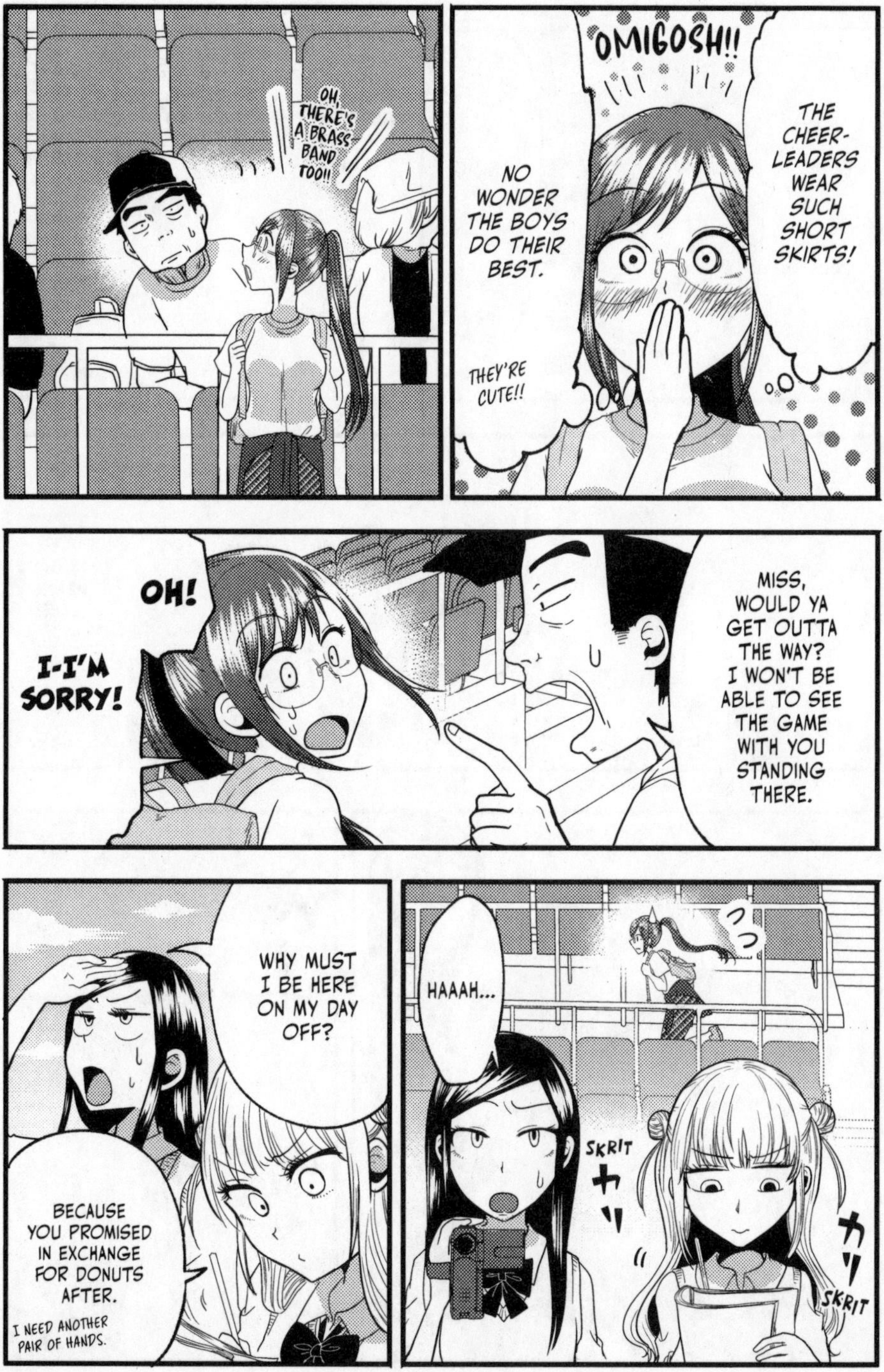
OMIGOSH!!
THE CHEER-LEADERS WEAR SUCH SHORT SKIRTS!
NO WONDER THE BOYS DO THEIR BEST.
THEY'RE CUTE!!
OH, THERE'S A BRASS BAND TOO!!
MISS, WOULD YA GET OUTTA THE WAY? I WON'T BE ABLE TO SEE THE GAME WITH YOU STANDING THERE.
OH!
I-I'M SORRY!
HAAAH...
SKRIT
SKRIT
WHY MUST I BE HERE ON MY DAY OFF?
BECAUSE YOU PROMISED IN EXCHANGE FOR DONUTS AFTER.
I NEED ANOTHER PAIR OF HANDS.

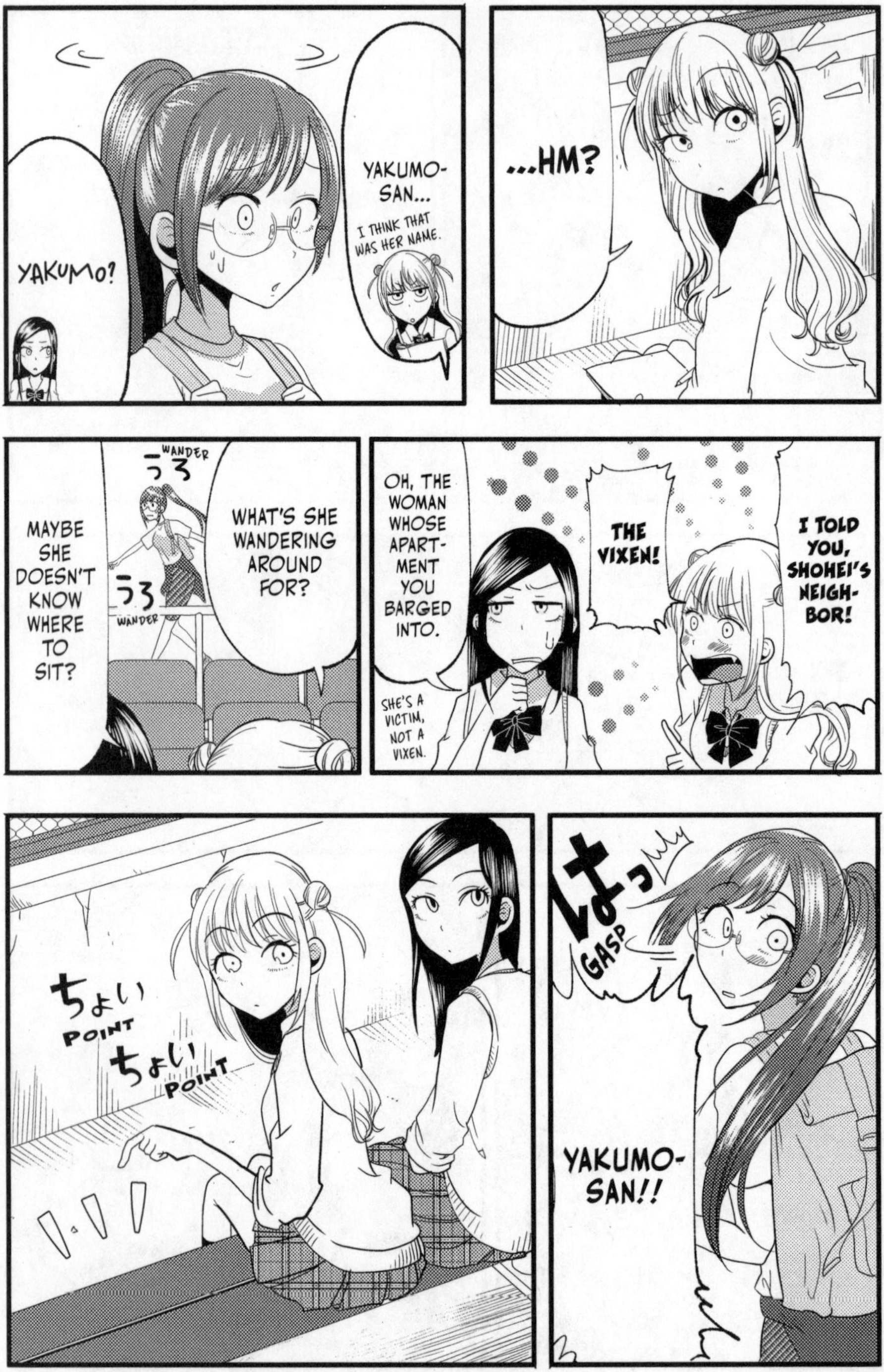
...HM?
YAKUMO-SAN...
I THINK THAT WAS HER NAME.
YAKUMO?
I TOLD YOU, SHOHEI'S NEIGHBOR!
THE VIXEN!
OH, THE WOMAN WHOSE APARTMENT YOU BARGED INTO.
SHE'S A VICTIM, NOT A VIXEN.
うろ WANDER
うろ WANDER
WHAT'S SHE WANDERING AROUND FOR?
MAYBE SHE DOESN'T KNOW WHERE TO SIT?
はっ GASP
YAKUMO-SAN!!
ちょい POINT
ちょい POINT

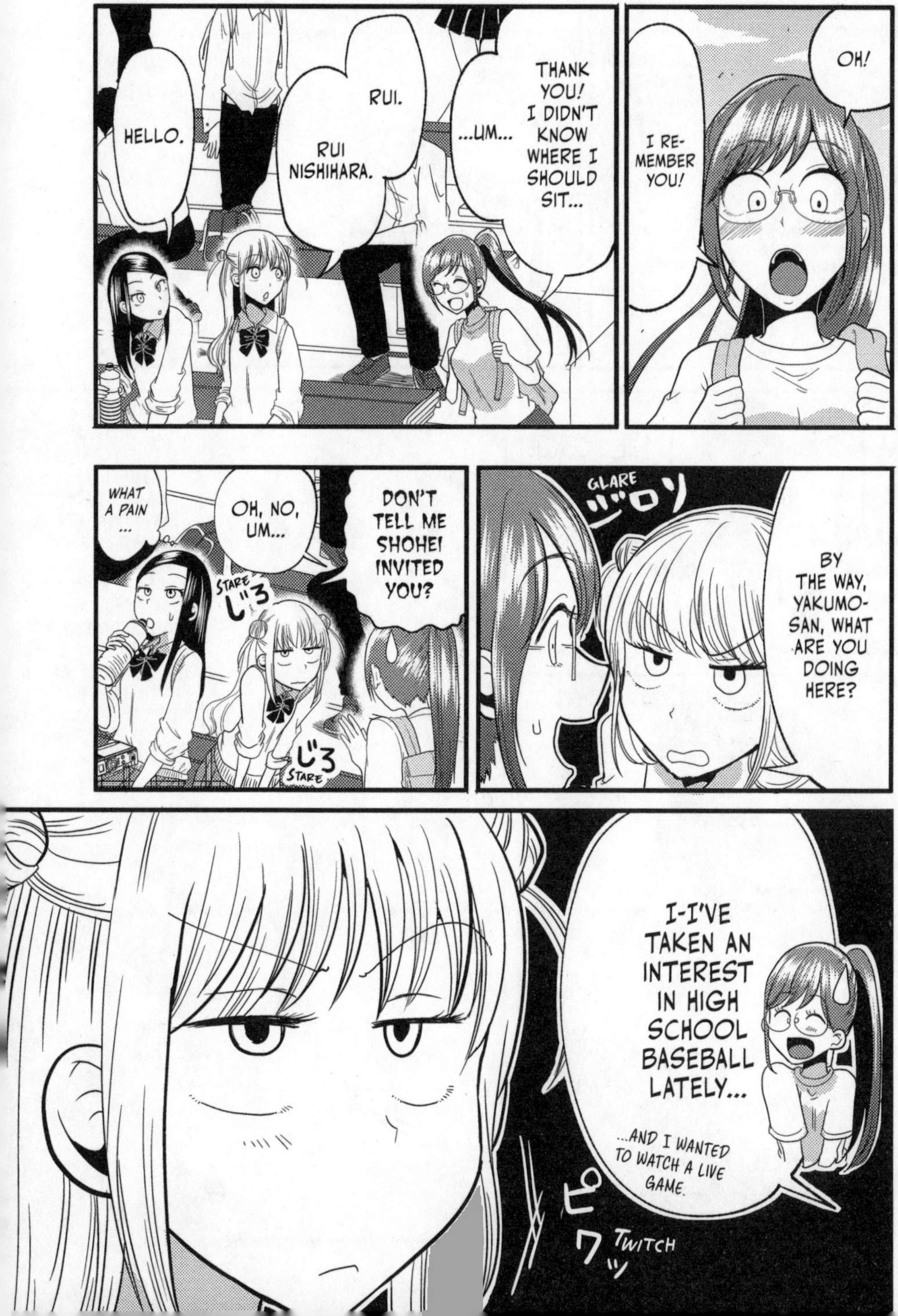
OH!
I RE-MEMBER YOU!
THANK YOU! I DIDN'T KNOW WHERE I SHOULD SIT...
...UM...
RUI.
RUI NISHIHARA.
HELLO.
GLARE
BY THE WAY, YAKUMO-SAN, WHAT ARE YOU DOING HERE?
DON'T TELL ME SHOHEI INVITED YOU?
OH, NO, UM...
WHAT A PAIN ...
STARE
STARE
I-I'VE TAKEN AN INTEREST IN HIGH SCHOOL BASEBALL LATELY...
...AND I WANTED TO WATCH A LIVE GAME.
TWITCH

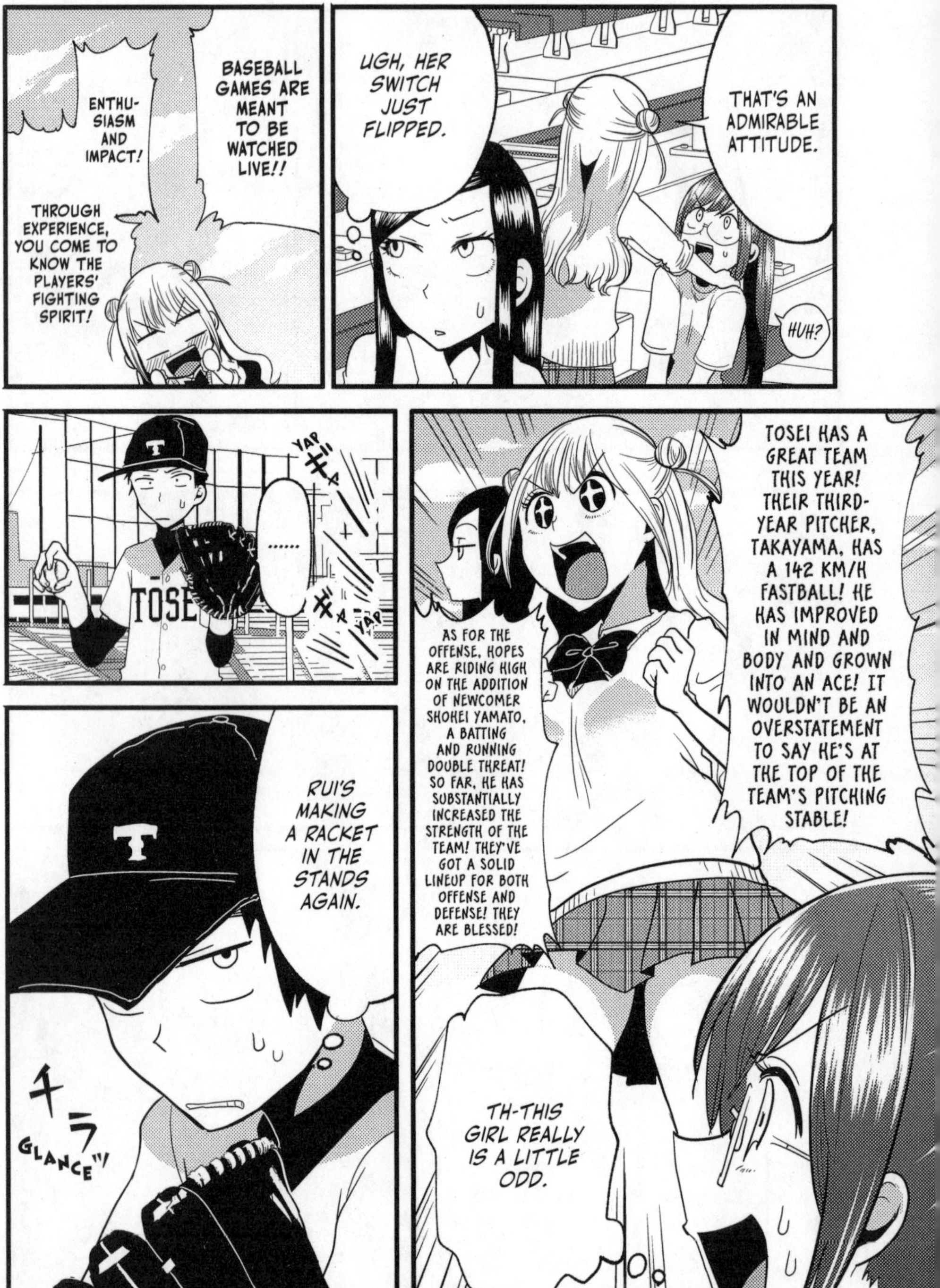
THAT'S AN ADMIRABLE ATTITUDE.
UGH, HER SWITCH JUST FLIPPED.
HUH?
BASEBALL GAMES ARE MEANT TO BE WATCHED LIVE!!
ENTHUSIASM AND IMPACT!
THROUGH EXPERIENCE, YOU COME TO KNOW THE PLAYERS' FIGHTING SPIRIT!
TOSEI HAS A GREAT TEAM THIS YEAR! THEIR THIRD-YEAR PITCHER, TAKAYAMA, HAS A 142 KM/H FASTBALL! HE HAS IMPROVED IN MIND AND BODY AND GROWN INTO AN ACE! IT WOULDN'T BE AN OVERSTATEMENT TO SAY HE'S AT THE TOP OF THE TEAM'S PITCHING STABLE!
AS FOR THE OFFENSE, HOPES ARE RIDING HIGH ON THE ADDITION OF NEWCOMER SHOHEI YAMATO, A BATTING AND RUNNING DOUBLE THREAT! SO FAR, HE HAS SUBSTANTIALLY INCREASED THE STRENGTH OF THE TEAM! THEY'VE GOT A SOLID LINEUP FOR BOTH OFFENSE AND DEFENSE! THEY ARE BLESSED!
TH-THIS GIRL REALLY IS A LITTLE ODD.
YAP
......
YAP
TOSEI
RUI'S MAKING A RACKET IN THE STANDS AGAIN.
GLANCE

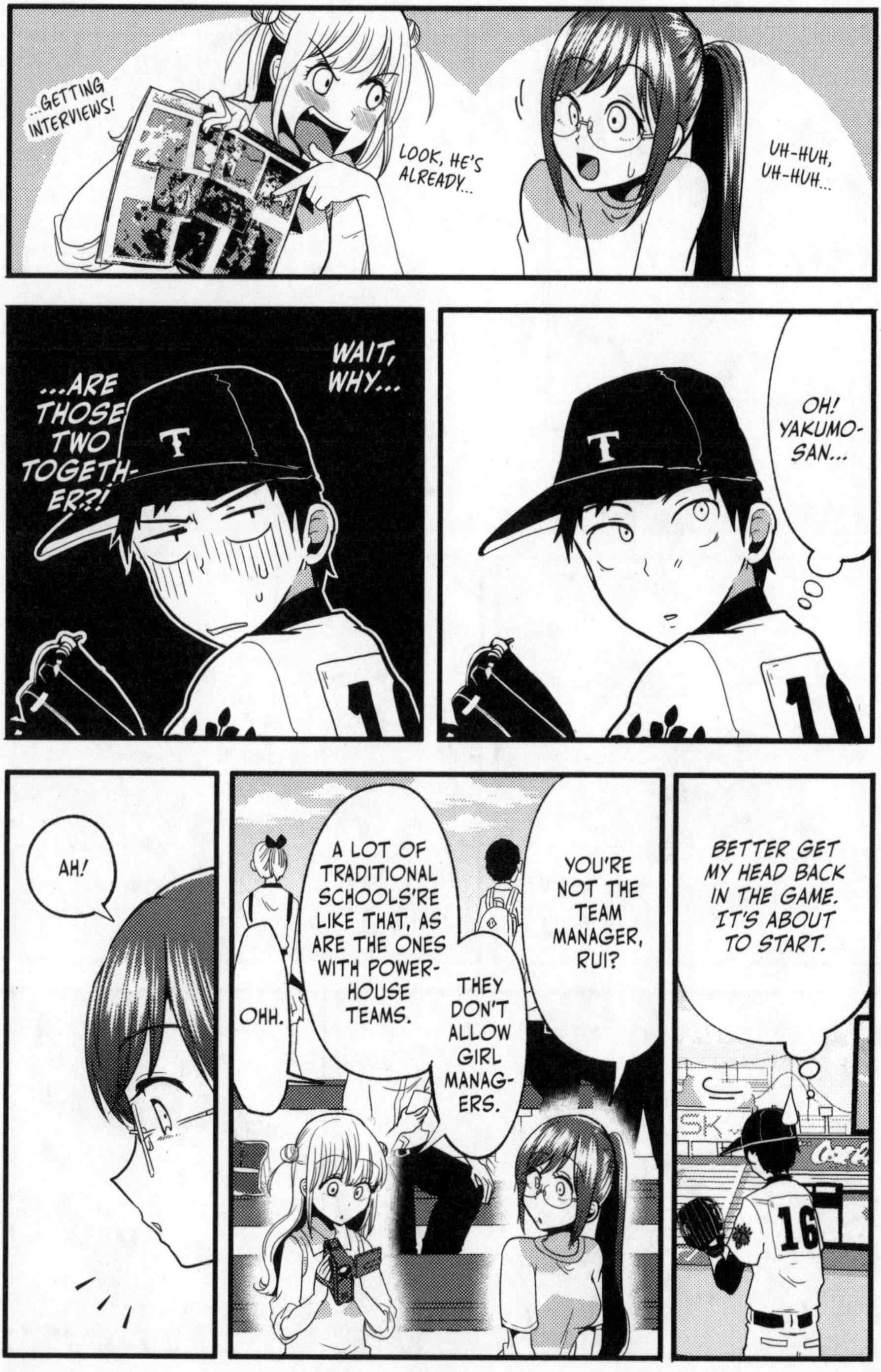
UH-HUH, UH-HUH...
LOOK, HE'S ALREADY...
...GETTING INTERVIEWS!
OH! YAKUMO-SAN...
WAIT, WHY...
...ARE THOSE TWO TOGETHER?!
BETTER GET MY HEAD BACK IN THE GAME. IT'S ABOUT TO START.
YOU'RE NOT THE TEAM MANAGER, RUI?
THEY DON'T ALLOW GIRL MANAGERS.
A LOT OF TRADITIONAL SCHOOLS'RE LIKE THAT, AS ARE THE ONES WITH POWERHOUSE TEAMS.
OHH.
AH!

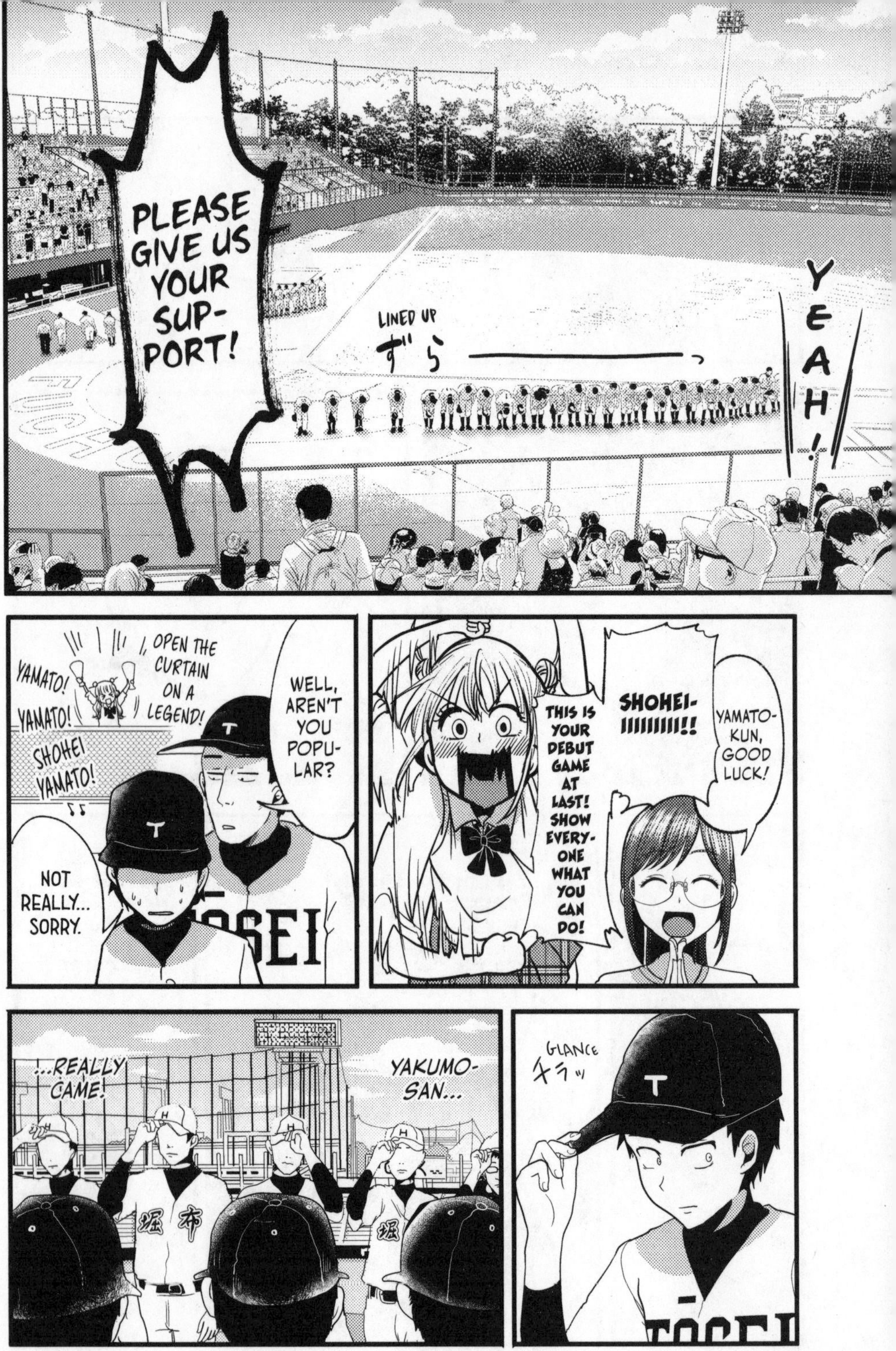
PLEASE GIVE US YOUR SUP-PORT!
LINED UP
ずら
YEAH!!
SHOHEI-IIIIIIIII!!
YAMATO-KUN, GOOD LUCK!
THIS IS YOUR DEBUT GAME AT LAST! SHOW EVERY-ONE WHAT YOU CAN DO!
WELL, AREN'T YOU POPU-LAR?
OPEN THE CURTAIN ON A LEGEND!
YAMATO!
YAMATO!
SHOHEI YAMATO!
NOT REALLY... SORRY.
GLANCE
チラッ
YAKUMO-SAN...
...REALLY CAME!

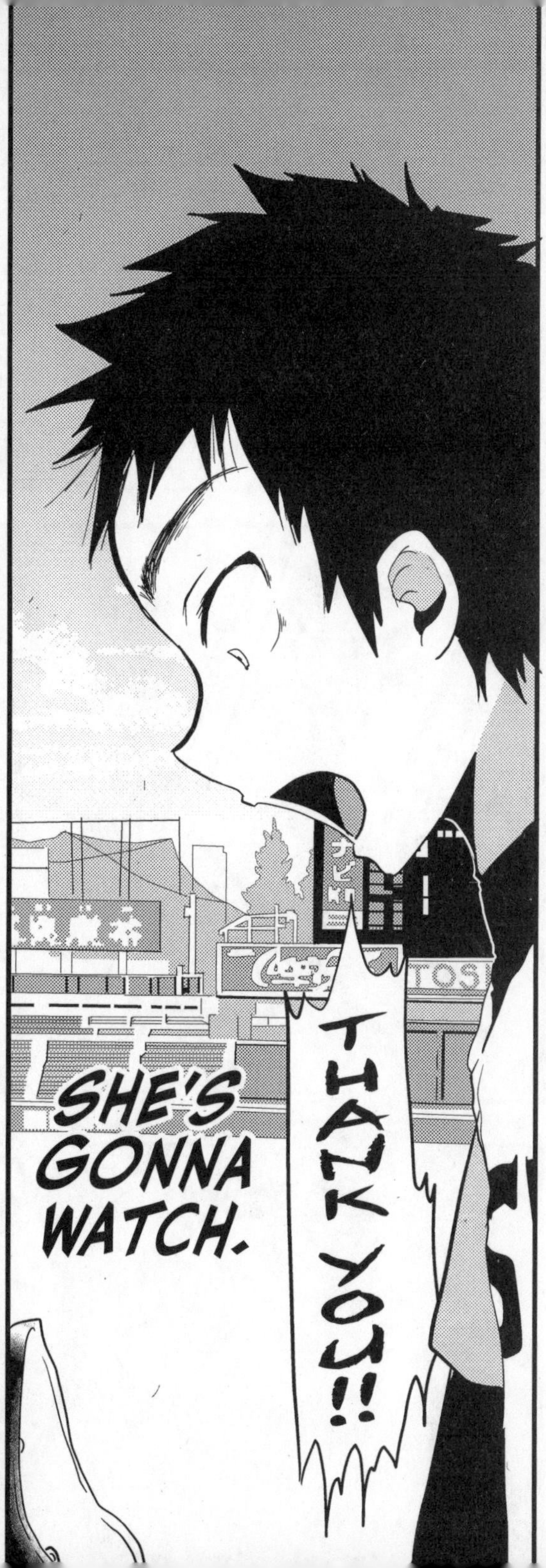
THANK YOU!!
SHE'S GONNA WATCH.
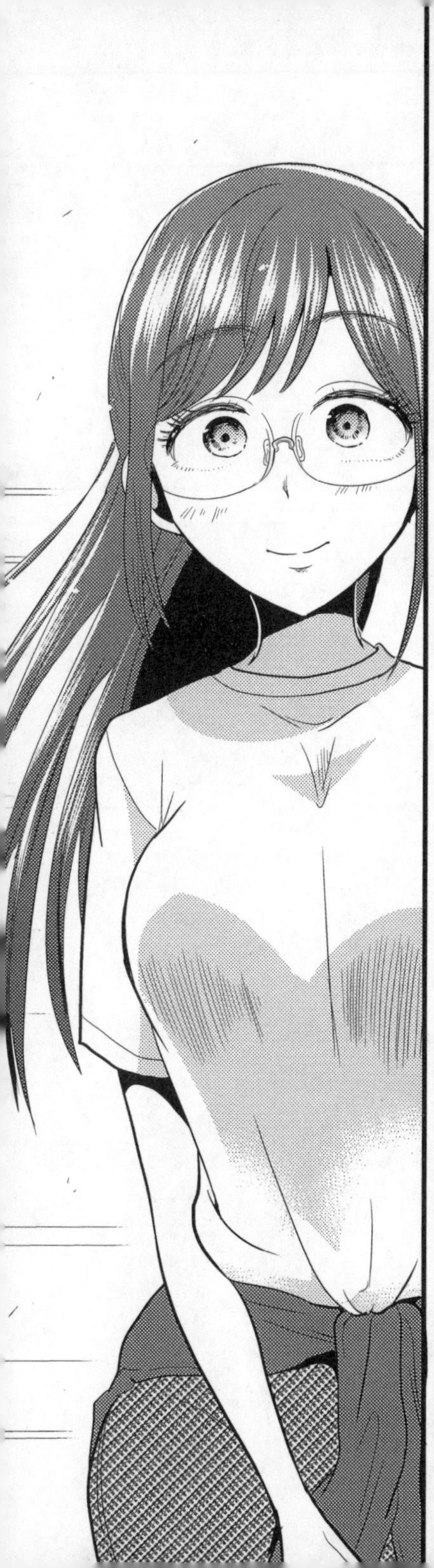

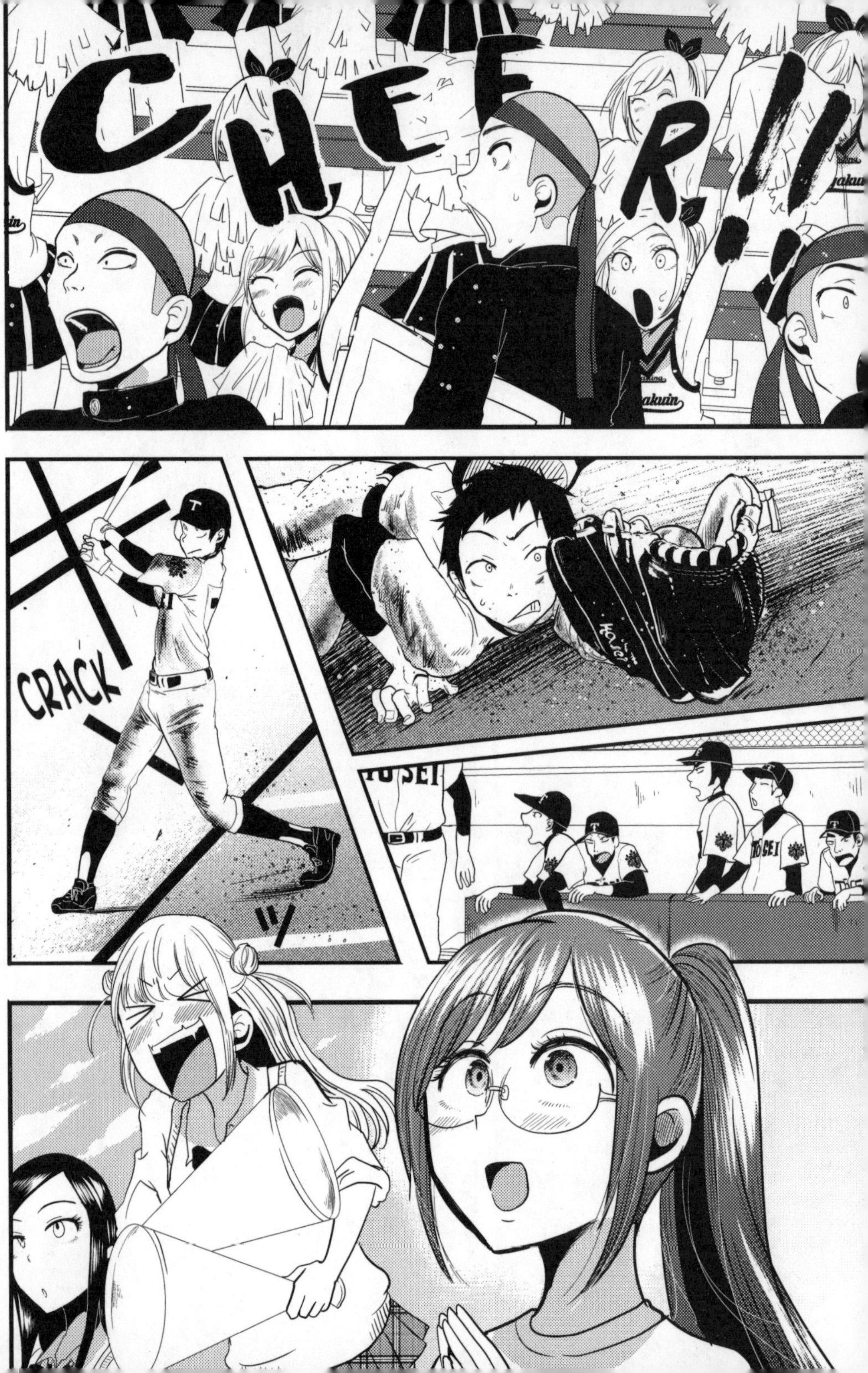
CHEER!!
CRACK

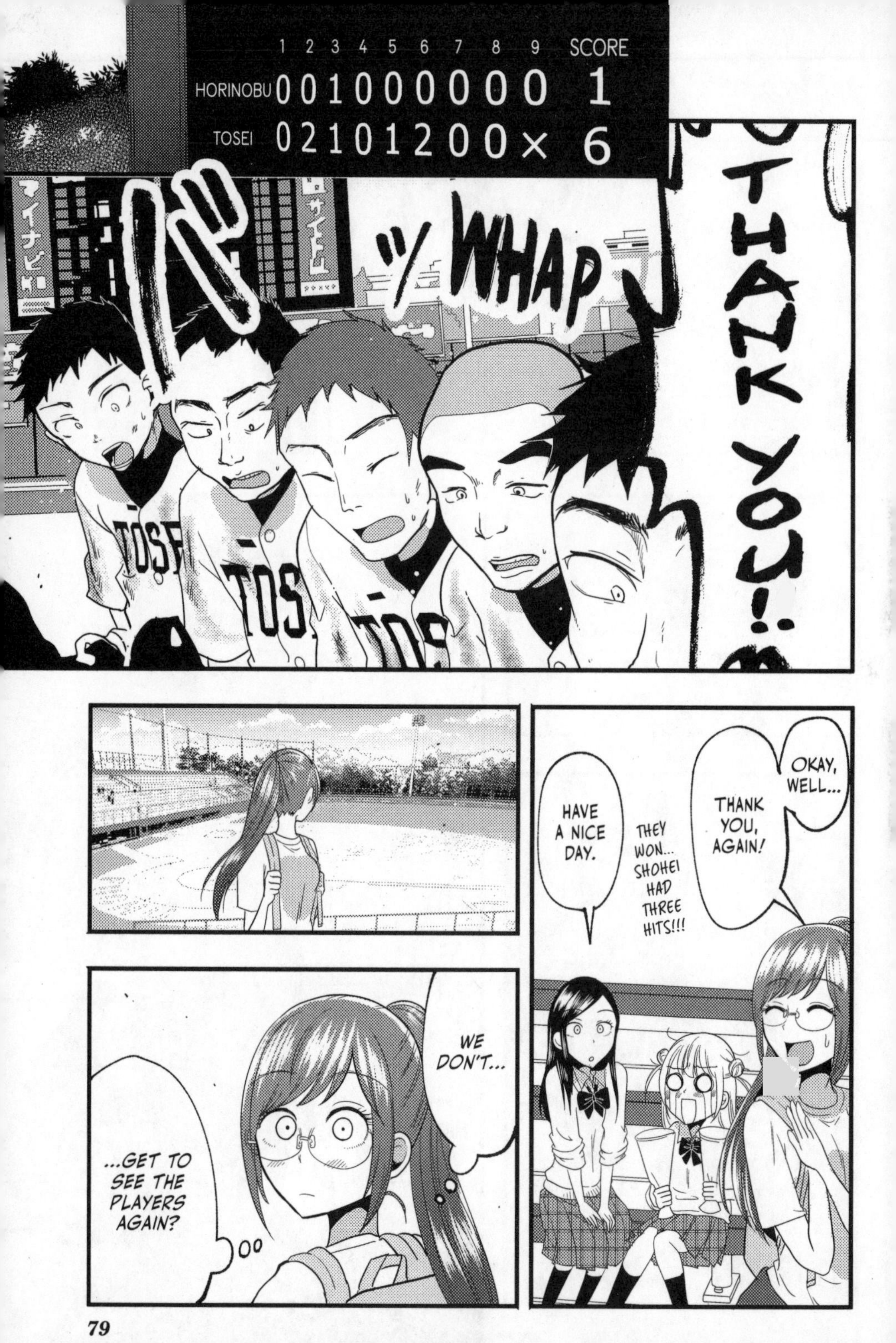
1 2 3 4 5 6 7 8 9 SCORE
HORINOBU 0 0 1 0 0 0 0 0 0 1
TOSEI 0 2 1 0 1 2 0 0 × 6
THANK YOU!!
パッ
WHAP
OKAY, WELL...
THANK YOU, AGAIN!
THEY WON... SHOHEI HAD THREE HITS!!!
HAVE A NICE DAY.
WE DON'T...
...GET TO SEE THE PLAYERS AGAIN?

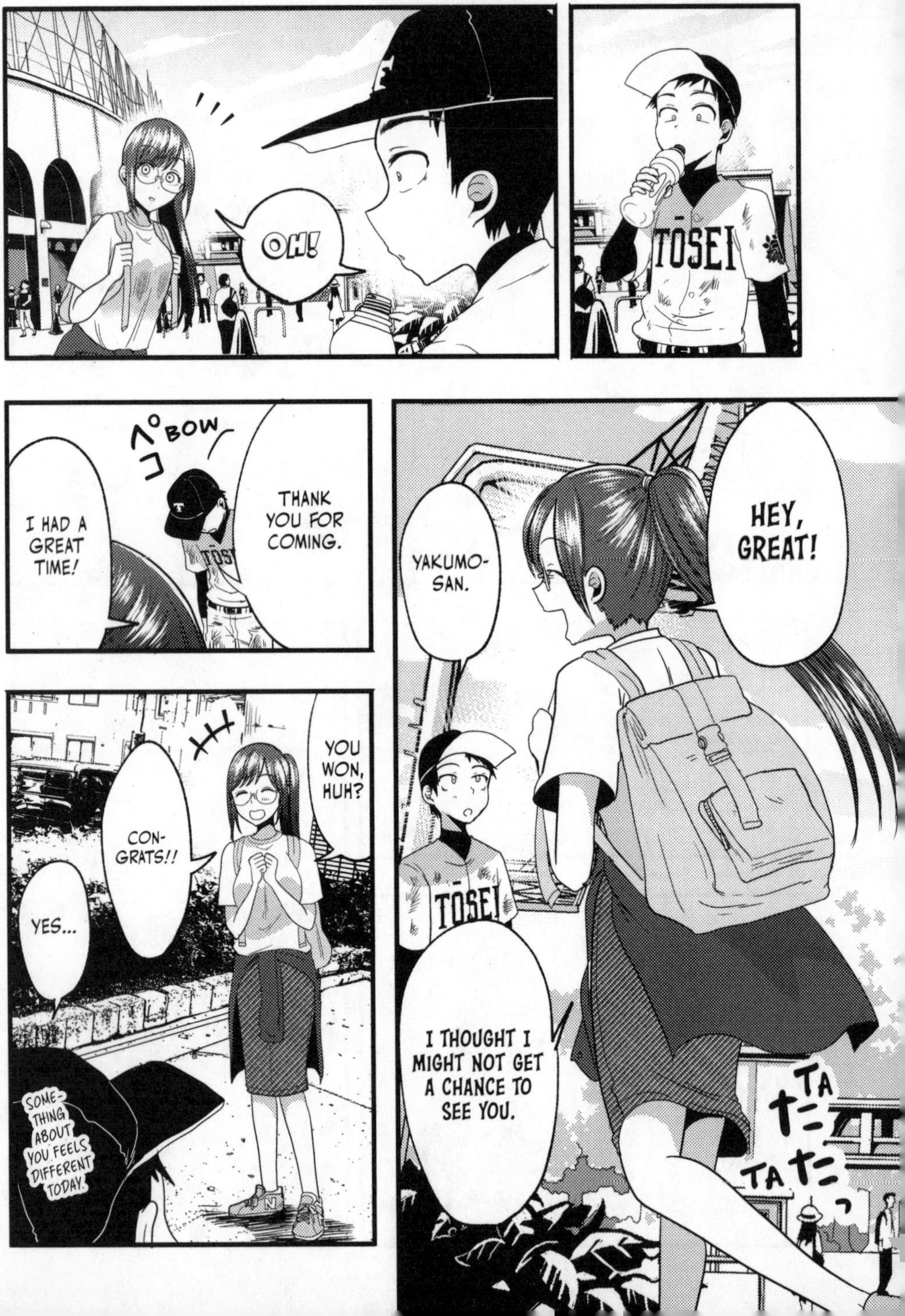
OH!
HEY, GREAT!
YAKUMO-SAN.
I THOUGHT I MIGHT NOT GET A CHANCE TO SEE YOU.
TA TA
THANK YOU FOR COMING.
BOW
I HAD A GREAT TIME!
YOU WON, HUH?
CON-GRATS!!
YES...
SOME-THING ABOUT YOU FEELS DIFFERENT TODAY.

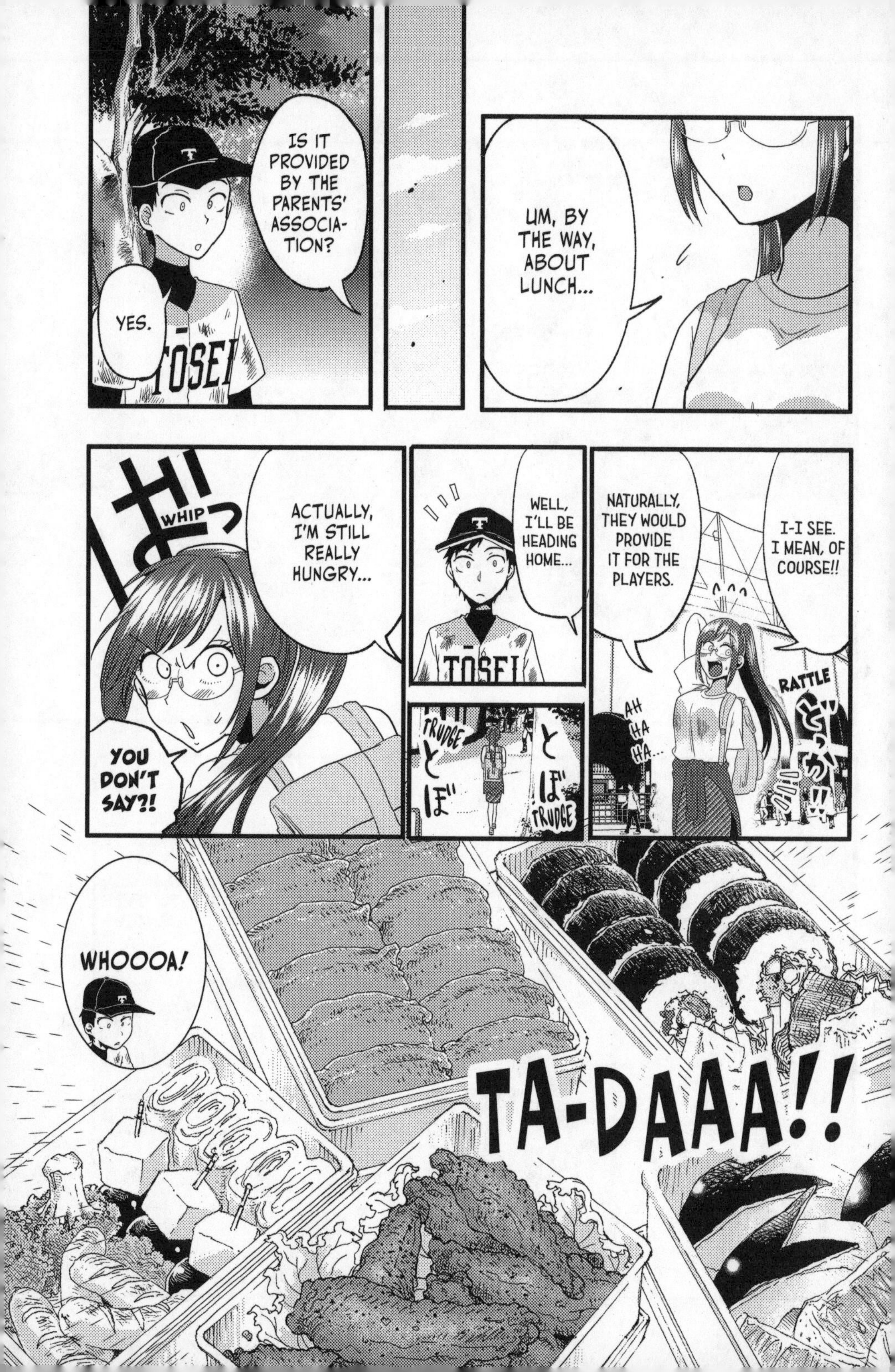
UM, BY THE WAY, ABOUT LUNCH...
IS IT PROVIDED BY THE PARENTS' ASSOCIATION?
YES.
I-I SEE. I MEAN, OF COURSE!!
NATURALLY, THEY WOULD PROVIDE IT FOR THE PLAYERS.
AH HA HA...
RATTLE
WELL, I'LL BE HEADING HOME...
TRUDGE
TRUDGE
ACTUALLY, I'M STILL REALLY HUNGRY...
WHIP
YOU DON'T SAY?!
TA-DAAA!!
WHOOOA!

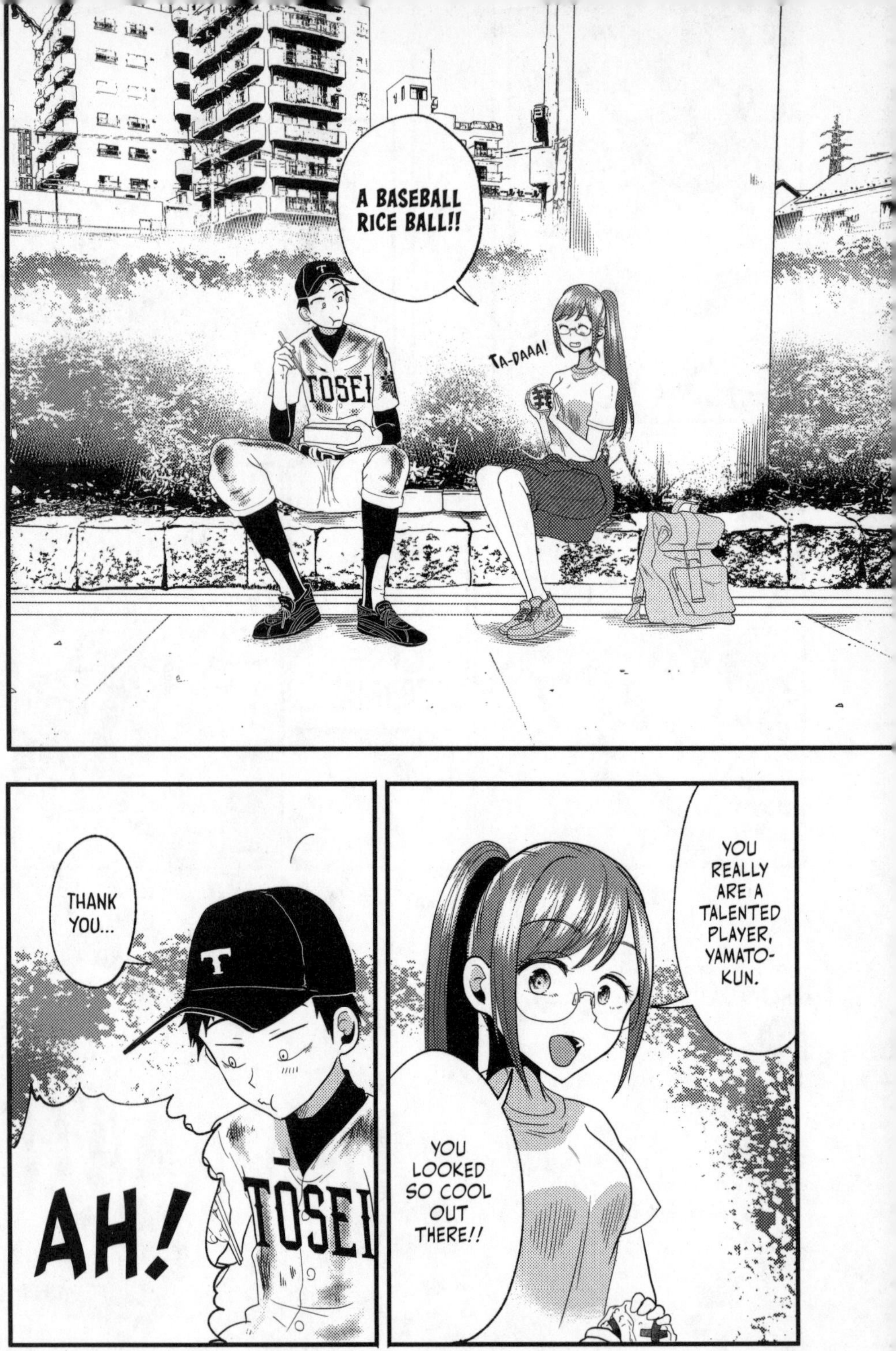
A BASEBALL RICE BALL!!
TA-DAAA!
YOU REALLY ARE A TALENTED PLAYER, YAMATO-KUN.
YOU LOOKED SO COOL OUT THERE!!
THANK YOU...
AH!

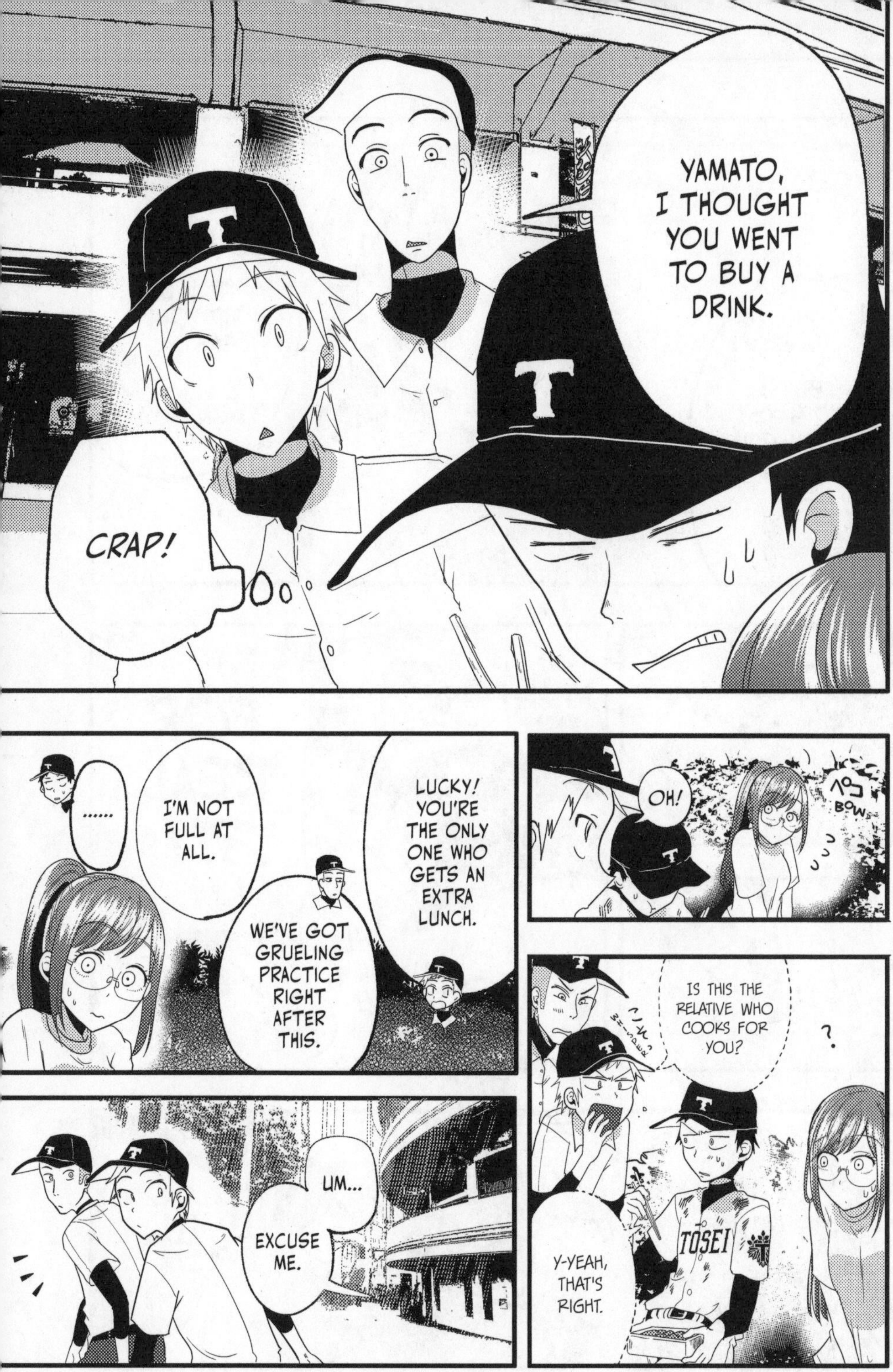
YAMATO, I THOUGHT YOU WENT TO BUY A DRINK.
CRAP!
OH!
ペコ BOW
LUCKY! YOU'RE THE ONLY ONE WHO GETS AN EXTRA LUNCH.
I'M NOT FULL AT ALL.
......
WE'VE GOT GRUELING PRACTICE RIGHT AFTER THIS.
IS THIS THE RELATIVE WHO COOKS FOR YOU?
?
Y-YEAH, THAT'S RIGHT.
TOSEI
UM...
EXCUSE ME.

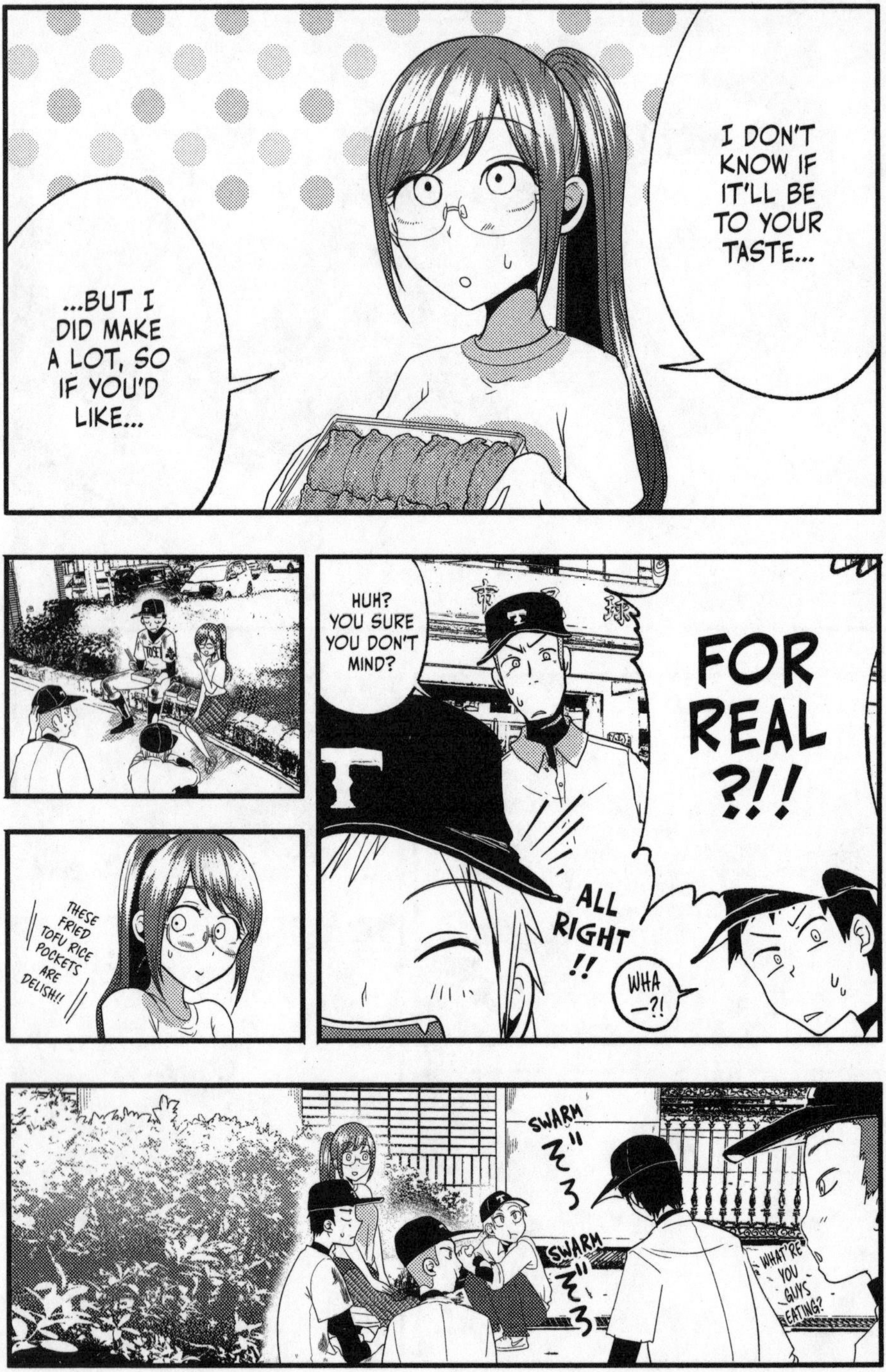

I DON'T KNOW IF IT'LL BE TO YOUR TASTE...
...BUT I DID MAKE A LOT, SO IF YOU'D LIKE...
FOR REAL ?!!
HUH? YOU SURE YOU DON'T MIND?
WHA —?!
ALL RIGHT !!
THESE FRIED TOFU RICE POCKETS ARE DELISH!!
SWARM ぞろ
SWARM ぞろ
WHAT'RE YOU GUYS EATING?

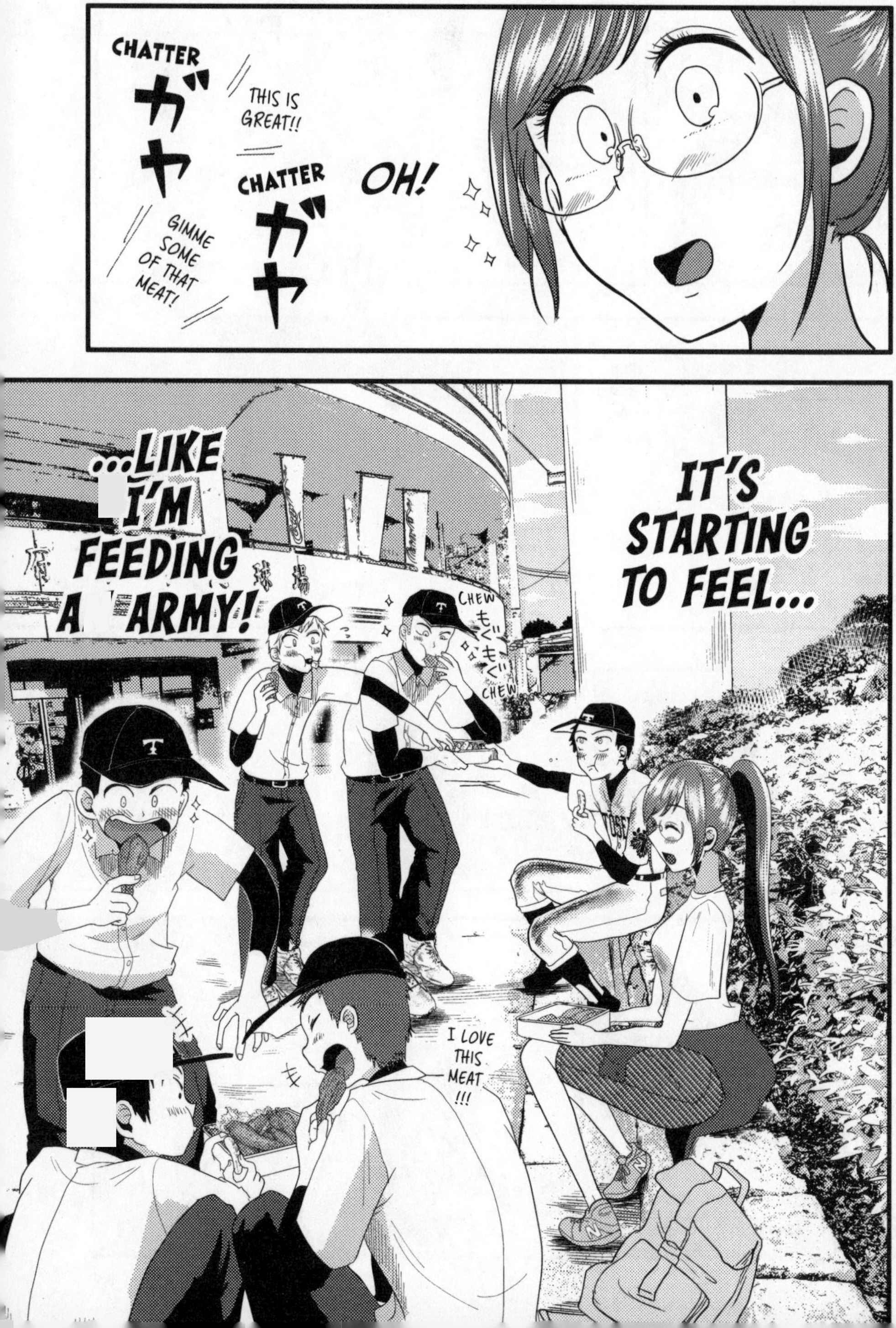
OH!
CHATTER ガヤ
THIS IS GREAT!!
CHATTER ガヤ
GIMME SOME OF THAT MEAT!
IT'S STARTING TO FEEL...
...LIKE I'M FEEDING A ARMY!
CHEW もぐもぐ CHEW
I LOVE THIS MEAT!!!

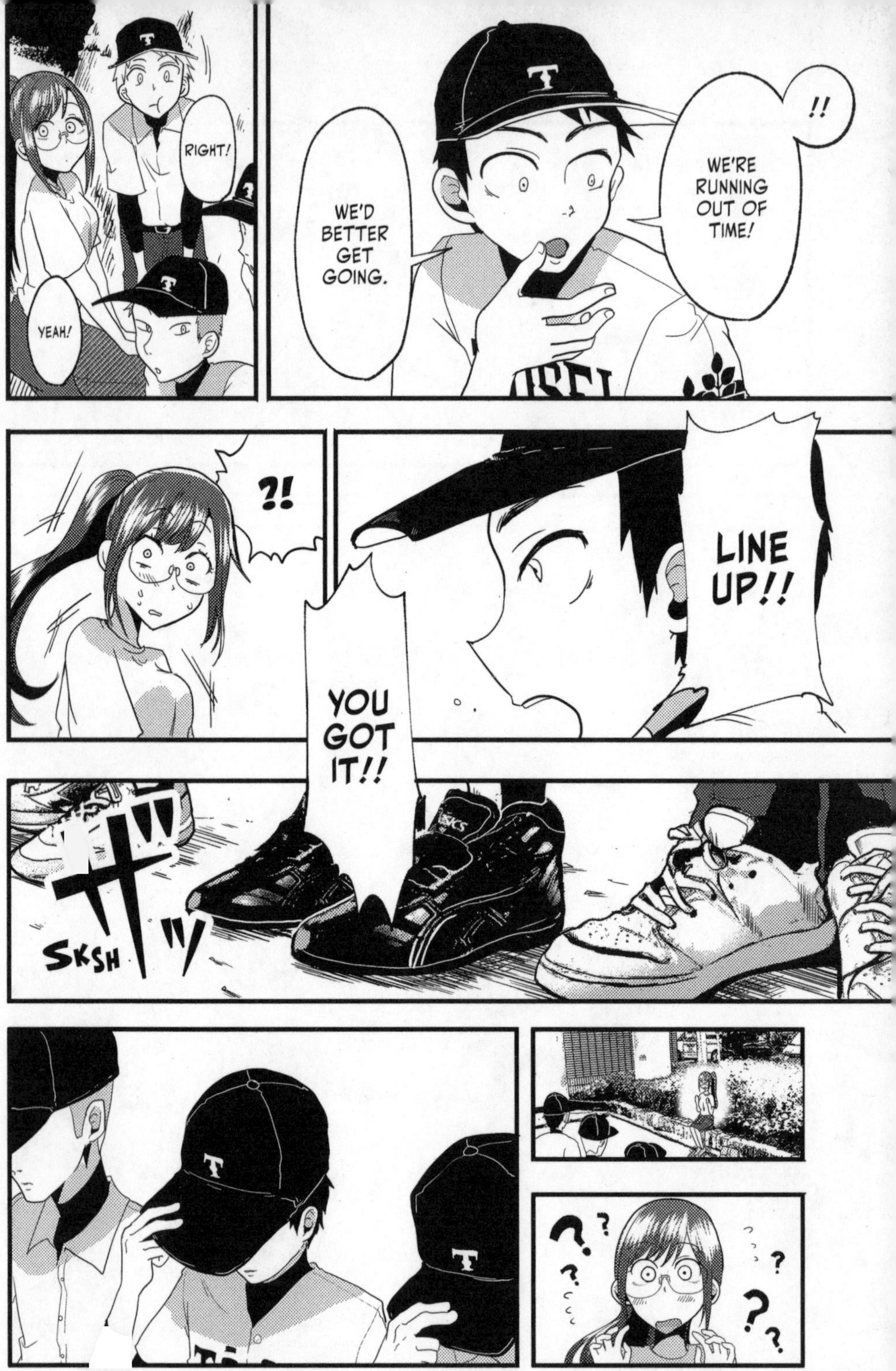
!!
WE'RE RUNNING OUT OF TIME!
WE'D BETTER GET GOING.
RIGHT!
YEAH!
LINE UP!!
YOU GOT IT!!
?!
SKSH

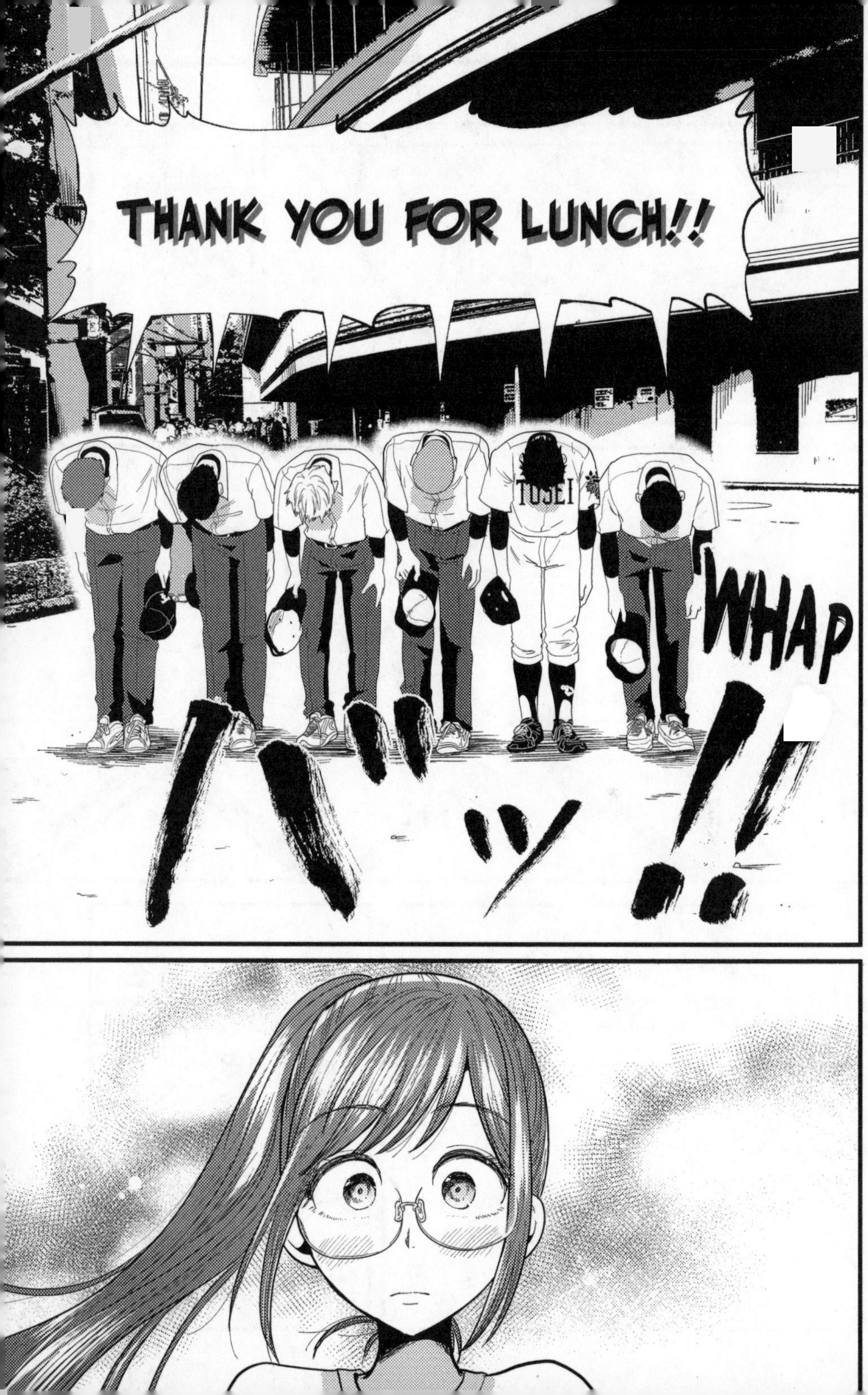
THANK YOU FOR LUNCH!!
TOSEI
WHAP
バッ!!

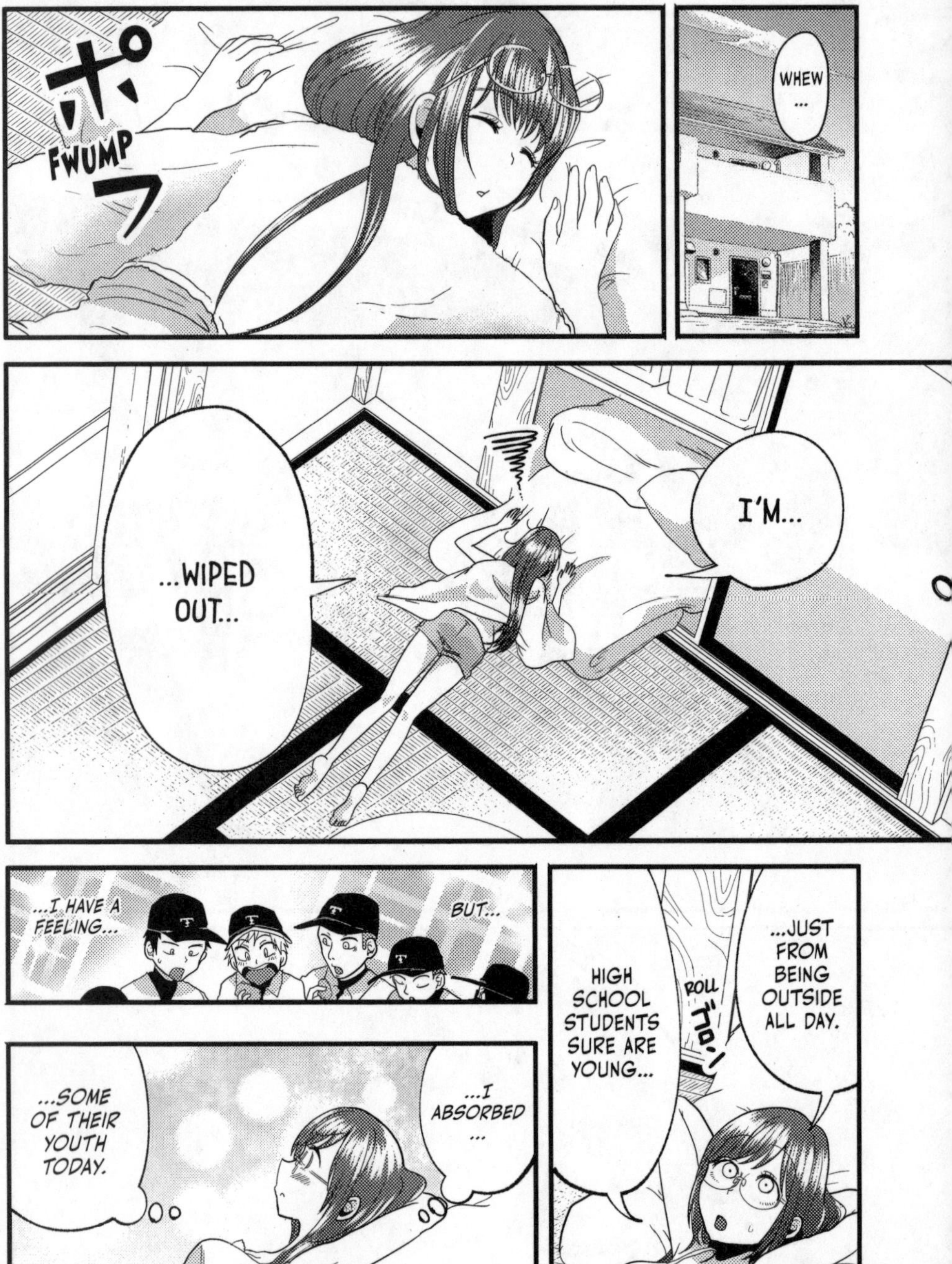
WHEW ...
ポフ
FWUMP
I'M...
...WIPED OUT...
...JUST FROM BEING OUTSIDE ALL DAY.
ROLL
ゴロッ
HIGH SCHOOL STUDENTS SURE ARE YOUNG...
BUT...
...I HAVE A FEELING...
...I ABSORBED ...
...SOME OF THEIR YOUTH TODAY.

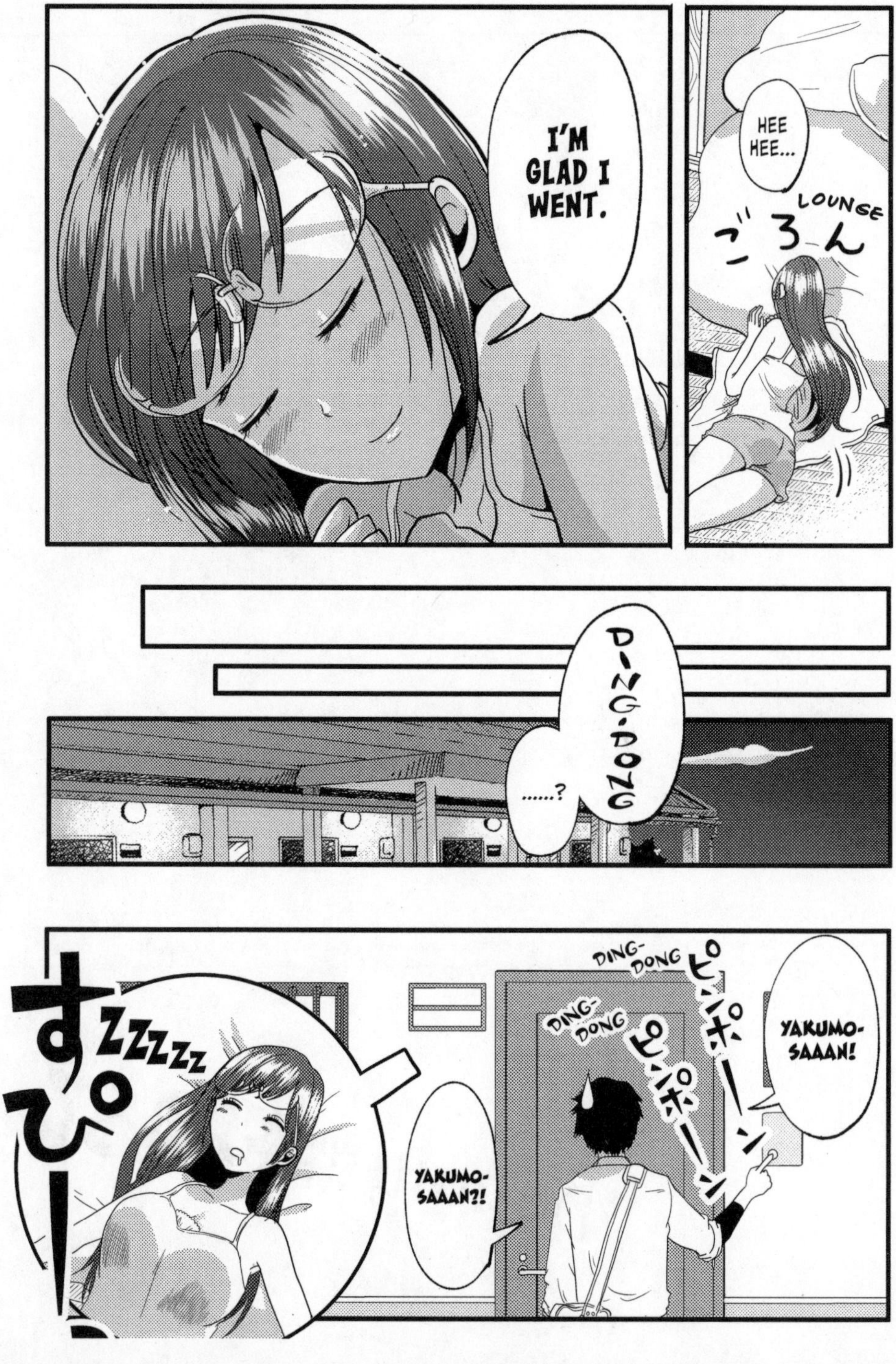
HEE HEE...
LOUNGE
ごろん
I'M GLAD I WENT.
DING-DONG
......?
YAKUMO-SAAAN!
DING-DONG
ピンポーン
DING-DONG
ピンポーン
YAKUMO-SAAAN?!
ZZZZZZ
すぴー!

Beauty and the FEAST.

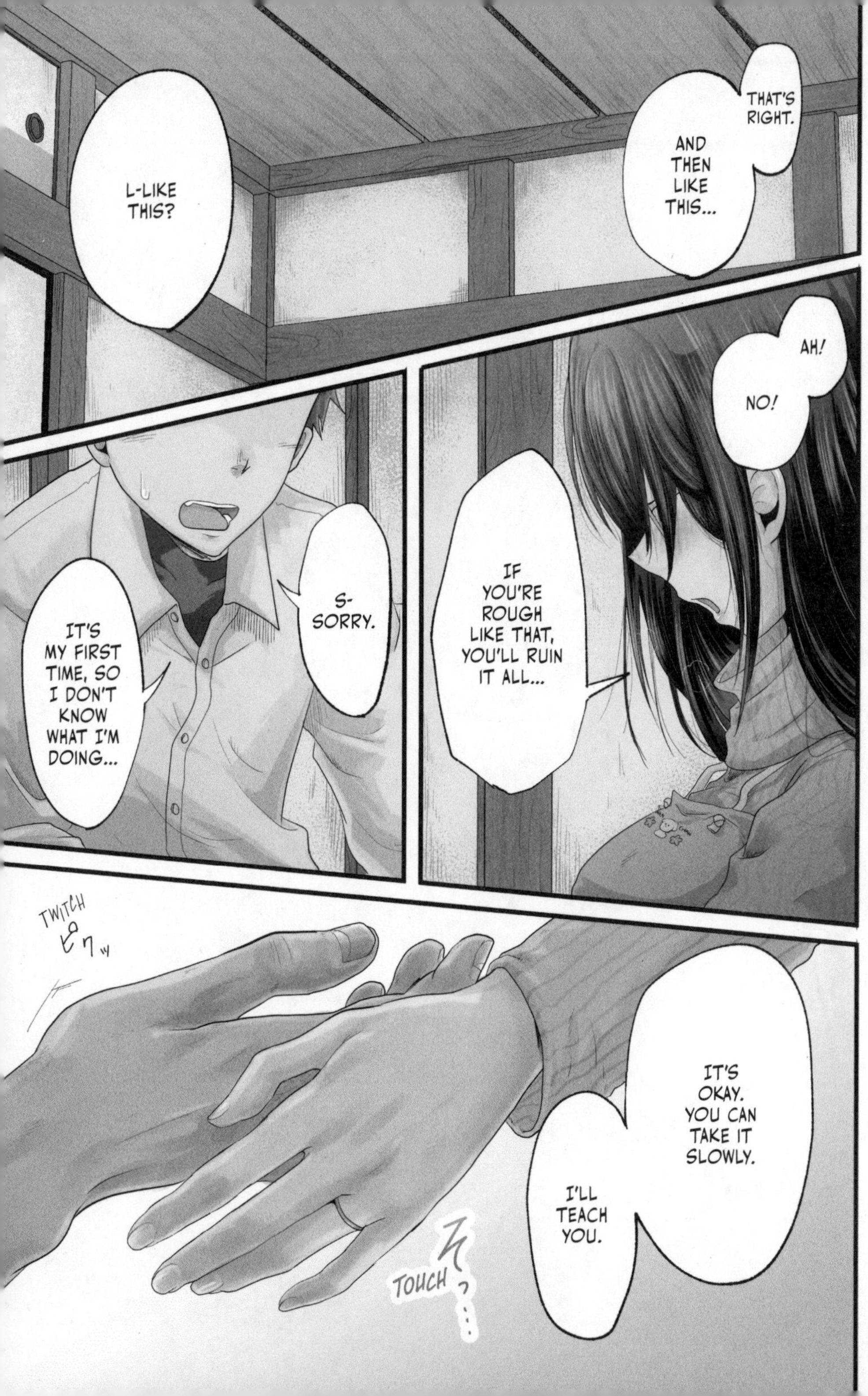
THAT'S RIGHT.
AND THEN LIKE THIS...
L-LIKE THIS?
AH!
NO!
IF YOU'RE ROUGH LIKE THAT, YOU'LL RUIN IT ALL...
S- SORRY.
IT'S MY FIRST TIME, SO I DON'T KNOW WHAT I'M DOING...
IT'S OKAY. YOU CAN TAKE IT SLOWLY.
I'LL TEACH YOU.
TWITCH
ピクッ
TOUCH

Meal 12: Yakumo-san Cooks a Reward

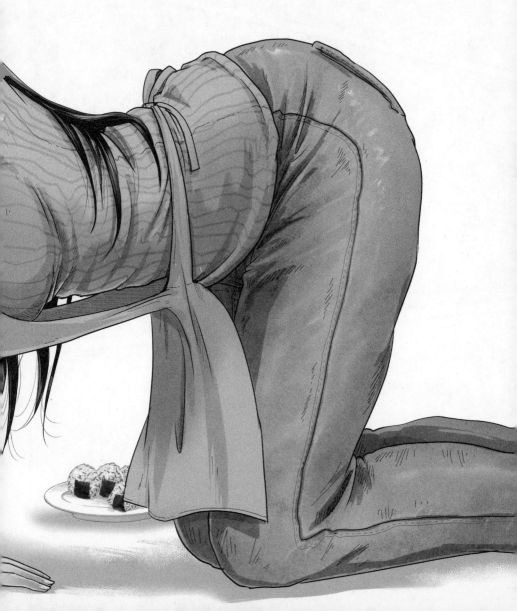

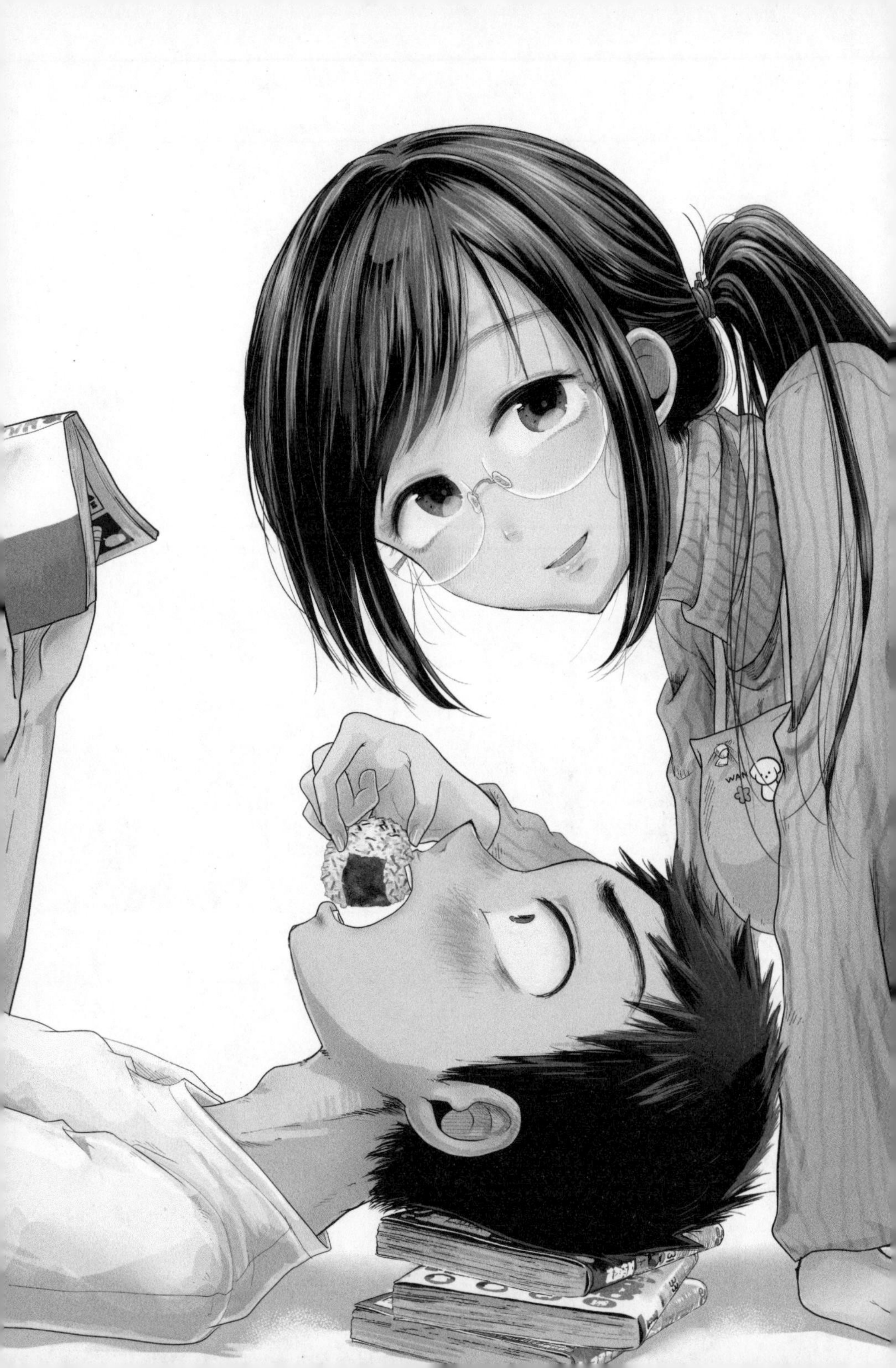
WAN

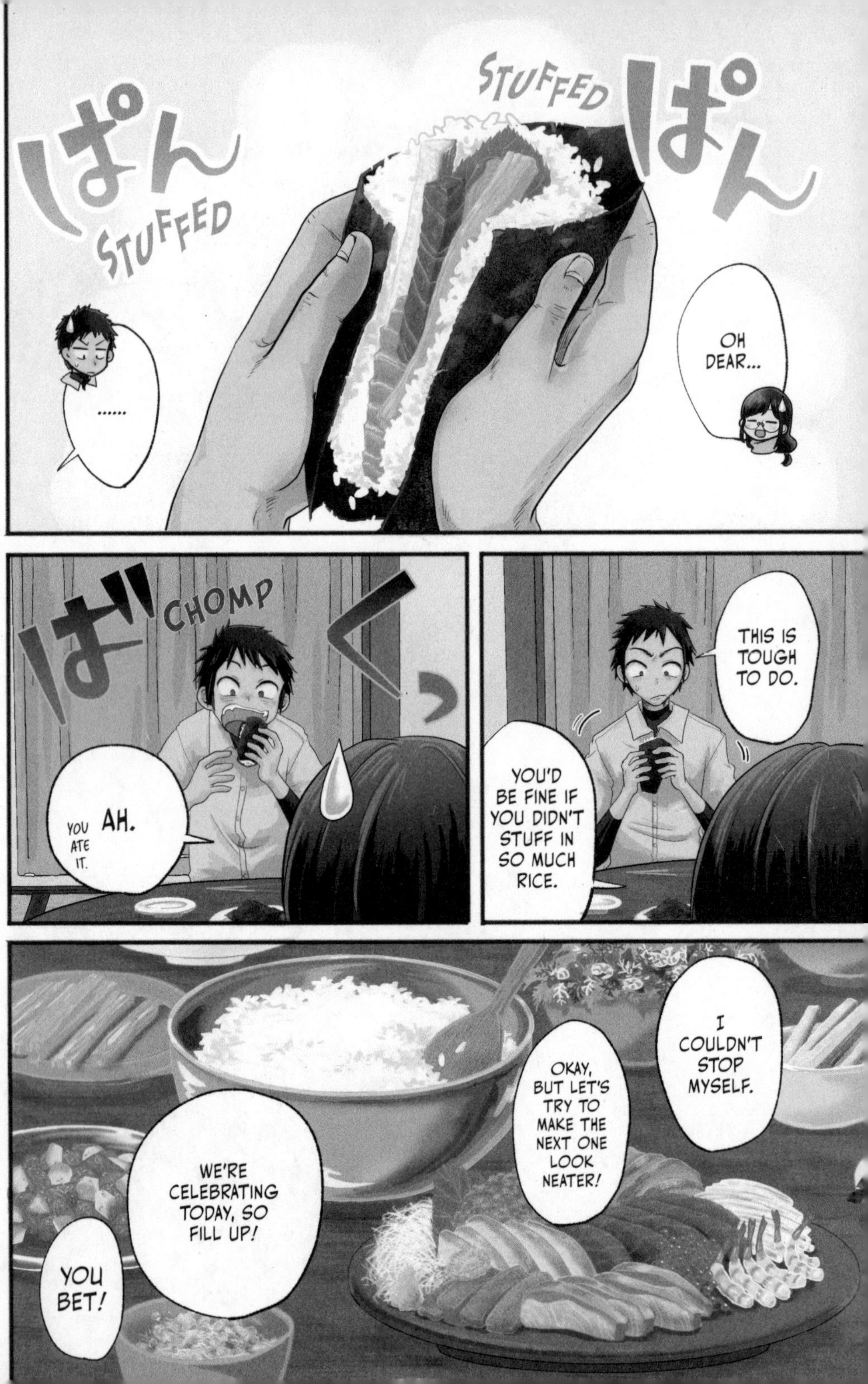
STUFFED
ぱん～
OH DEAR...
ぱん～
STUFFED
......
THIS IS TOUGH TO DO.
YOU'D BE FINE IF YOU DIDN'T STUFF IN SO MUCH RICE.
CHOMP
ばっ
AH.
YOU ATE IT.
I COULDN'T STOP MYSELF.
OKAY, BUT LET'S TRY TO MAKE THE NEXT ONE LOOK NEATER!
WE'RE CELEBRATING TODAY, SO FILL UP!
YOU BET!

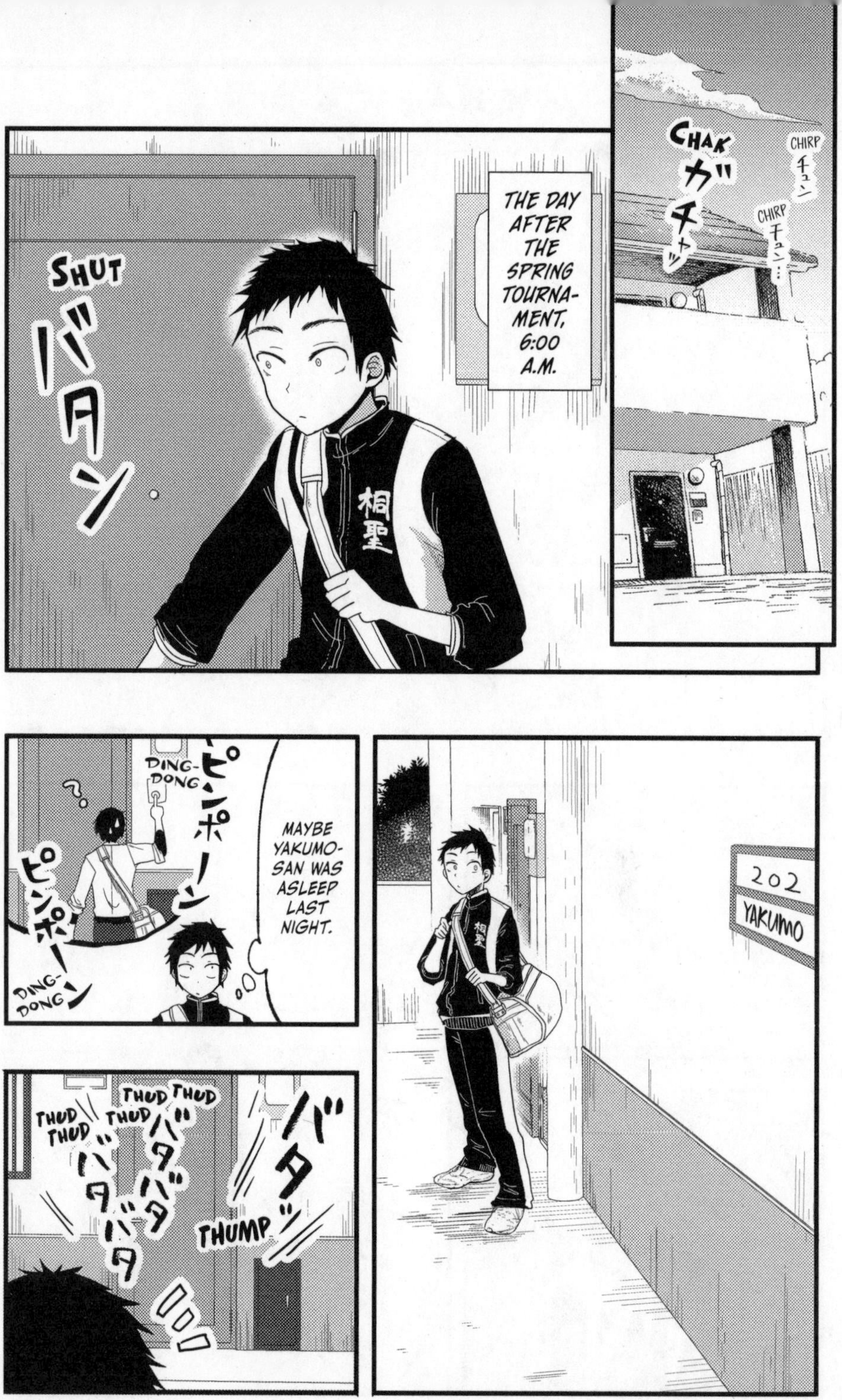
CHAK
ガチャッ
CHIRP
チュン
CHIRP
チュン…
THE DAY AFTER THE SPRING TOURNAMENT, 6:00 A.M.
SHUT
バタン
202
YAKUMO
DING-DONG
ピンポーン
DING-DONG
ピンポーン
MAYBE YAKUMO-SAN WAS ASLEEP LAST NIGHT.
THUMP
バタッ
THUD THUD
バタバタ
THUD THUD
バタバタ

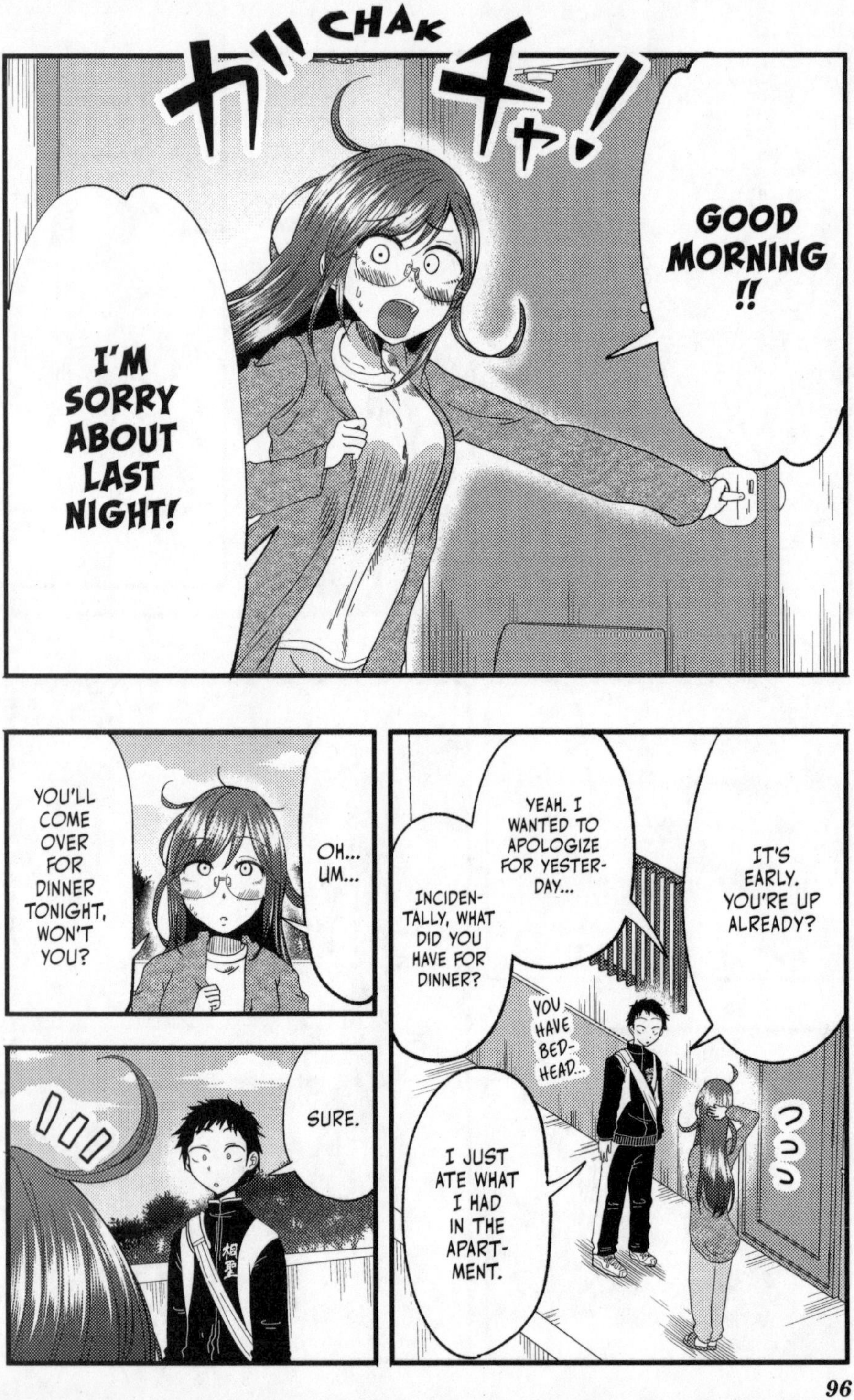
ガチャ! CHAK
GOOD MORNING!!
I'M SORRY ABOUT LAST NIGHT!
IT'S EARLY. YOU'RE UP ALREADY?
YEAH. I WANTED TO APOLOGIZE FOR YESTER-DAY...
INCIDEN-TALLY, WHAT DID YOU HAVE FOR DINNER?
YOU HAVE BED-HEAD..
I JUST ATE WHAT I HAD IN THE APART-MENT.
OH... UM...
YOU'LL COME OVER FOR DINNER TONIGHT, WON'T YOU?
SURE.

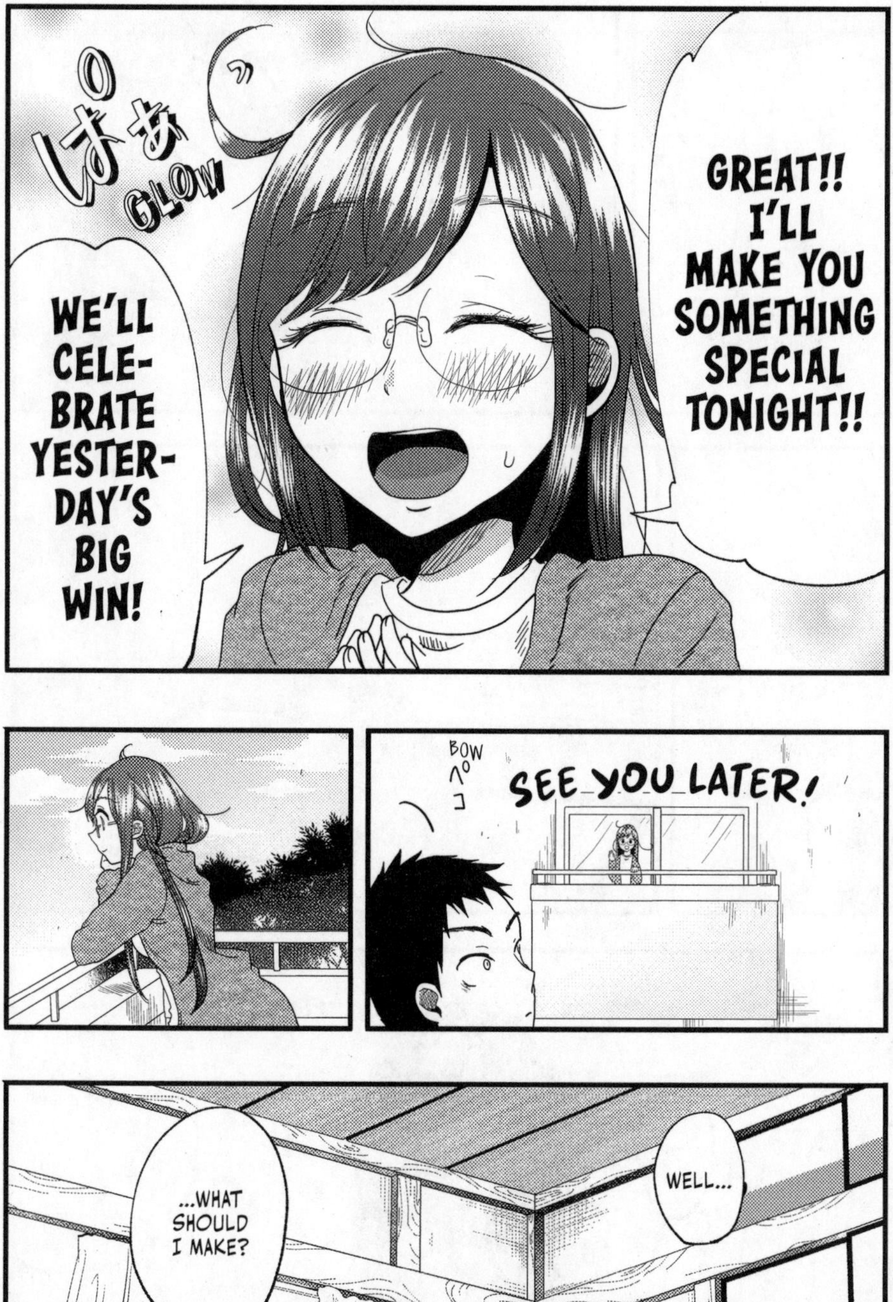
GREAT!! I'LL MAKE YOU SOMETHING SPECIAL TONIGHT!!
ぱあっ
GLOW
WE'LL CELE-BRATE YESTER-DAY'S BIG WIN!
ペコ
BOW
SEE YOU LATER!
WELL...
...WHAT SHOULD I MAKE?

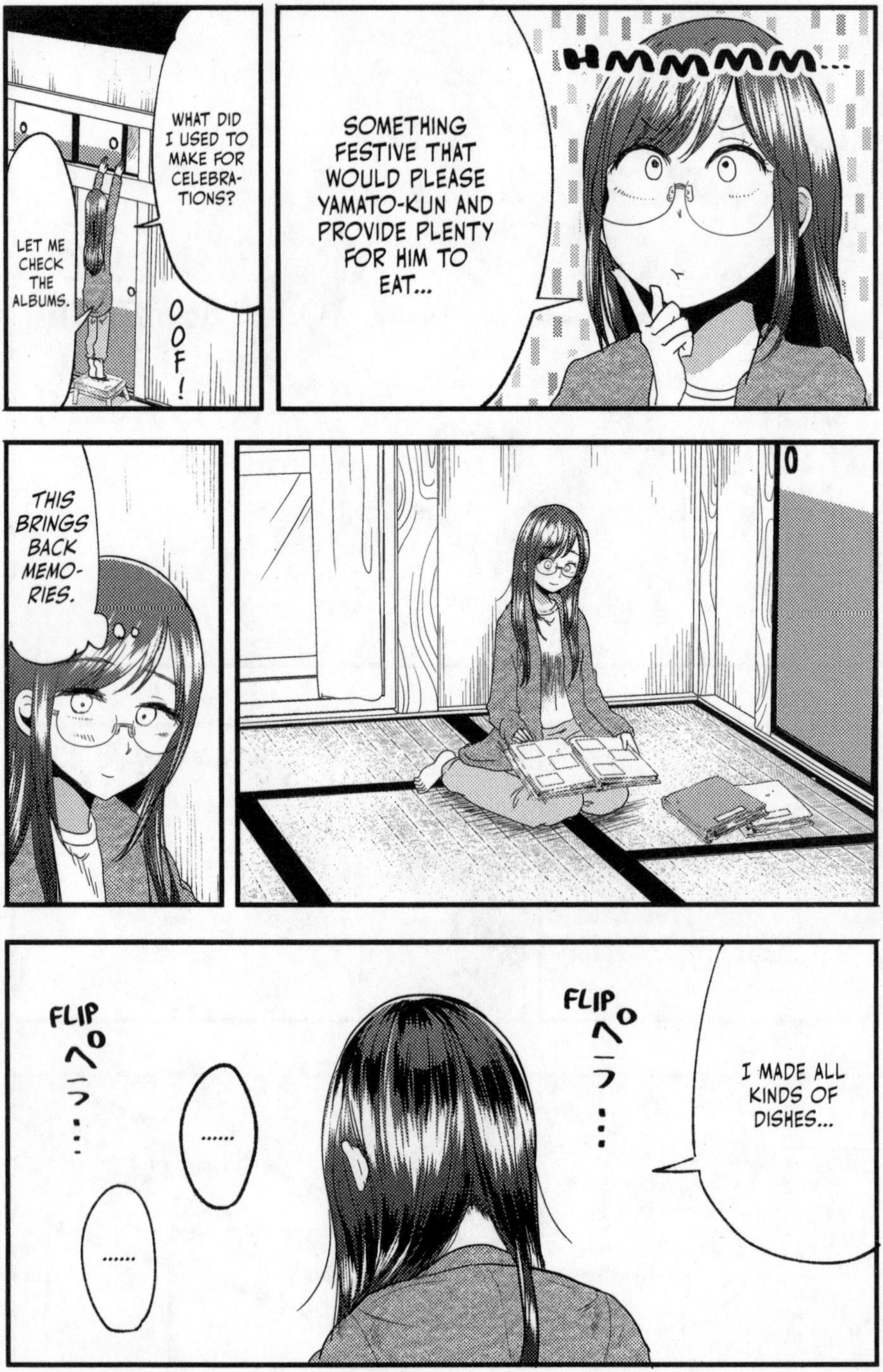
HMMMM...
SOMETHING FESTIVE THAT WOULD PLEASE YAMATO-KUN AND PROVIDE PLENTY FOR HIM TO EAT...
WHAT DID I USED TO MAKE FOR CELEBRATIONS?
OOF!
LET ME CHECK THE ALBUMS.
THIS BRINGS BACK MEMORIES.
I MADE ALL KINDS OF DISHES...
FLIP
ペラ...
......
......
FLIP
ペラ...

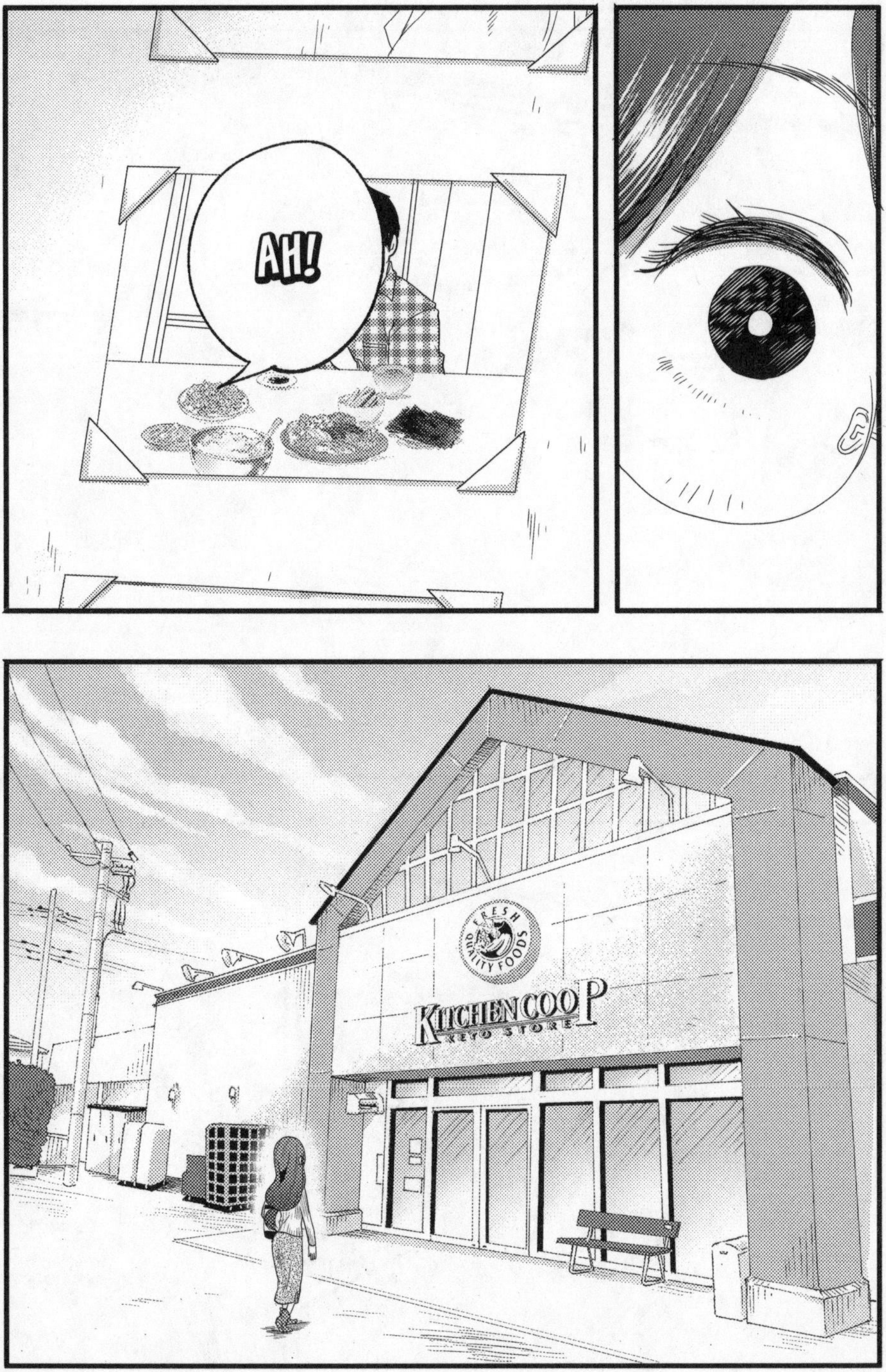
AH!
FRESH
QUALITY FOODS
KITCHEN COOP
KEYO STORE

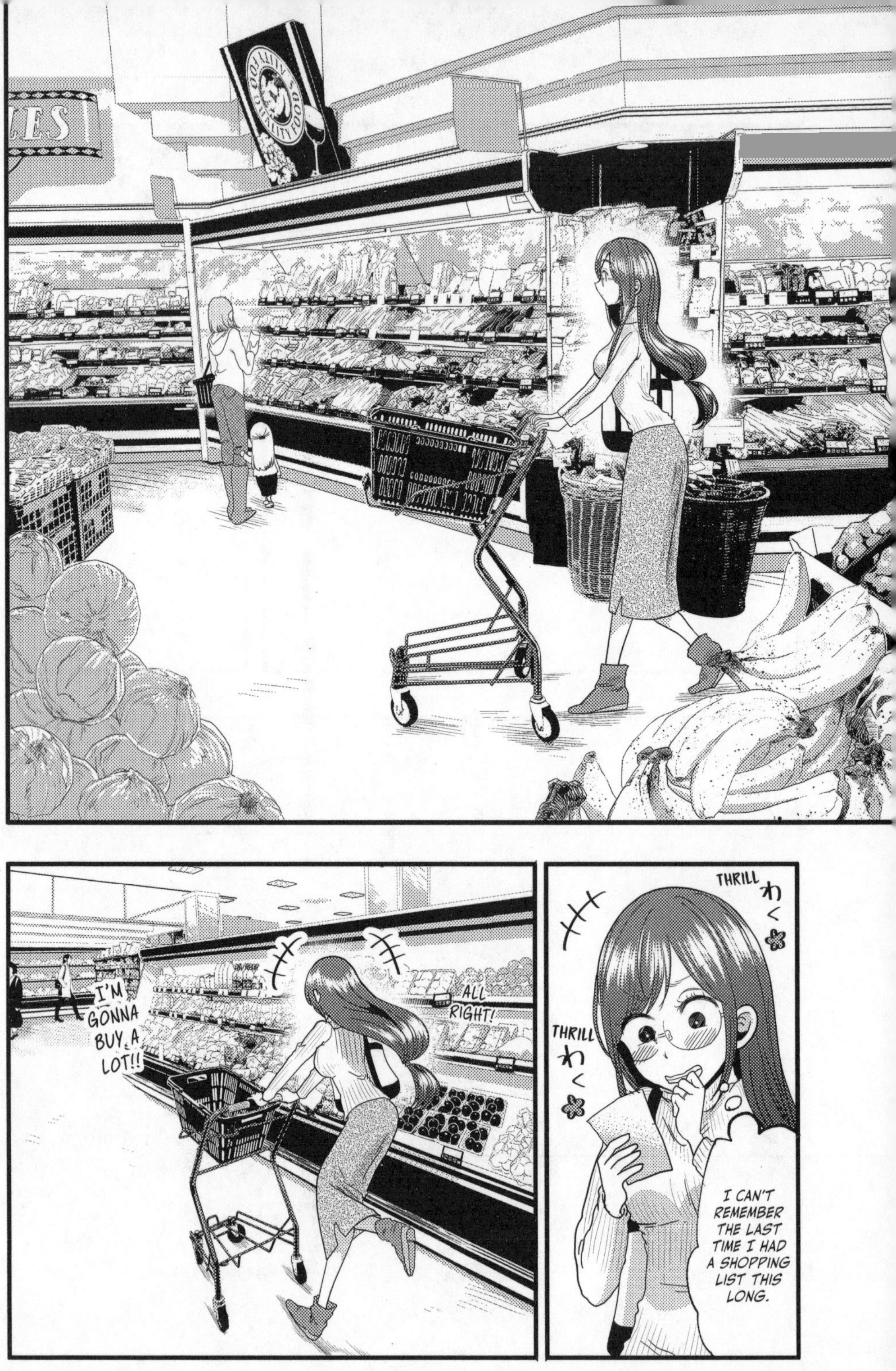
THRILL わく
THRILL わく
I CAN'T REMEMBER THE LAST TIME I HAD A SHOPPING LIST THIS LONG.
ALL RIGHT!
I'M GONNA BUY A LOT!!

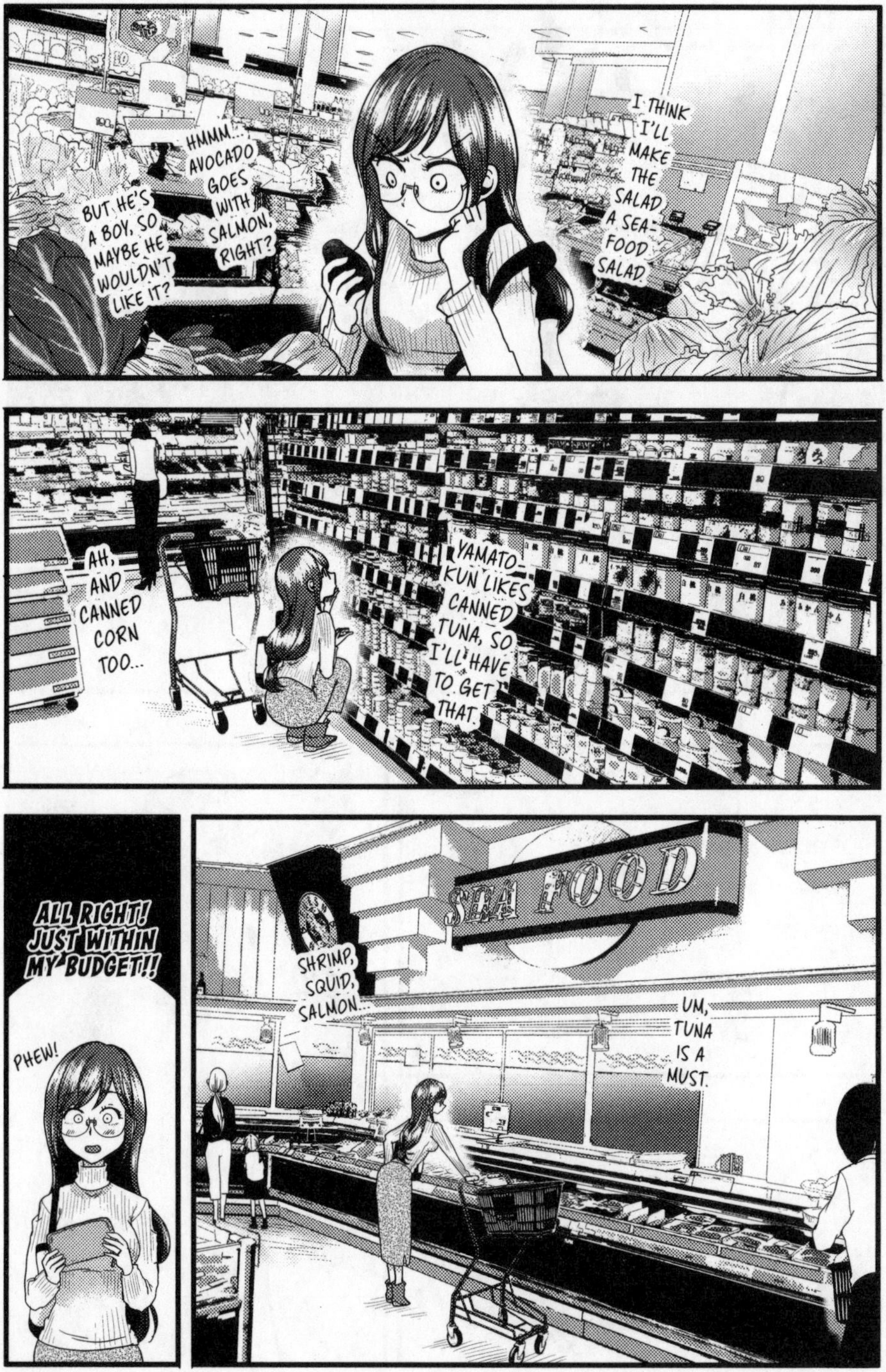
I THINK I'LL MAKE THE SALAD A SEA-FOOD SALAD.
HMMM... AVOCADO GOES WITH SALMON, RIGHT?
BUT HE'S A BOY, SO MAYBE HE WOULDN'T LIKE IT?
YAMATO-KUN LIKES CANNED TUNA, SO I'LL HAVE TO GET THAT.
AH, AND CANNED CORN TOO...
SEA FOOD
UM, TUNA IS A MUST.
SHRIMP, SQUID, SALMON...
ALL RIGHT! JUST WITHIN MY BUDGET!!
PHEW!

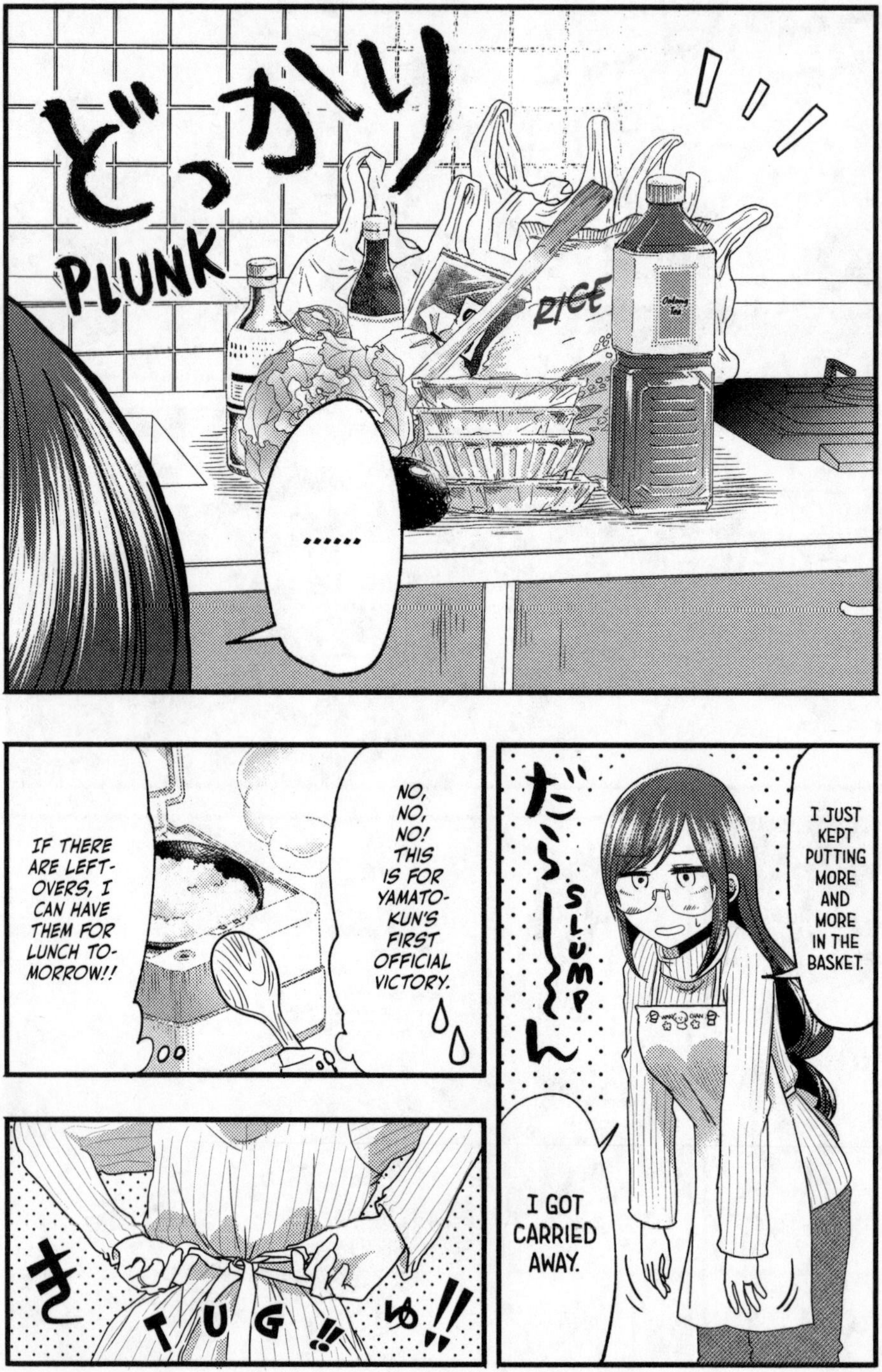
どっかり
PLUNK
......
I JUST KEPT PUTTING MORE AND MORE IN THE BASKET.
だら〜ん
SLUMP
I GOT CARRIED AWAY.
NO, NO, NO! THIS IS FOR YAMATO-KUN'S FIRST OFFICIAL VICTORY.
IF THERE ARE LEFT-OVERS, I CAN HAVE THEM FOR LUNCH TO-MORROW!!
きゅ!!
TUG!!

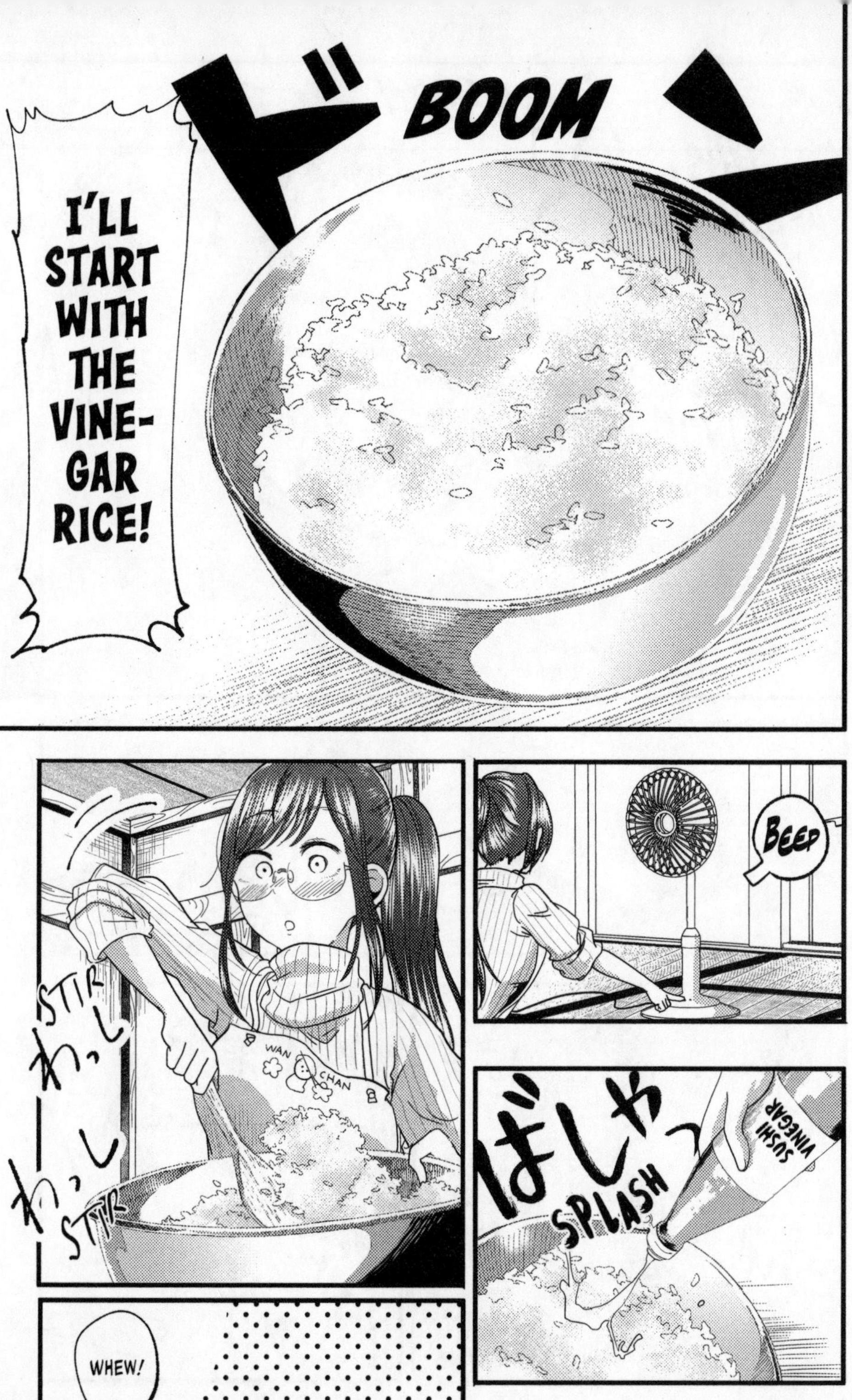
ド
BOOM
I'LL START WITH THE VINE-GAR RICE!
BEEP
ぱしゃっ
SPLASH
SUSHI VINEGAR
わっし
STIR
わっし
STIR
WAN CHAN
WHEW!

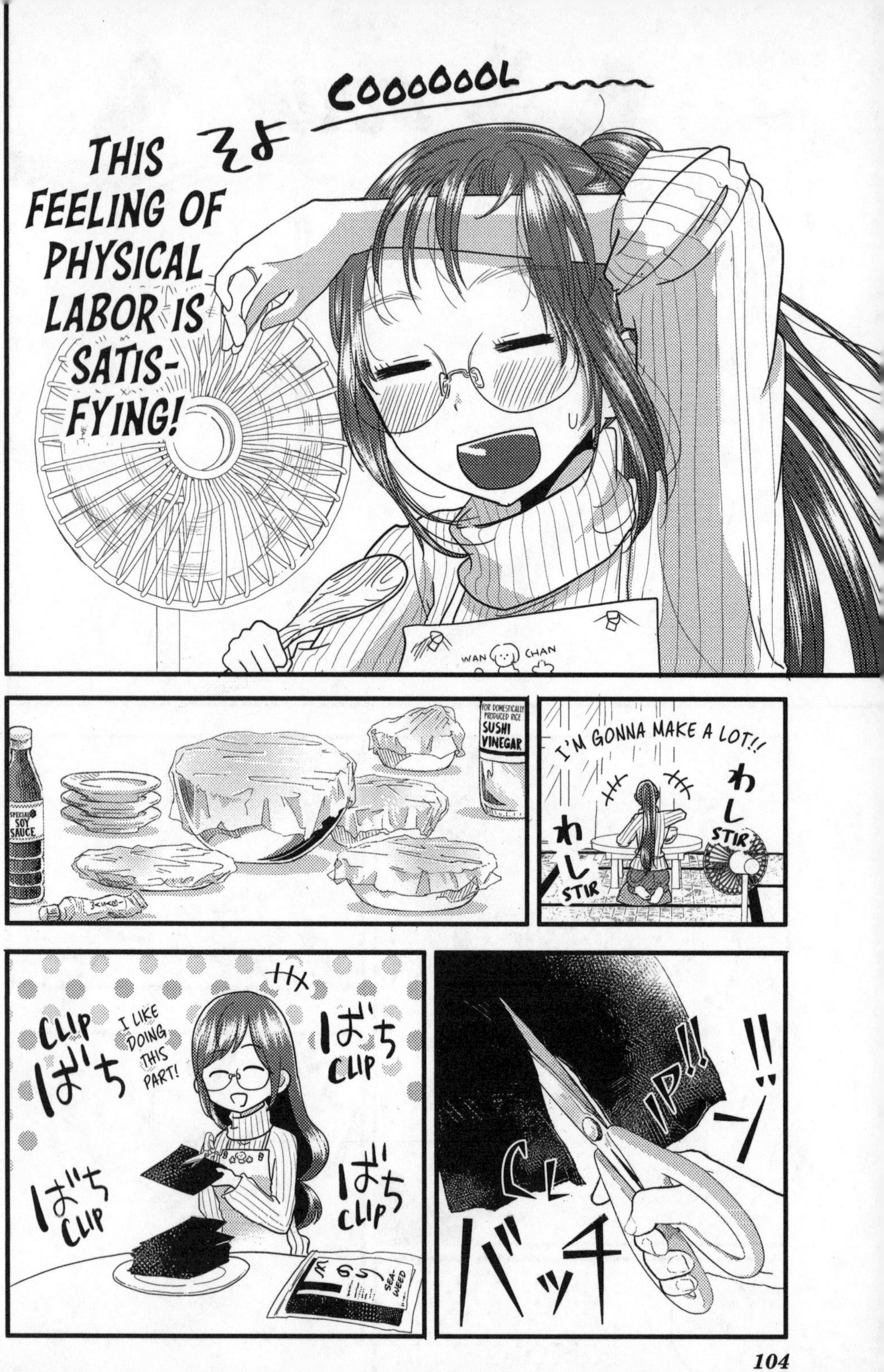
そよ
COOOOOOL
THIS FEELING OF PHYSICAL LABOR IS SATIS-FYING!
WAN CHAN
I'M GONNA MAKE A LOT!!
わし STIR
わし STIR
FOR DOMESTICALLY PRODUCED RICE SUSHI VINEGAR
SPECIAL SOY SAUCE
バッチ
CLIP!!
ぱち CLIP
I LIKE DOING THIS PART!
CLIP ぱち
ぱち CLIP
ぱち CLIP
SEA-WEED

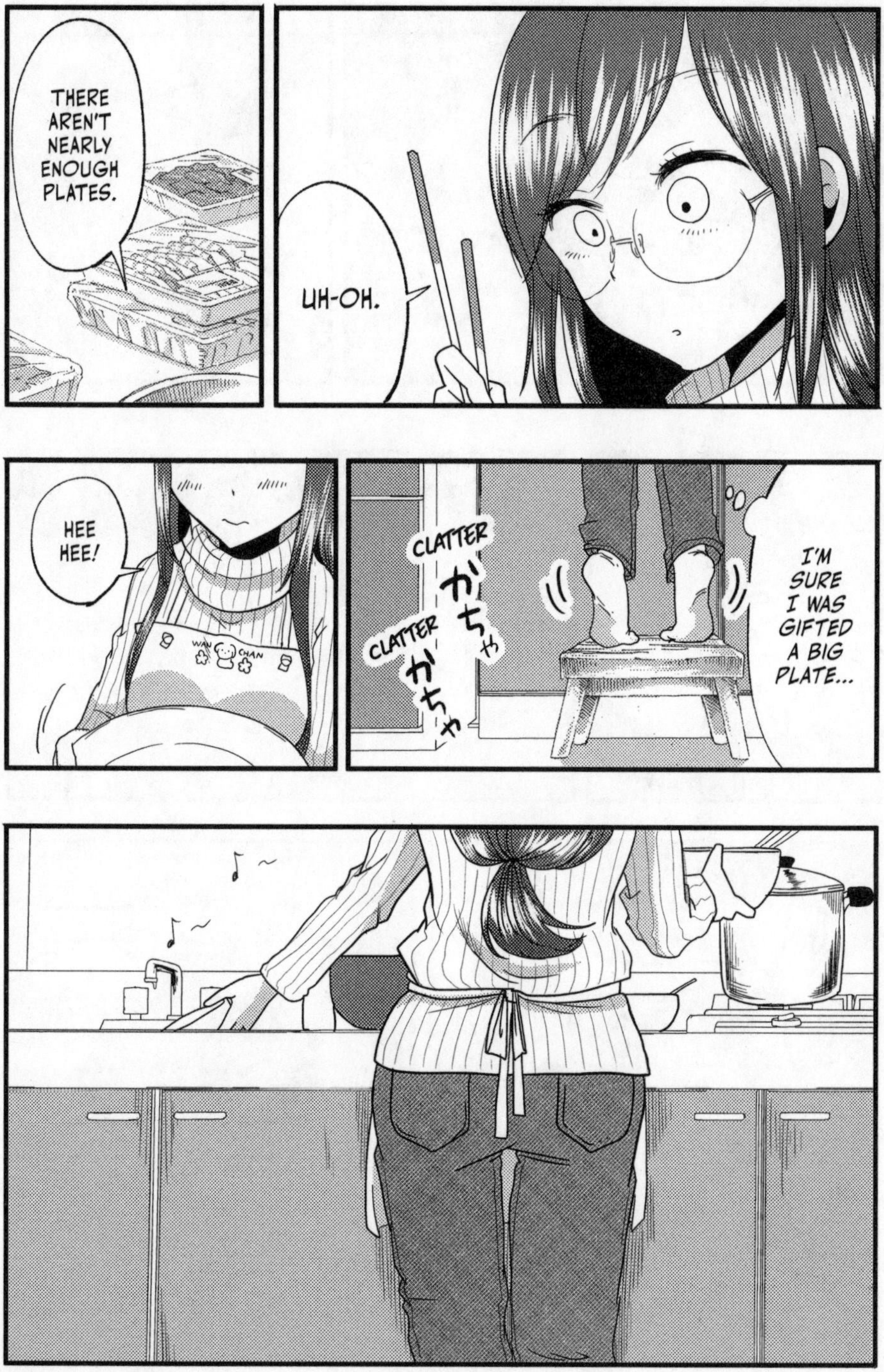
UH-OH.
THERE AREN'T NEARLY ENOUGH PLATES.
I'M SURE I WAS GIFTED A BIG PLATE...
CLATTER がちゃ
CLATTER がちゃ
HEE HEE!
WAN CHAN

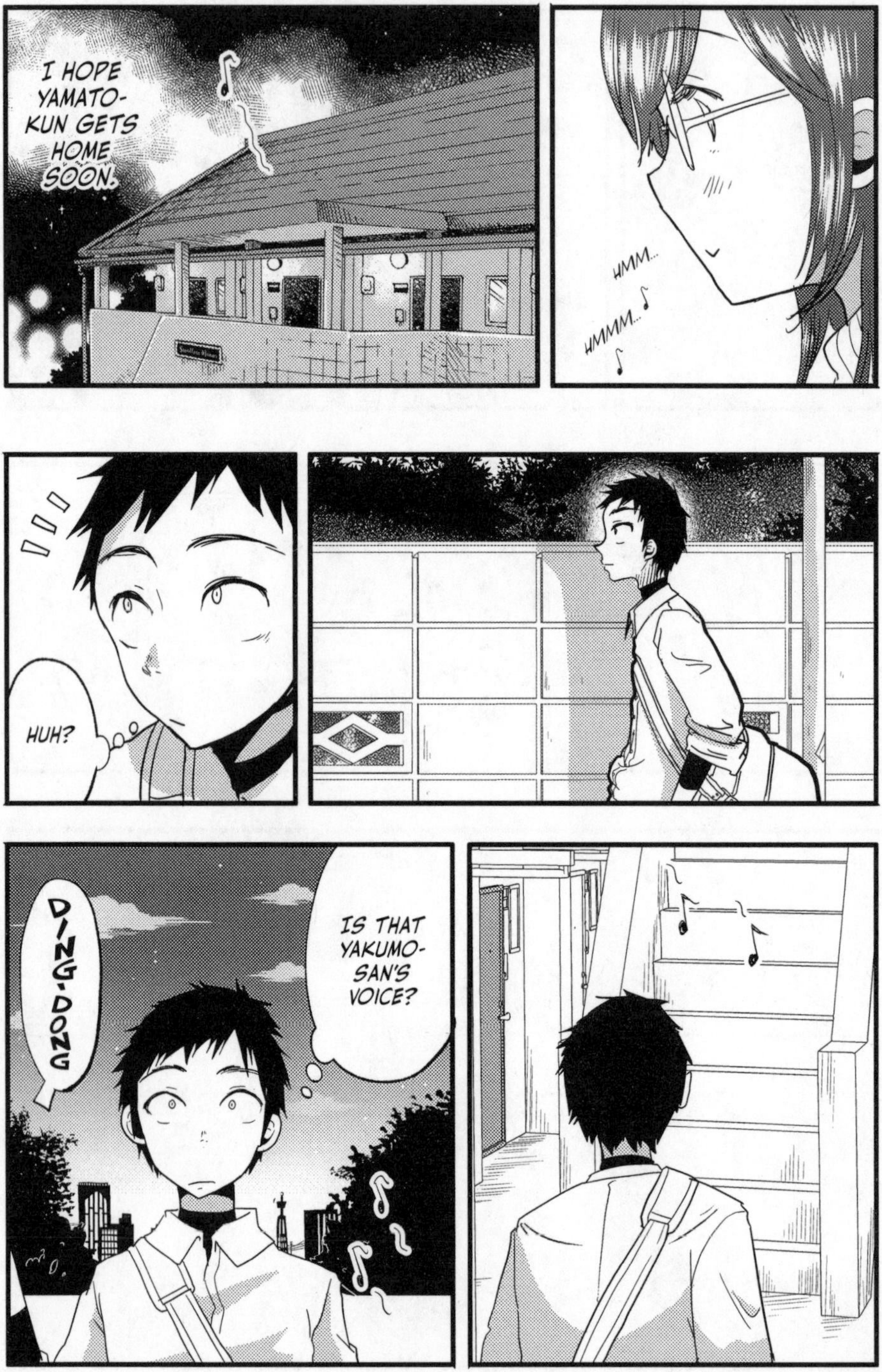
HMM...
HMMM...
I HOPE YAMATO-KUN GETS HOME SOON.
HUH?
IS THAT YAKUMO-SAN'S VOICE?
DING-DONG

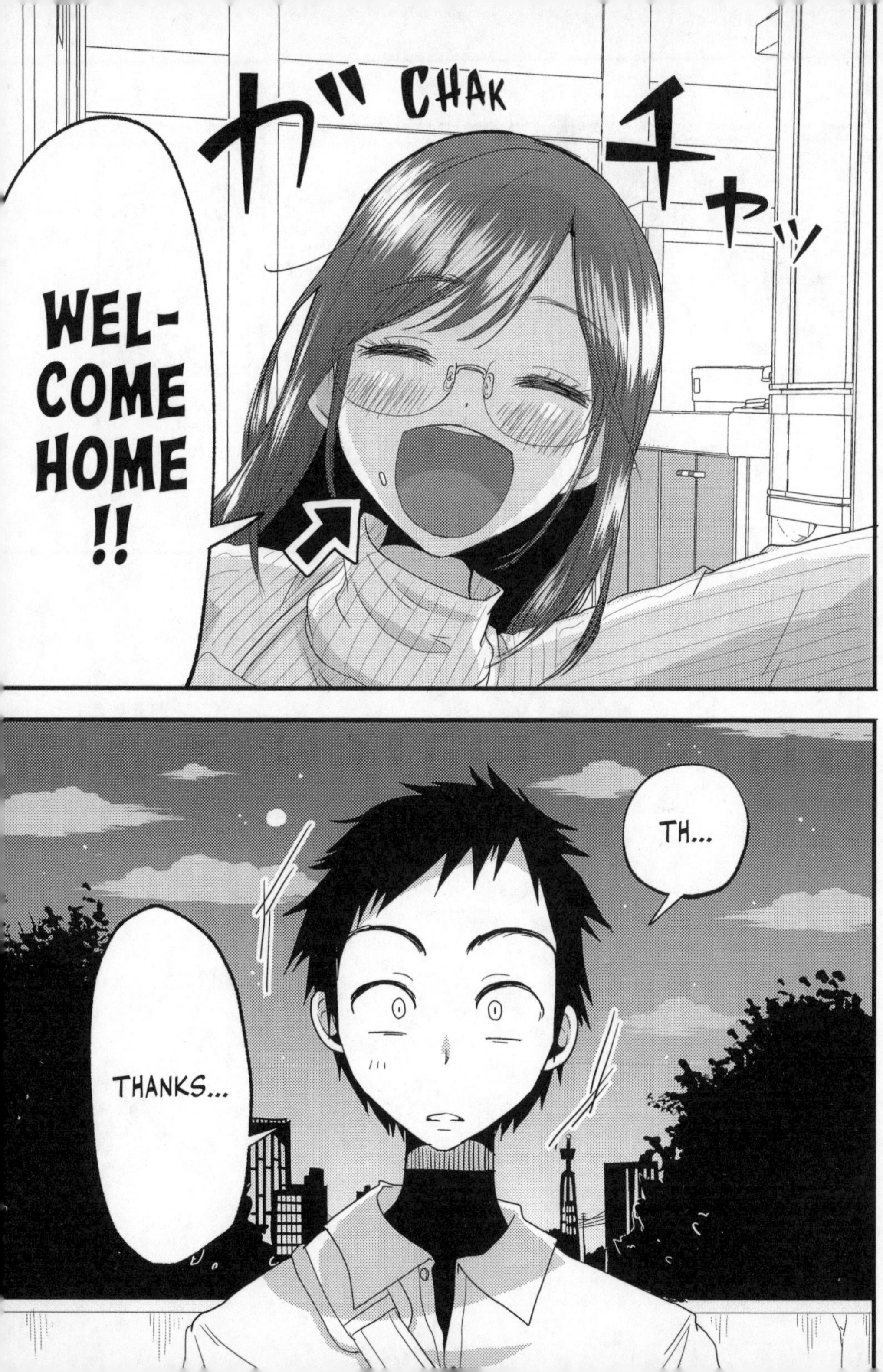
ガチャッ
CHAK
WEL-COME HOME!!
TH...
THANKS...

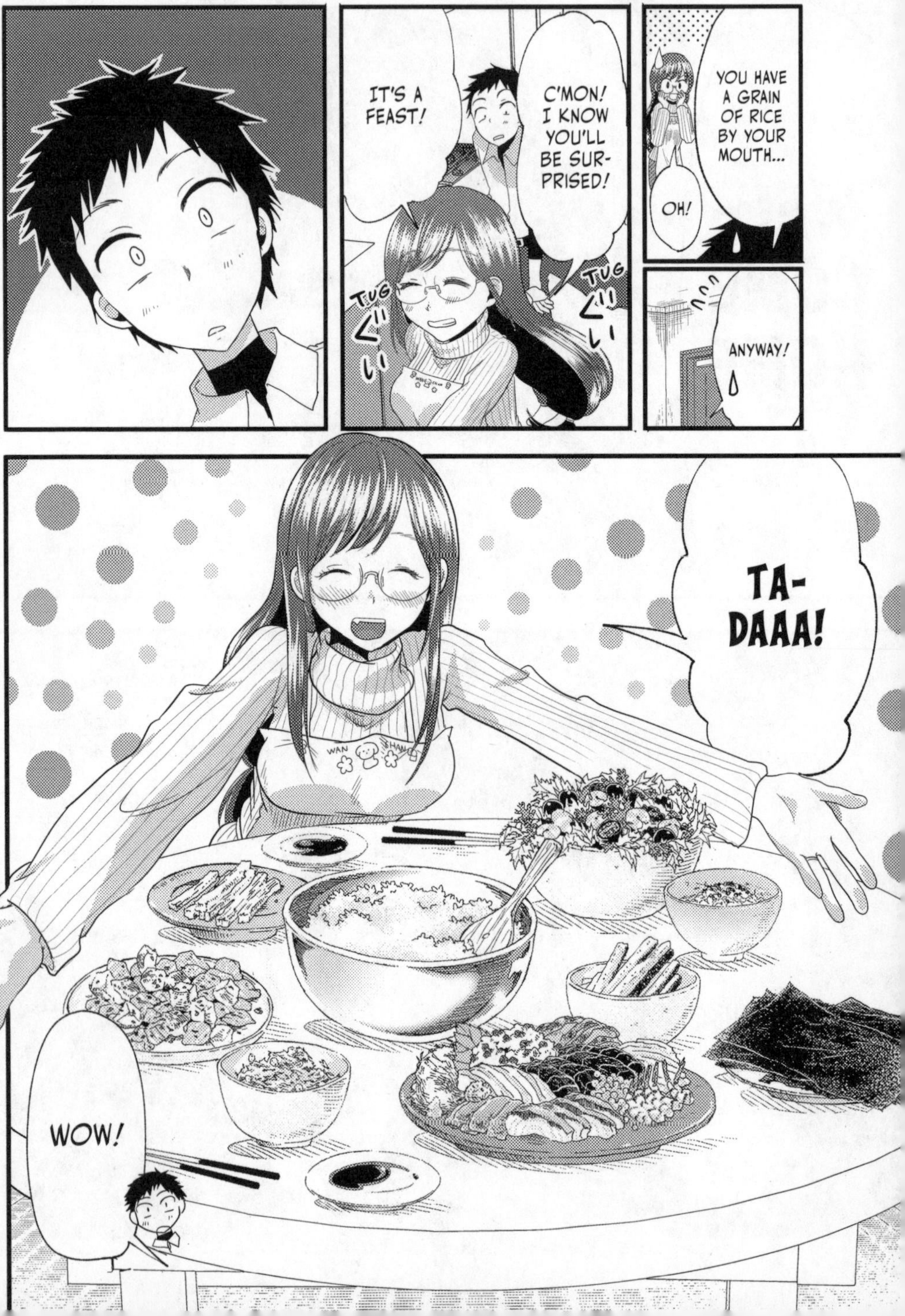

YOU HAVE A GRAIN OF RICE BY YOUR MOUTH...
OH!
ANYWAY!
C'MON! I KNOW YOU'LL BE SURPRISED!
IT'S A FEAST!
TUG ぐいい
TUG ぐいい
TA-DAAA!
WOW!

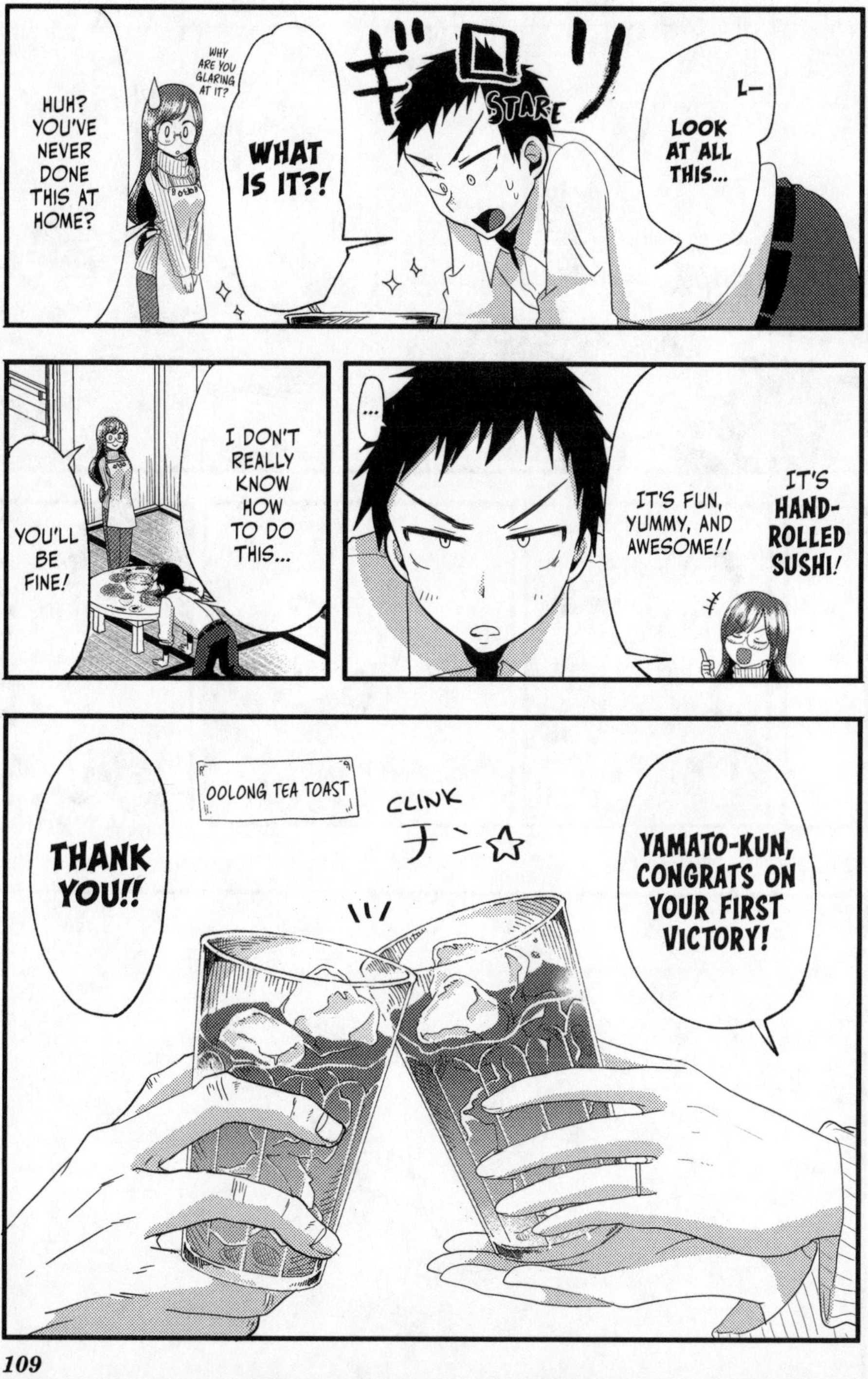
L— LOOK AT ALL THIS...
ギロリ
STARE
WHAT IS IT?!
WHY ARE YOU GLARING AT IT?
HUH? YOU'VE NEVER DONE THIS AT HOME?
IT'S HAND-ROLLED SUSHI!
IT'S FUN, YUMMY, AND AWESOME!!
...
I DON'T REALLY KNOW HOW TO DO THIS...
YOU'LL BE FINE!
YAMATO-KUN, CONGRATS ON YOUR FIRST VICTORY!
CLINK
チン☆
OOLONG TEA TOAST
THANK YOU!!

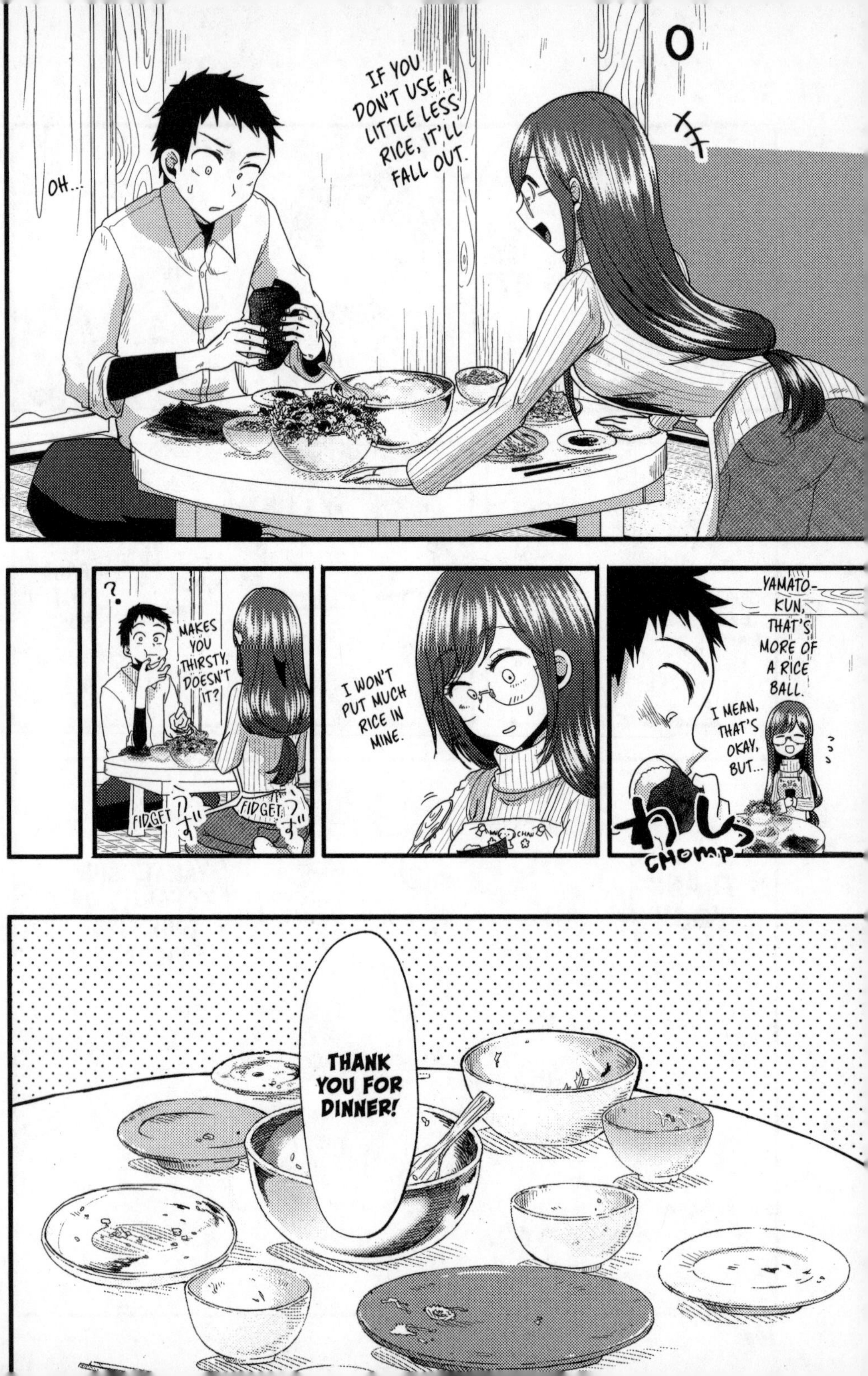
IF YOU DON'T USE A LITTLE LESS RICE, IT'LL FALL OUT.
OH...
YAMATO-KUN, THAT'S MORE OF A RICE BALL.
I MEAN, THAT'S OKAY, BUT...
CHOMP
I WON'T PUT MUCH RICE IN MINE.
?
MAKES YOU THIRSTY, DOESN'T IT?
FIDGET
FIDGET
THANK YOU FOR DINNER!

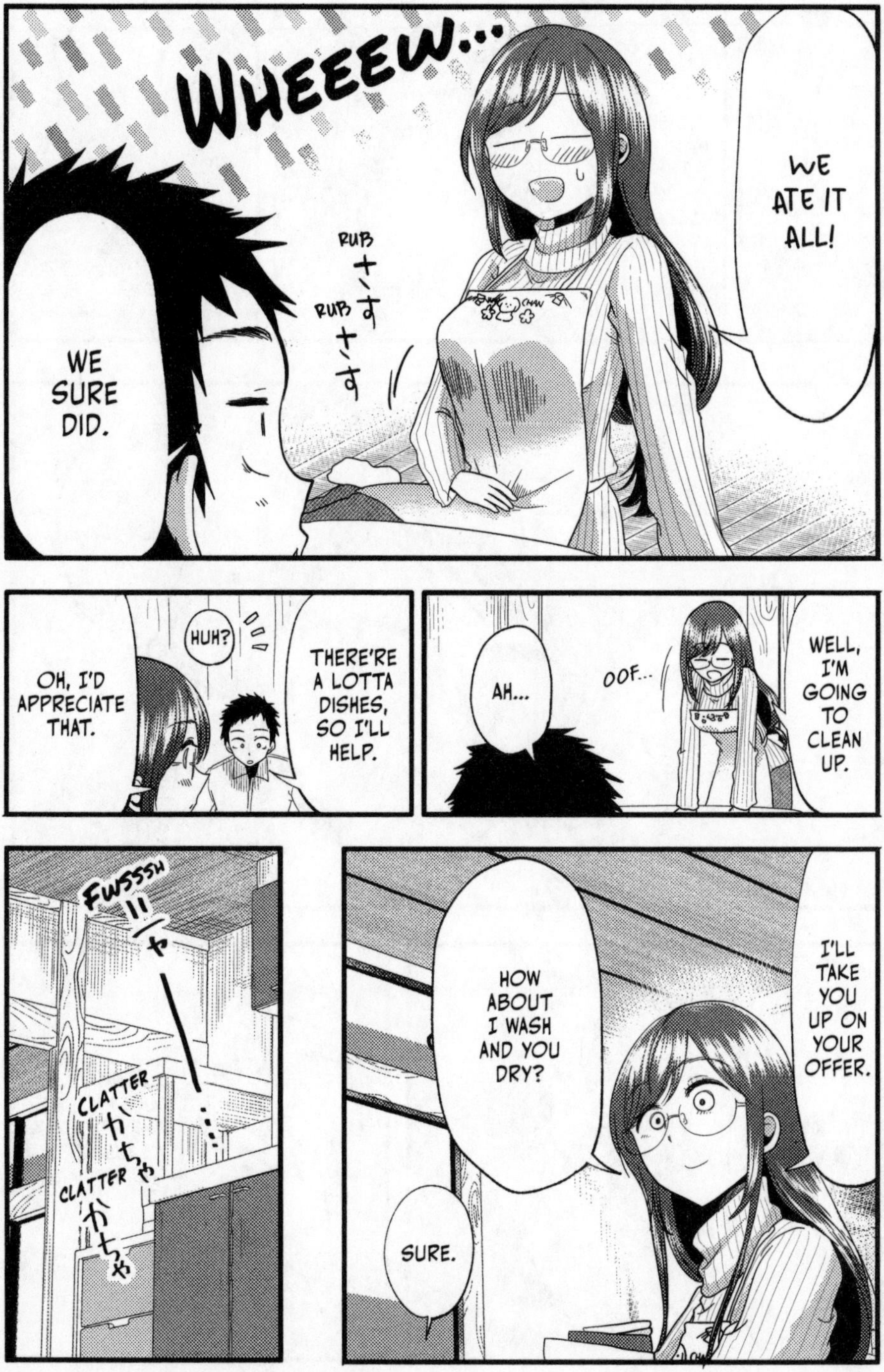
WE ATE IT ALL!
WHEEEW...
RUB さす
RUB さす
WE SURE DID.
WELL, I'M GOING TO CLEAN UP.
OOF...
AH...
THERE'RE A LOTTA DISHES, SO I'LL HELP.
HUH?
OH, I'D APPRECIATE THAT.
I'LL TAKE YOU UP ON YOUR OFFER.
HOW ABOUT I WASH AND YOU DRY?
SURE.
FWSSSH ジャー…
CLATTER かちゃ
CLATTER かちゃ

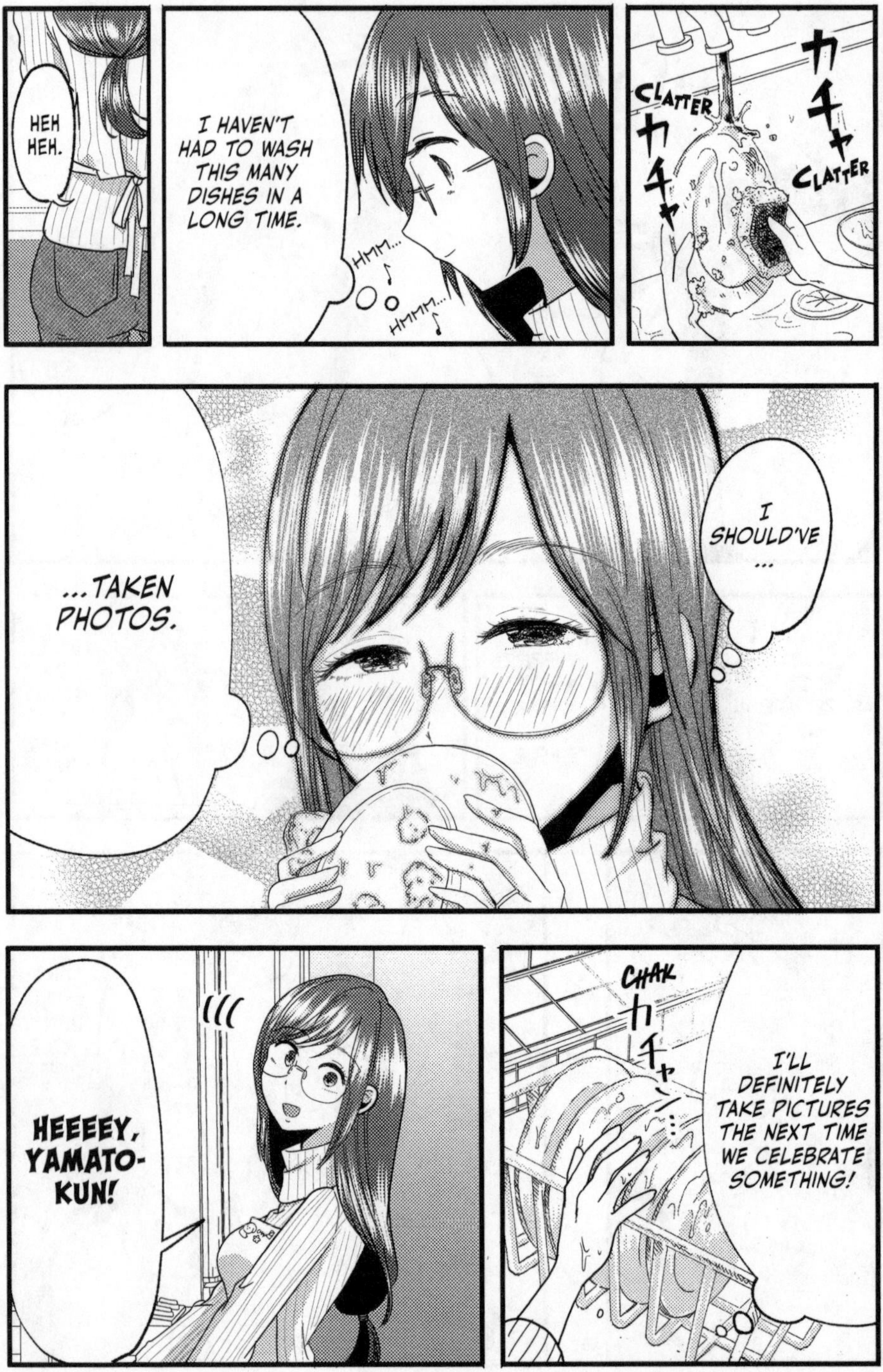
CLATTER
カチャ
カチャ
CLATTER
I HAVEN'T HAD TO WASH THIS MANY DISHES IN A LONG TIME.
HMM... ♪
HMMM... ♪
HEH HEH.
I SHOULD'VE ...
...TAKEN PHOTOS.
CHAK
カチャン…
I'LL DEFINITELY TAKE PICTURES THE NEXT TIME WE CELEBRATE SOMETHING!
HEEEEY, YAMATO-KUN!

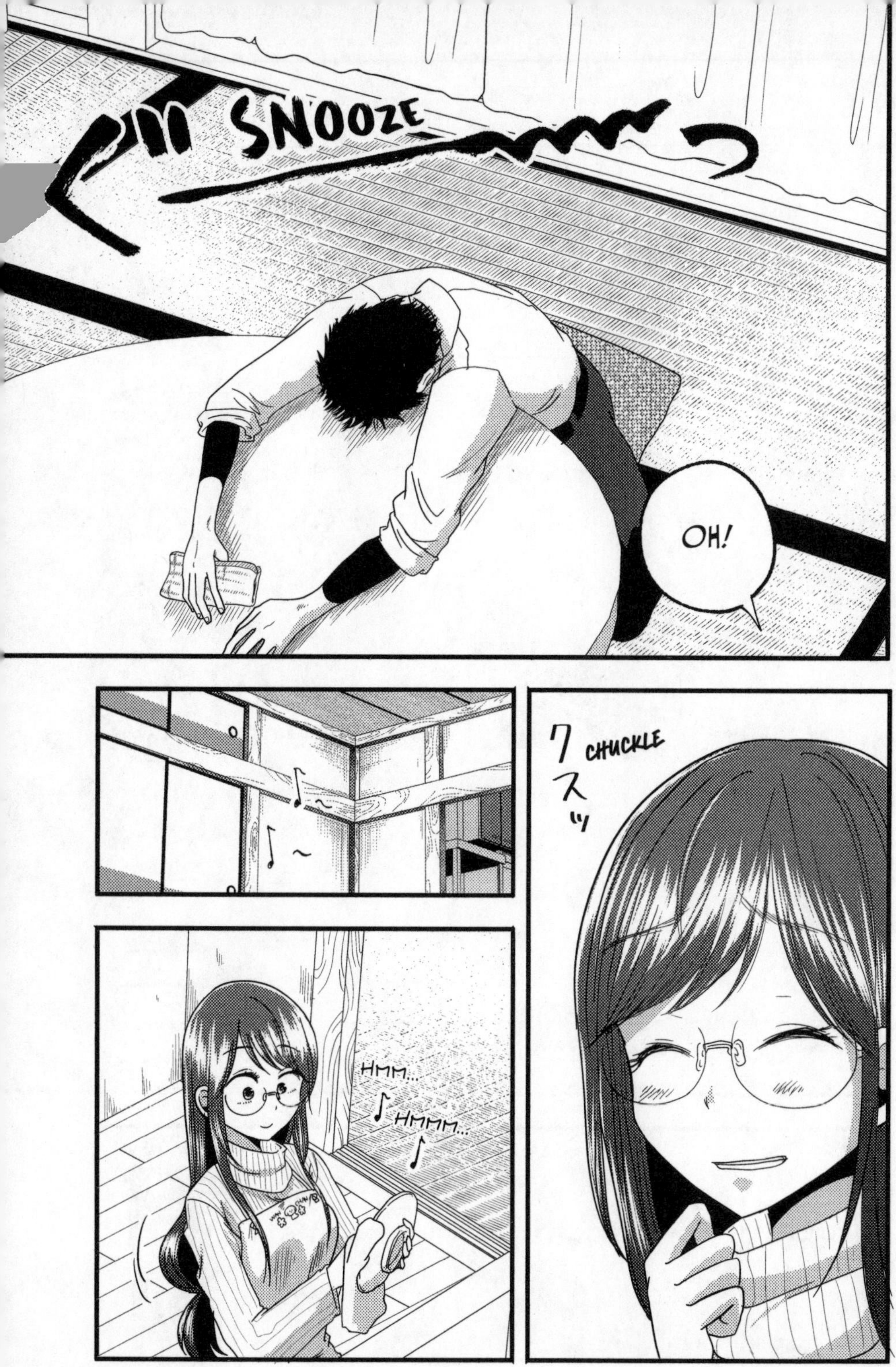
SNOOZE
OH!
クスッ
CHUCKLE
HMM...
HMMM...

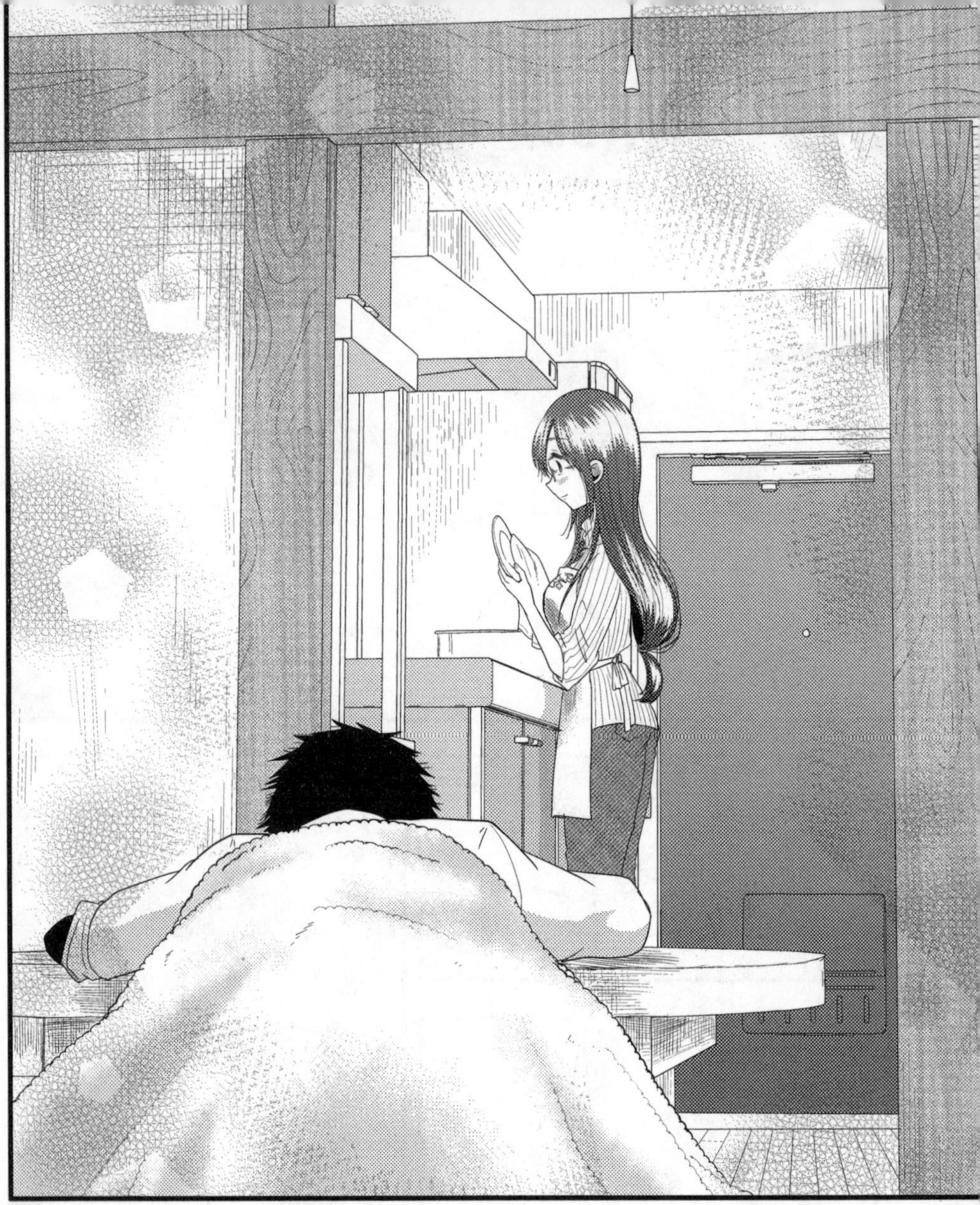

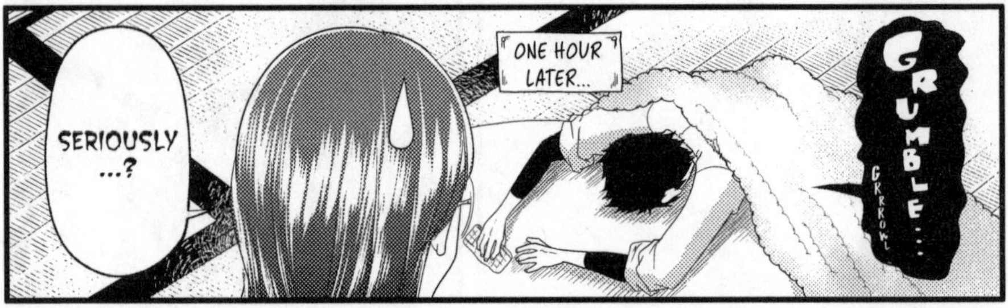
GRUMBLE...
GRRROWL
ONE HOUR LATER...
SERIOUSLY ...?

Beauty and the FEAST

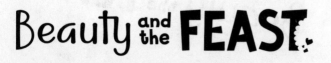

Beauty and the FEAST

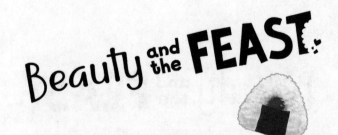

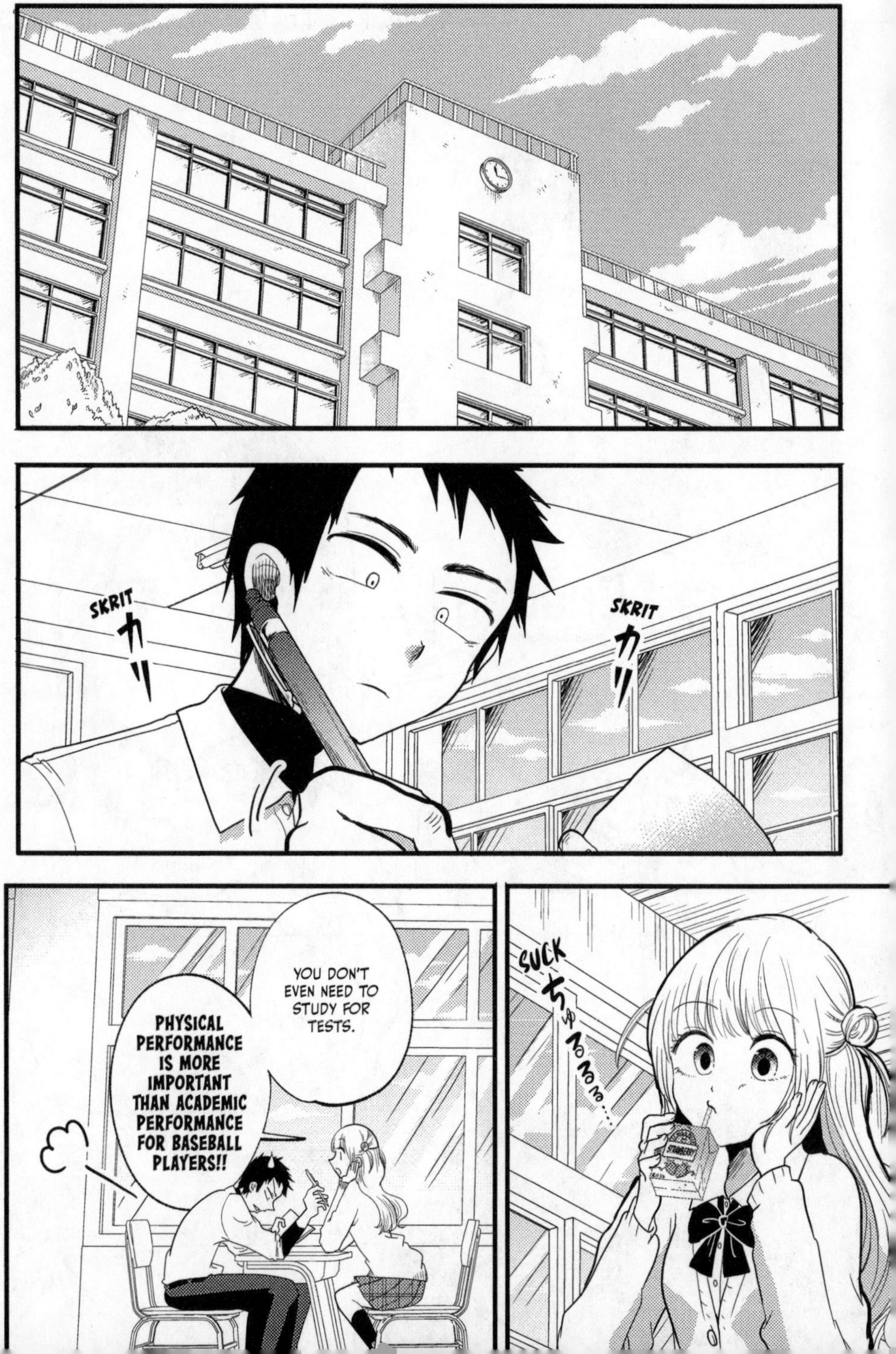
SKRIT
SKRIT
SUCK
YOU DON'T EVEN NEED TO STUDY FOR TESTS.
PHYSICAL PERFORMANCE IS MORE IMPORTANT THAN ACADEMIC PERFORMANCE FOR BASEBALL PLAYERS!!

Meal 13: Let's Enjoy English!

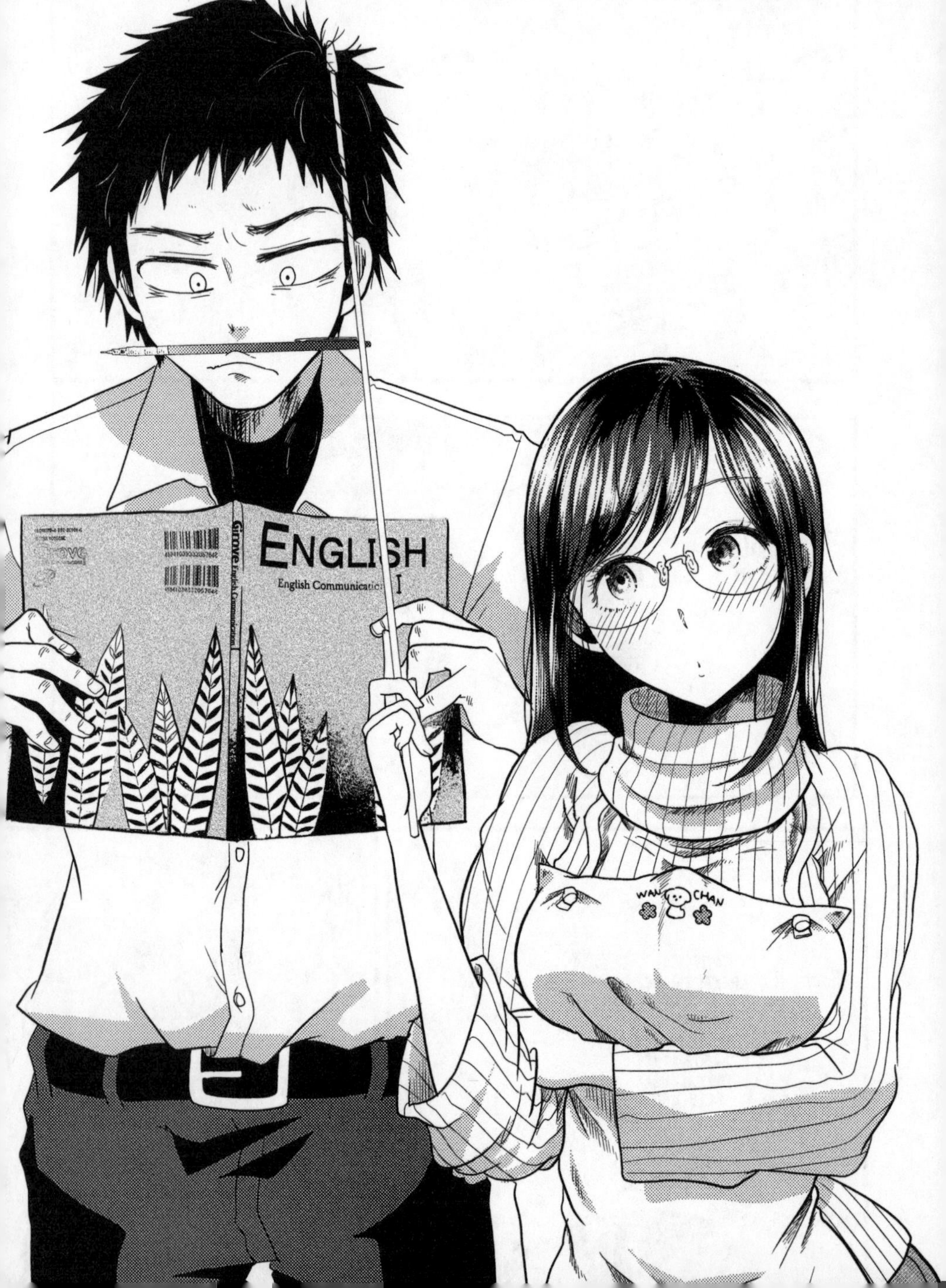
ENGLISH
English Communication I
WAN
CHAN

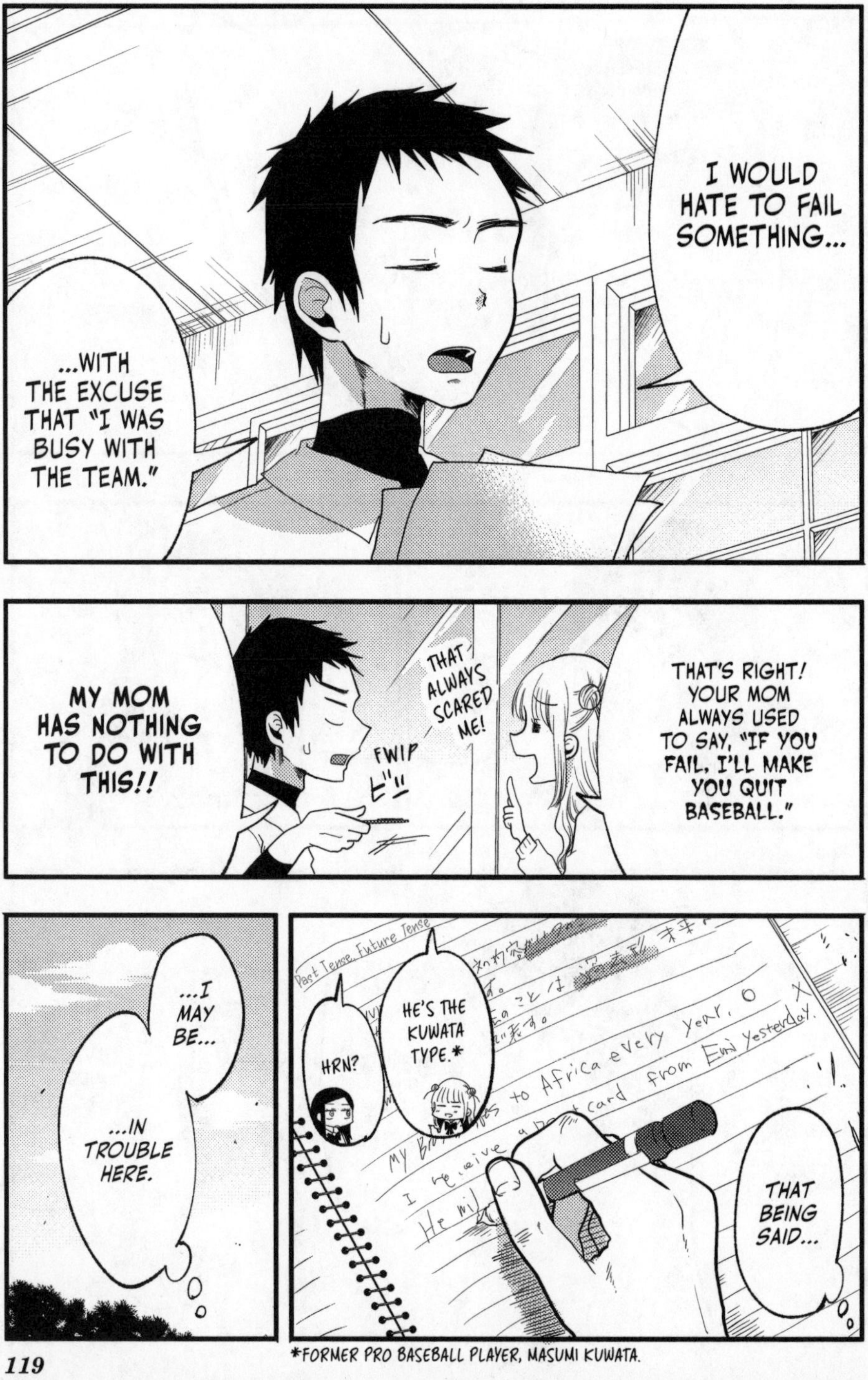
I WOULD HATE TO FAIL SOMETHING...
...WITH THE EXCUSE THAT "I WAS BUSY WITH THE TEAM."
THAT'S RIGHT! YOUR MOM ALWAYS USED TO SAY, "IF YOU FAIL, I'LL MAKE YOU QUIT BASEBALL."
THAT ALWAYS SCARED ME!
FWIP
ビッ
MY MOM HAS NOTHING TO DO WITH THIS!!
THAT BEING SAID...
Past Tense, Future Tense
HE'S THE KUWATA TYPE.*
HRN?
...I MAY BE...
...IN TROUBLE HERE.

*FORMER PRO BASEBALL PLAYER, MASUMI KUWATA.

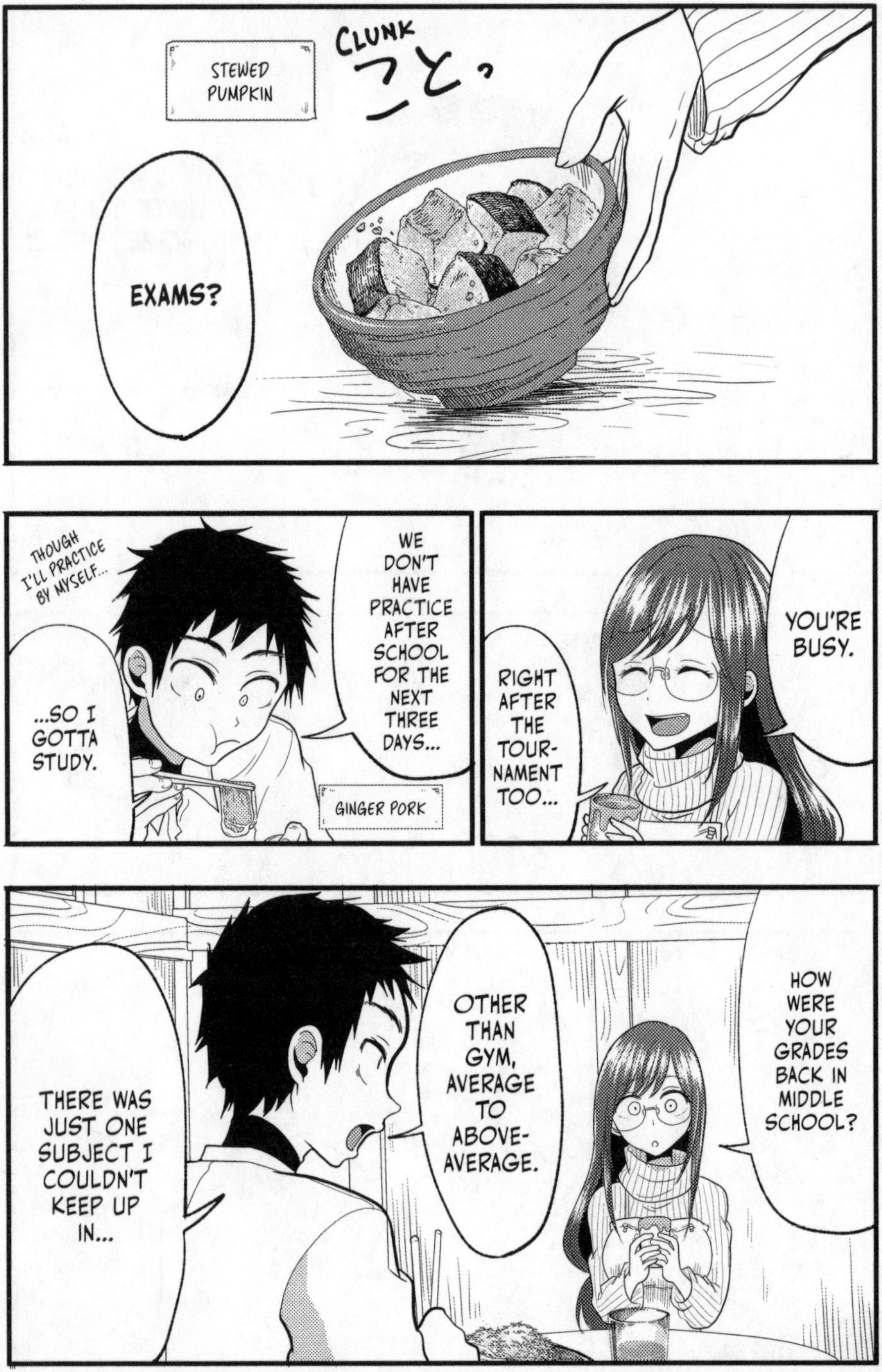
CLUNK
こと
STEWED PUMPKIN
EXAMS?
YOU'RE BUSY.
RIGHT AFTER THE TOURNAMENT TOO...
WE DON'T HAVE PRACTICE AFTER SCHOOL FOR THE NEXT THREE DAYS...
THOUGH I'LL PRACTICE BY MYSELF...
...SO I GOTTA STUDY.
GINGER PORK
HOW WERE YOUR GRADES BACK IN MIDDLE SCHOOL?
OTHER THAN GYM, AVERAGE TO ABOVE-AVERAGE.
THERE WAS JUST ONE SUBJECT I COULDN'T KEEP UP IN...

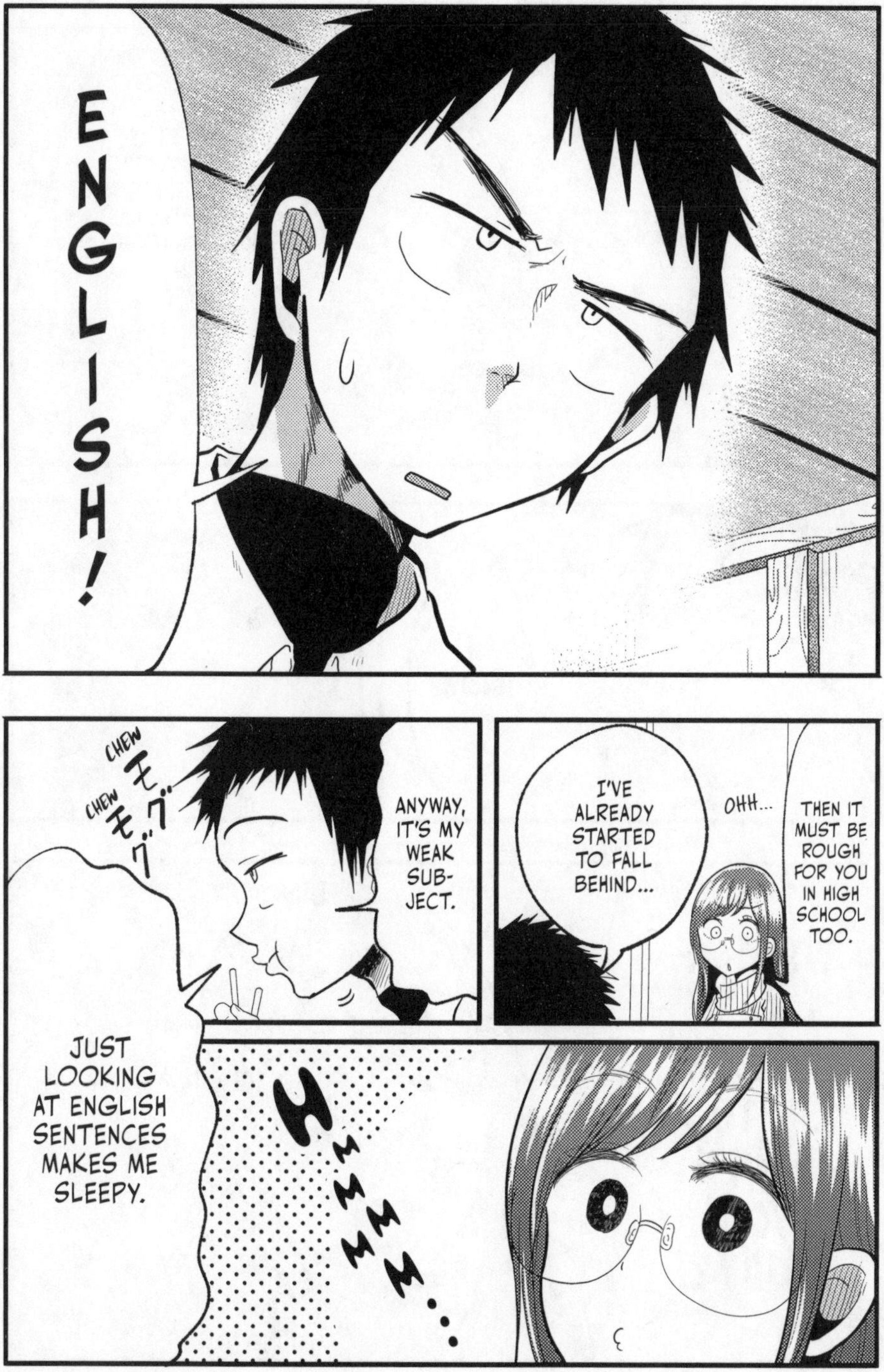
ENGLISH!
I'VE ALREADY STARTED TO FALL BEHIND...
OHH...
THEN IT MUST BE ROUGH FOR YOU IN HIGH SCHOOL TOO.
CHEW CHEW モグモグ
ANYWAY, IT'S MY WEAK SUB-JECT.
JUST LOOKING AT ENGLISH SENTENCES MAKES ME SLEEPY.
HMMMMM...

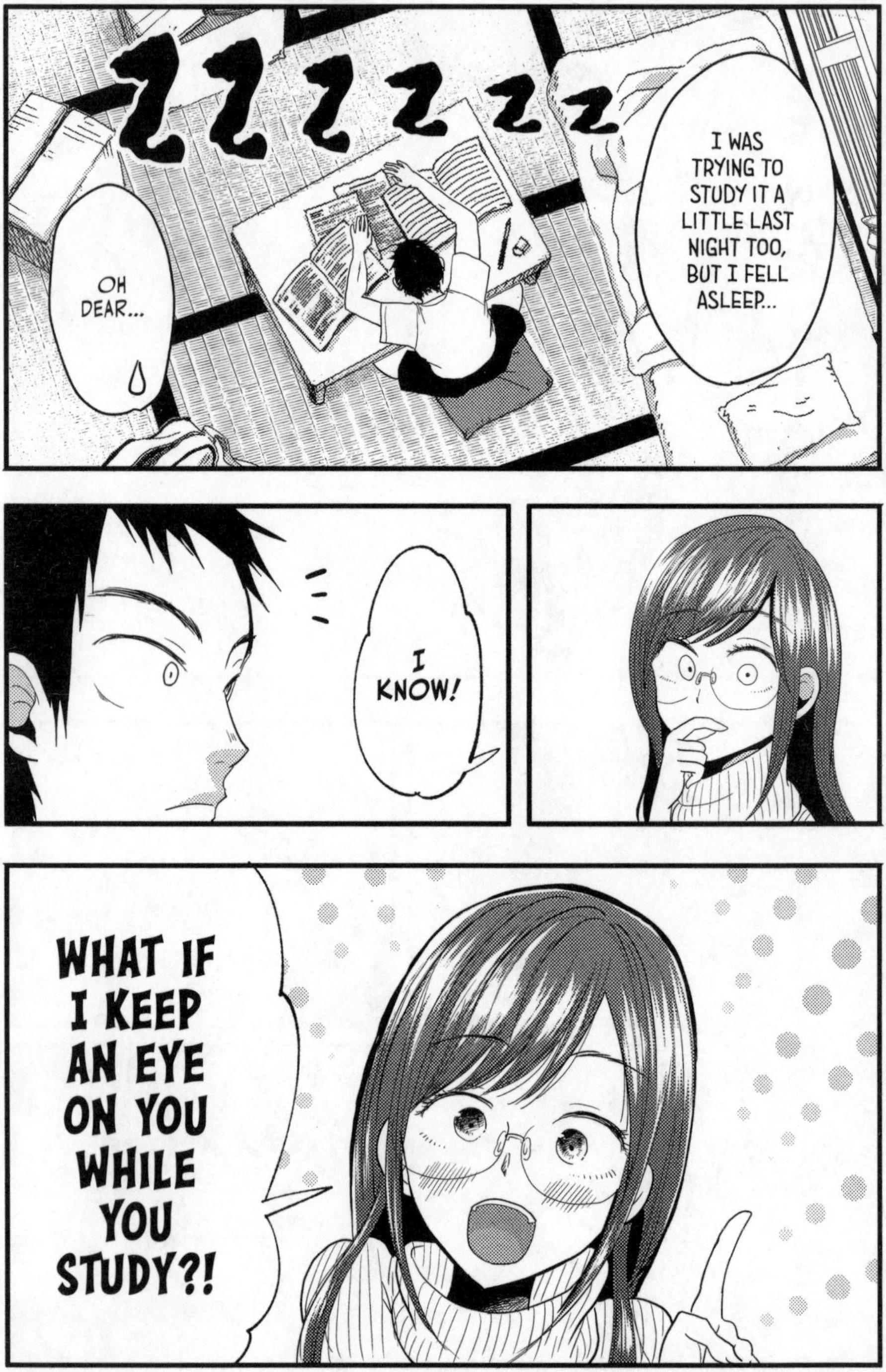
I WAS TRYING TO STUDY IT A LITTLE LAST NIGHT TOO, BUT I FELL ASLEEP...
ZZZZZZZ
OH DEAR...
I KNOW!
WHAT IF I KEEP AN EYE ON YOU WHILE YOU STUDY?!

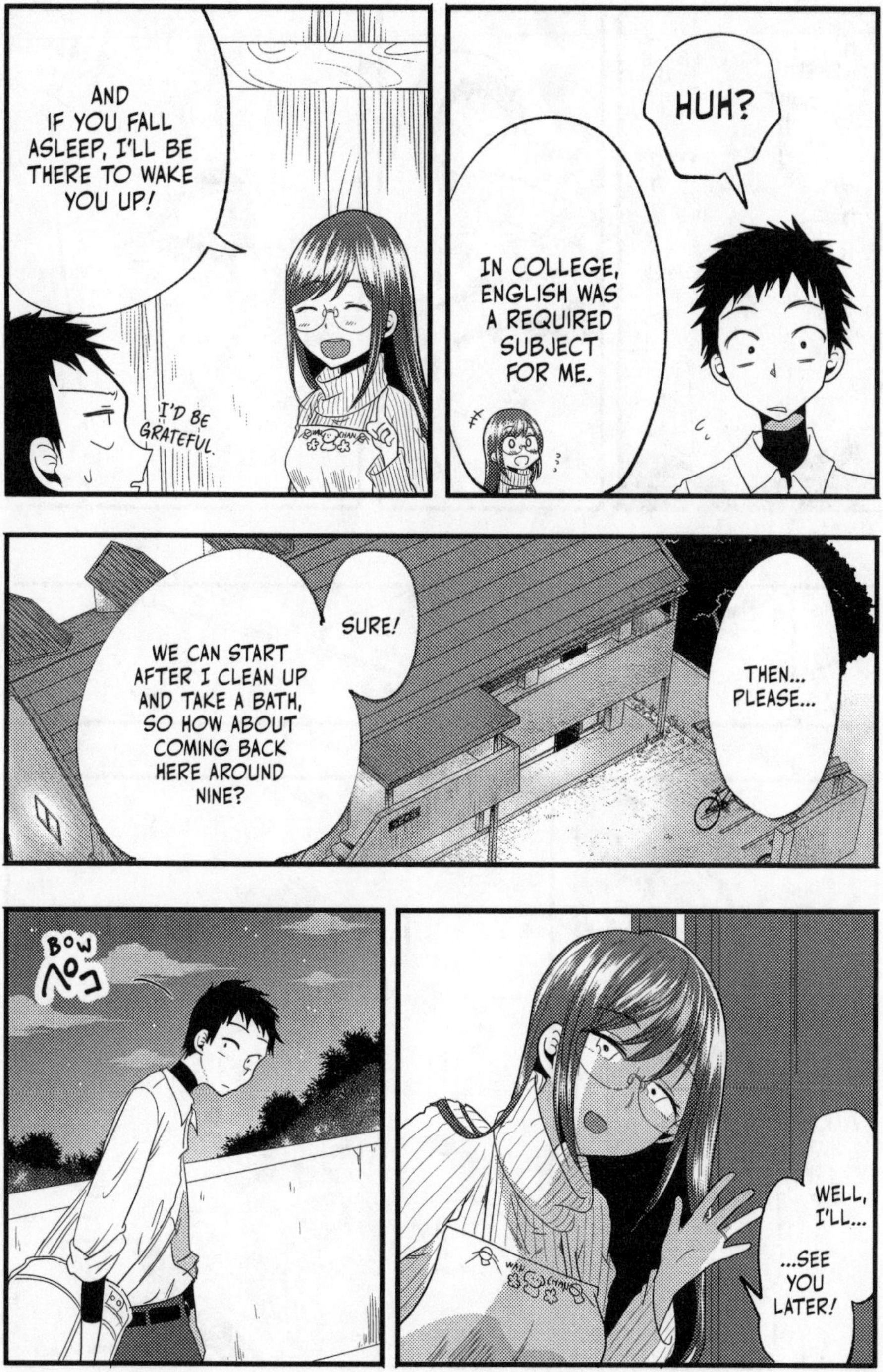
HUH?
IN COLLEGE, ENGLISH WAS A REQUIRED SUBJECT FOR ME.
AND IF YOU FALL ASLEEP, I'LL BE THERE TO WAKE YOU UP!
I'D BE GRATEFUL.
THEN... PLEASE...
SURE!
WE CAN START AFTER I CLEAN UP AND TAKE A BATH, SO HOW ABOUT COMING BACK HERE AROUND NINE?
WELL, I'LL...
...SEE YOU LATER!
BOW
ペコ

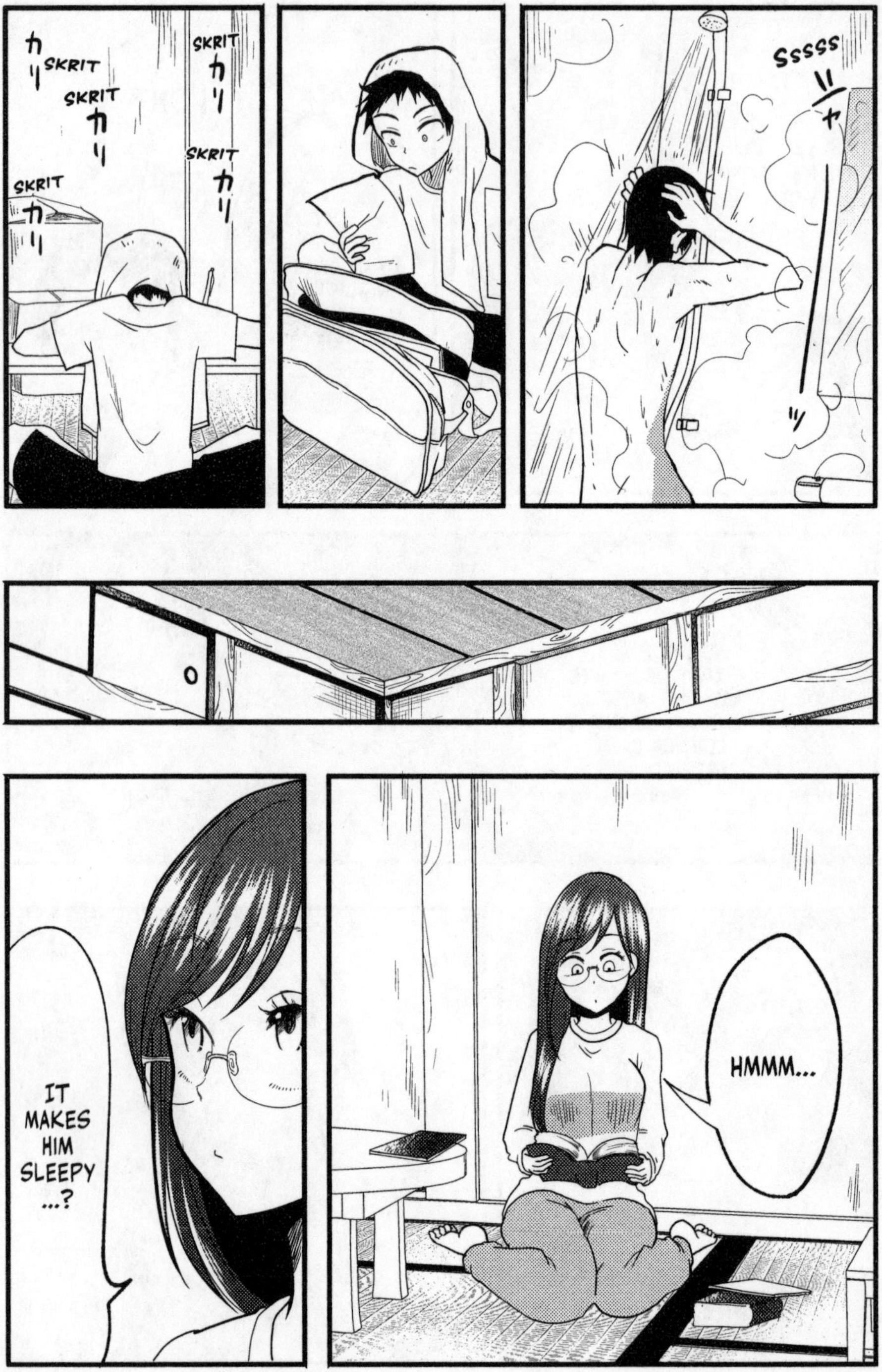
SSSSS
シャ
ッ
SKRIT
カリ
SKRIT
カリ
SKRIT
カリ
SKRIT
カリ
SKRIT
カリ
HMMM...
IT MAKES HIM SLEEPY ...?

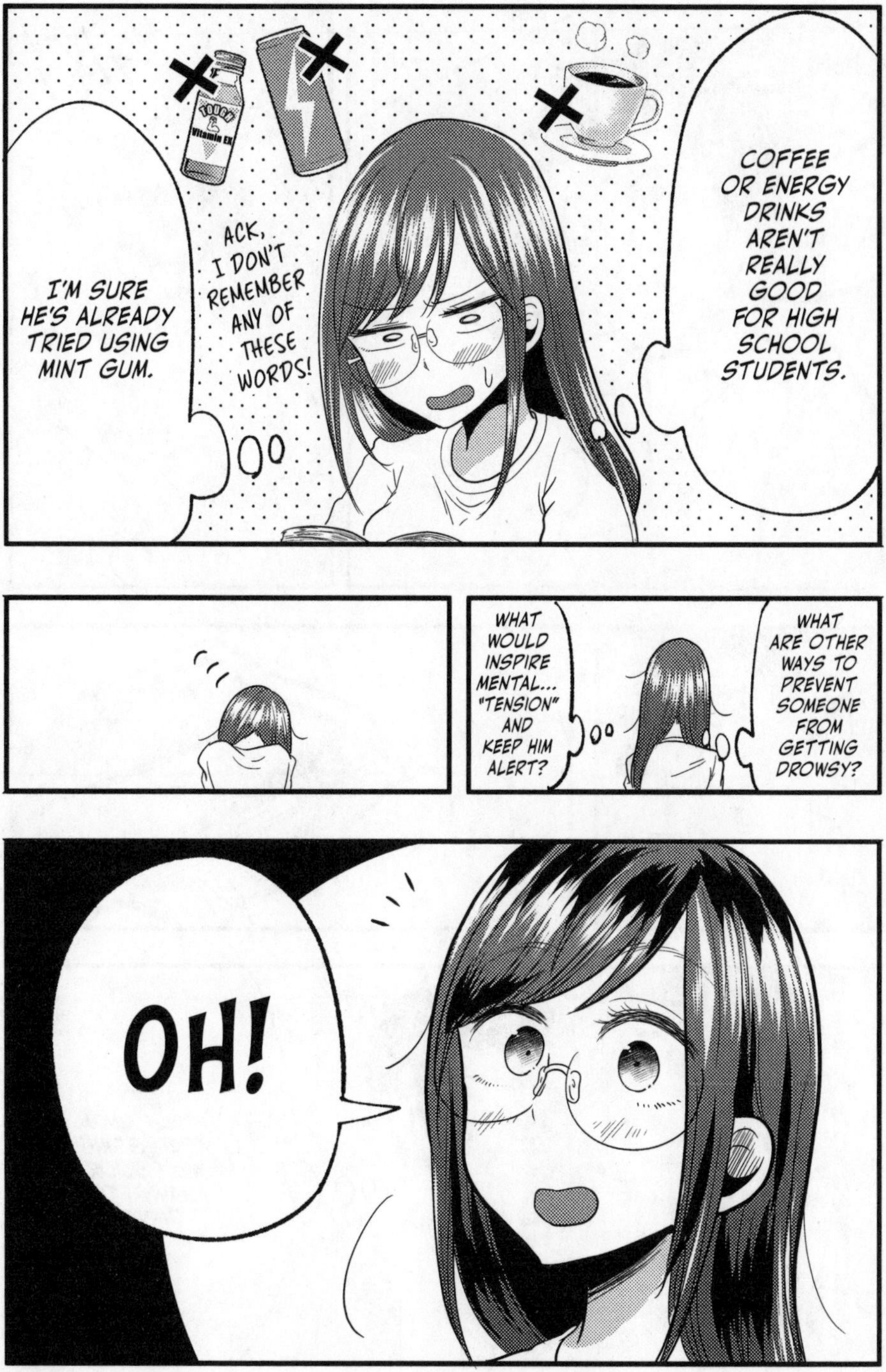
COFFEE OR ENERGY DRINKS AREN'T REALLY GOOD FOR HIGH SCHOOL STUDENTS.
ACK, I DON'T REMEMBER ANY OF THESE WORDS!
I'M SURE HE'S ALREADY TRIED USING MINT GUM.
WHAT ARE OTHER WAYS TO PREVENT SOMEONE FROM GETTING DROWSY?
WHAT WOULD INSPIRE MENTAL... "TENSION" AND KEEP HIM ALERT?
OH!

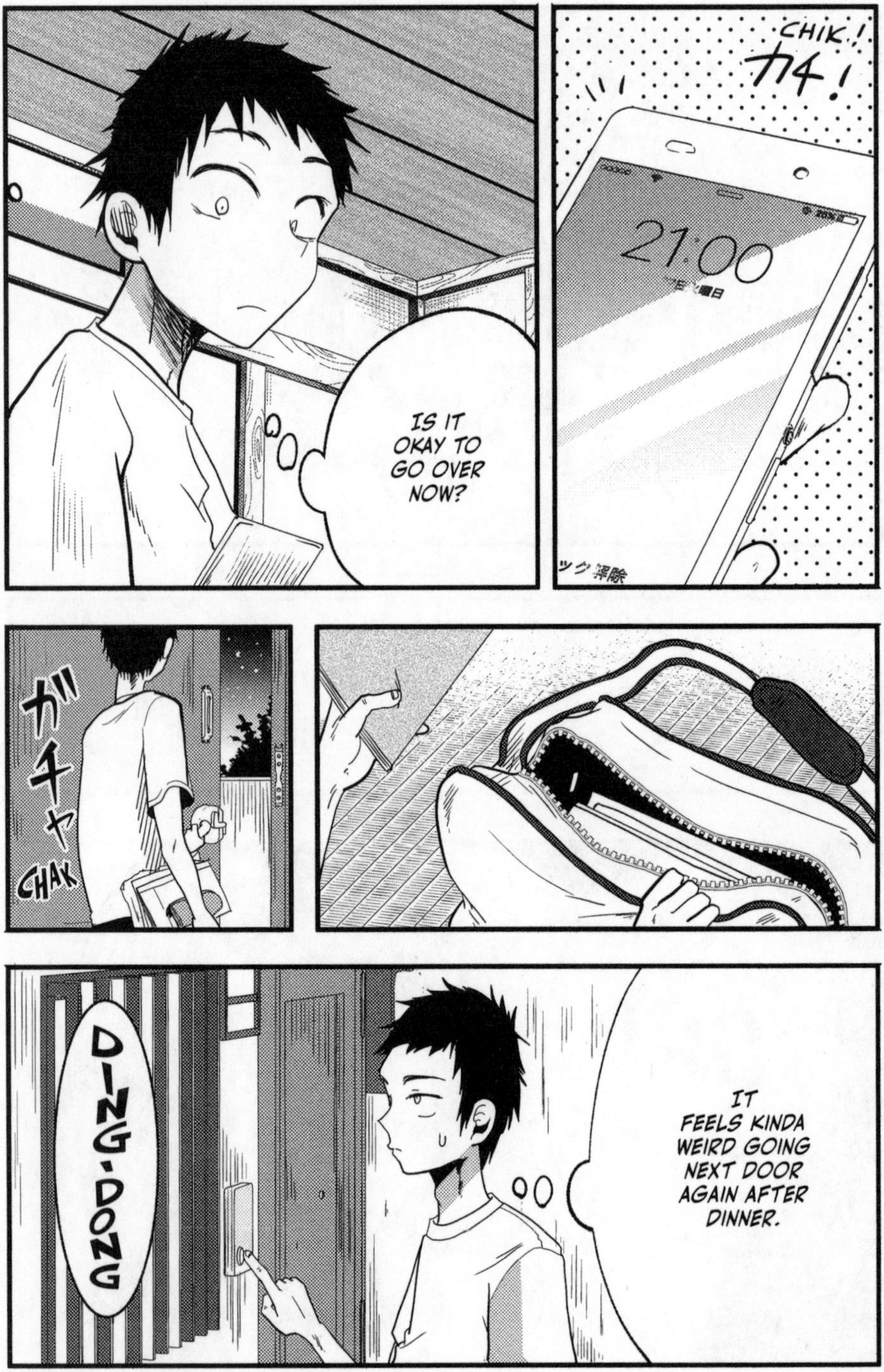
CHIK!
カチ!
21:00
IS IT OKAY TO GO OVER NOW?
ガチャ
CHAK
IT FEELS KINDA WEIRD GOING NEXT DOOR AGAIN AFTER DINNER.
DING-DONG

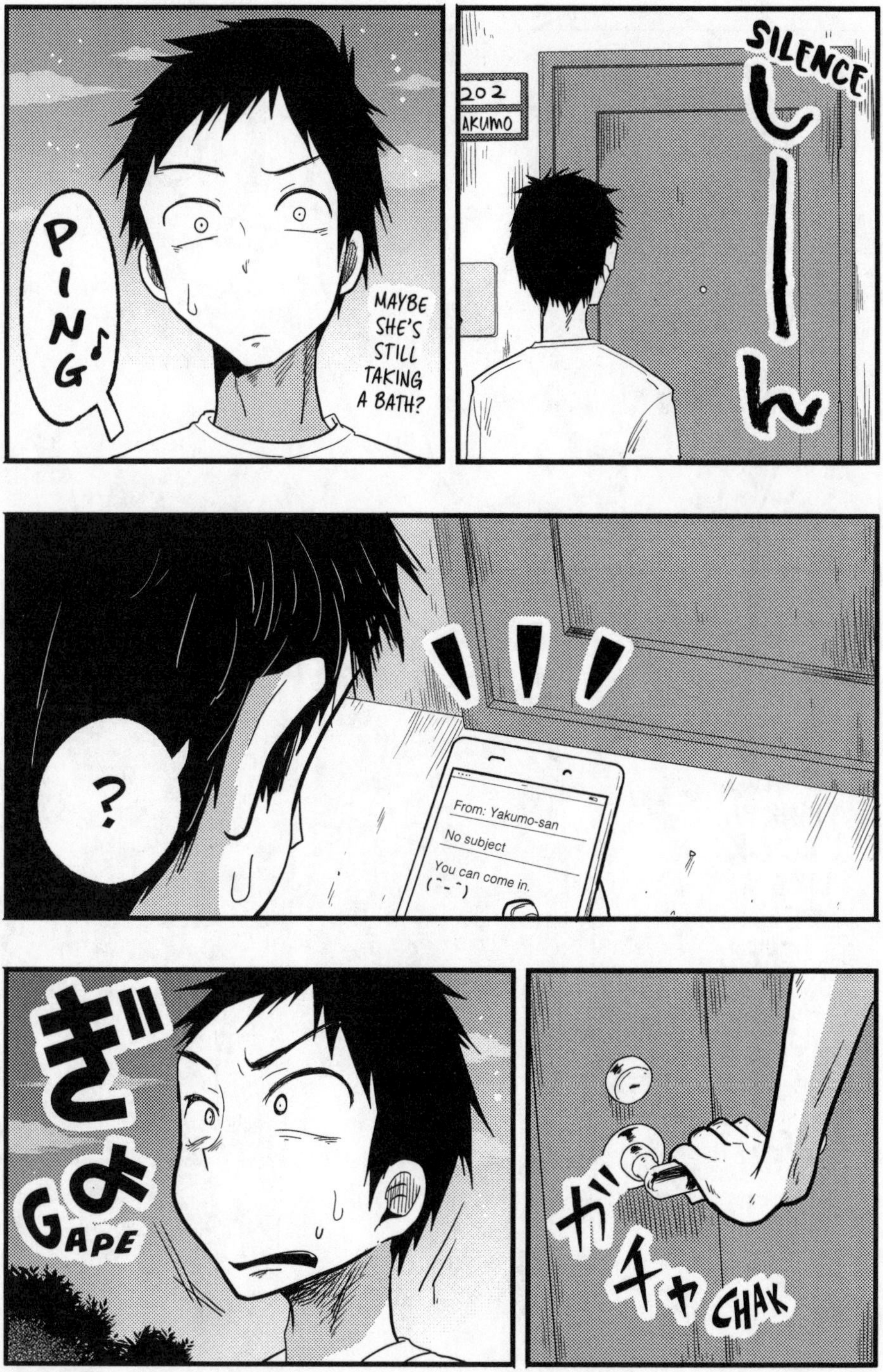
202
AKUMO
SILENCE
しーん
PING♪
MAYBE SHE'S STILL TAKING A BATH?
From: Yakumo-san
No subject
You can come in.
(ˆ-ˆ)
?
ガチャ
CHAK
ぎょ
GAPE

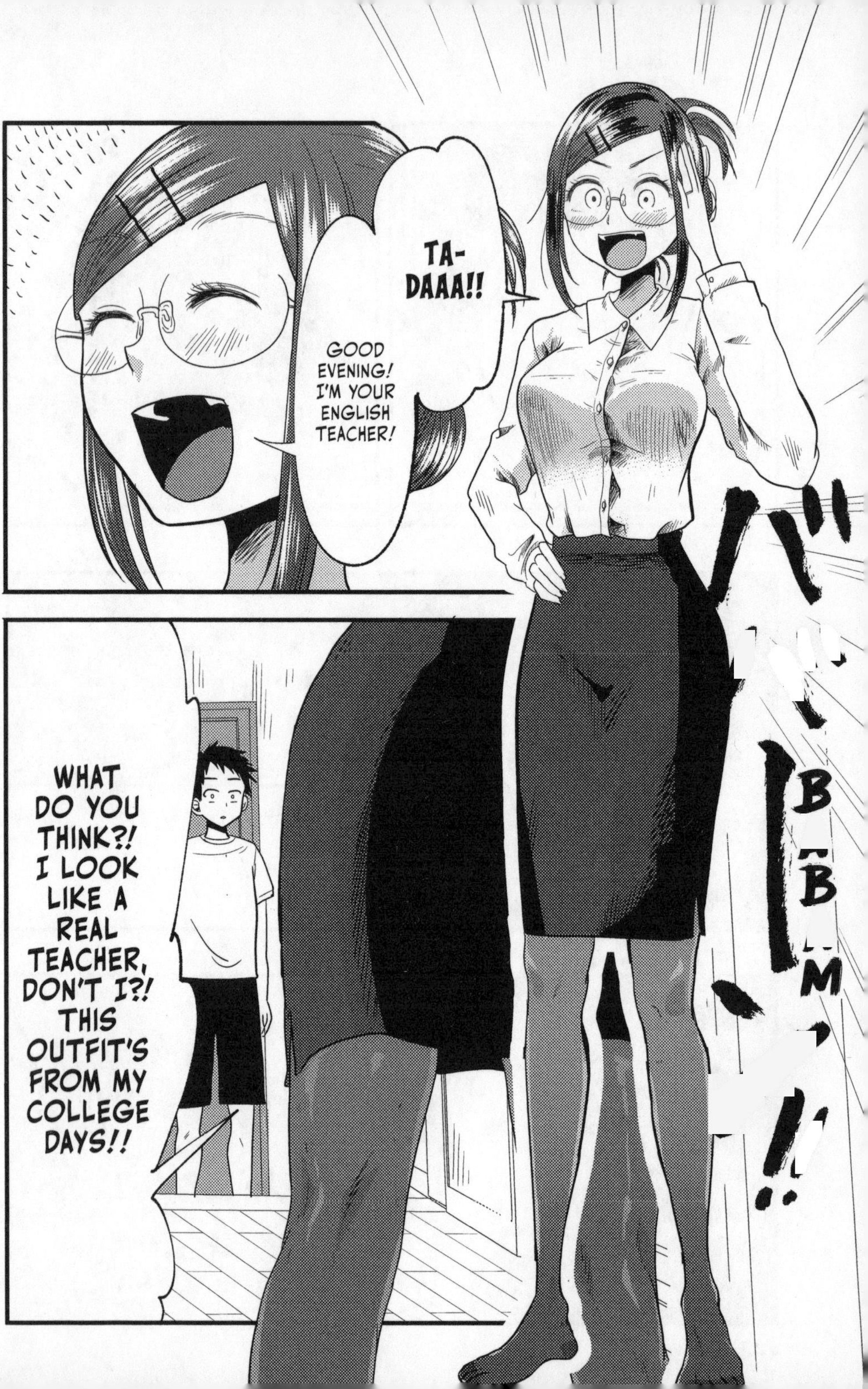
TA-DAAA!!
B B M!!
GOOD EVENING! I'M YOUR ENGLISH TEACHER!
WHAT DO YOU THINK?! I LOOK LIKE A REAL TEACHER, DON'T I?! THIS OUTFIT'S FROM MY COLLEGE DAYS!!

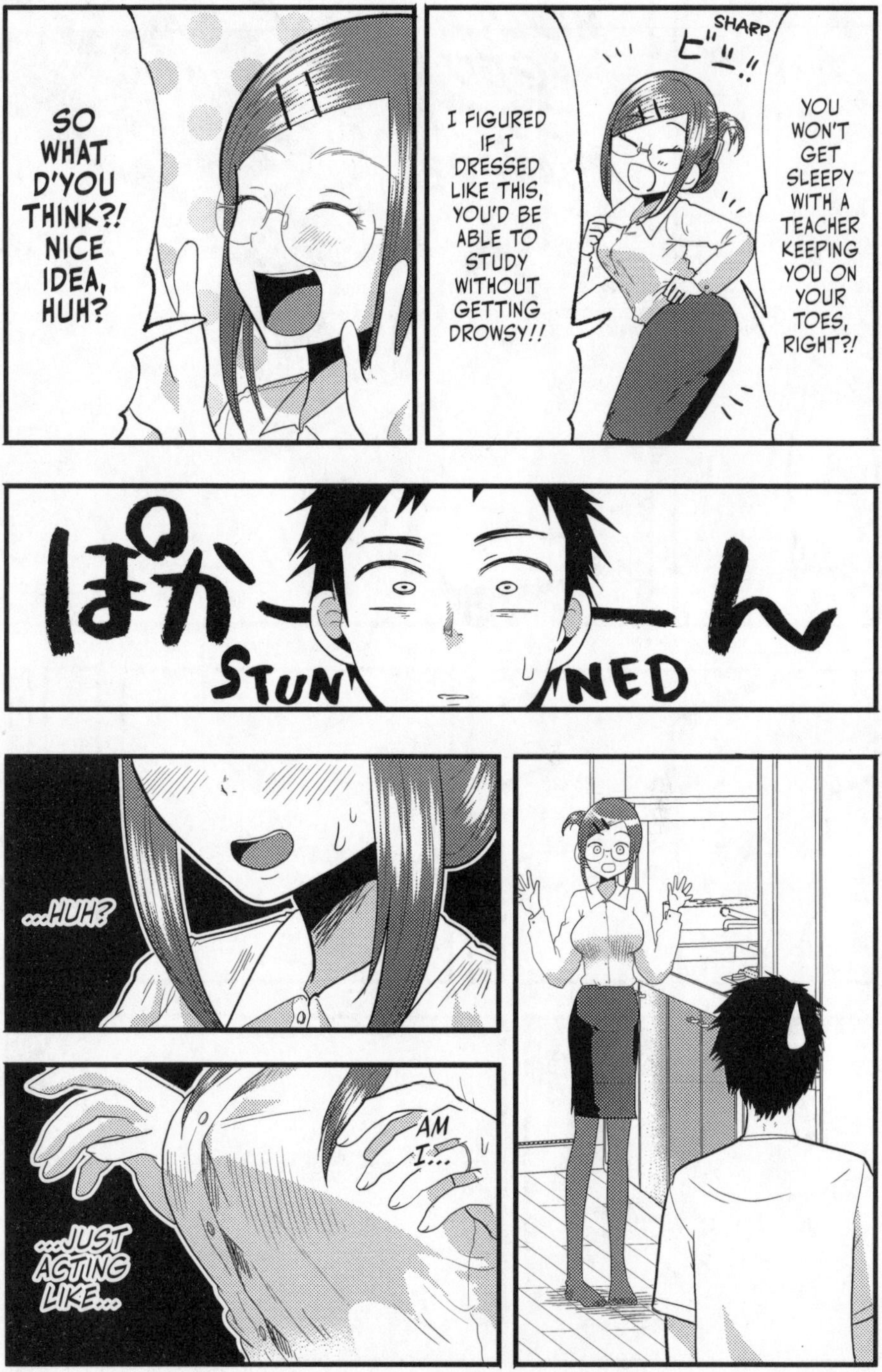
SHARP
ビッ!!
YOU WON'T GET SLEEPY WITH A TEACHER KEEPING YOU ON YOUR TOES, RIGHT?!
I FIGURED IF I DRESSED LIKE THIS, YOU'D BE ABLE TO STUDY WITHOUT GETTING DROWSY!!
SO WHAT D'YOU THINK?! NICE IDEA, HUH?
ぱかーーーん
STUNNED
...HUH?
AM I...
...JUST ACTING LIKE...

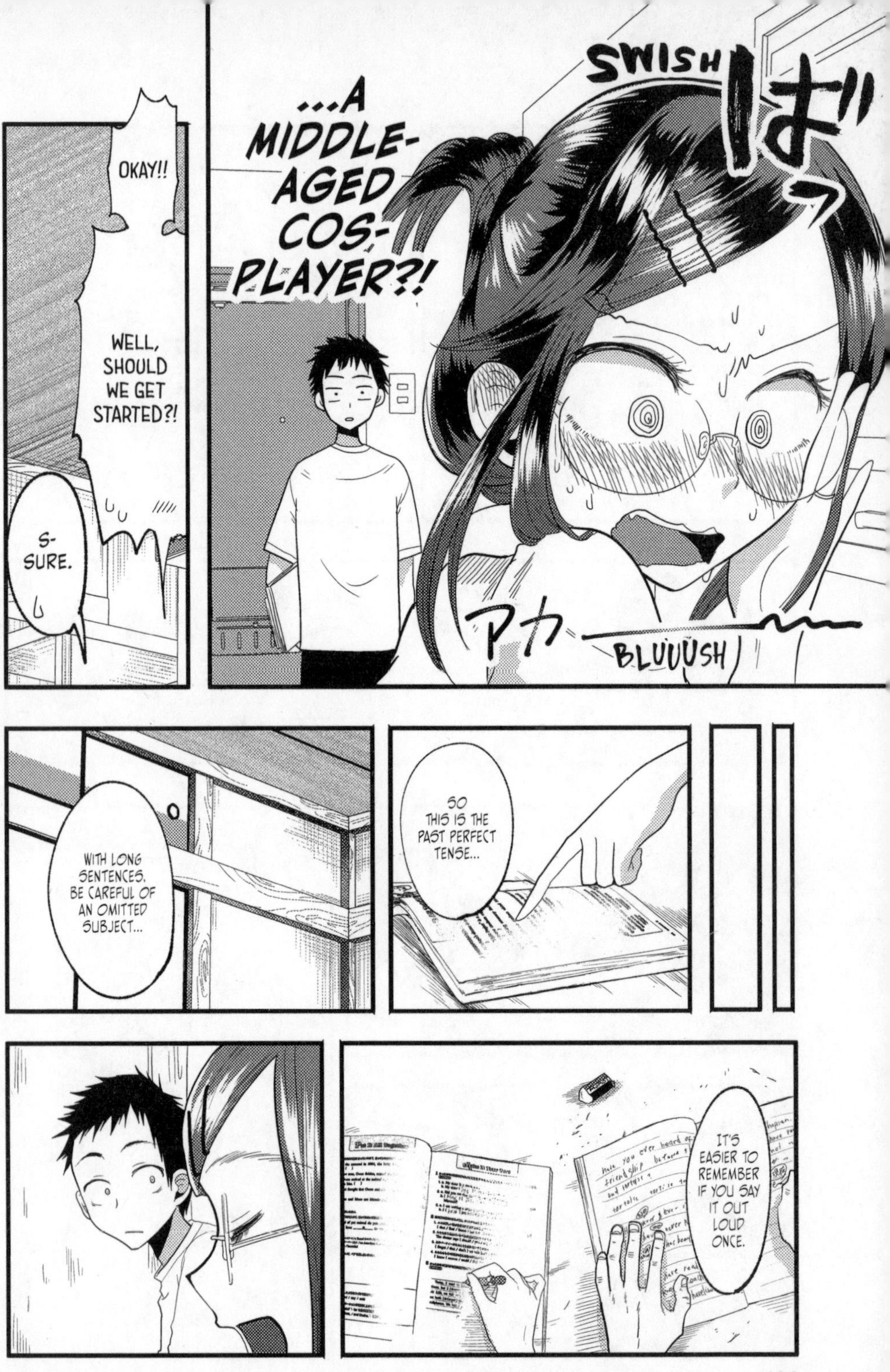
SWISH
ばっ
...A MIDDLE-AGED COS-PLAYER?!
アカ
BLUUUSH
OKAY!!
WELL, SHOULD WE GET STARTED?!
S-SURE.
SO THIS IS THE PAST PERFECT TENSE...
WITH LONG SENTENCES, BE CAREFUL OF AN OMITTED SUBJECT...
IT'S EASIER TO REMEMBER IF YOU SAY IT OUT LOUD ONCE.

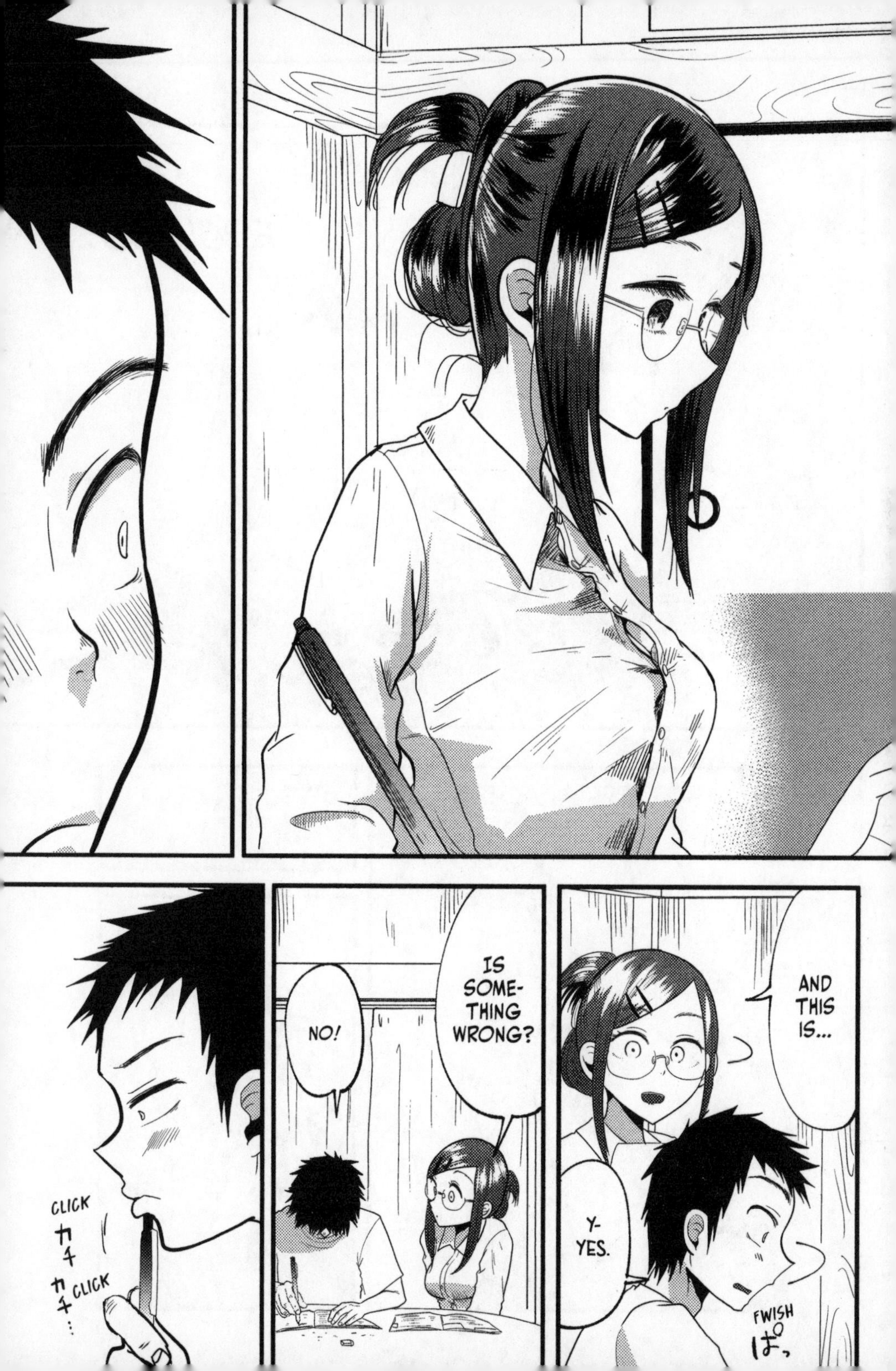
AND THIS IS...
Y- YES.
FWISH
ぱっ
IS SOME-THING WRONG?
NO!
CLICK
カチ
カチ…
CLICK

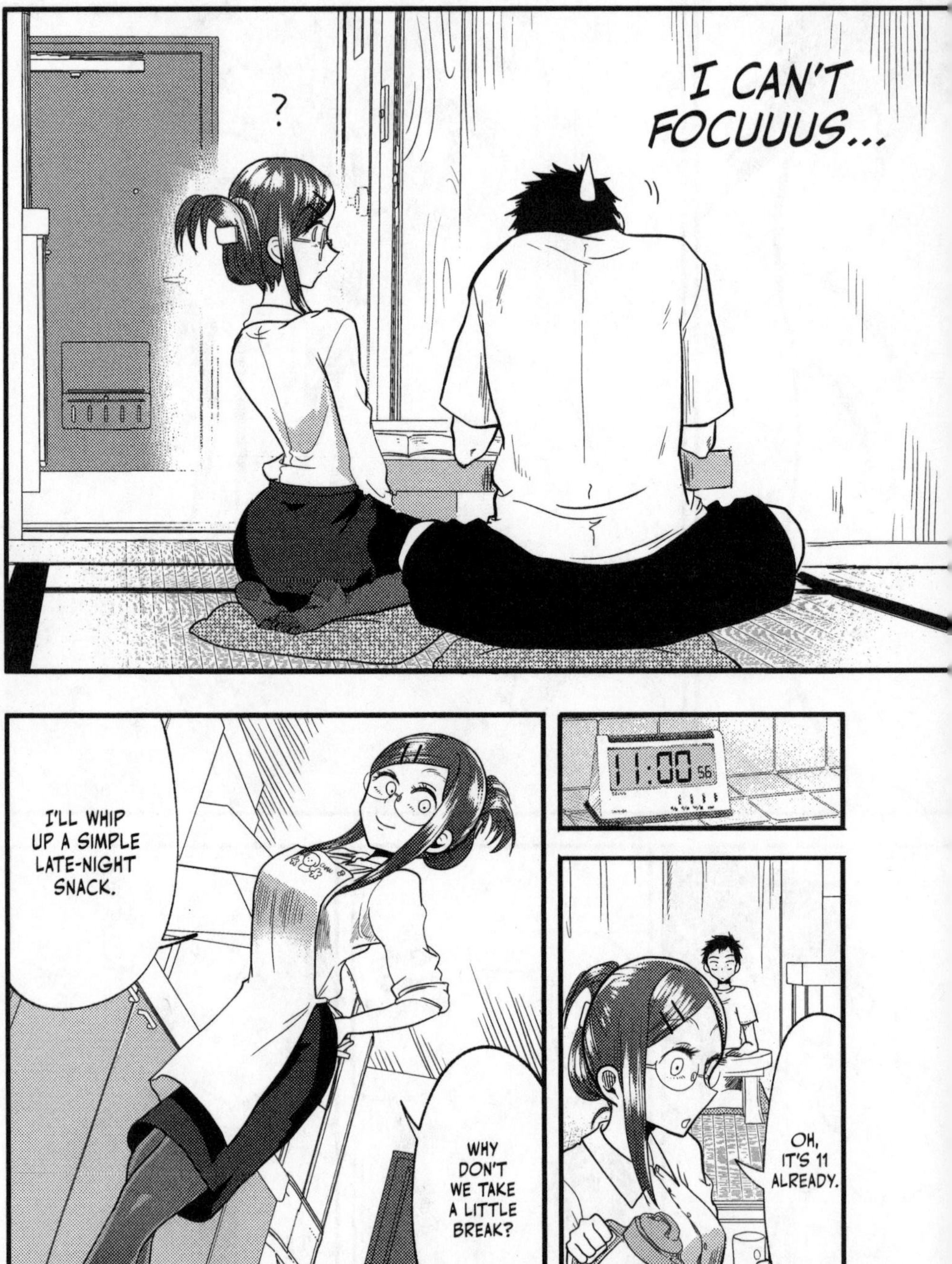

I CAN'T FOCUUUS...
?
11:00
OH, IT'S 11 ALREADY.
WHY DON'T WE TAKE A LITTLE BREAK?
I'LL WHIP UP A SIMPLE LATE-NIGHT SNACK.

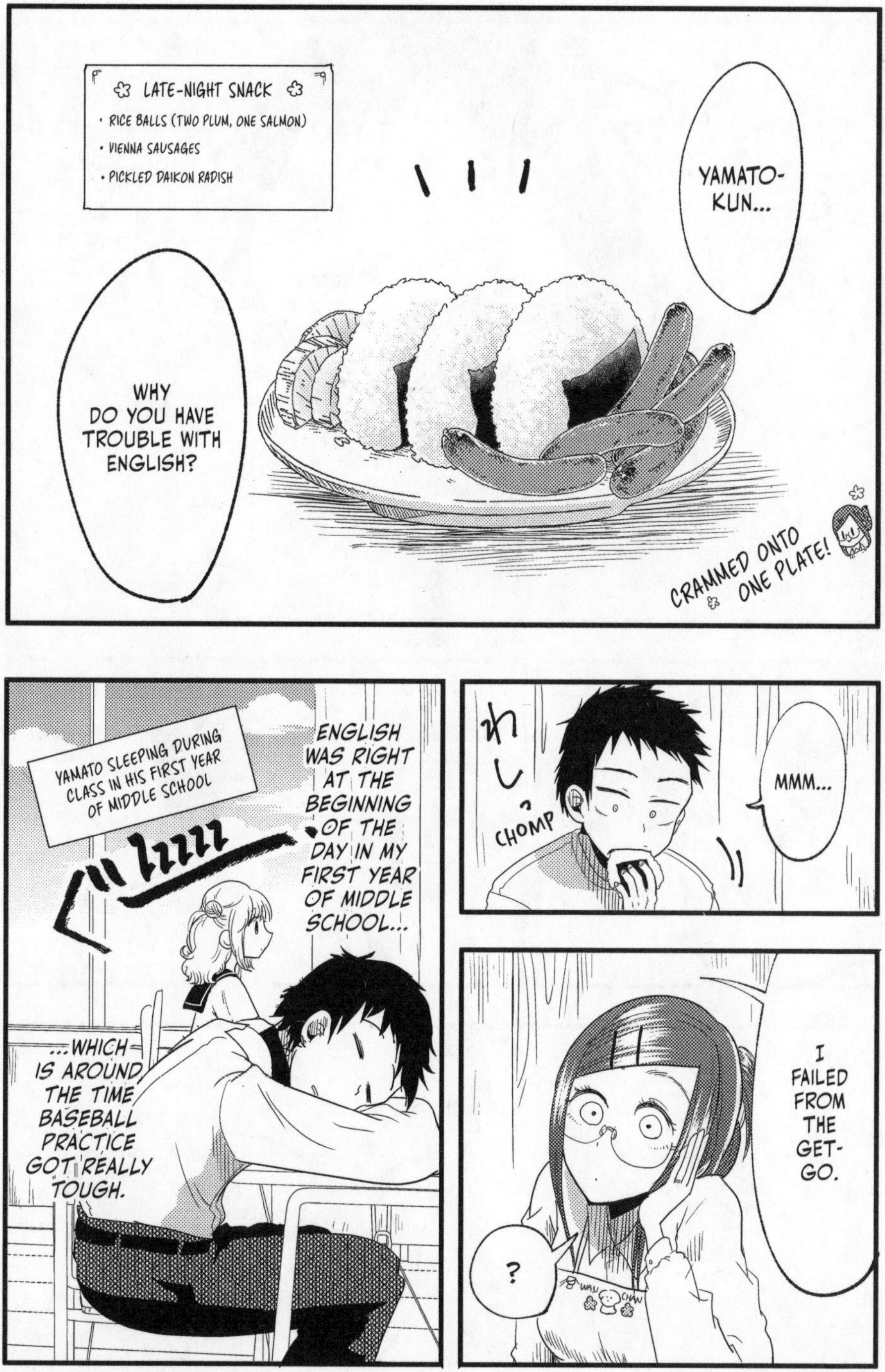
YAMATO-KUN...
LATE-NIGHT SNACK
• RICE BALLS (TWO PLUM, ONE SALMON)
• VIENNA SAUSAGES
• PICKLED DAIKON RADISH
WHY DO YOU HAVE TROUBLE WITH ENGLISH?
CRAMMED ONTO ONE PLATE!
わし
CHOMP
MMM...
I FAILED FROM THE GET-GO.
?
YAMATO SLEEPING DURING CLASS IN HIS FIRST YEAR OF MIDDLE SCHOOL
ENGLISH WAS RIGHT AT THE BEGINNING OF THE DAY IN MY FIRST YEAR OF MIDDLE SCHOOL...
ZZZZZ
...WHICH IS AROUND THE TIME BASEBALL PRACTICE GOT REALLY TOUGH.

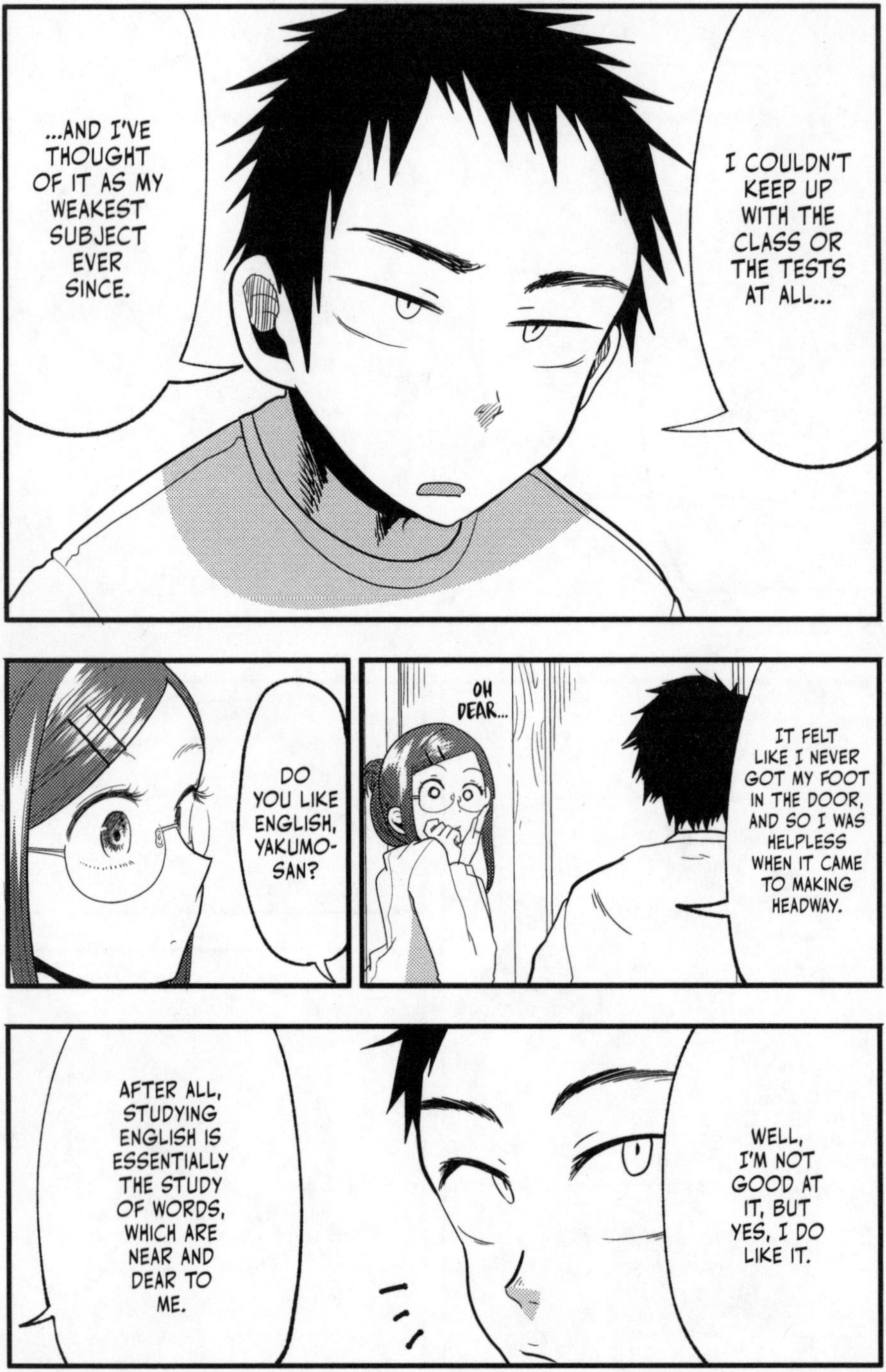
I COULDN'T KEEP UP WITH THE CLASS OR THE TESTS AT ALL...
...AND I'VE THOUGHT OF IT AS MY WEAKEST SUBJECT EVER SINCE.
IT FELT LIKE I NEVER GOT MY FOOT IN THE DOOR, AND SO I WAS HELPLESS WHEN IT CAME TO MAKING HEADWAY.
OH DEAR...
DO YOU LIKE ENGLISH, YAKUMO-SAN?
WELL, I'M NOT GOOD AT IT, BUT YES, I DO LIKE IT.
AFTER ALL, STUDYING ENGLISH IS ESSENTIALLY THE STUDY OF WORDS, WHICH ARE NEAR AND DEAR TO ME.

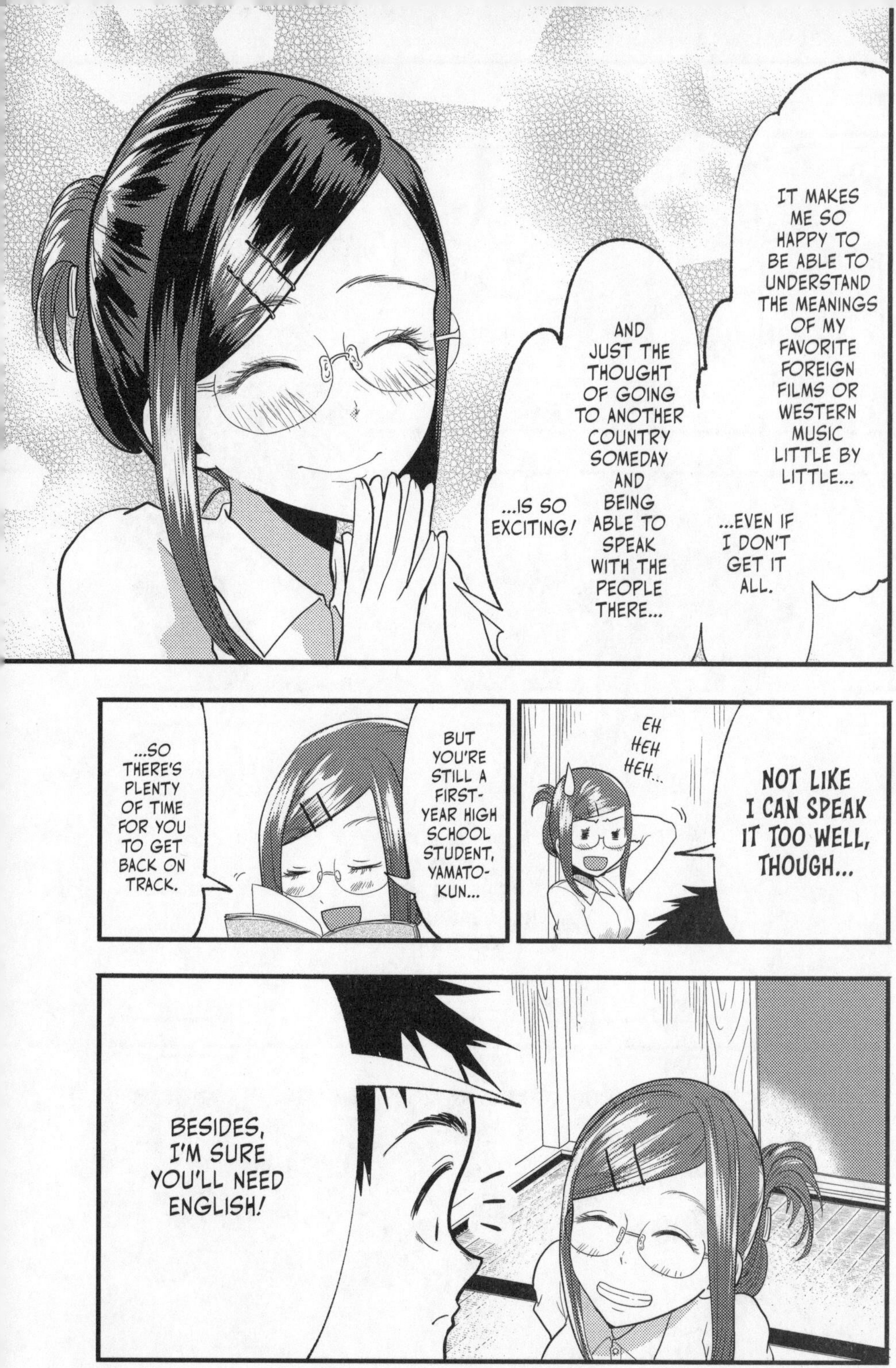
IT MAKES ME SO HAPPY TO BE ABLE TO UNDERSTAND THE MEANINGS OF MY FAVORITE FOREIGN FILMS OR WESTERN MUSIC LITTLE BY LITTLE...
...EVEN IF I DON'T GET IT ALL.
AND JUST THE THOUGHT OF GOING TO ANOTHER COUNTRY SOMEDAY AND BEING ABLE TO SPEAK WITH THE PEOPLE THERE...
...IS SO EXCITING!
NOT LIKE I CAN SPEAK IT TOO WELL, THOUGH...
EH HEH HEH...
BUT YOU'RE STILL A FIRST-YEAR HIGH SCHOOL STUDENT, YAMATO-KUN...
...SO THERE'S PLENTY OF TIME FOR YOU TO GET BACK ON TRACK.
BESIDES, I'M SURE YOU'LL NEED ENGLISH!

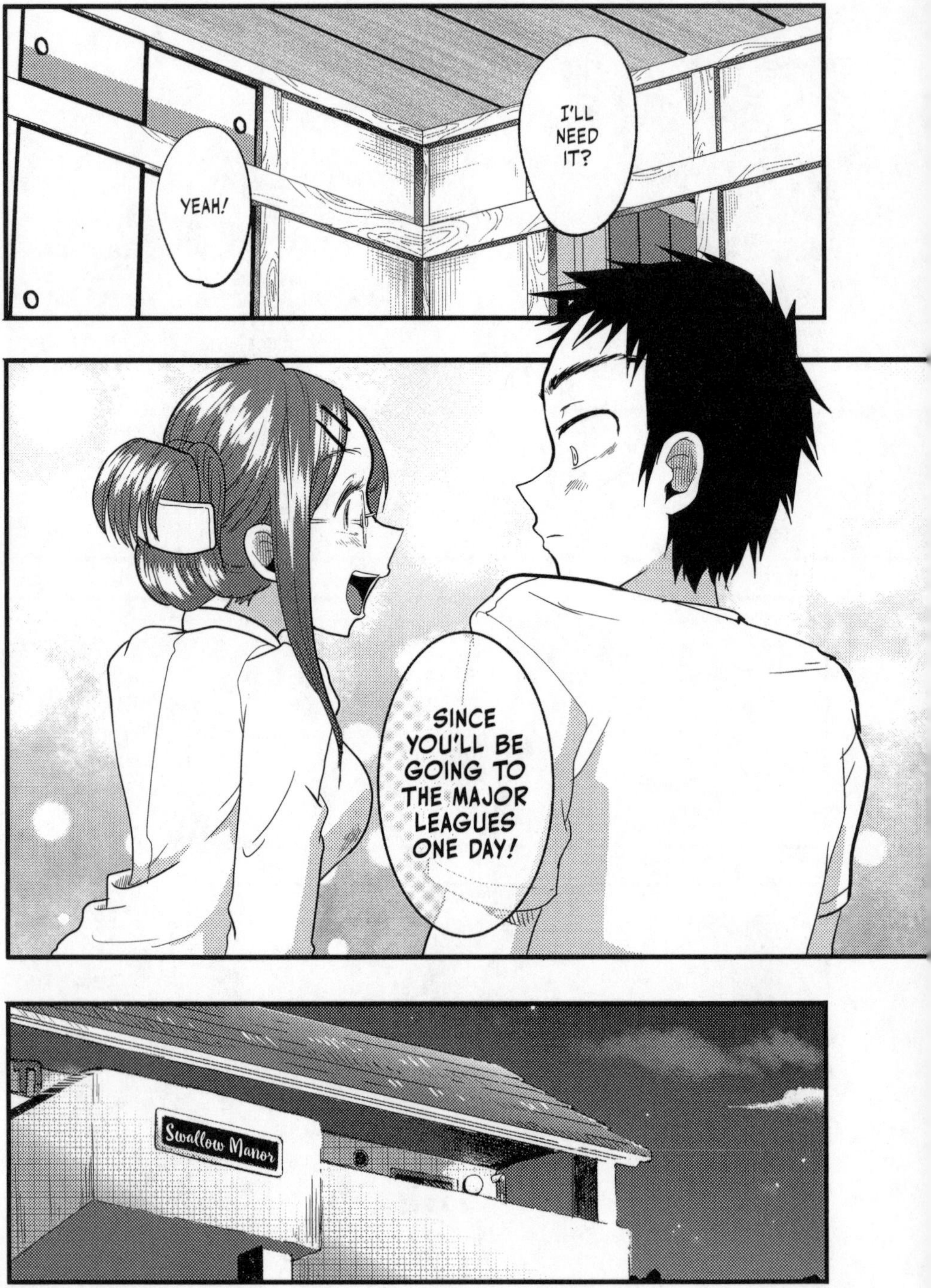
I'LL NEED IT?
YEAH!
SINCE YOU'LL BE GOING TO THE MAJOR LEAGUES ONE DAY!
Swallow Manor

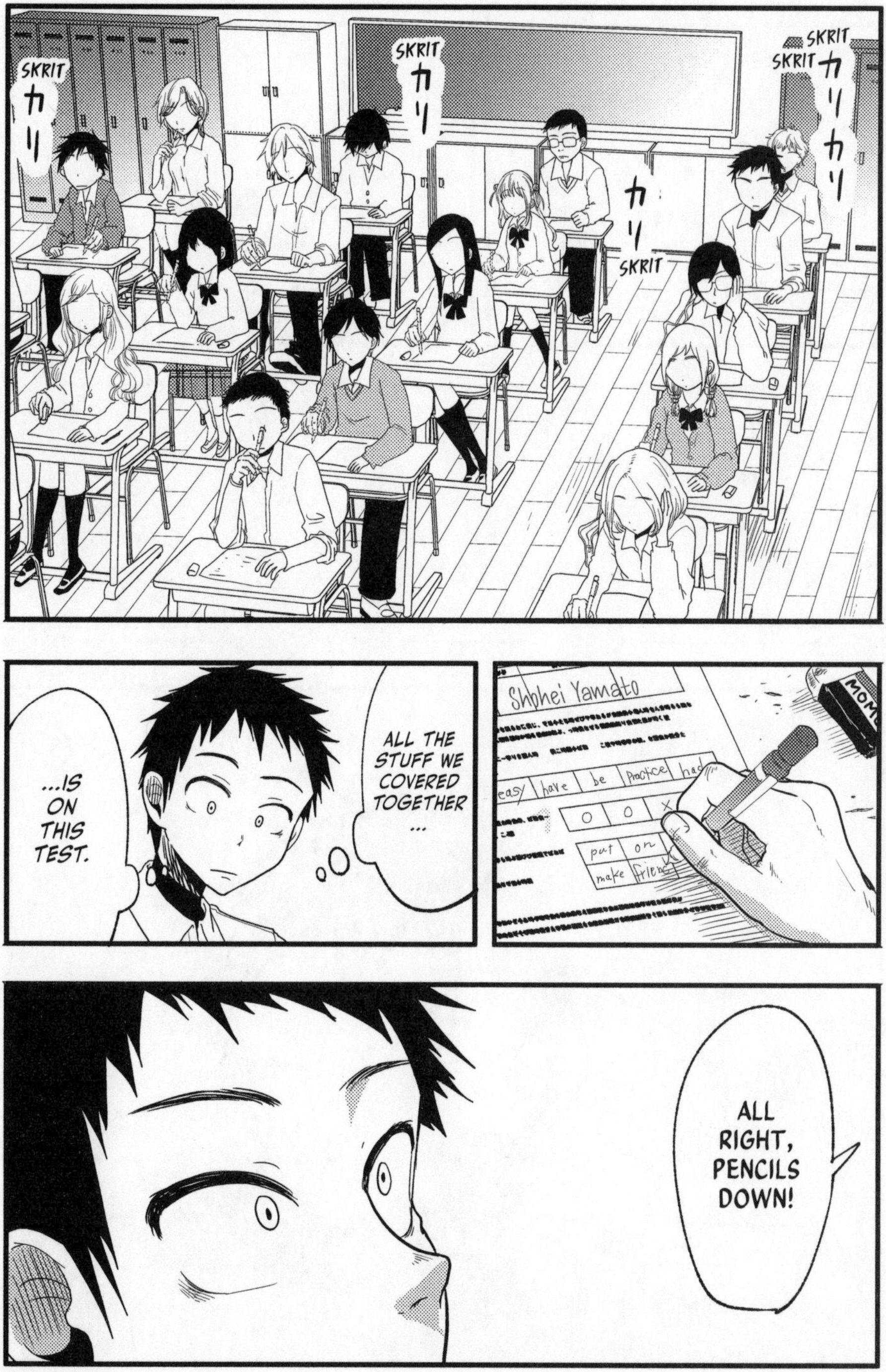
SKRIT SKRIT
カリカリ
カリ
SKRIT
SKRIT
カリ
SKRIT
カリ
Shohei Yamato
easy have be practice
put on
make
ALL THE STUFF WE COVERED TOGETHER ...
...IS ON THIS TEST.
ALL RIGHT, PENCILS DOWN!

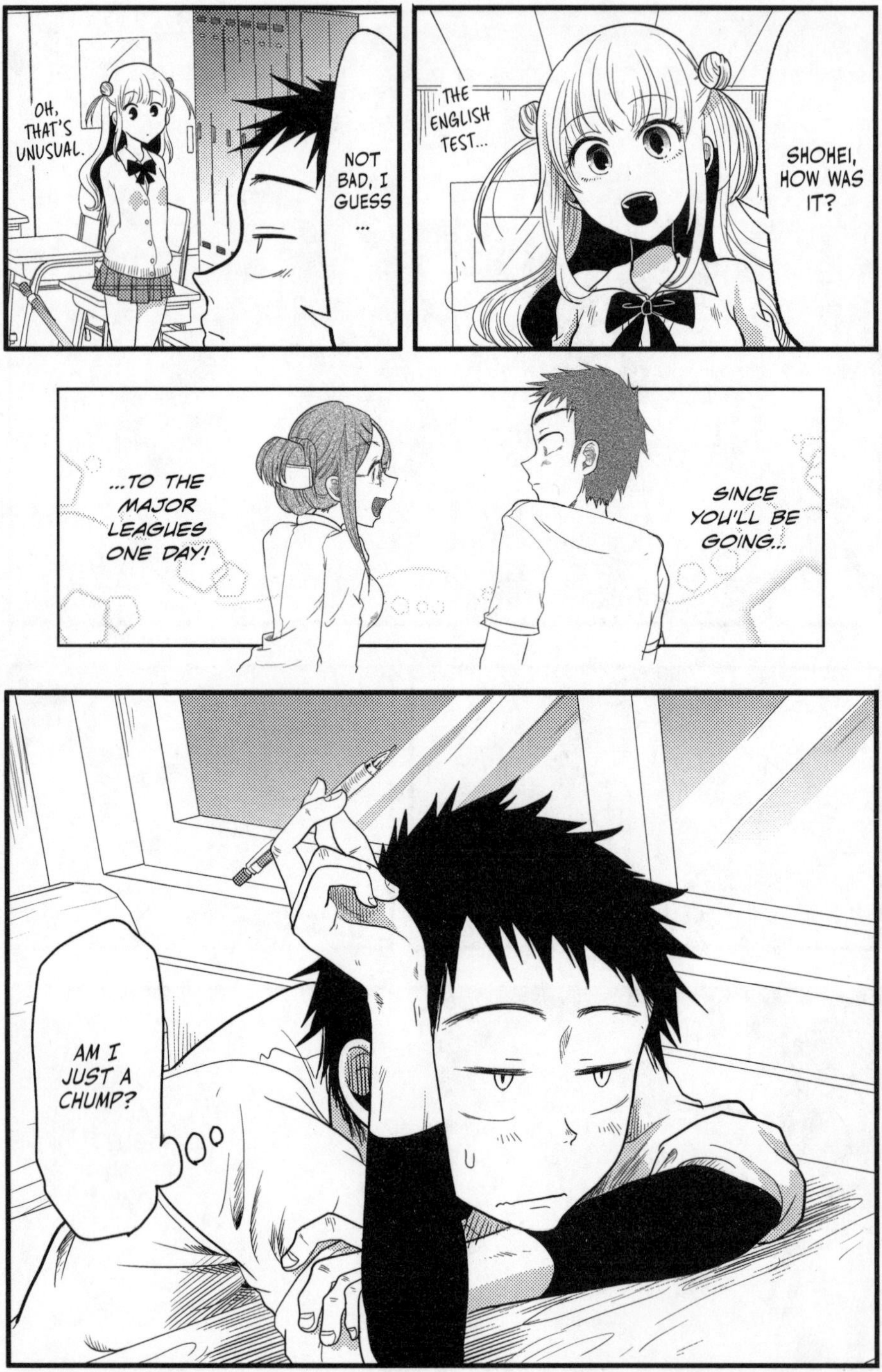
SHOHEI, HOW WAS IT?
THE ENGLISH TEST...
NOT BAD, I GUESS ...
OH, THAT'S UNUSUAL.
SINCE YOU'LL BE GOING...
...TO THE MAJOR LEAGUES ONE DAY!
AM I JUST A CHUMP?

Beauty and the FEAST.

Beauty and the FEAST.

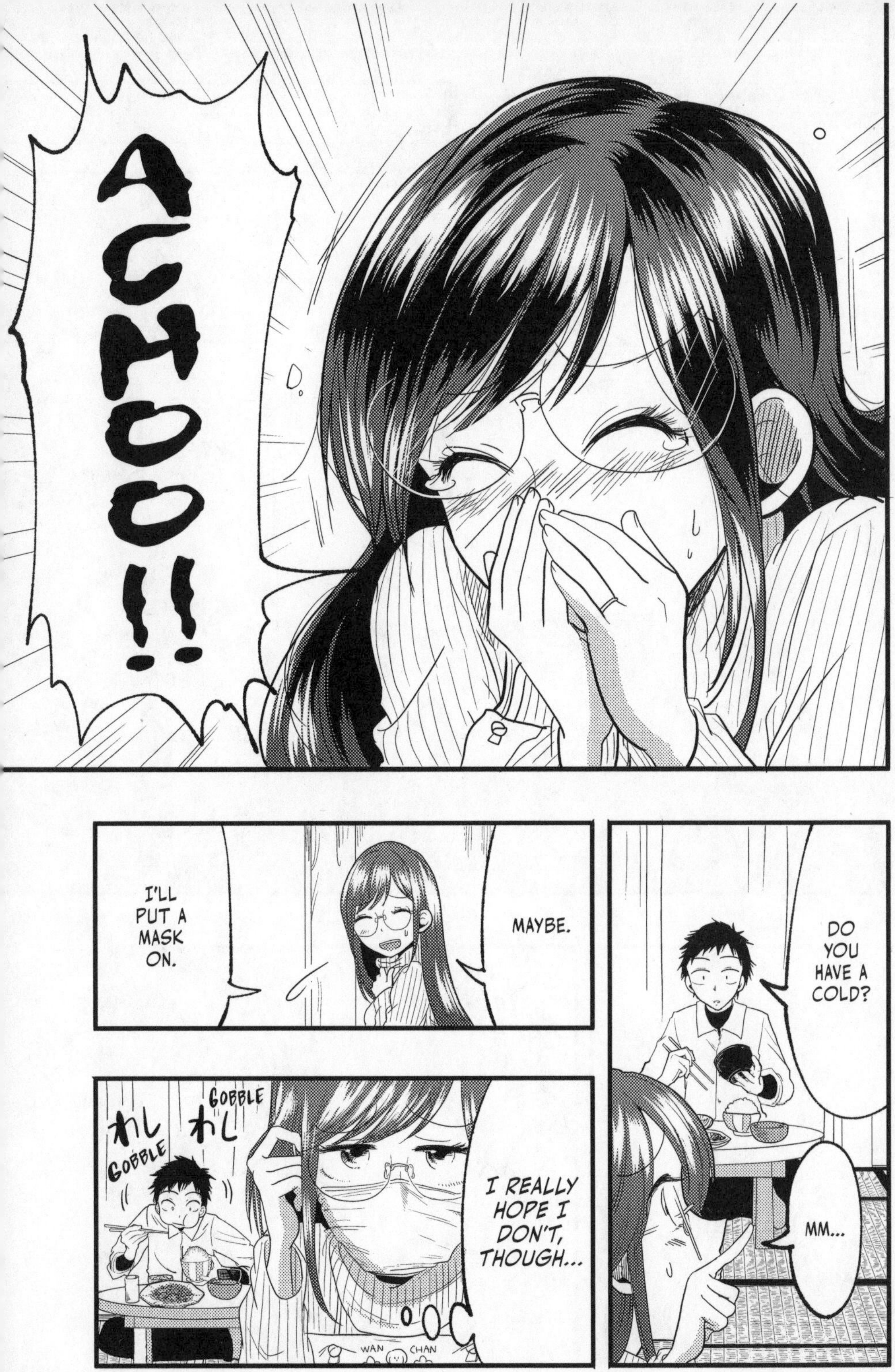
ACHOO!!
DO YOU HAVE A COLD?
MM...
MAYBE.
I'LL PUT A MASK ON.
I REALLY HOPE I DON'T, THOUGH...
わし わし
GOBBLE
GOBBLE
WAN CHAN

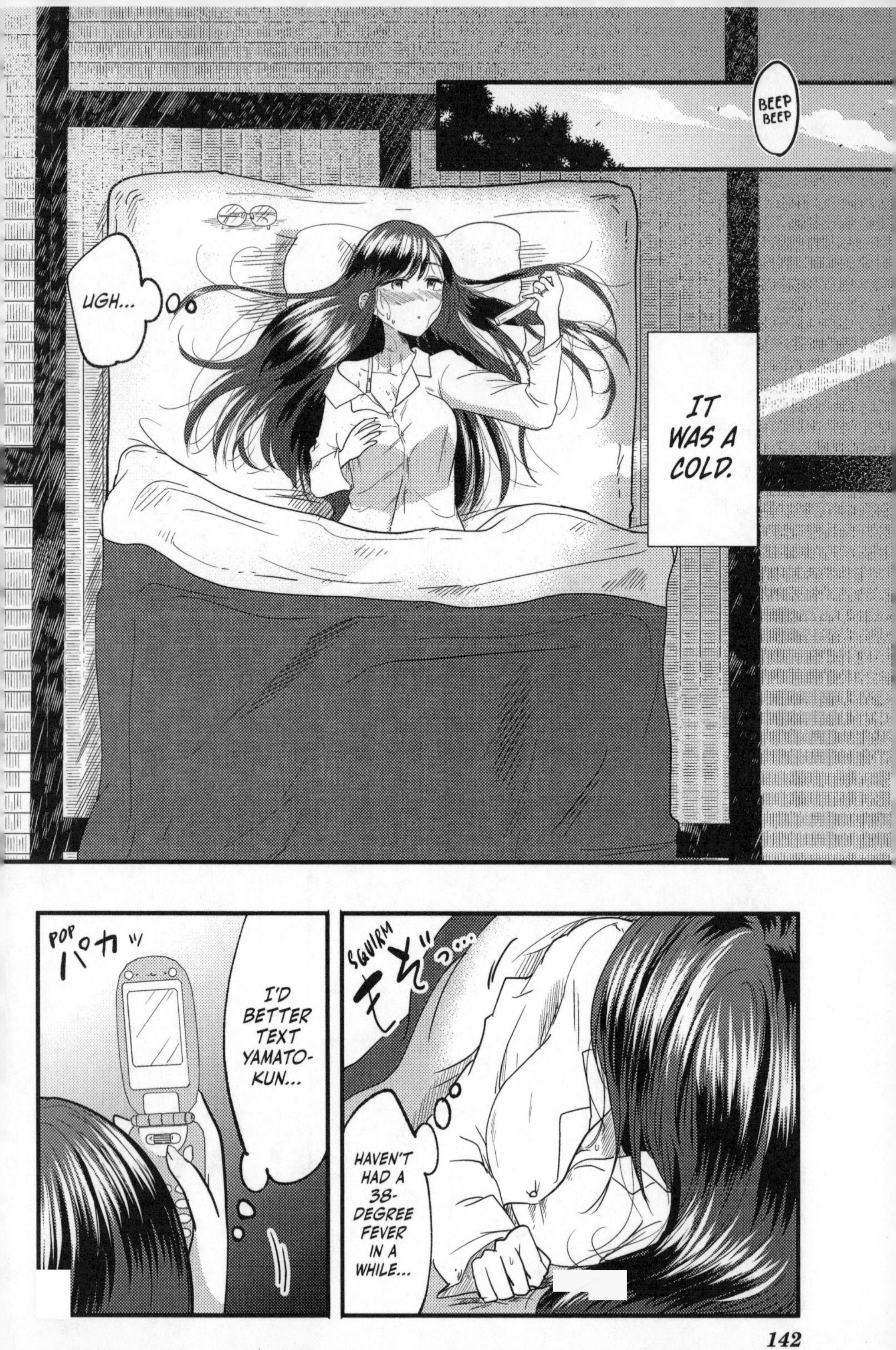
BEEP BEEP
IT WAS A COLD.
UGH...
SQUIRM
もぞっ...
HAVEN'T HAD A 38-DEGREE FEVER IN A WHILE...
POP
パカッ
I'D BETTER TEXT YAMATO-KUN...

Meal 14: Yamato's Payback

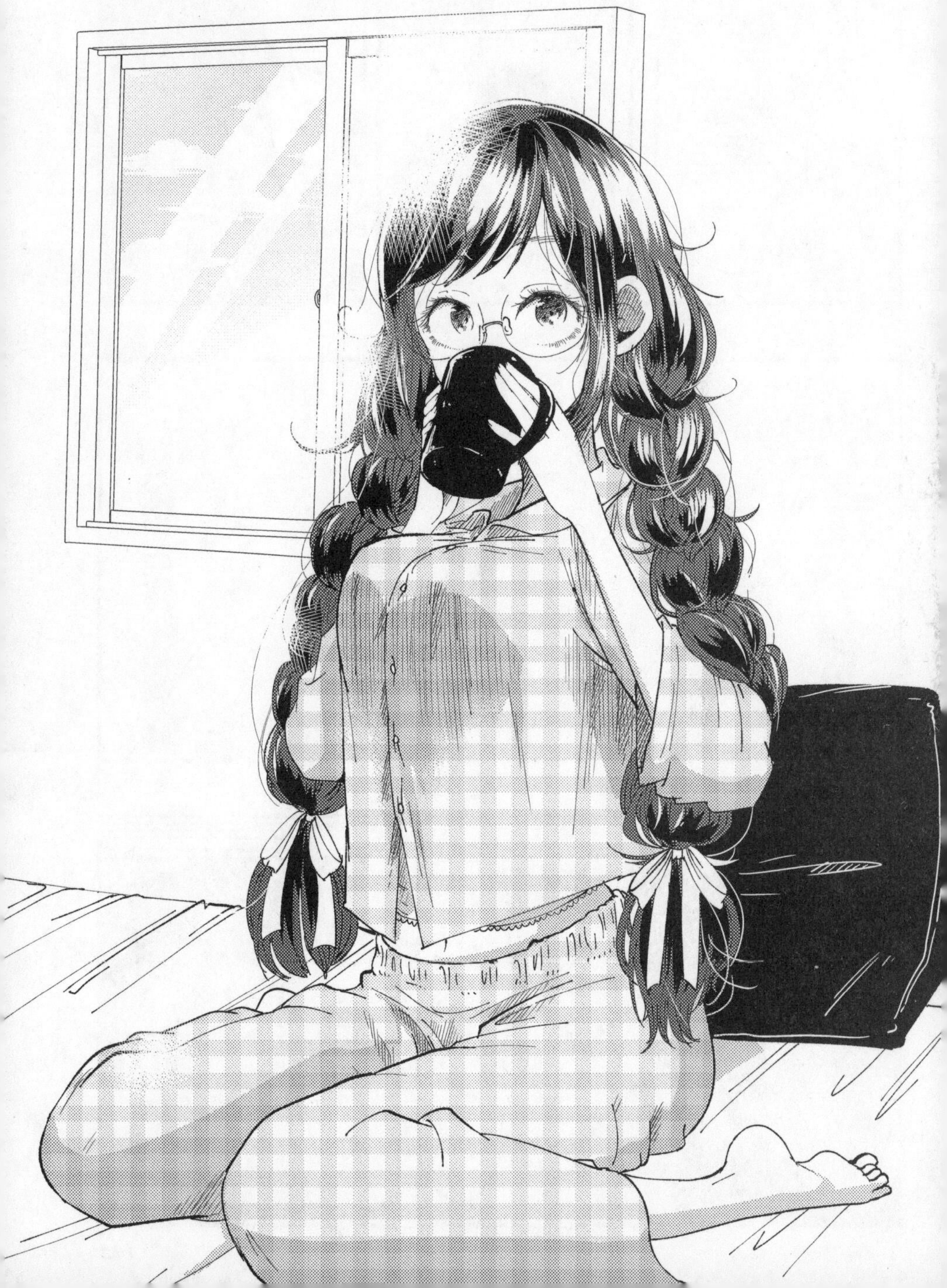

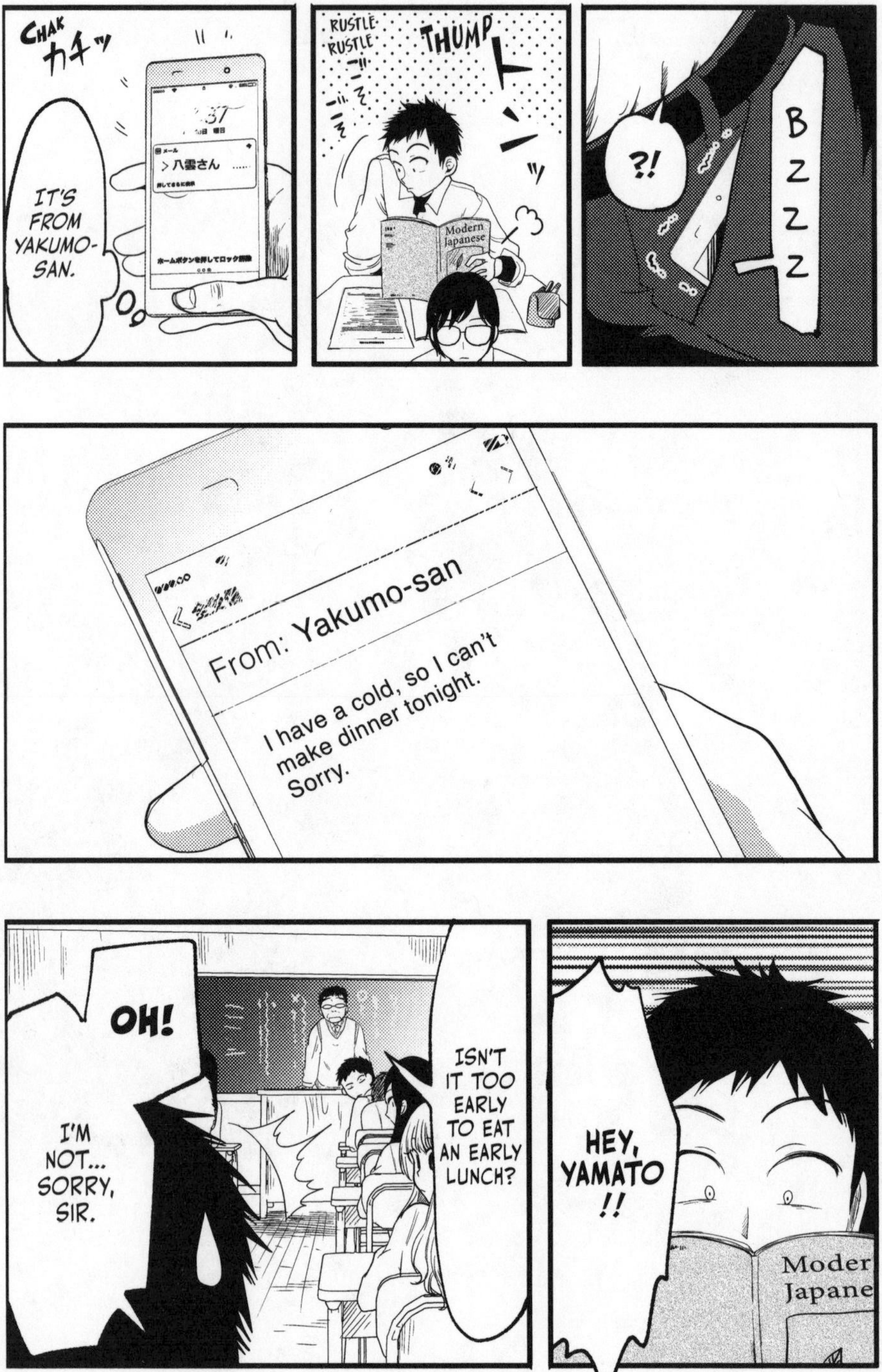
B Z Z Z
?!
RUSTLE RUSTLE
THUMP
ドンッ
Modern Japanese
CHAK
カチッ
八雲さん
IT'S FROM YAKUMO-SAN.
From: Yakumo-san
I have a cold, so I can't make dinner tonight. Sorry.
HEY, YAMATO!!
Moder Japane
ISN'T IT TOO EARLY TO EAT AN EARLY LUNCH?
OH!
I'M NOT... SORRY, SIR.

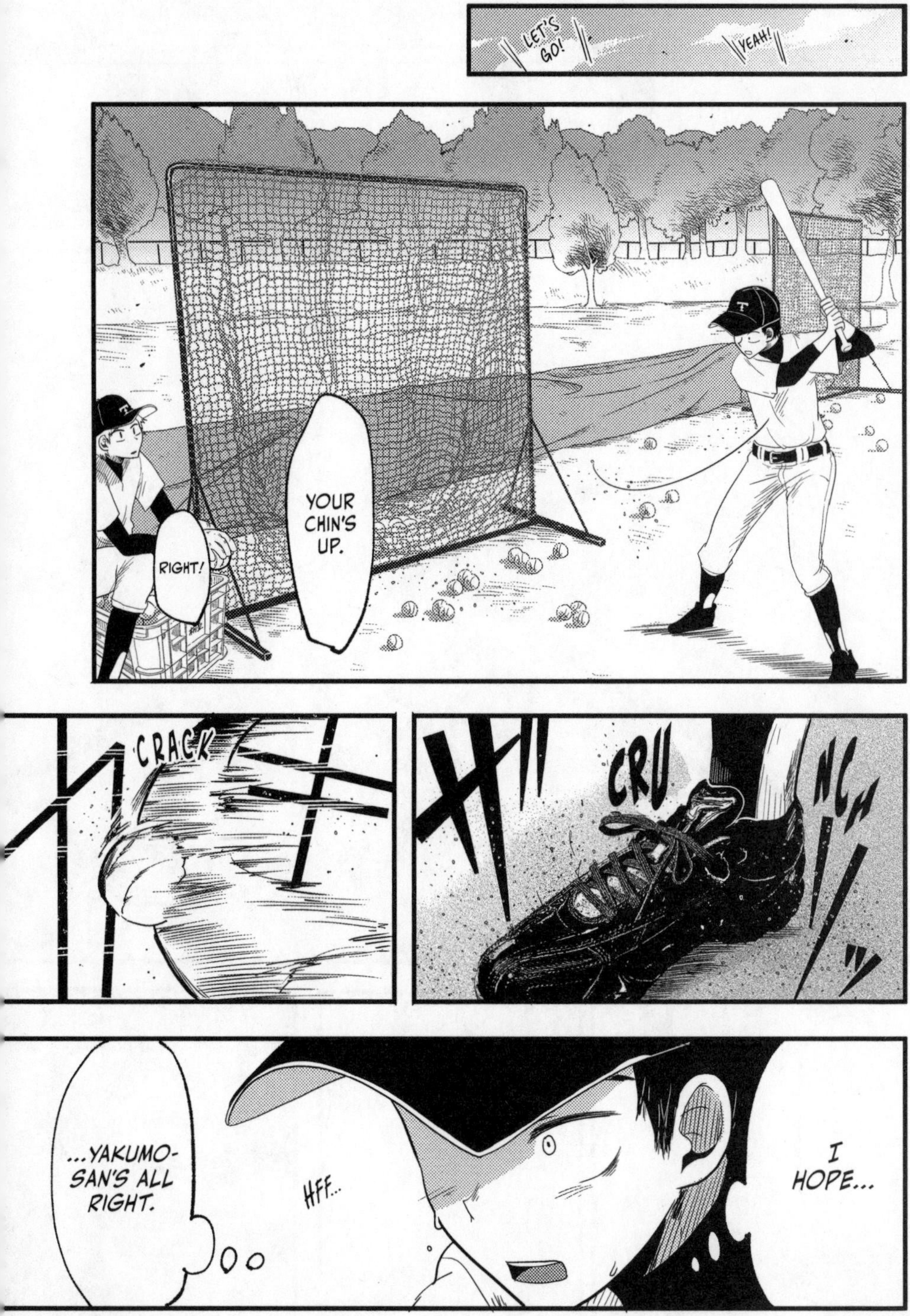
YEAH!
LET'S GO!
YOUR CHIN'S UP.
RIGHT!
CRUNCH
CRACK
I HOPE...
HFF...
...YAKUMO-SAN'S ALL RIGHT.

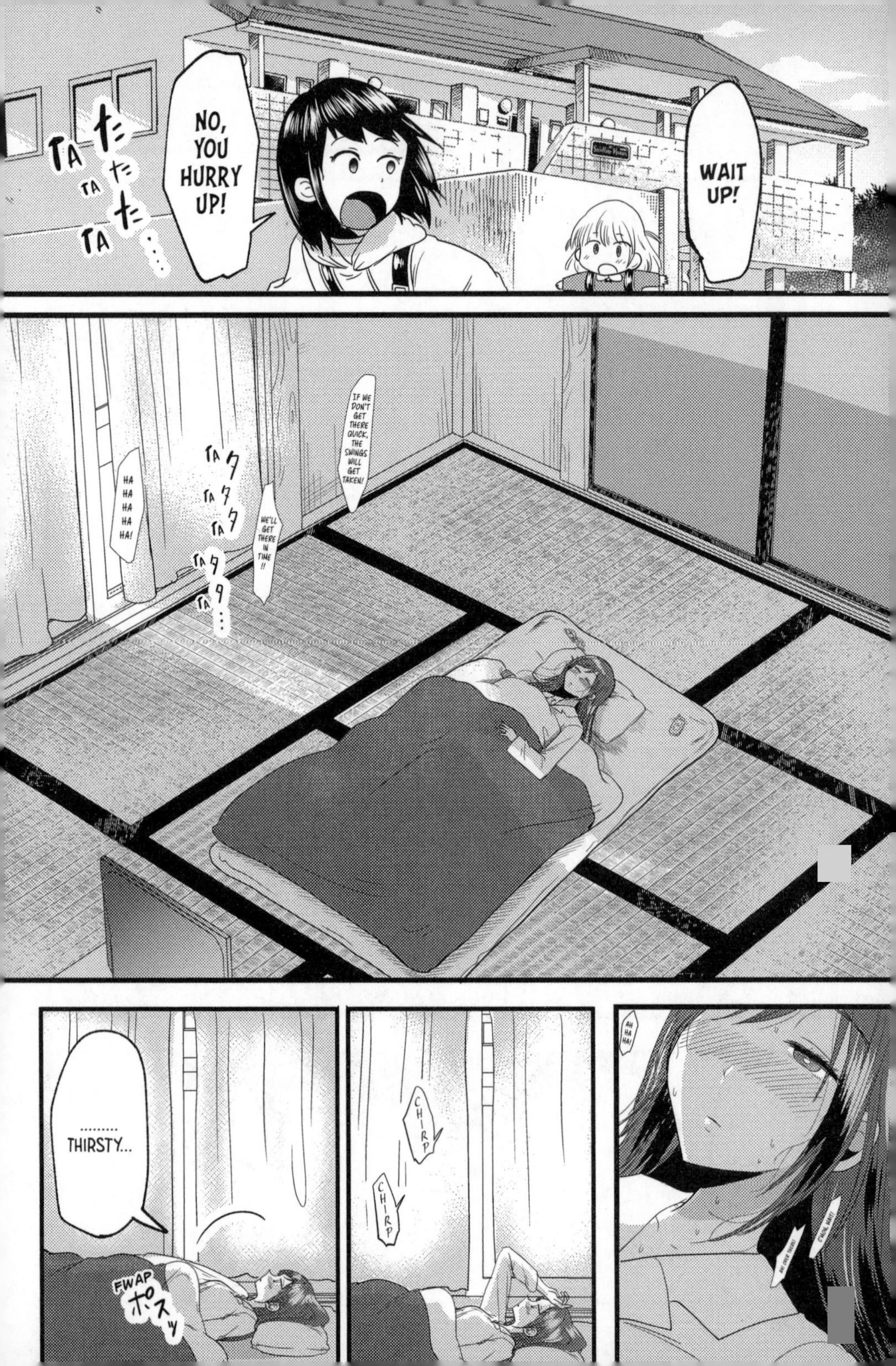
WAIT UP!
NO, YOU HURRY UP!
TA た TA た TA た...
IF WE DON'T GET THERE QUICK, THE SWINGS WILL GET TAKEN!
WE'LL GET THERE IN TIME!!
TA タ TA タ TA タ TA タ TA タ...
HA HA HA HA HA!
AH HA HA!
C'MON, WAIT!
AH! OVER THERE!
CHIRP
CHIRP
....
THIRSTY...
FWAP ポスッ

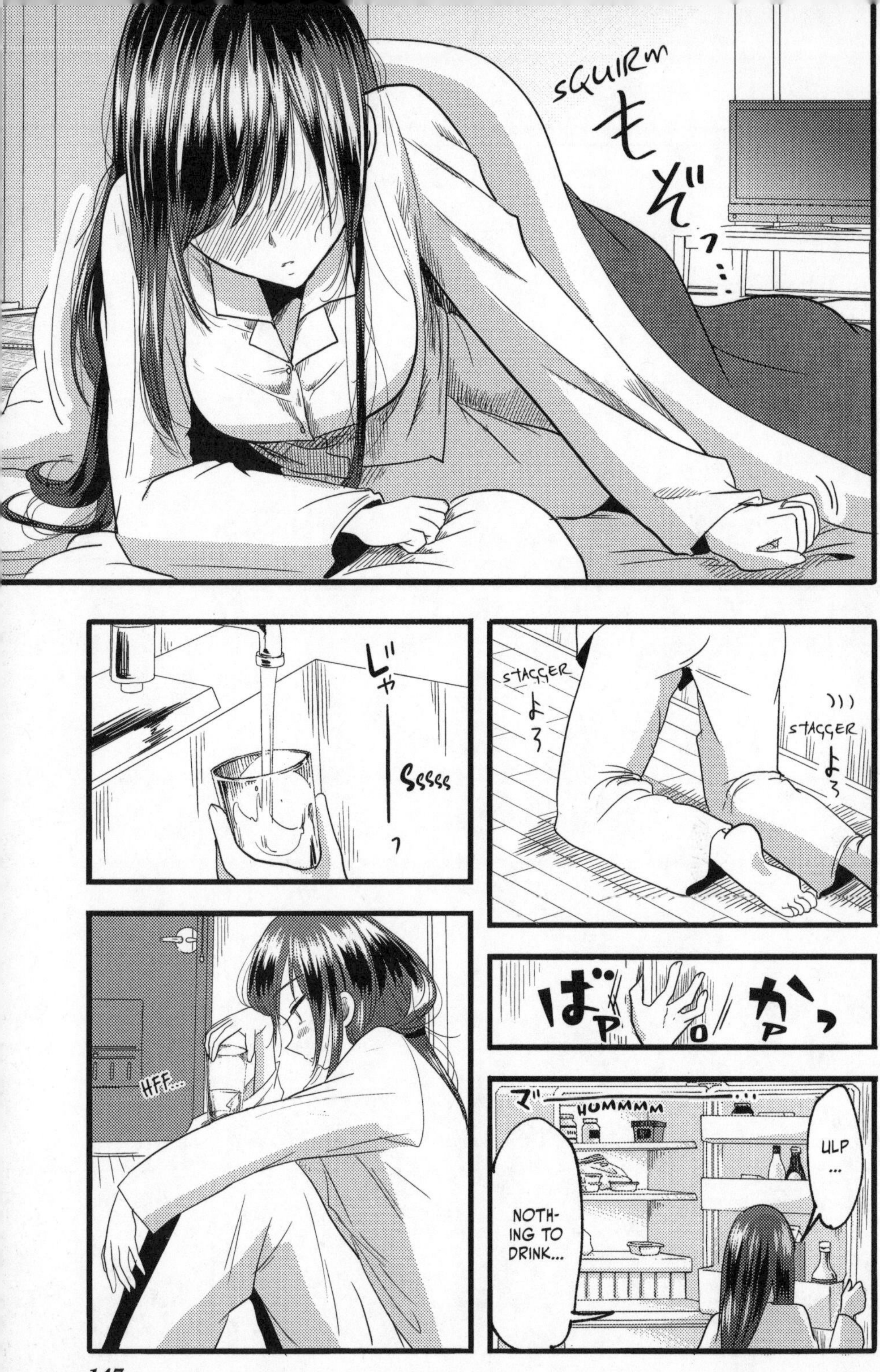

SQUIRM
もぞっ…
STAGGER
よろ
STAGGER
よろ
じゃーっ
SSSSS
ばっ
POP
かっ
HUMMMM
ULP...
NOTHING TO DRINK...
HFF...

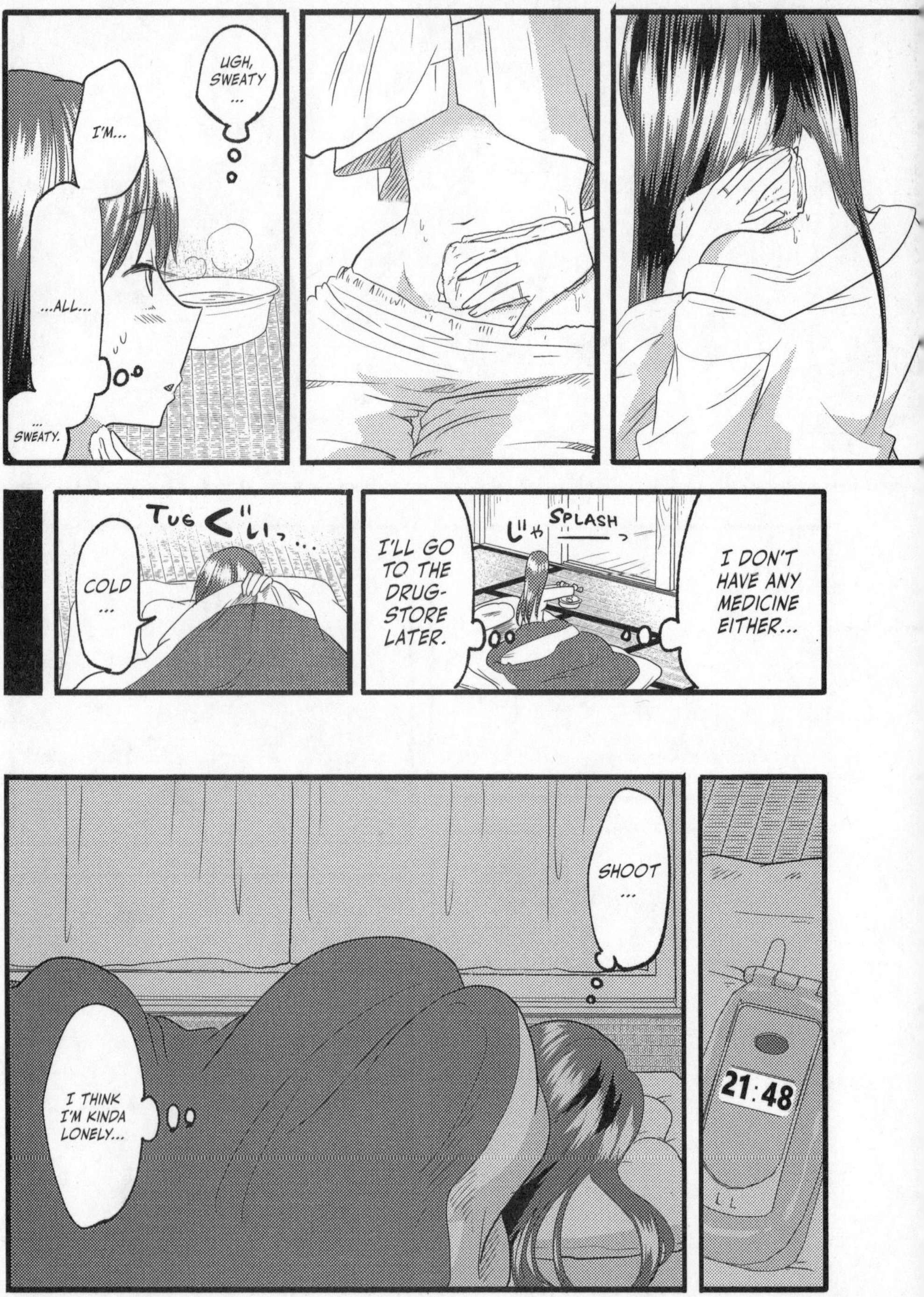
UGH, SWEATY ...
I'M...
...ALL...
... SWEATY.
I DON'T HAVE ANY MEDICINE EITHER...
じゃ SPLASH
I'LL GO TO THE DRUG-STORE LATER.
TUG ぐいっ...
COLD ...
21:48
SHOOT ...
I THINK I'M KINDA LONELY...

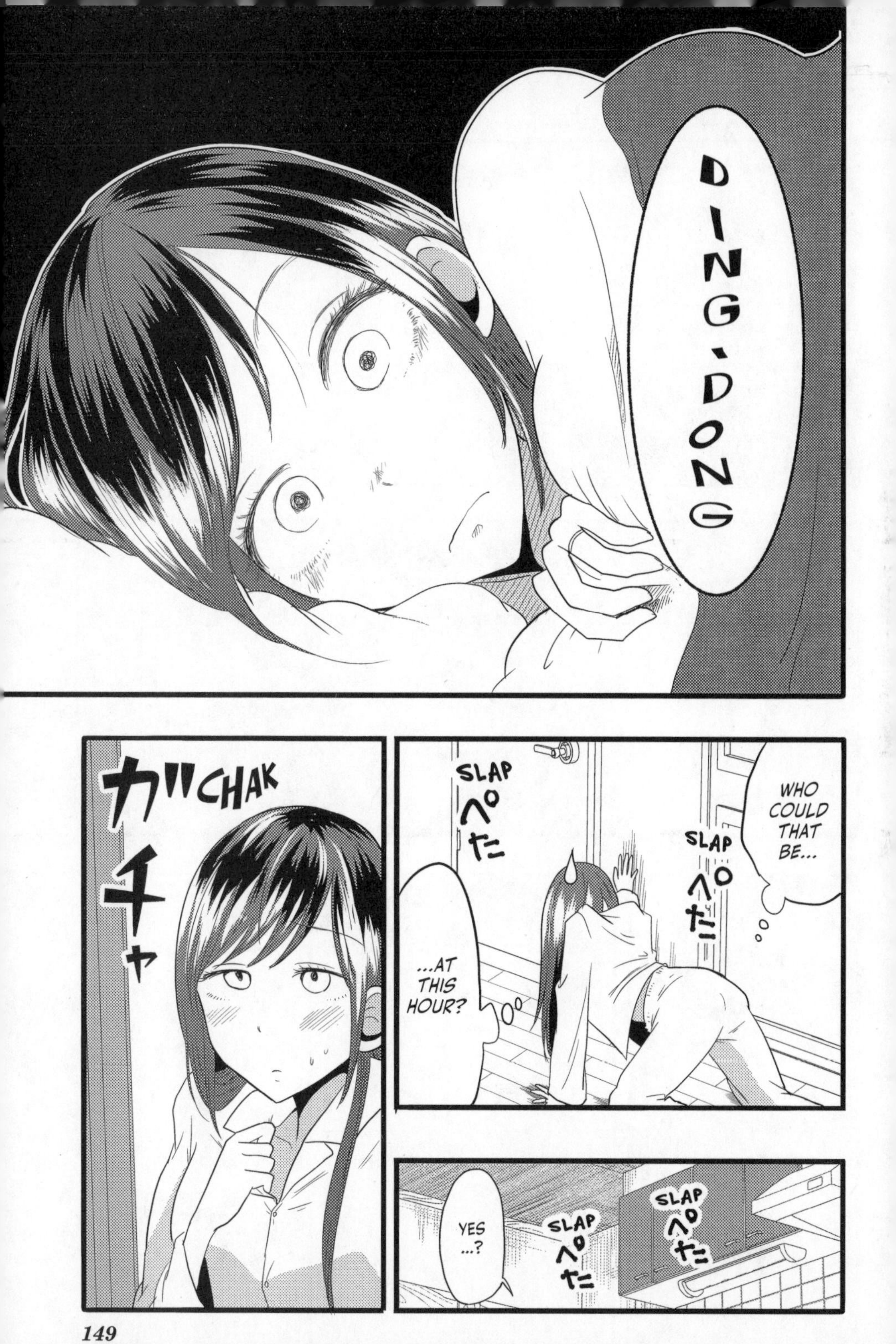
DING-DONG
WHO COULD THAT BE...
SLAP ぺた
SLAP ぺた
...AT THIS HOUR?
SLAP ぺた
SLAP ぺた
YES ...?
ガCHAK チャ

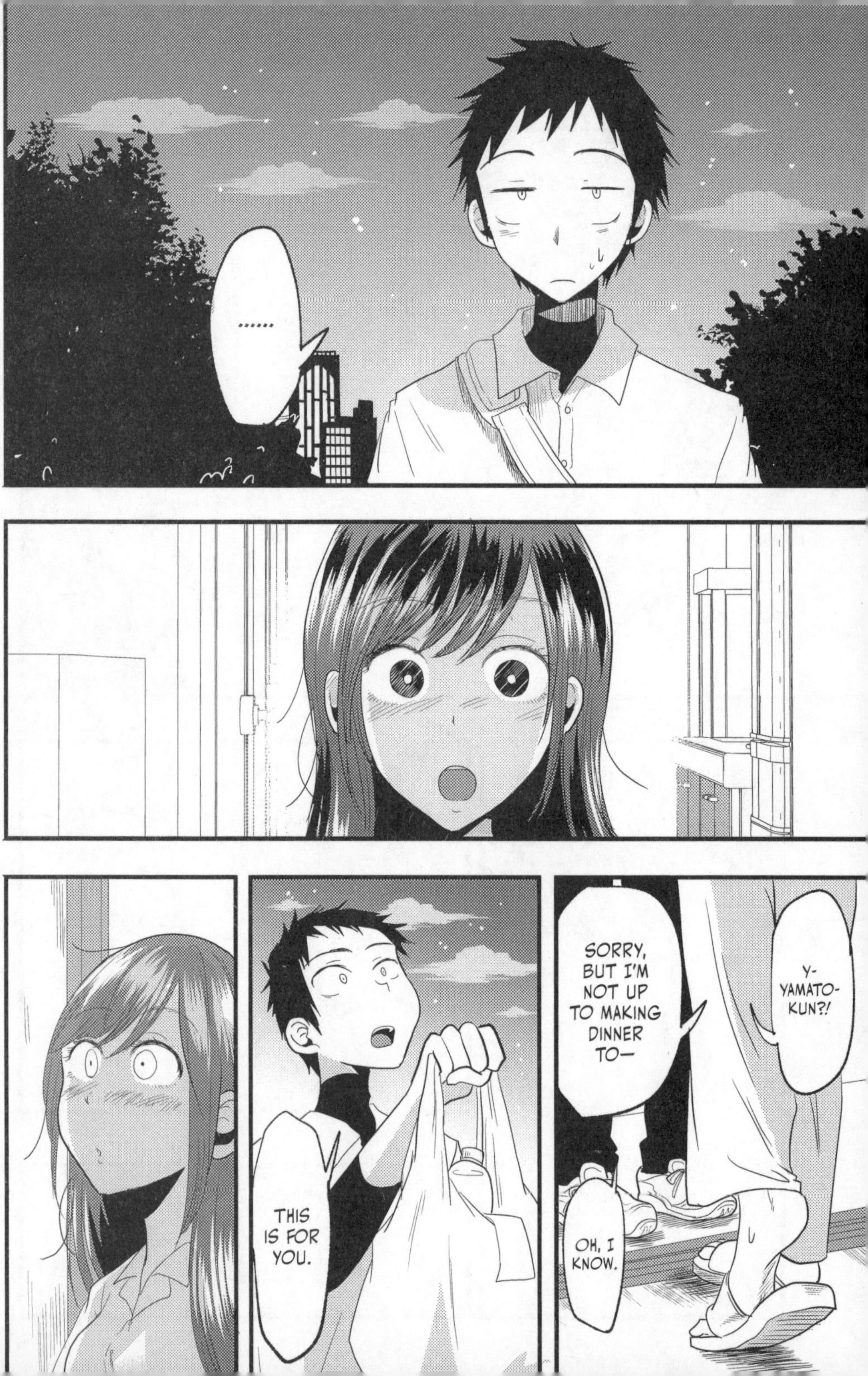
......
Y-YAMATO-KUN?!
SORRY, BUT I'M NOT UP TO MAKING DINNER TO—
OH, I KNOW.
THIS IS FOR YOU.

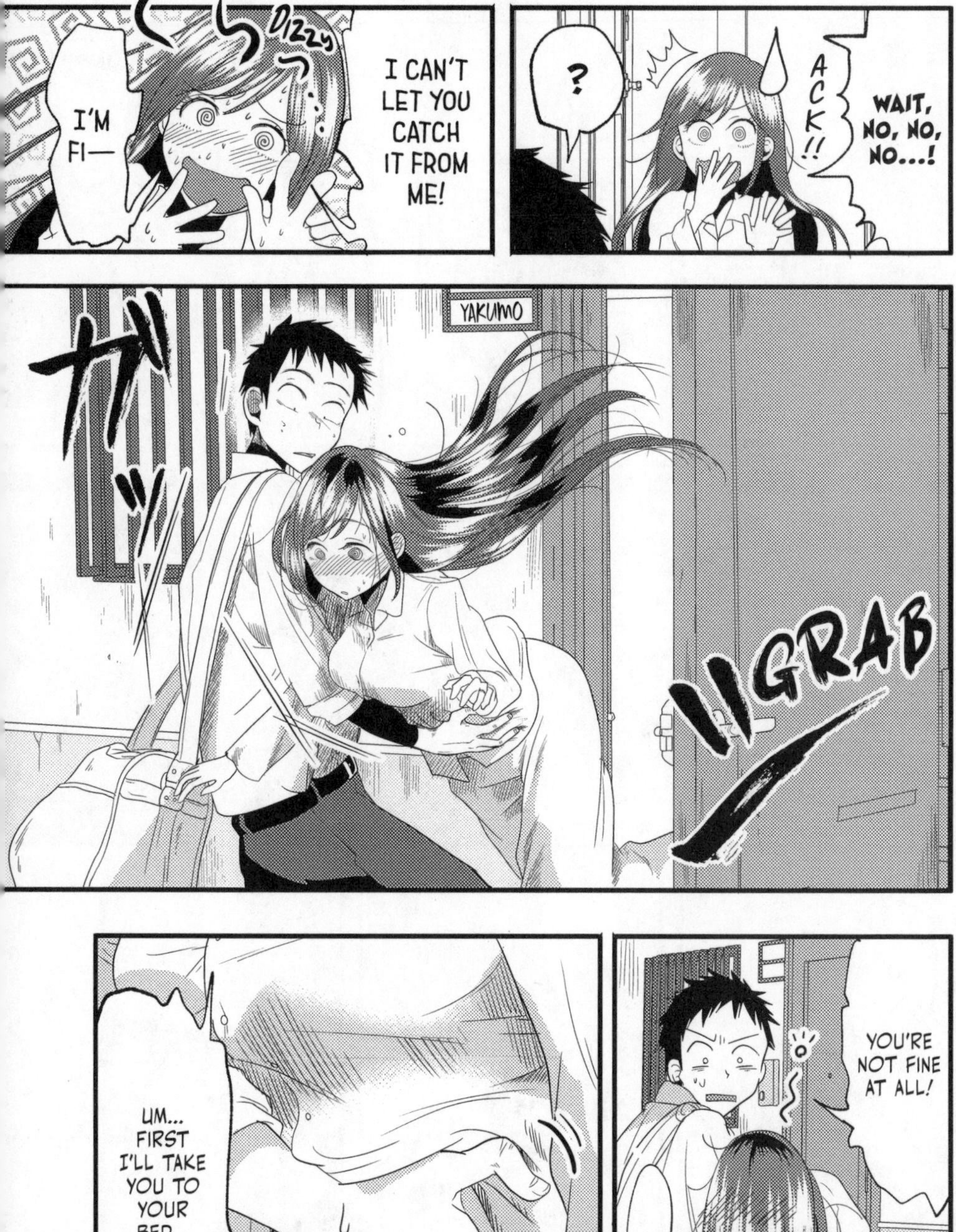
WAIT, NO, NO, NO...!
ACK!!
?
I CAN'T LET YOU CATCH IT FROM ME!
くら
DIZZY
I'M FI—
YAKUMO
GRAB
YOU'RE NOT FINE AT ALL!
......
UM... FIRST I'LL TAKE YOU TO YOUR BED...

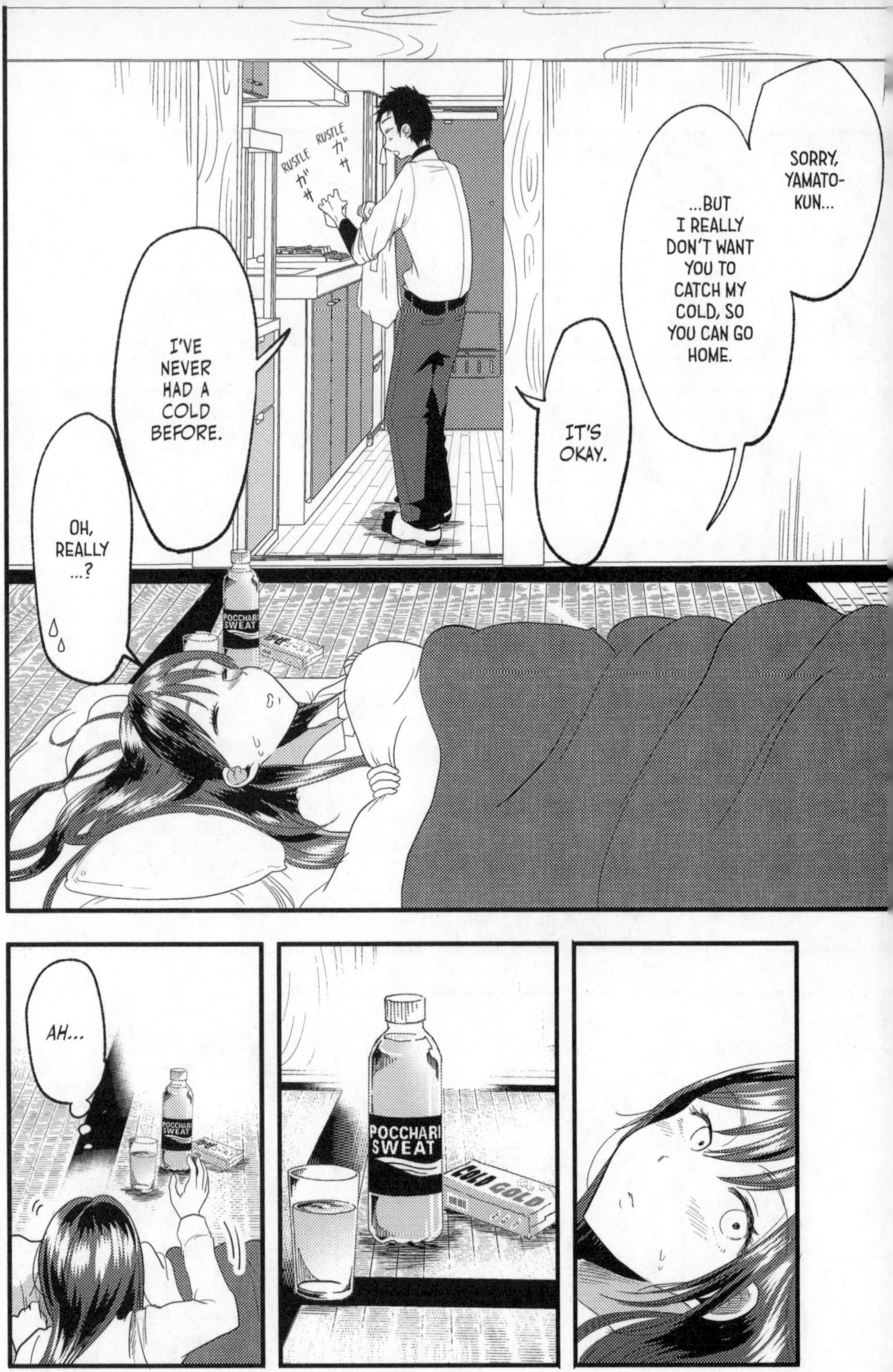

SORRY, YAMATO-KUN...
...BUT I REALLY DON'T WANT YOU TO CATCH MY COLD, SO YOU CAN GO HOME.
RUSTLE ガサ
RUSTLE ガサ
IT'S OKAY.
I'VE NEVER HAD A COLD BEFORE.
OH, REALLY ...?
POCCHARI SWEAT
POCCHARI SWEAT
COLD GOLD
AH...
POCCHARI SWEAT

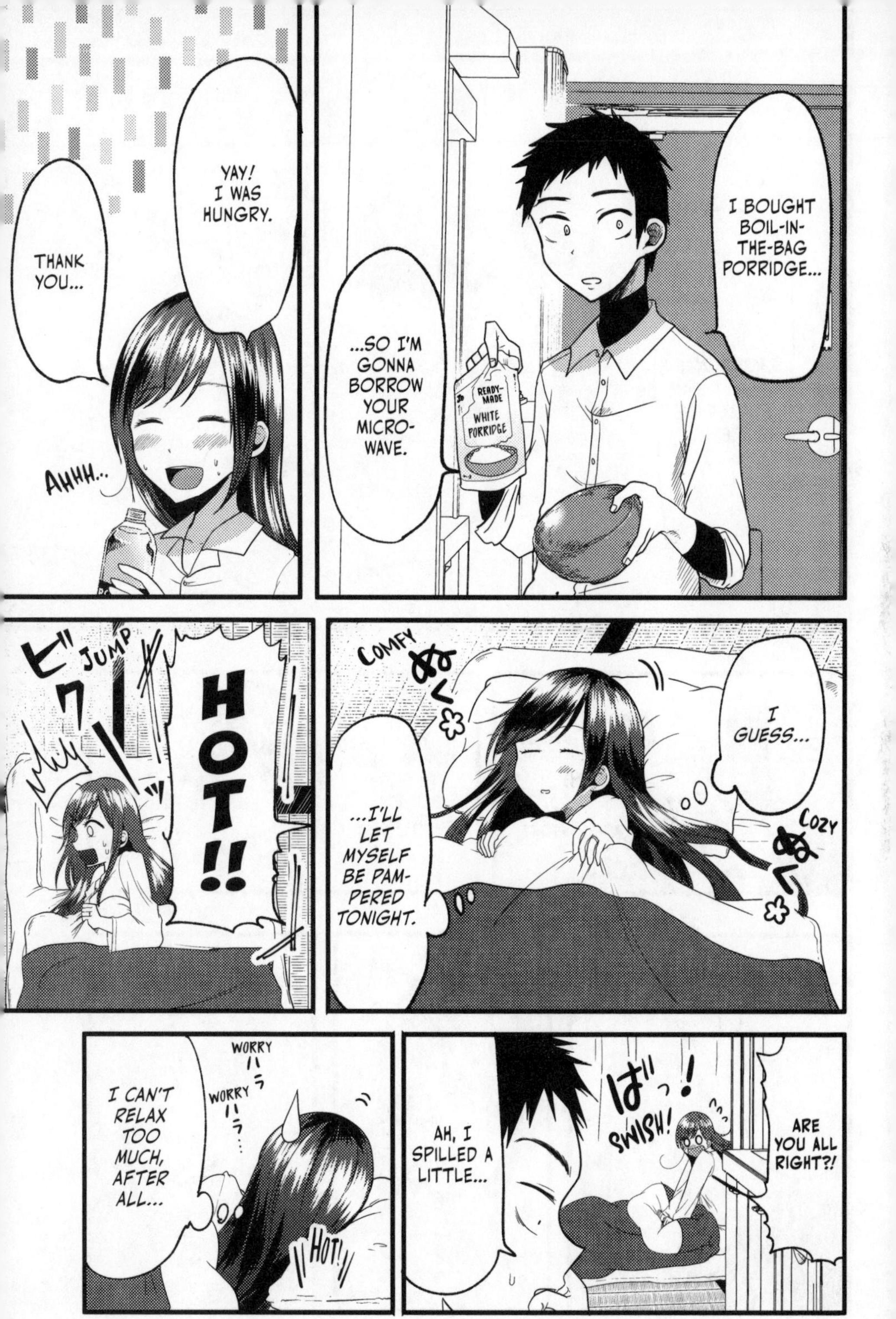
I BOUGHT BOIL-IN-THE-BAG PORRIDGE...
READY-MADE WHITE PORRIDGE
...SO I'M GONNA BORROW YOUR MICRO-WAVE.
YAY! I WAS HUNGRY.
THANK YOU...
AHHH...
COMFY ぬく
I GUESS...
...I'LL LET MYSELF BE PAM-PERED TONIGHT.
COZY ぬく
ビクッ JUMP
HOT!!
ばっ! SWISH!
ARE YOU ALL RIGHT?!
AH, I SPILLED A LITTLE...
WORRY ハラ
WORRY ハラ...
I CAN'T RELAX TOO MUCH, AFTER ALL...
HOT!

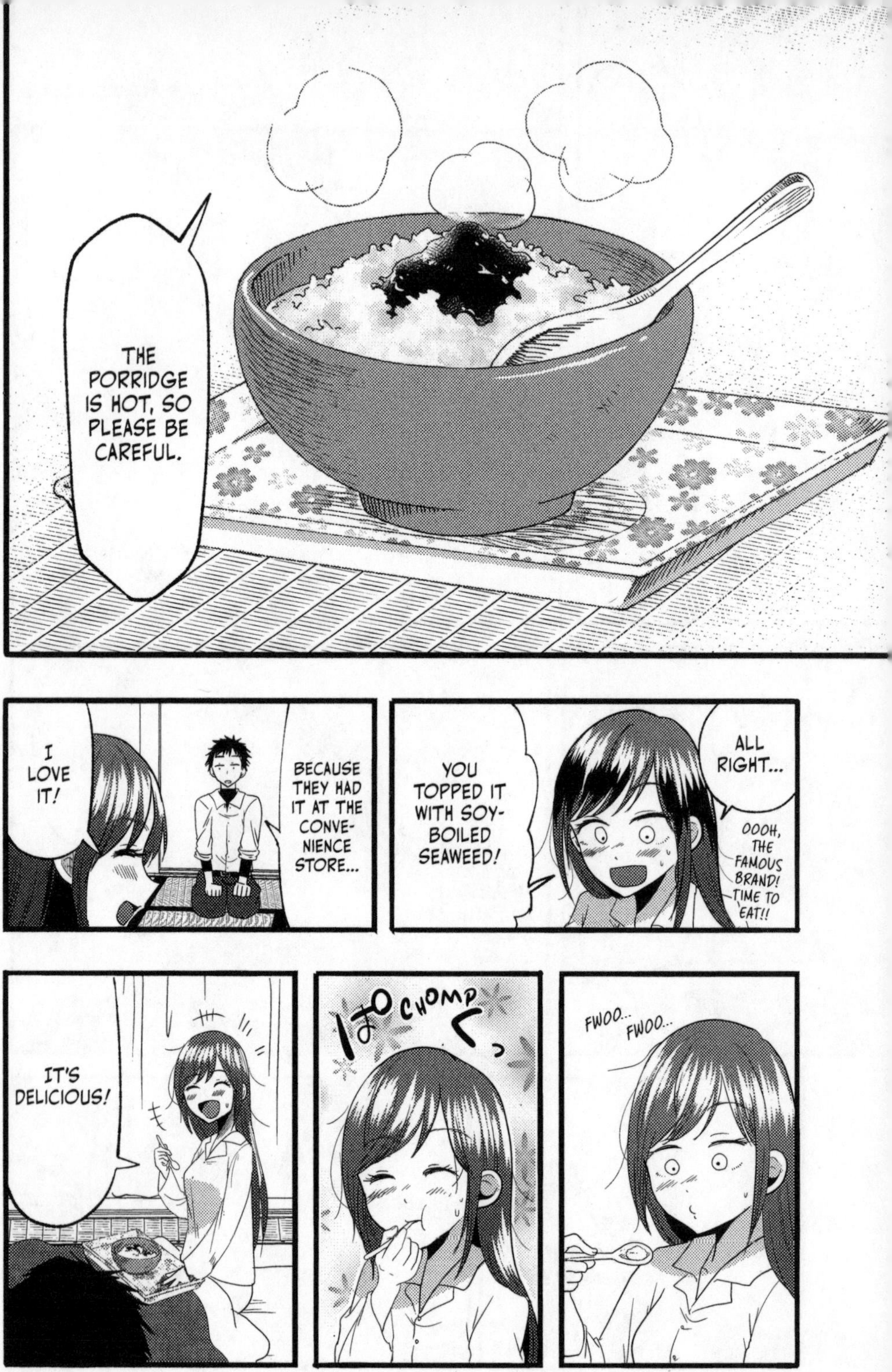
THE PORRIDGE IS HOT, SO PLEASE BE CAREFUL.
ALL RIGHT...
OOOH, THE FAMOUS BRAND! TIME TO EAT!!
YOU TOPPED IT WITH SOY-BOILED SEAWEED!
BECAUSE THEY HAD IT AT THE CONVENIENCE STORE...
I LOVE IT!
FWOO... FWOO...
ぱくっ
CHOMP
IT'S DELICIOUS!

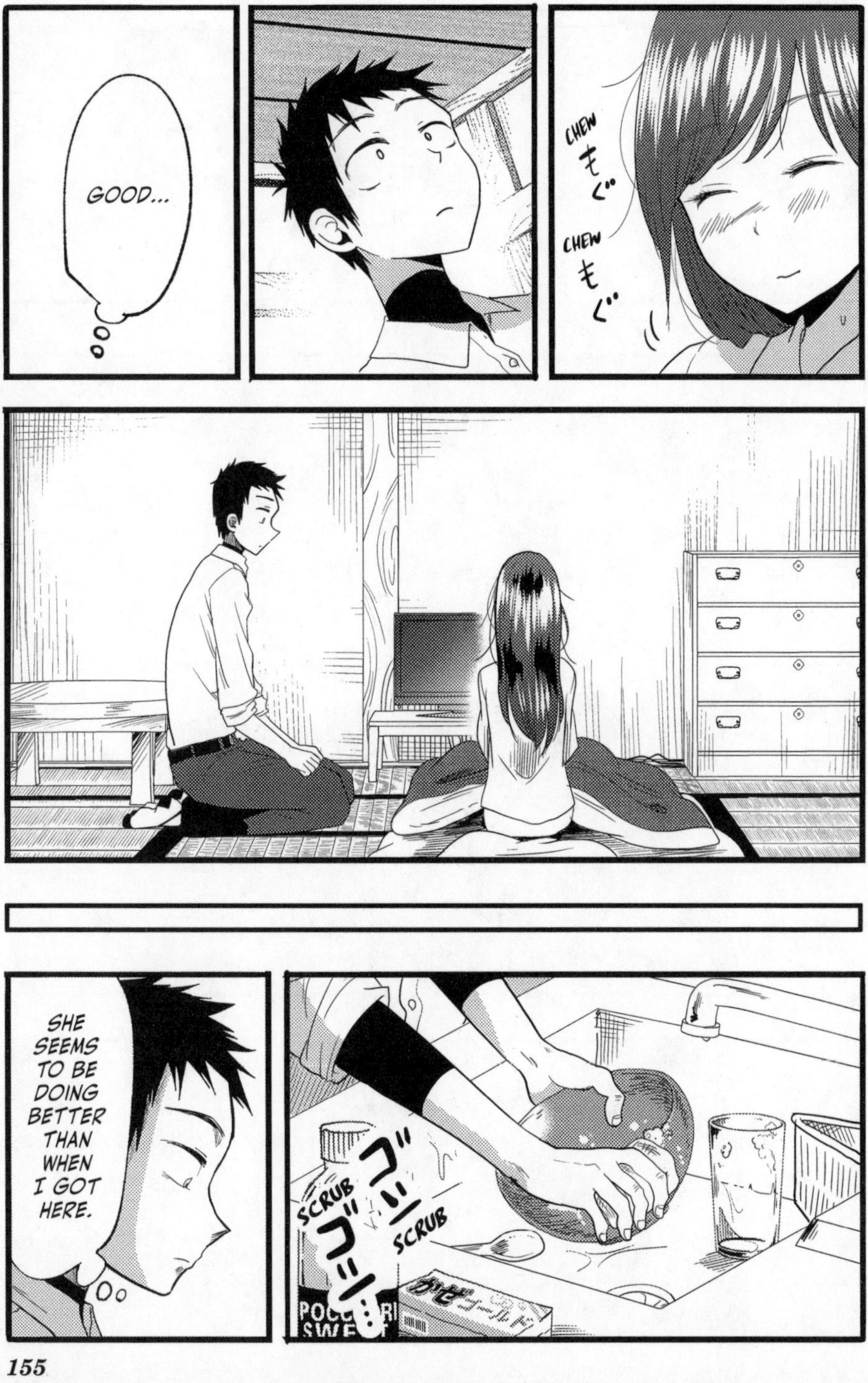
CHEW
もぐ
CHEW
もぐ
GOOD...
SCRUB
ゴシ
SCRUB
ゴシ...
SHE SEEMS TO BE DOING BETTER THAN WHEN I GOT HERE.

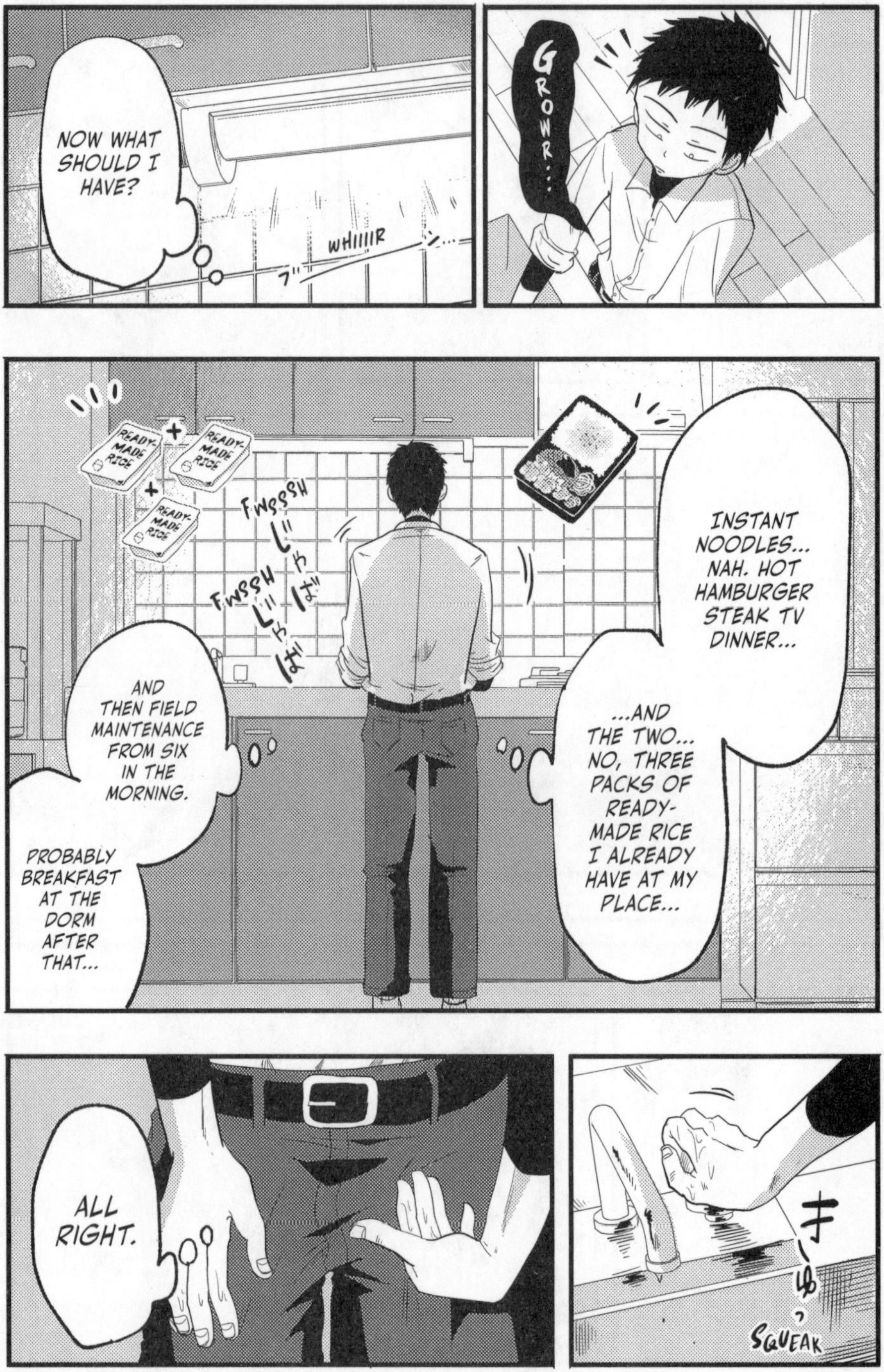
GROWR...
NOW WHAT SHOULD I HAVE?
WHIIIIR
INSTANT NOODLES... NAH. HOT HAMBURGER STEAK TV DINNER...
READY-MADE RICE
READY-MADE RICE
READY-MADE RICE
...AND THE TWO... NO, THREE PACKS OF READY-MADE RICE I ALREADY HAVE AT MY PLACE...
FWSSH
FWSSH
AND THEN FIELD MAINTENANCE FROM SIX IN THE MORNING.
PROBABLY BREAKFAST AT THE DORM AFTER THAT...
SQUEAK
ALL RIGHT.

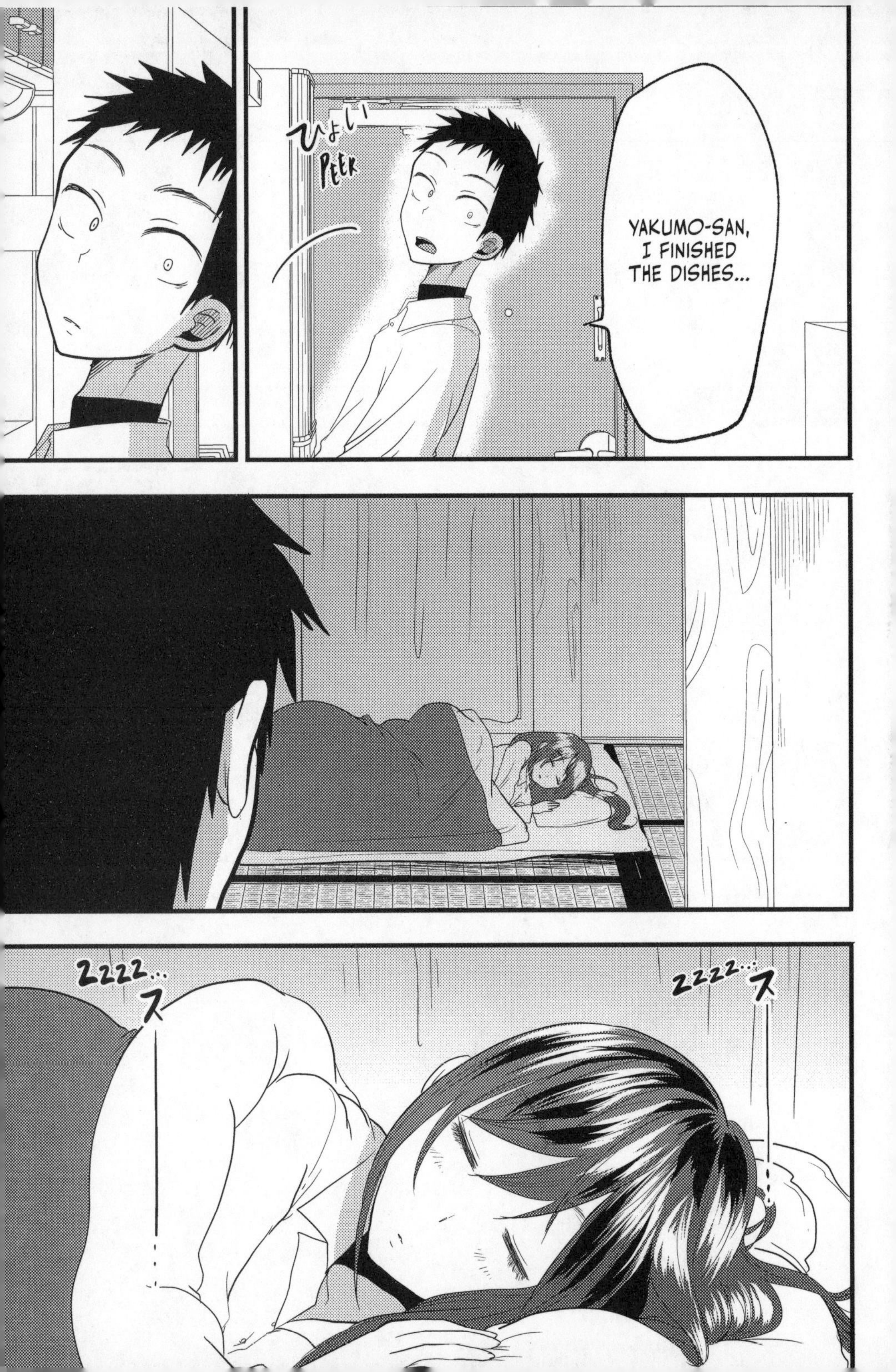
YAKUMO-SAN, I FINISHED THE DISHES...
ひょい
PEEK
ZZZZ...
ス
ZZZZ...
ス

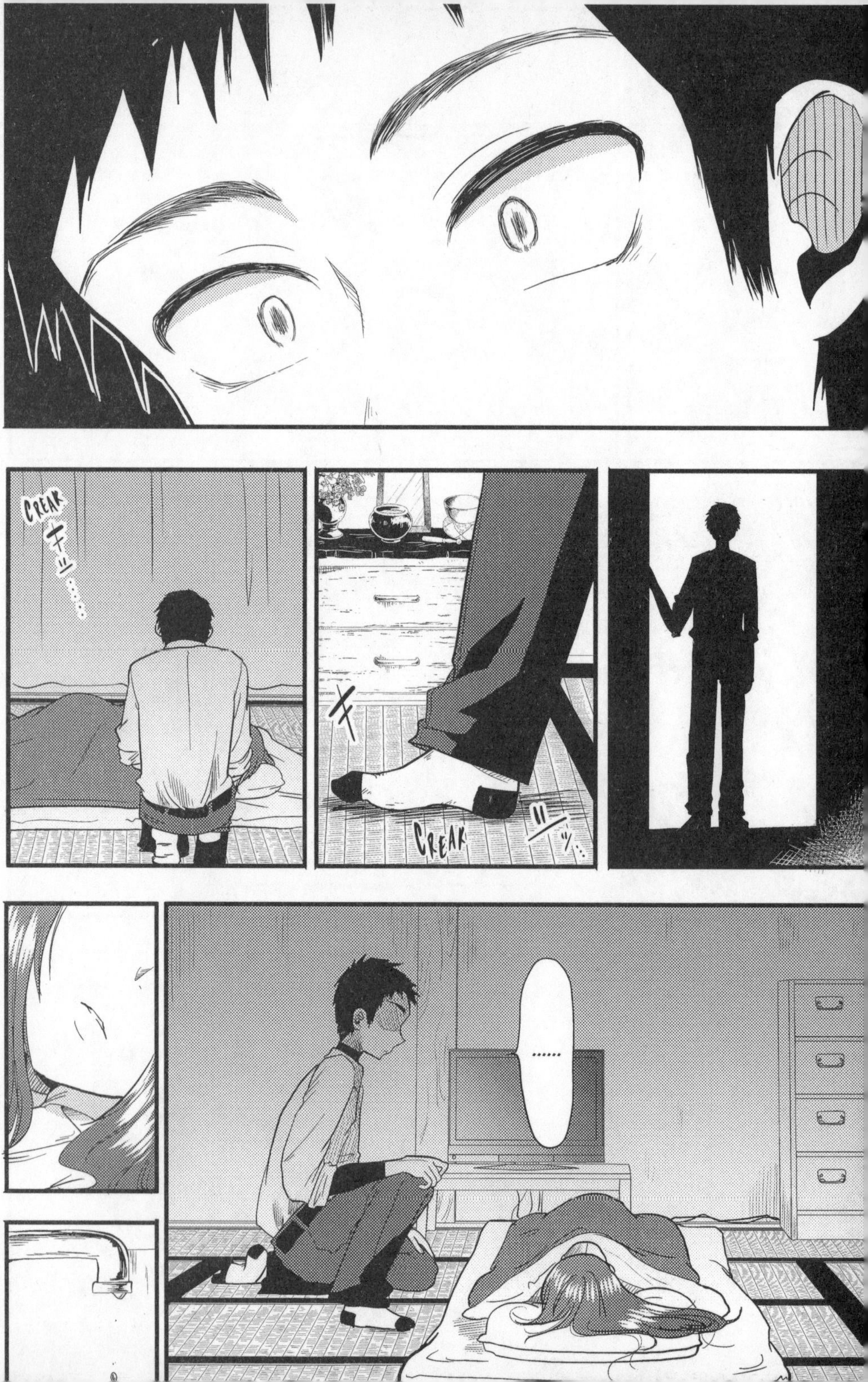
ギシッ…
CREAK
CREAK
キシ……
……

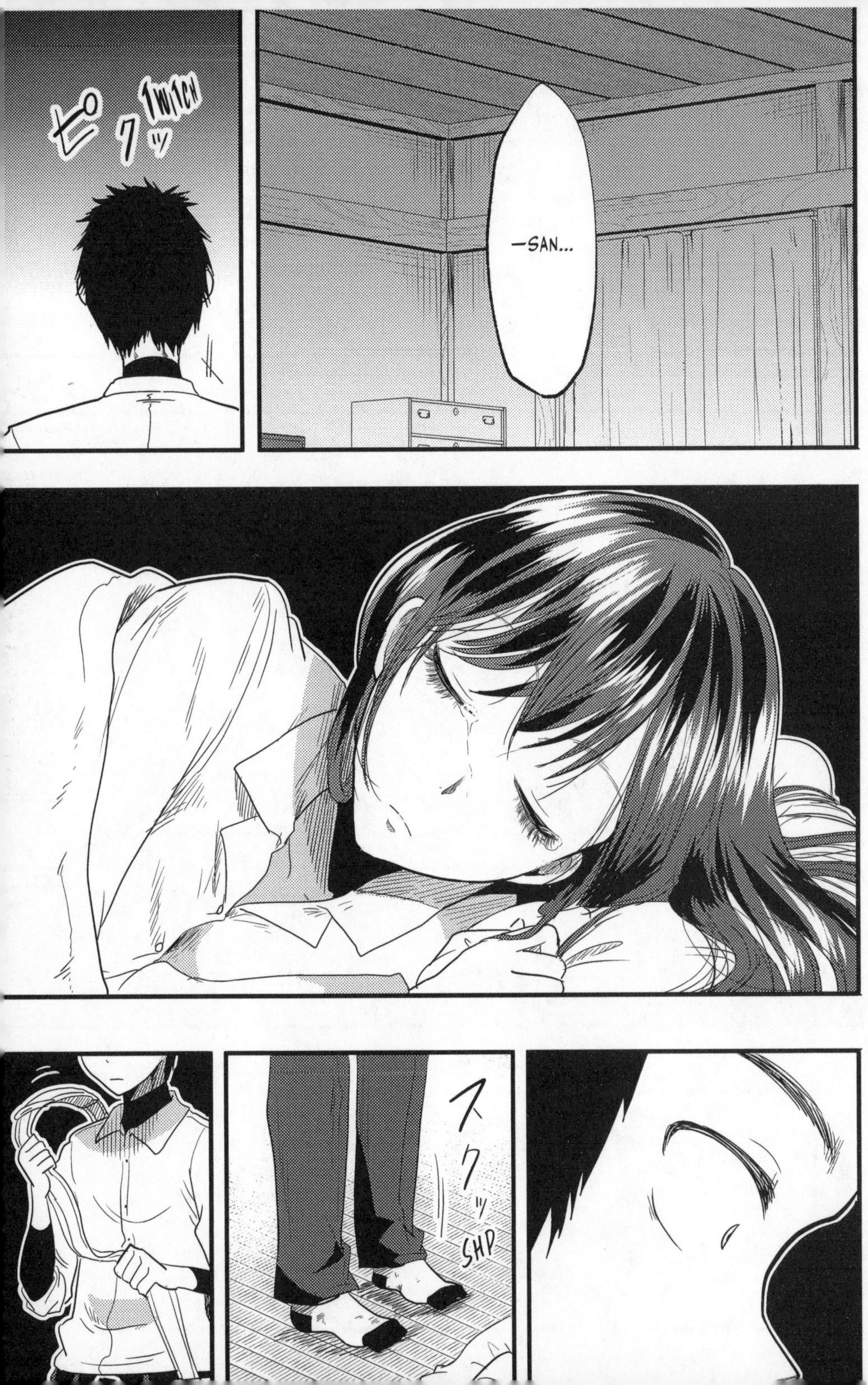
—SAN...
ピクッ
TWITCH
スクッ
SHP

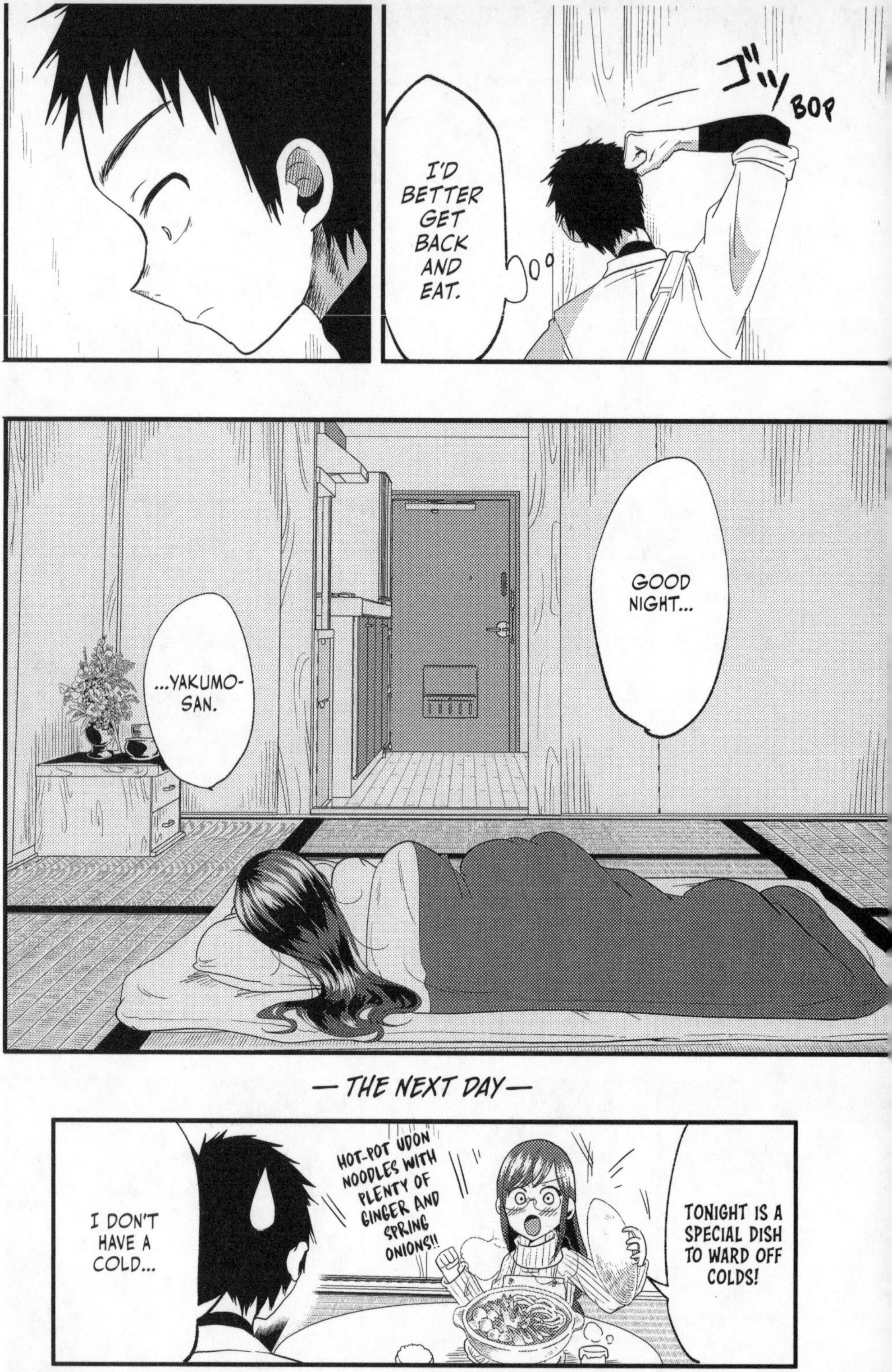
ゴッ
BOP
I'D BETTER GET BACK AND EAT.
GOOD NIGHT...
...YAKUMO-SAN.
—THE NEXT DAY—
TONIGHT IS A SPECIAL DISH TO WARD OFF COLDS!
HOT-POT UDON NOODLES WITH PLENTY OF GINGER AND SPRING ONIONS!!
I DON'T HAVE A COLD...

Beauty and the **FEAST**

A SPECIAL SIDE STORY
BEGINS NOW! ☆

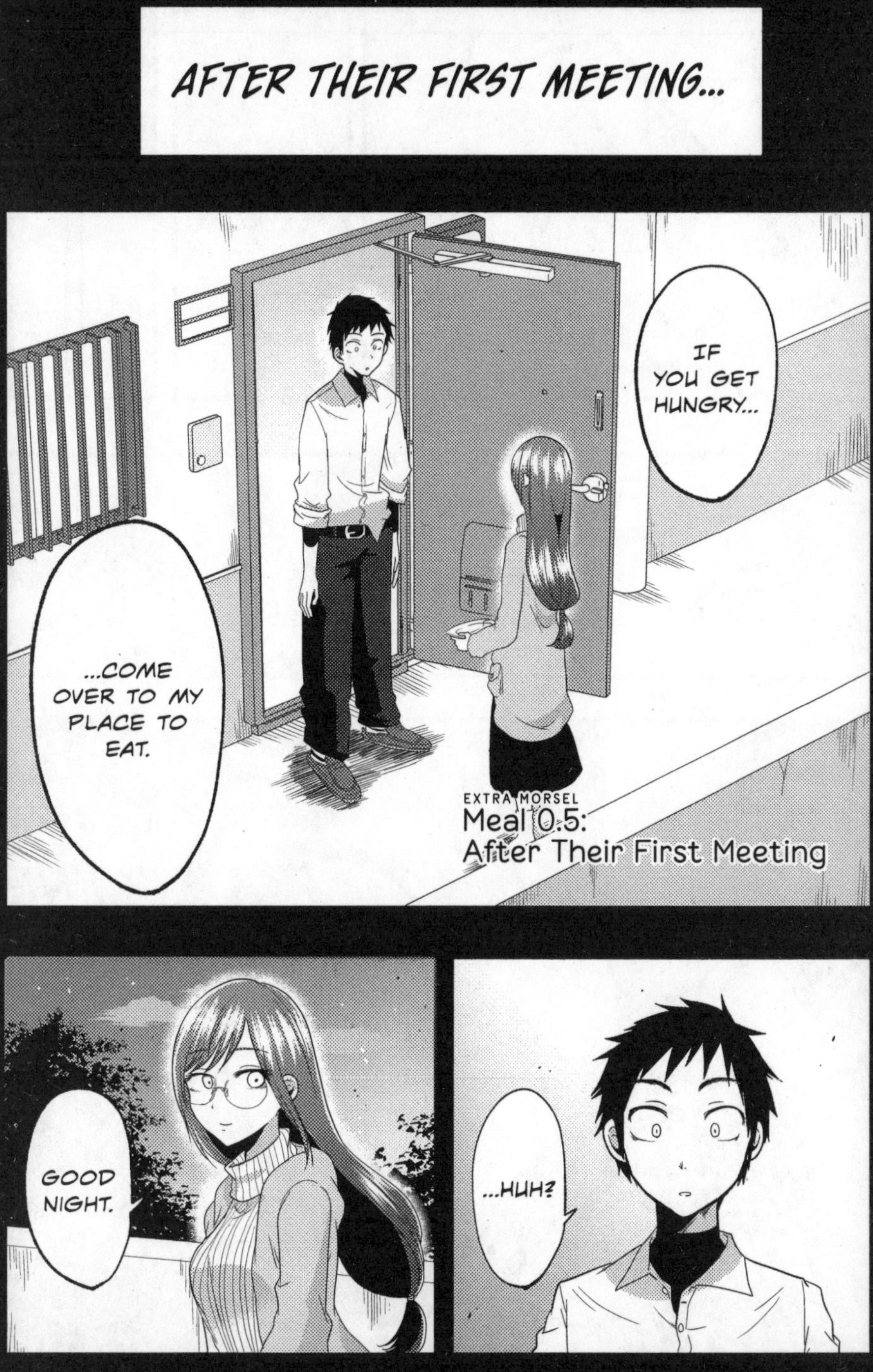
AFTER THEIR FIRST MEETING...
IF YOU GET HUNGRY...
...COME OVER TO MY PLACE TO EAT.
EXTRA MORSEL
Meal 0.5: After Their First Meeting
...HUH?
GOOD NIGHT.

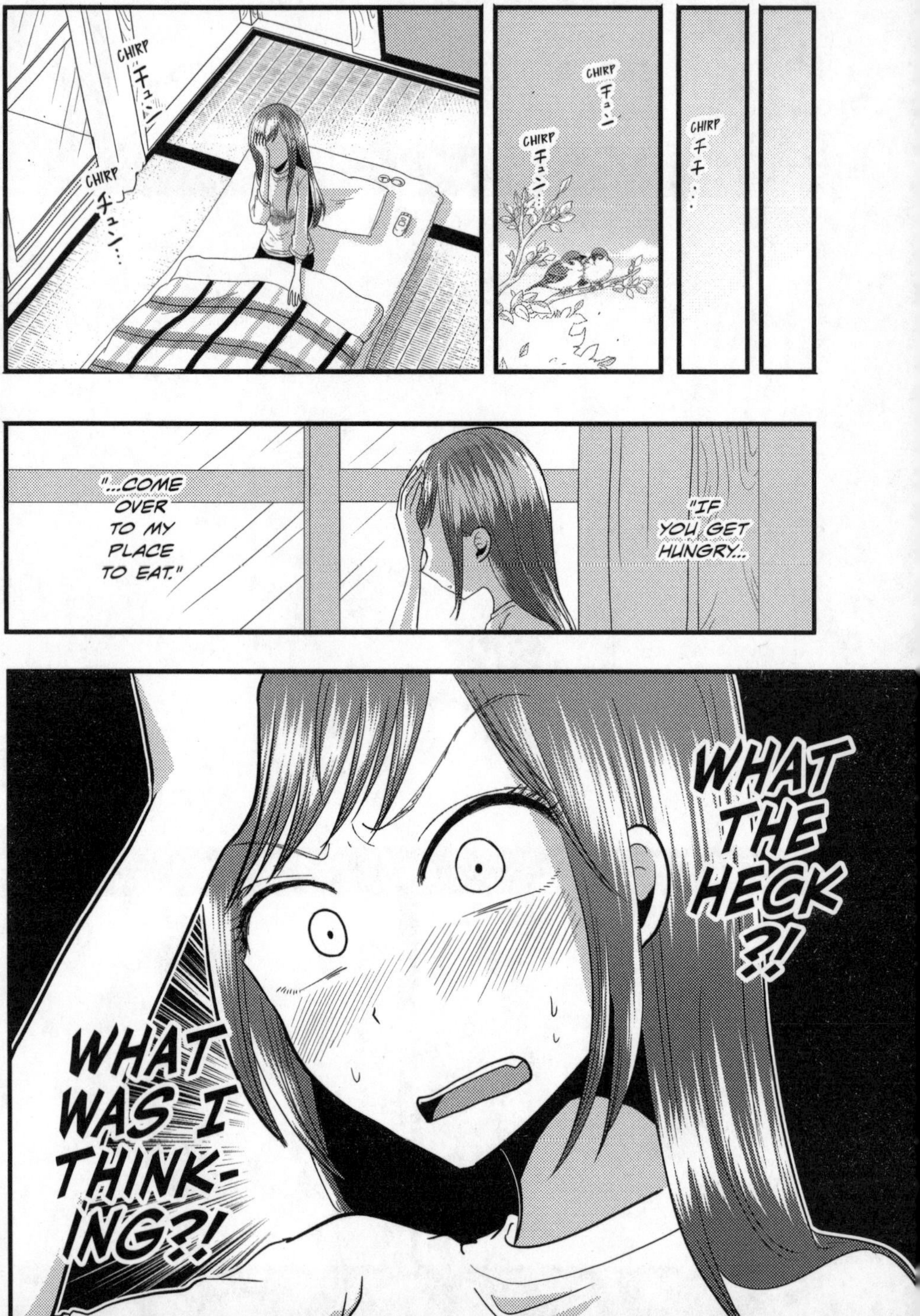
CHIRP
チチ…
CHIRP
チュン
CHIRP
チュン…
CHIRP
チュン
CHIRP
チュン…
"IF YOU GET HUNGRY...
"...COME OVER TO MY PLACE TO EAT."
WHAT THE HECK?!
WHAT WAS I THINK-ING?!

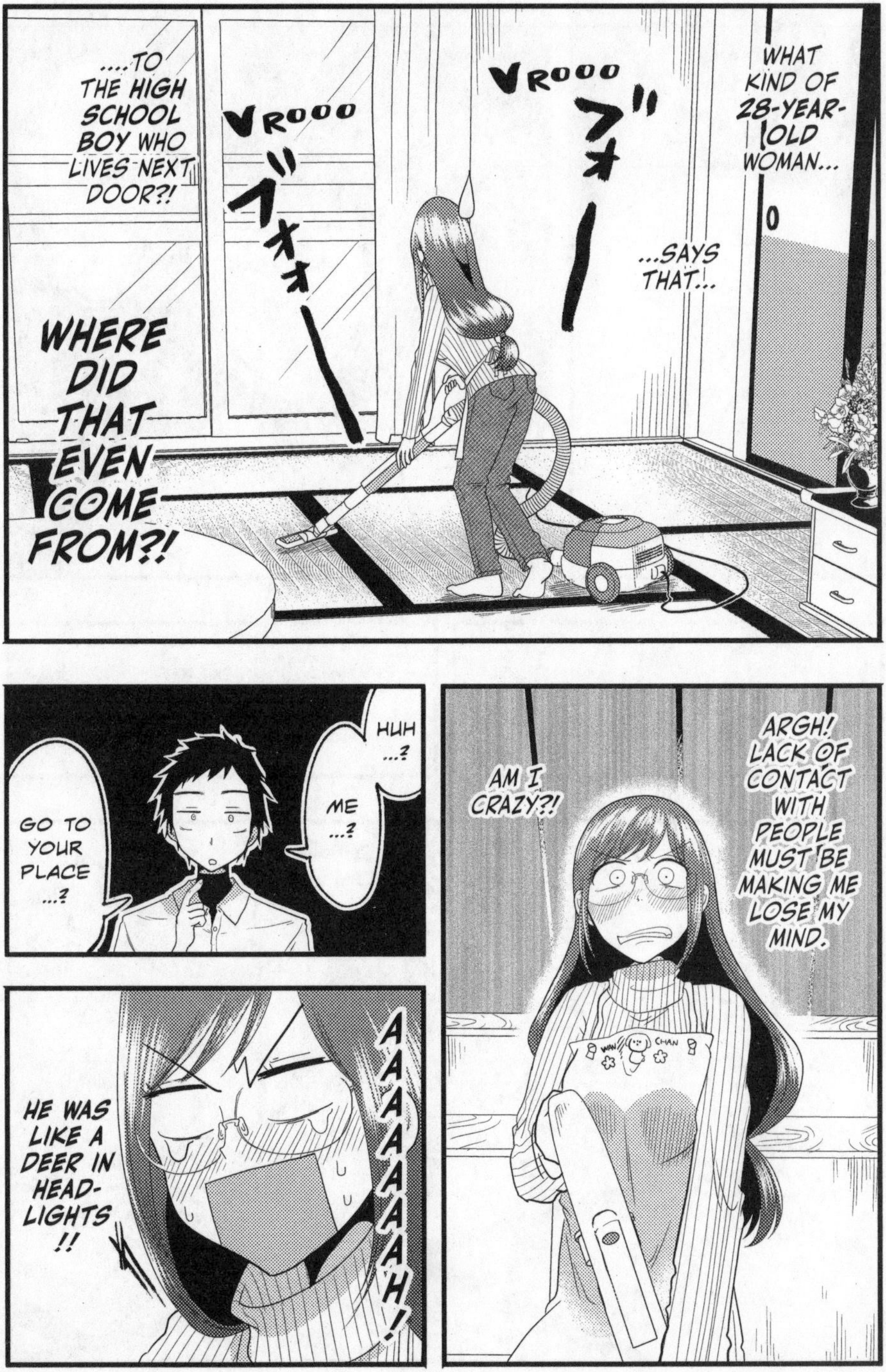

WHAT KIND OF 28-YEAR-OLD WOMAN...
...SAYS THAT...
VROOO
ブォー
VROOO
ブォォー
....TO THE HIGH SCHOOL BOY WHO LIVES NEXT DOOR?!
WHERE DID THAT EVEN COME FROM?!
ARGH! LACK OF CONTACT WITH PEOPLE MUST BE MAKING ME LOSE MY MIND.
AM I CRAZY?!
WAN
CHAN
HUH ...?
ME ...?
GO TO YOUR PLACE ...?
AAAAAAAAAH!
HE WAS LIKE A DEER IN HEAD-LIGHTS!!

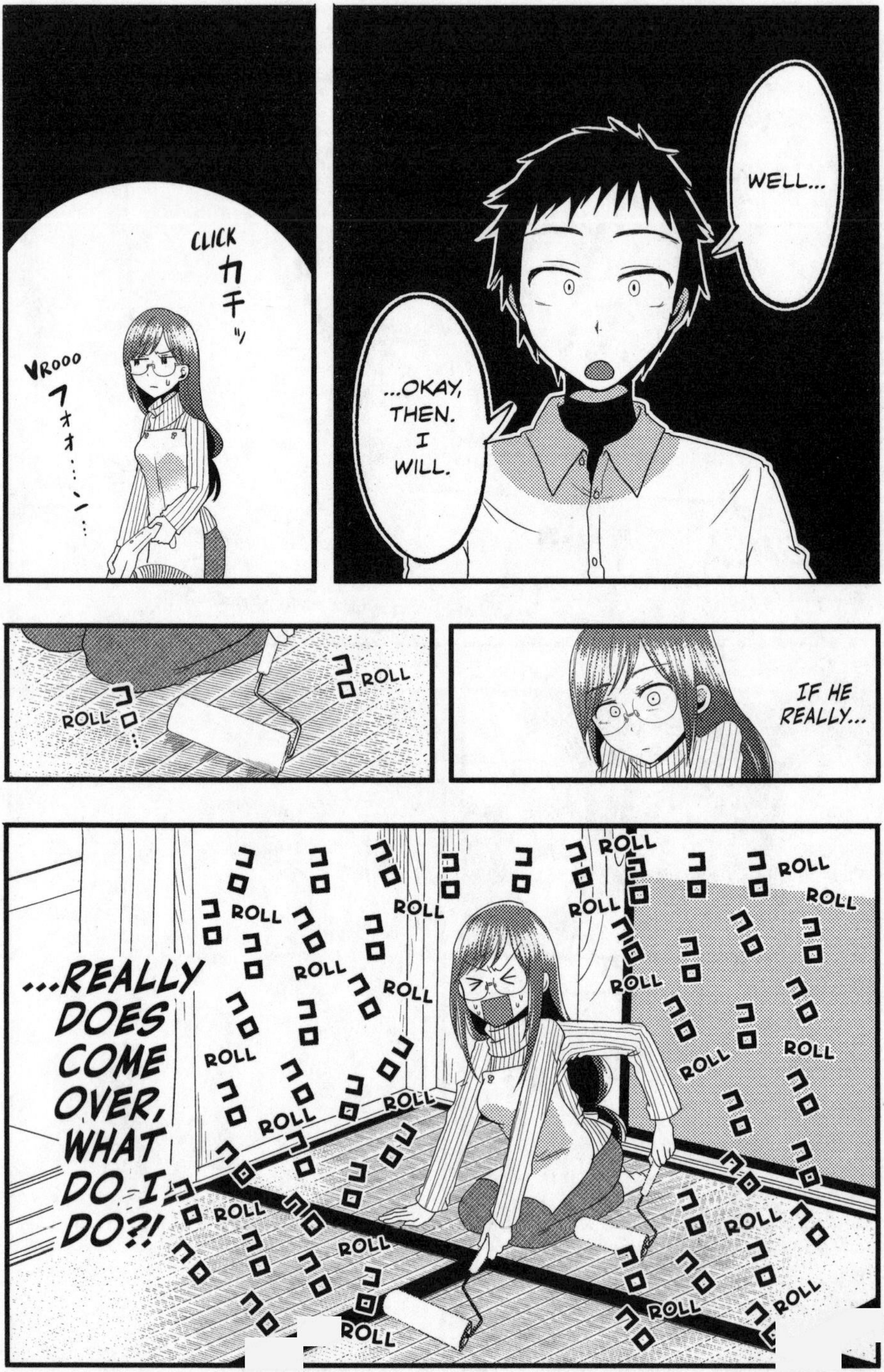
WELL...
...OKAY, THEN. I WILL.
CLICK カチッ
VROOO フォオ…ン…
IF HE REALLY...
ROLL コロ
ROLL コロ…
コロ ROLL コロ ROLL コロ ROLL コロ ROLL
...REALLY DOES COME OVER, WHAT DO I DO?!

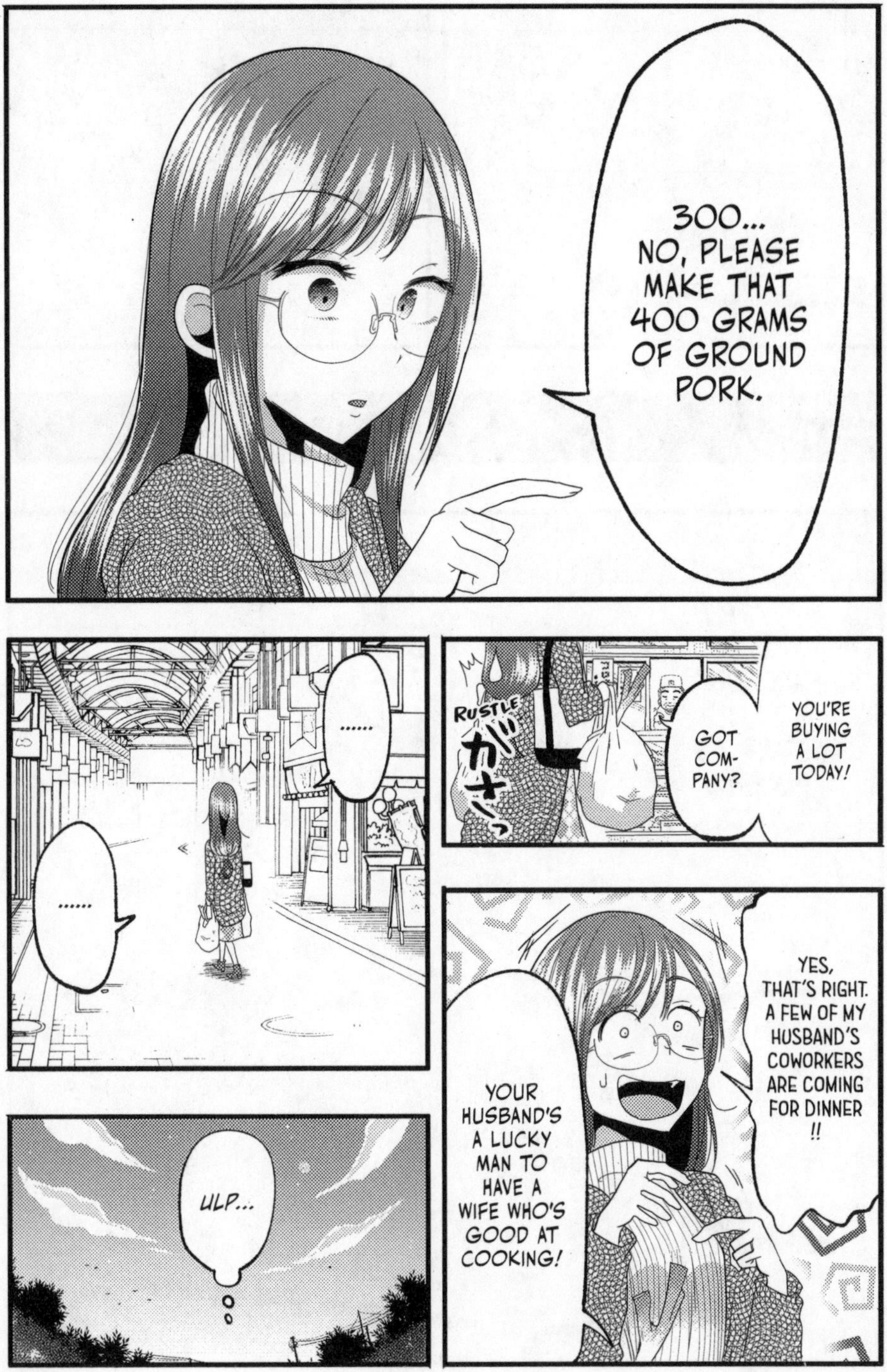
300... NO, PLEASE MAKE THAT 400 GRAMS OF GROUND PORK.
YOU'RE BUYING A LOT TODAY!
GOT COM-PANY?
RUSTLE
がさっ
YES, THAT'S RIGHT. A FEW OF MY HUSBAND'S COWORKERS ARE COMING FOR DINNER !!
YOUR HUSBAND'S A LUCKY MAN TO HAVE A WIFE WHO'S GOOD AT COOKING!
......
......
ULP...

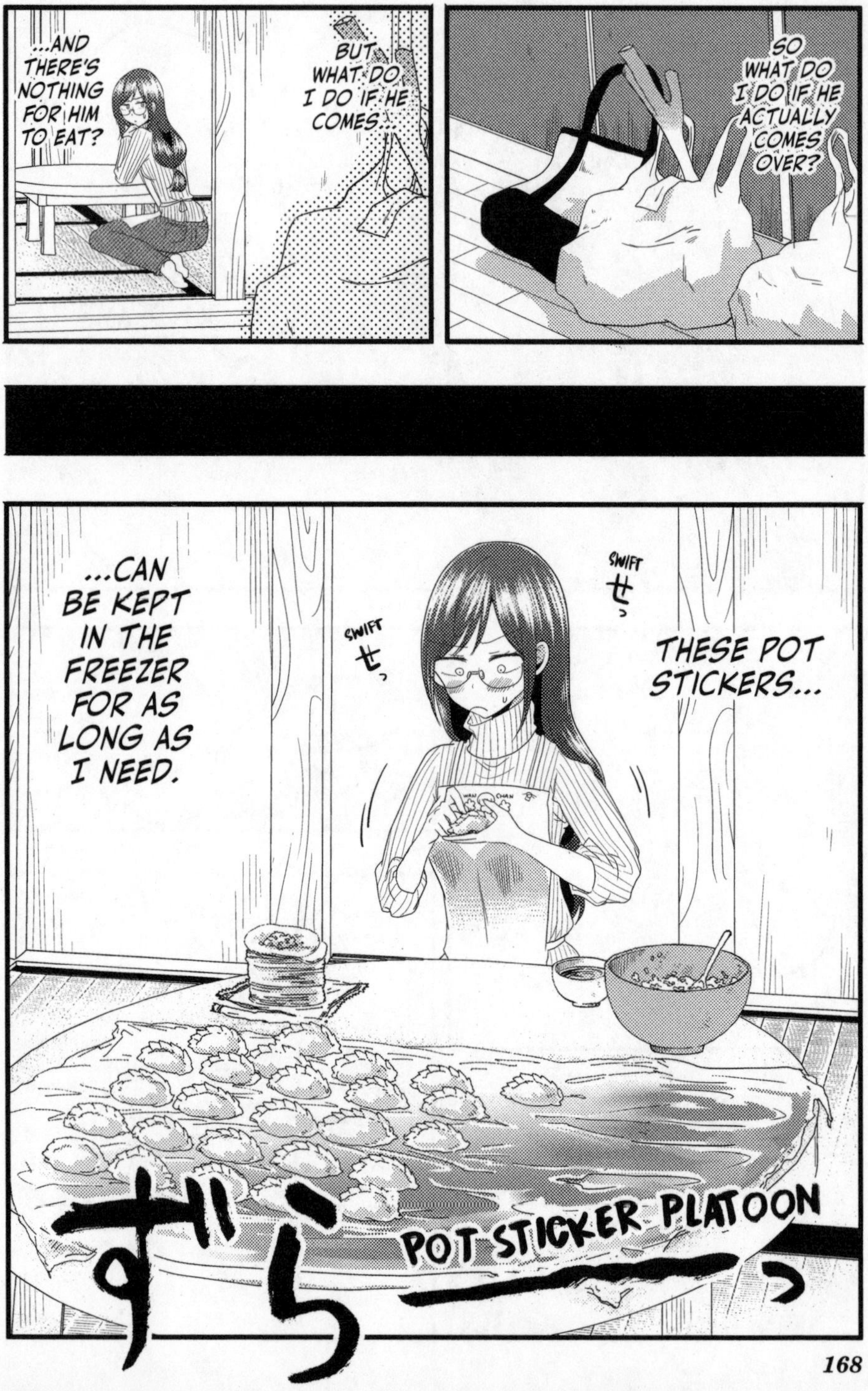
SO WHAT DO I DO IF HE ACTUALLY COMES OVER?
BUT WHAT DO I DO IF HE COMES...
...AND THERE'S NOTHING FOR HIM TO EAT?
SWIFT
SWIFT
THESE POT STICKERS...
...CAN BE KEPT IN THE FREEZER FOR AS LONG AS I NEED.
POT STICKER PLATOON

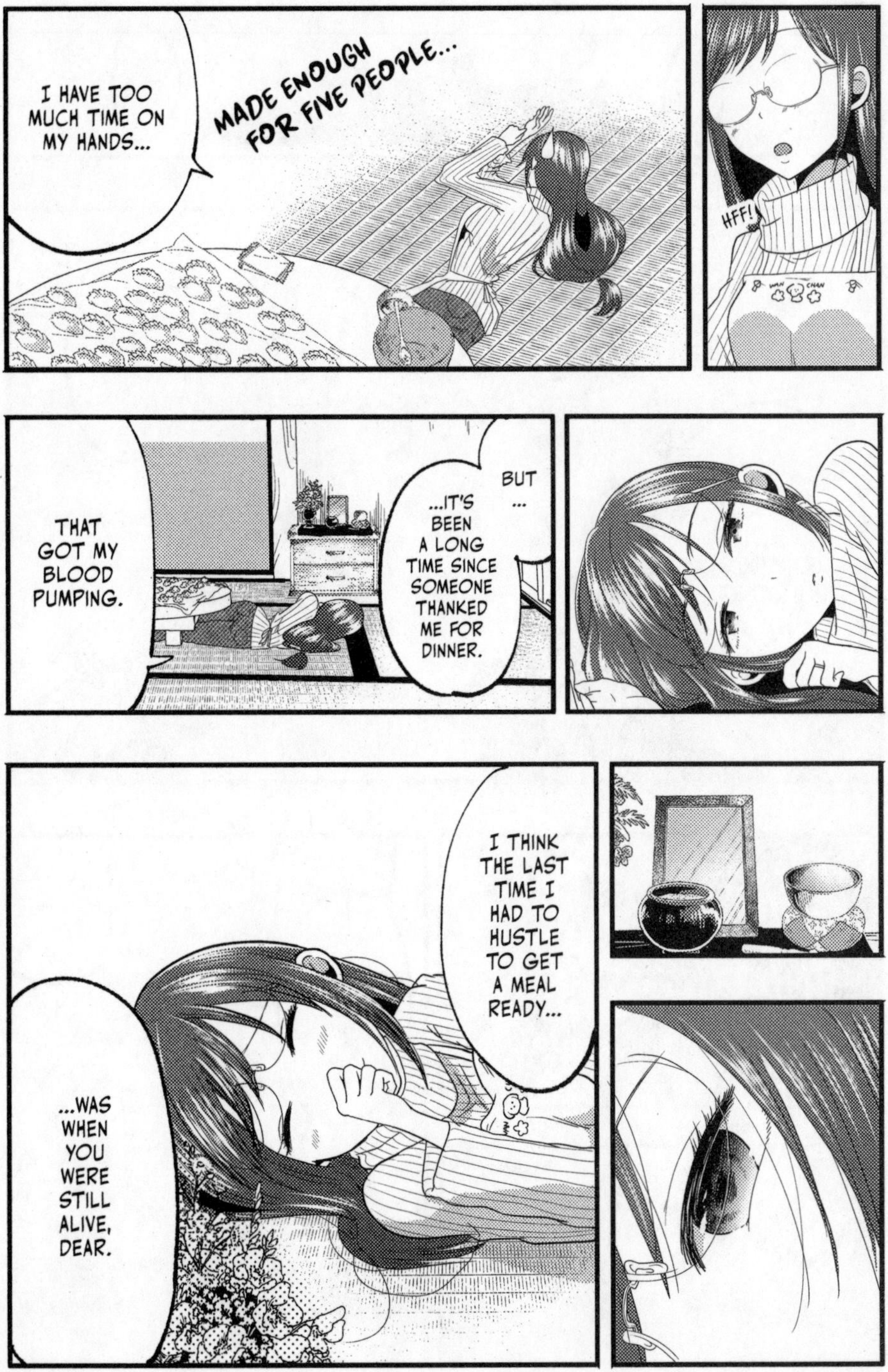
HFF!
WAN CHAN
I HAVE TOO MUCH TIME ON MY HANDS...
MADE ENOUGH FOR FIVE PEOPLE...
BUT ...
...IT'S BEEN A LONG TIME SINCE SOMEONE THANKED ME FOR DINNER.
THAT GOT MY BLOOD PUMPING.
I THINK THE LAST TIME I HAD TO HUSTLE TO GET A MEAL READY...
...WAS WHEN YOU WERE STILL ALIVE, DEAR.

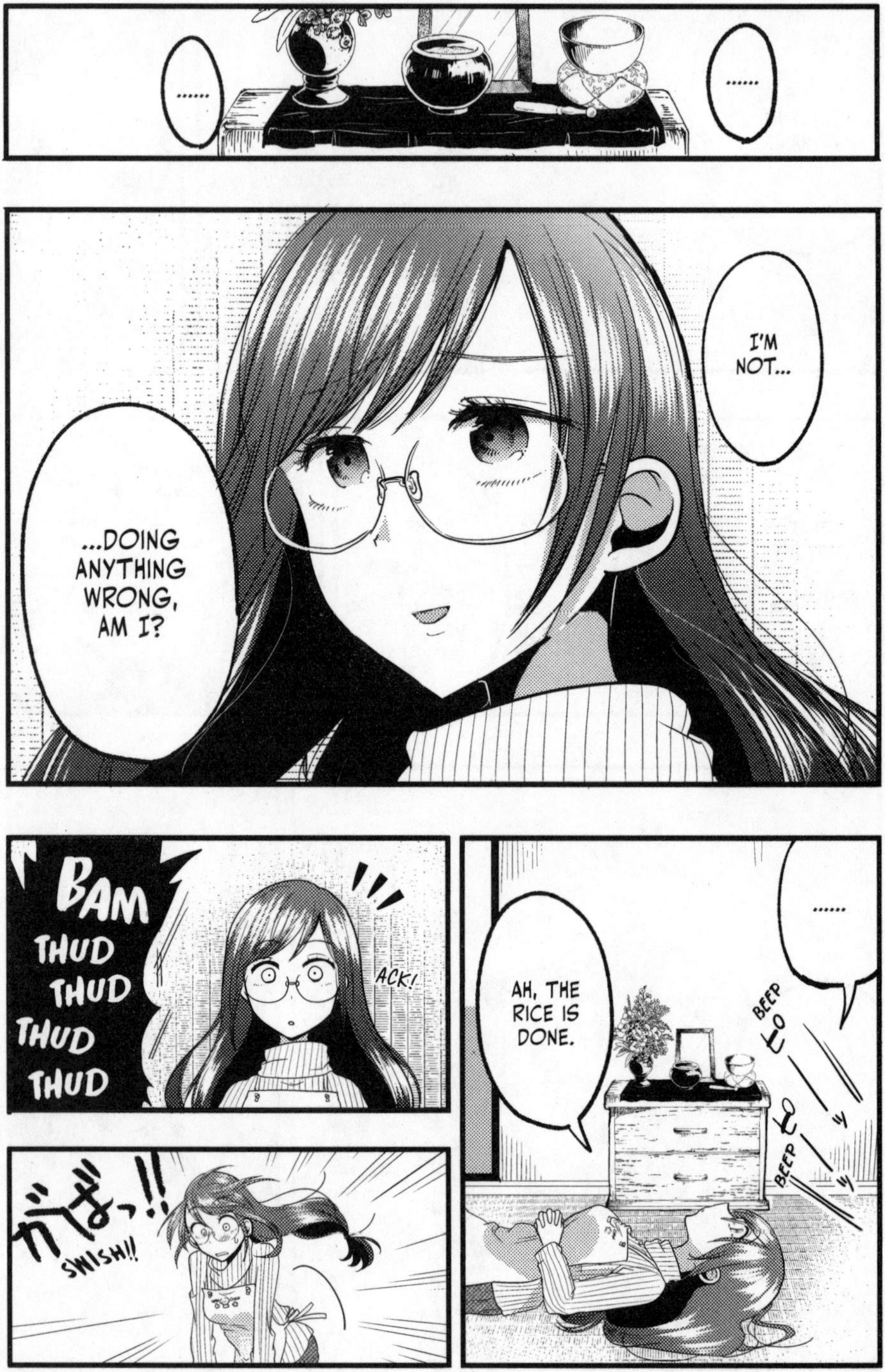
......
......
I'M NOT...
...DOING ANYTHING WRONG, AM I?
......
AH, THE RICE IS DONE.
BEEP
BEEP
BAM
THUD THUD THUD THUD
ACK!
SWISH!!

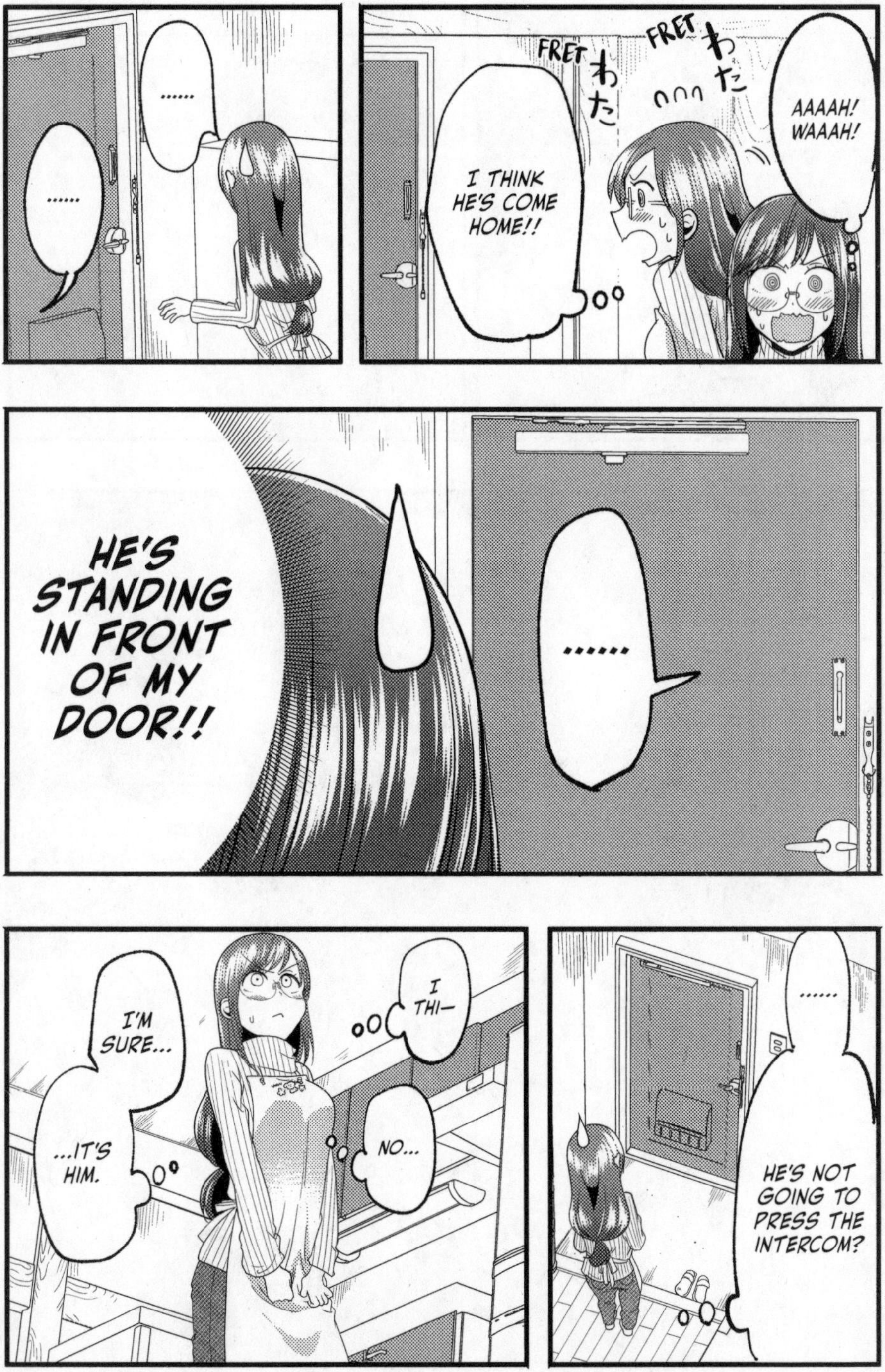
AAAAH! WAAAH!
FRET わた
FRET わた
I THINK HE'S COME HOME!!
......
......
......
HE'S STANDING IN FRONT OF MY DOOR!!
......
HE'S NOT GOING TO PRESS THE INTERCOM?
I THI—
NO...
I'M SURE...
...IT'S HIM.

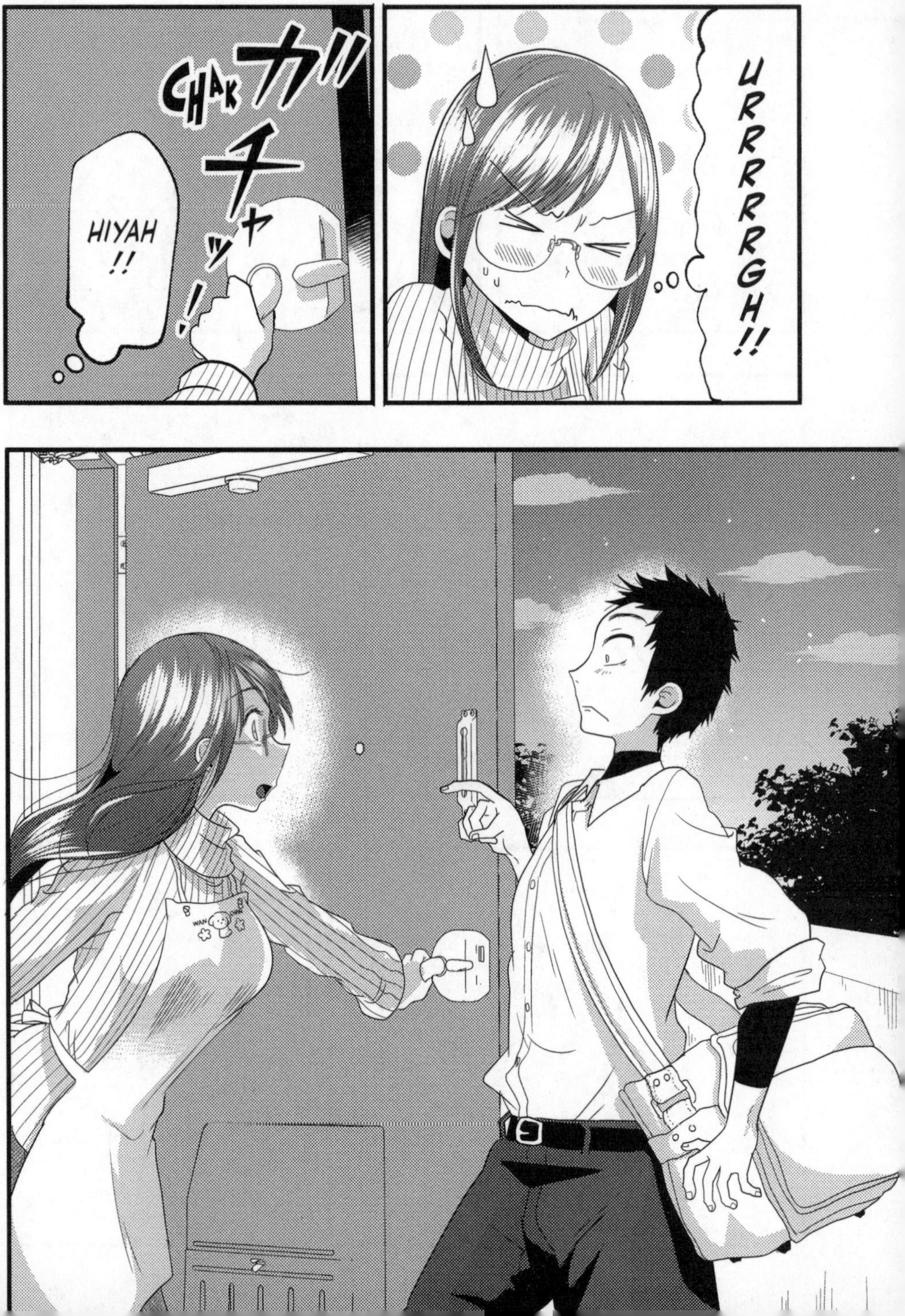
URRRRRGH!!
CHAK
カチャッ!
HIYAH!!

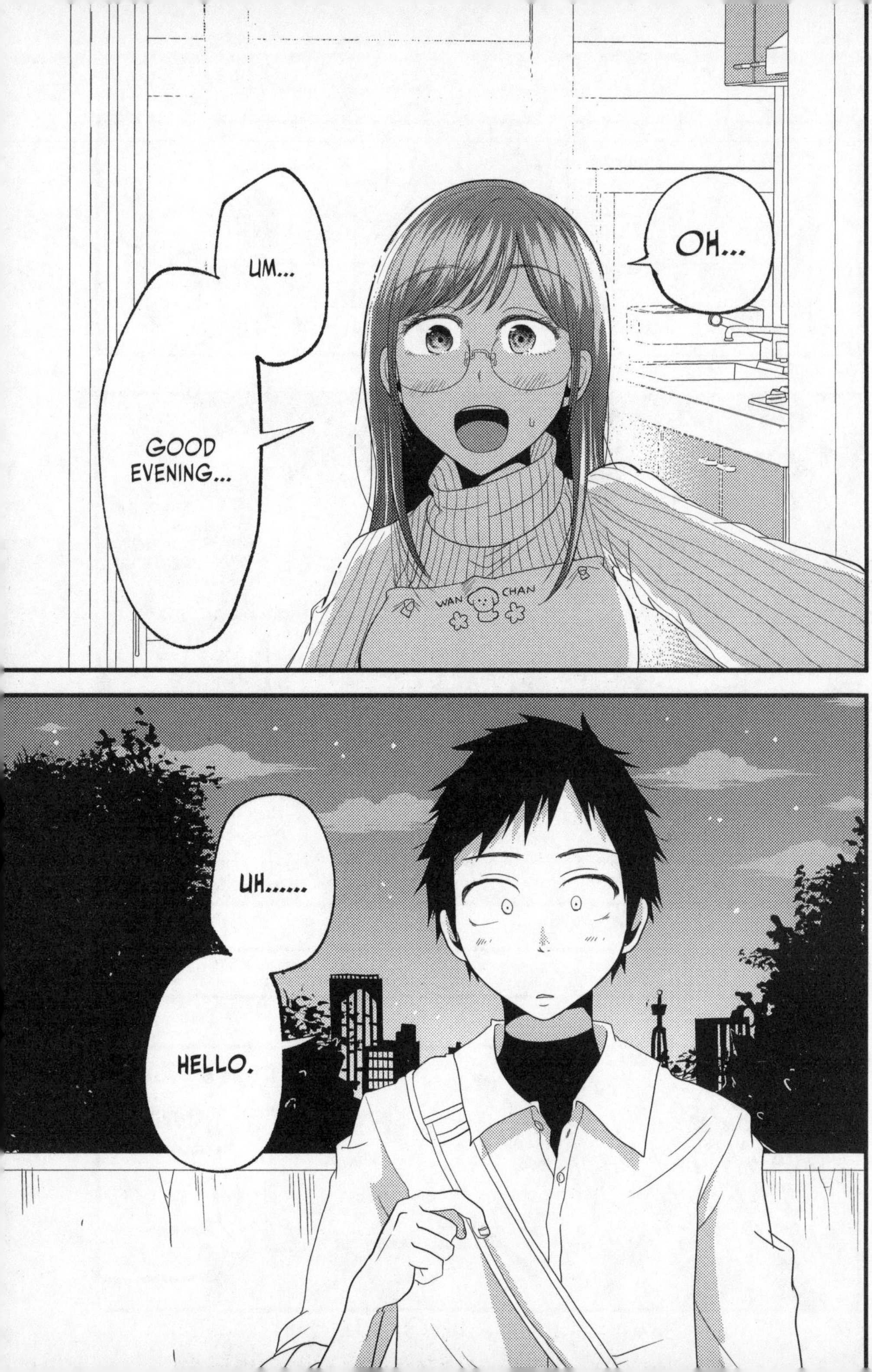
OH...
UM...
GOOD EVENING...
WAN CHAN
UH......
HELLO.

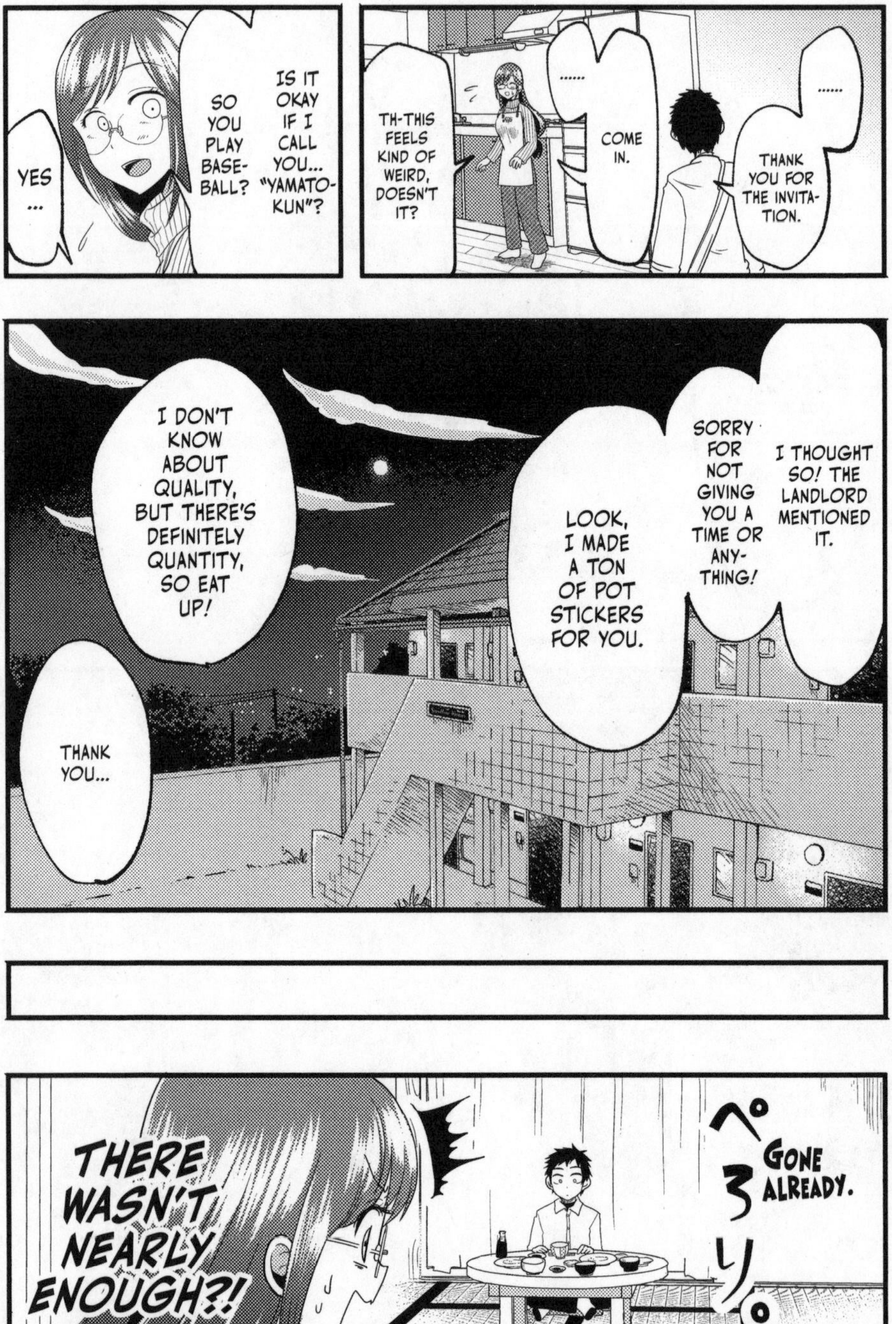
......
THANK YOU FOR THE INVITATION.
......
COME IN.
TH-THIS FEELS KIND OF WEIRD, DOESN'T IT?
IS IT OKAY IF I CALL YOU... "YAMATO-KUN"?
SO YOU PLAY BASEBALL?
YES...
I THOUGHT SO! THE LANDLORD MENTIONED IT.
SORRY FOR NOT GIVING YOU A TIME OR ANYTHING!
LOOK, I MADE A TON OF POT STICKERS FOR YOU.
I DON'T KNOW ABOUT QUALITY, BUT THERE'S DEFINITELY QUANTITY, SO EAT UP!
THANK YOU...
ぺろり。
GONE ALREADY.
THERE WASN'T NEARLY ENOUGH?!

Beauty and the Feast ② • THE END

Beauty and the FEAST.

Beauty and the FEAST

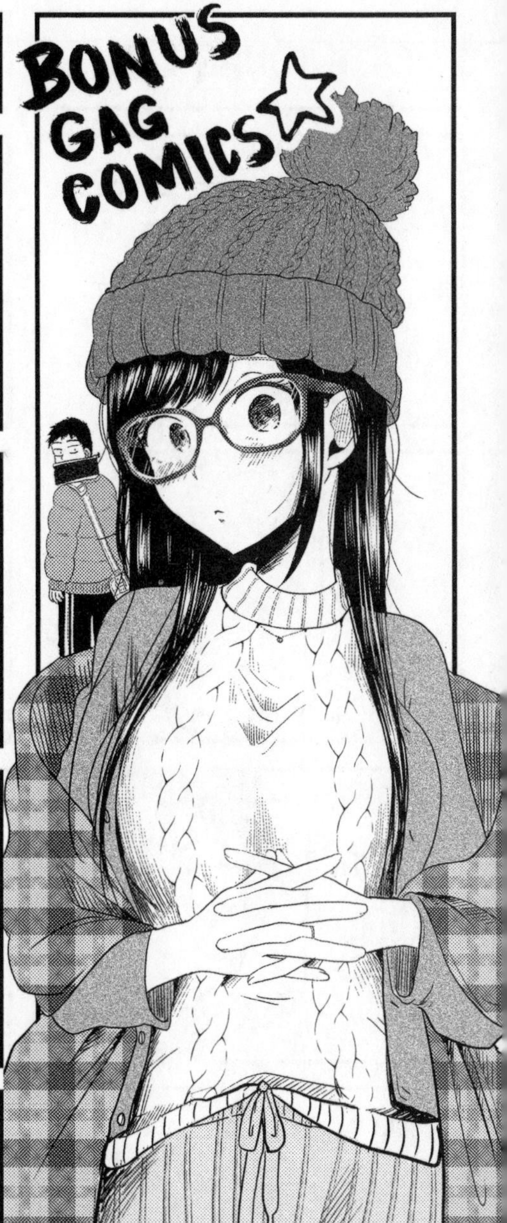
BONUS GAG COMICS☆

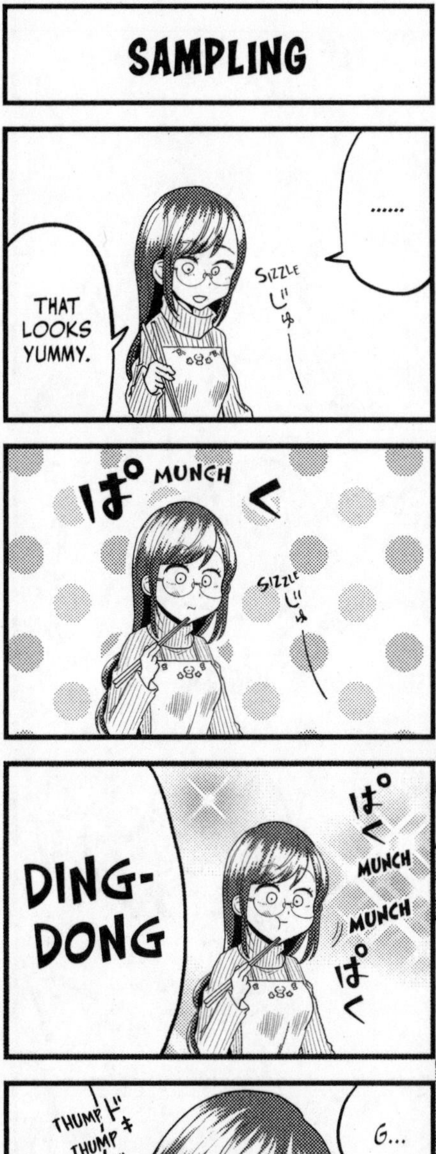
SAMPLING
......
SIZZLE じゅ
THAT LOOKS YUMMY.
ぱ MUNCH く
SIZZLE じゅ
ぱく MUNCH
MUNCH ぱく
DING-DONG
G...
THUMP, ドキ THUMP ドキ
GOME IG... (COME IN.)
MUNCH もぐ
MUNCH もぐ

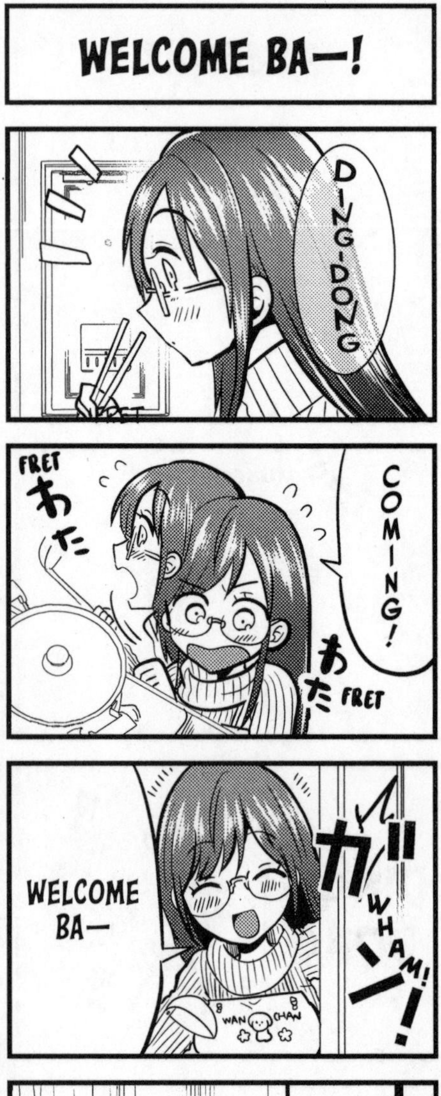
WELCOME BA—!
DING-DONG
FRET
COMING!
FRET
あた
あた
FRET
WELCOME BA—
WHAM!
WAN CHAN

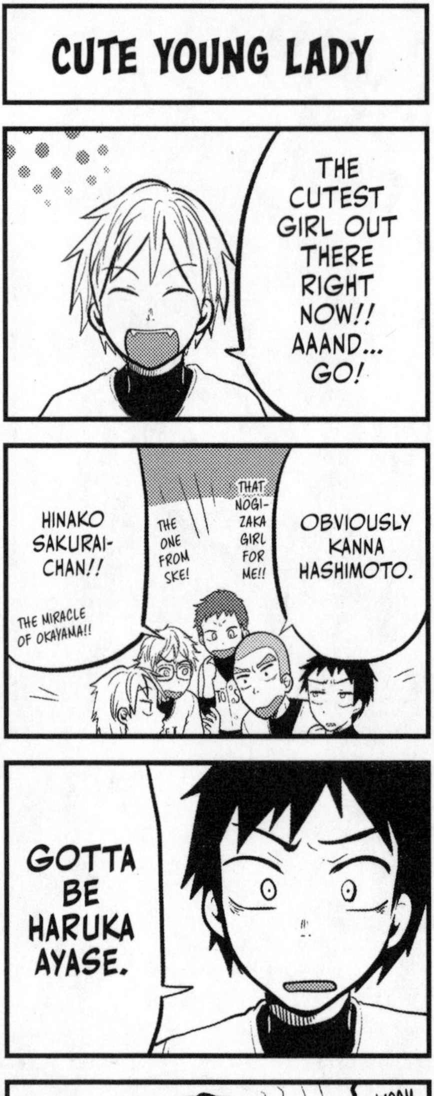
CUTE YOUNG LADY
THE CUTEST GIRL OUT THERE RIGHT NOW!! AAAND... GO!
OBVIOUSLY KANNA HASHIMOTO.
THAT NOGI-ZAKA GIRL FOR ME!!
THE ONE FROM SKE!
HINAKO SAKURAI-CHAN!!
THE MIRACLE OF OKAYAMA!!
GOTTA BE HARUKA AYASE.
WOAH...
AW, MAN...
YOU HAVE A DIRTY MIND...
AN OLDER WOMAN FETISH...
?!

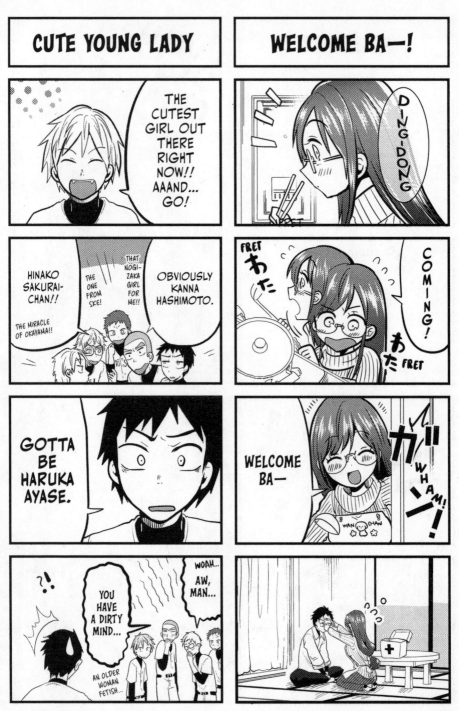

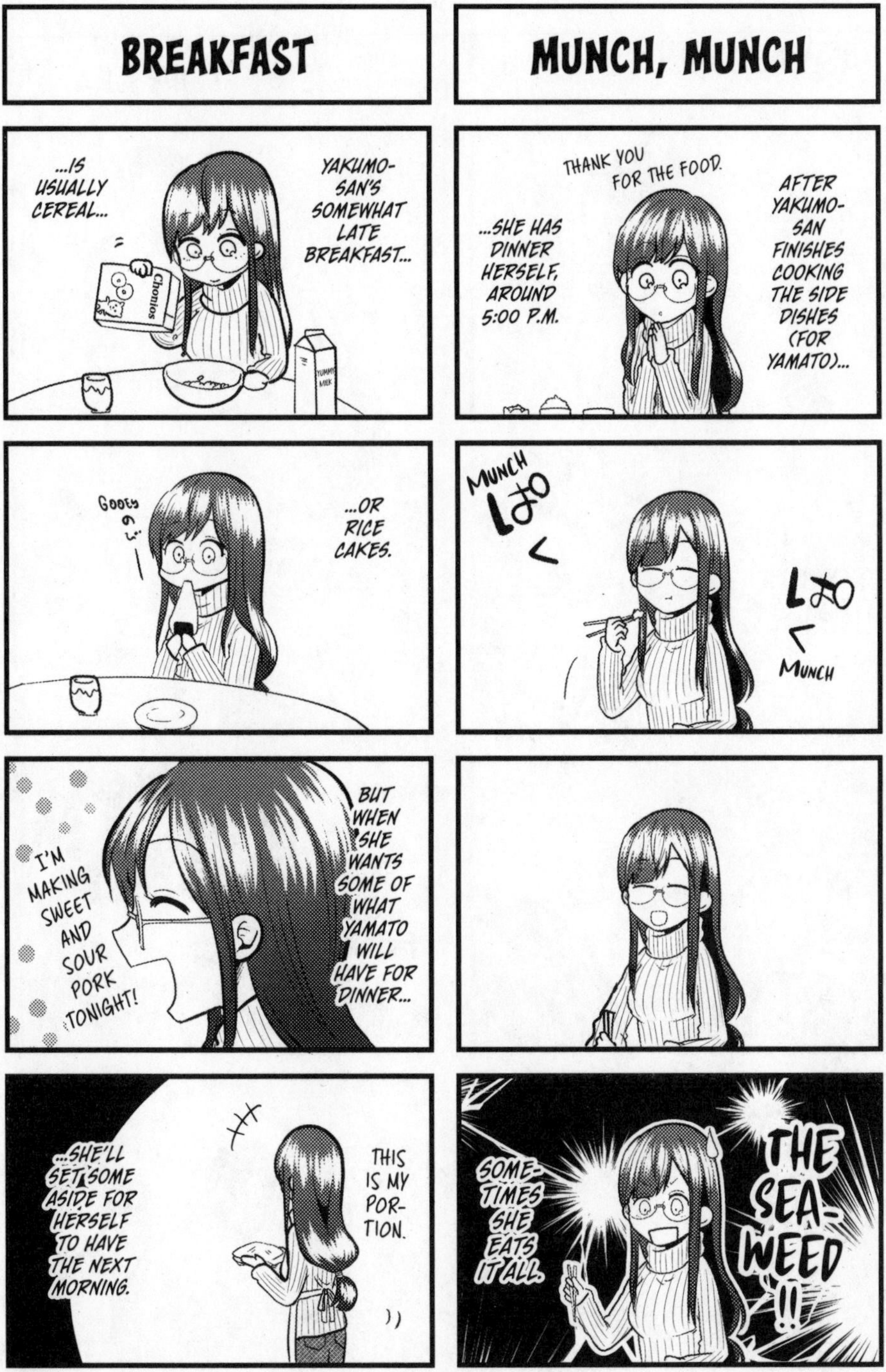
MUNCH, MUNCH
AFTER YAKUMO-SAN FINISHES COOKING THE SIDE DISHES (FOR YAMATO)...
THANK YOU FOR THE FOOD.
...SHE HAS DINNER HERSELF, AROUND 5:00 P.M.
MUNCH
MUNCH
THE SEA-WEED!!
SOME-TIMES SHE EATS IT ALL.
BREAKFAST
YAKUMO-SAN'S SOMEWHAT LATE BREAKFAST...
...IS USUALLY CEREAL...
Chomios
YUMMY MILK
...OR RICE CAKES.
GOOEY
BUT WHEN SHE WANTS SOME OF WHAT YAMATO WILL HAVE FOR DINNER...
I'M MAKING SWEET AND SOUR PORK TONIGHT!
THIS IS MY POR-TION.
...SHE'LL SET SOME ASIDE FOR HERSELF TO HAVE THE NEXT MORNING.

THE ANNOYING KID SISTER BESIDE ME

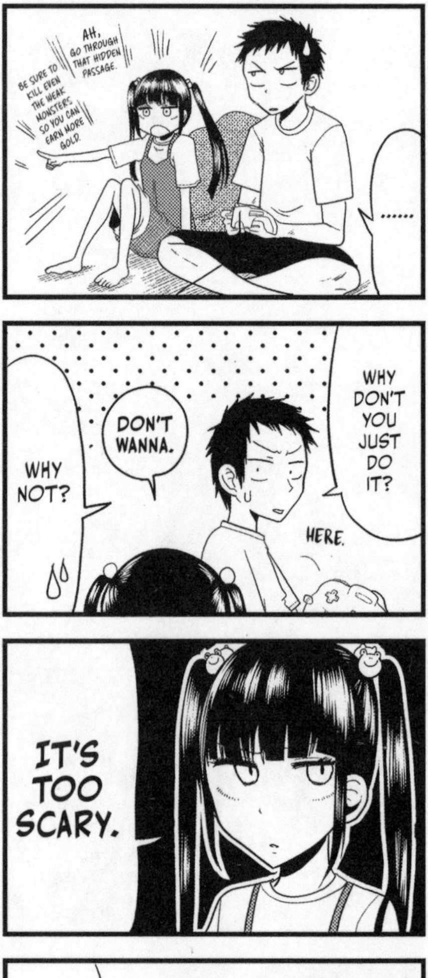
......
AH, GO THROUGH THAT HIDDEN PASSAGE.
BE SURE TO KILL EVEN THE WEAK MONSTERS SO YOU CAN EARN MORE GOLD.
WHY DON'T YOU JUST DO IT?
HERE.
DON'T WANNA.
WHY NOT?
IT'S TOO SCARY.
DO THIS!
DO THAT!
CHIK
I DON'T GET IT.
CHIK

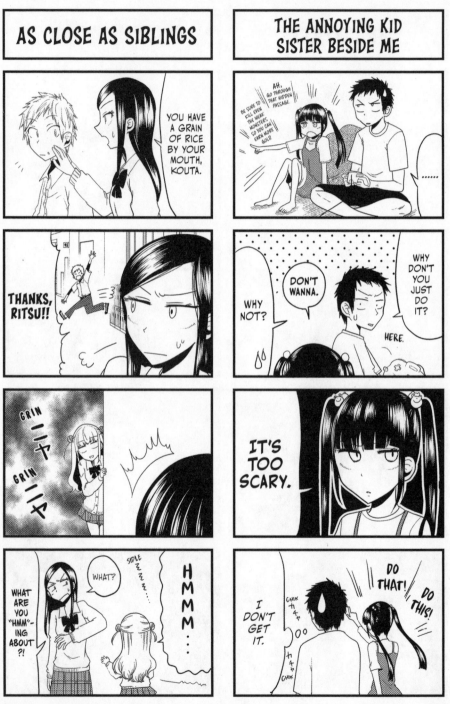

AS CLOSE AS SIBLINGS

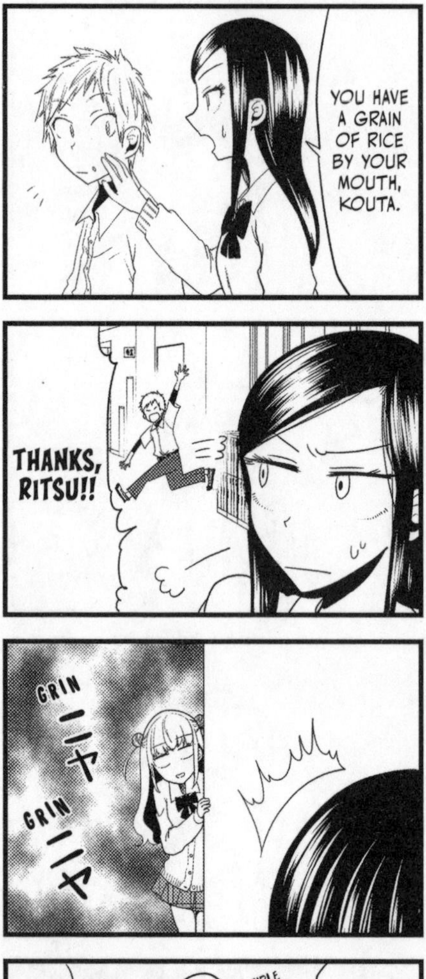
YOU HAVE A GRAIN OF RICE BY YOUR MOUTH, KOUTA.
THANKS, RITSU!!
GRIN
ニヤ
GRIN
ニヤ
HMMM...
SIDLE
WHAT?
WHAT ARE YOU "HMM"-ING ABOUT?!

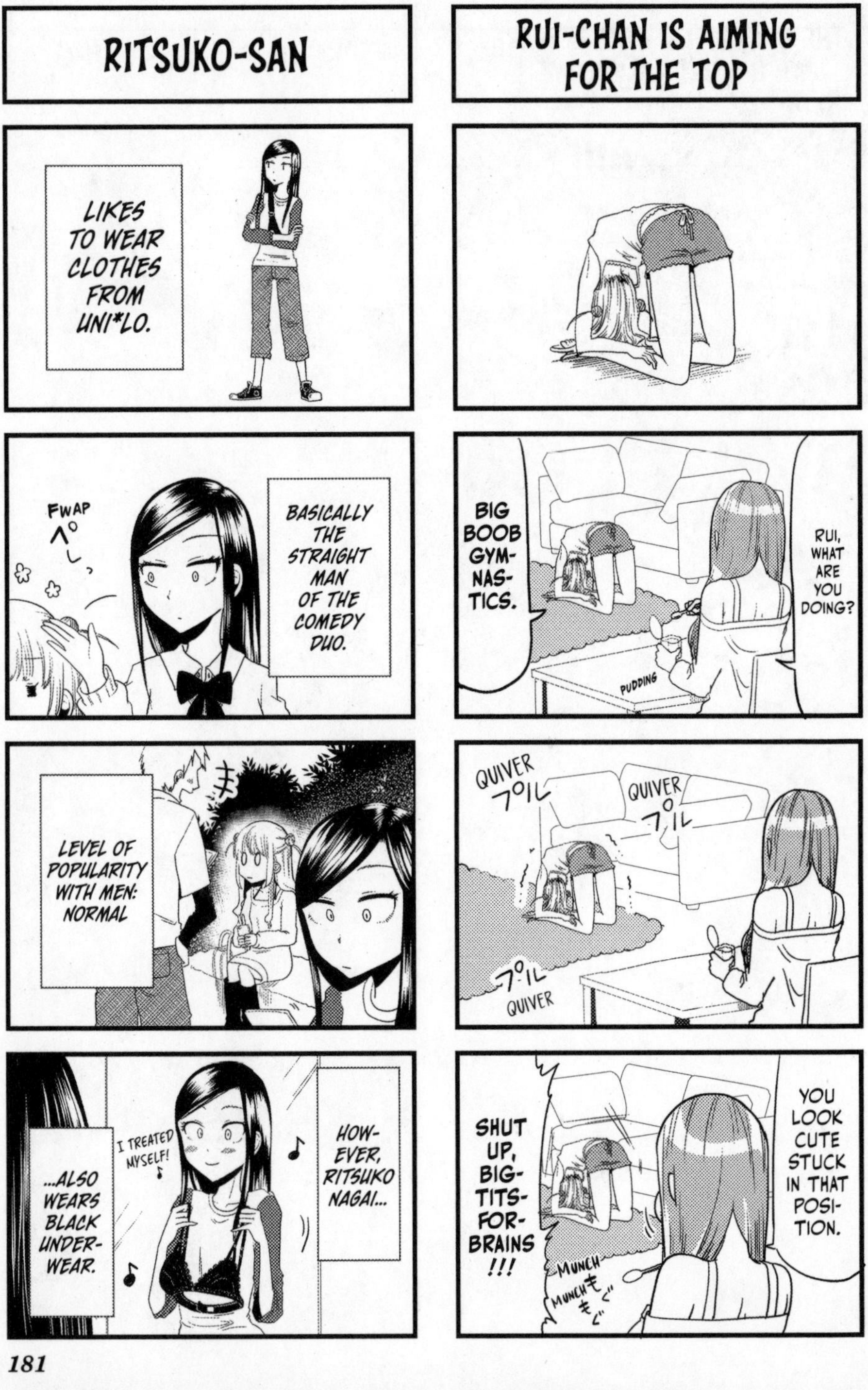
RUI-CHAN IS AIMING FOR THE TOP
RUI, WHAT ARE YOU DOING?
BIG BOOB GYMNASTICS.
PUDDING
QUIVER プル
QUIVER プル
プル QUIVER
YOU LOOK CUTE STUCK IN THAT POSITION.
SHUT UP, BIG-TITS-FOR-BRAINS!!!
MUNCH もぐ
MUNCH もぐ
RITSUKO-SAN
LIKES TO WEAR CLOTHES FROM UNI*LO.
BASICALLY THE STRAIGHT MAN OF THE COMEDY DUO.
FWAP ぺし
LEVEL OF POPULARITY WITH MEN: NORMAL
HOW-EVER, RITSUKO NAGAI...
I TREATED MYSELF! ♪
...ALSO WEARS BLACK UNDER-WEAR.

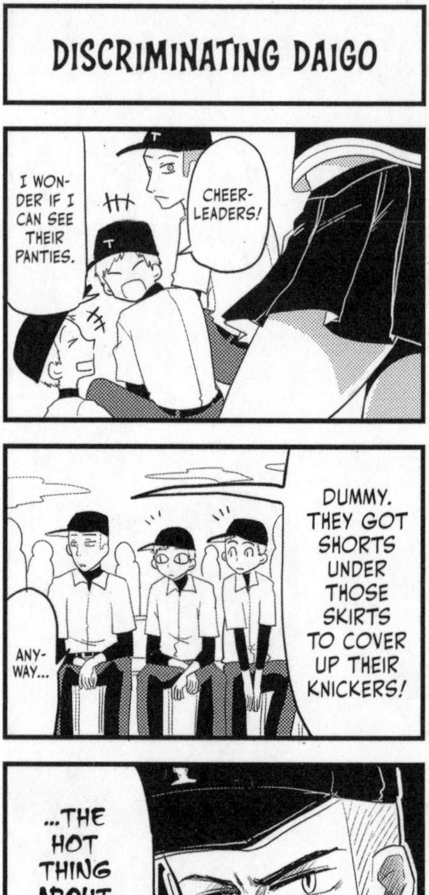
DISCRIMINATING DAIGO
CHEER-LEADERS!
I WON-DER IF I CAN SEE THEIR PANTIES.
DUMMY. THEY GOT SHORTS UNDER THOSE SKIRTS TO COVER UP THEIR KNICKERS!
ANY-WAY...
...THE HOT THING ABOUT CHEER-LEADERS IS THEIR ARMPITS.
UH...
OKAY ...

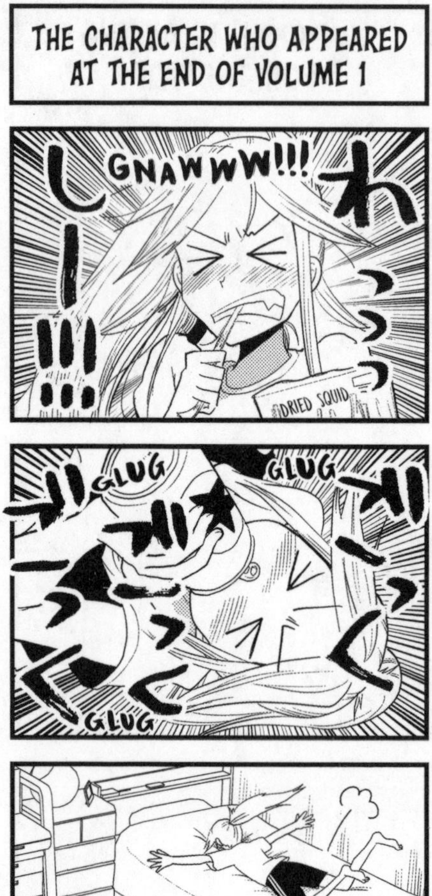
THE CHARACTER WHO APPEARED AT THE END OF VOLUME 1
GNAWWW!!!
DRIED SQUID
GLUG
GLUG
GLUG
FWUMP
THERE WAS NOTH-ING...
...FOR ME TO DO.

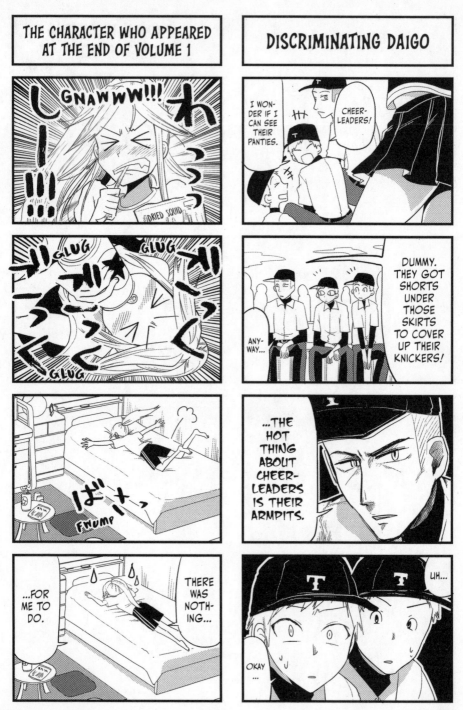

BANGS

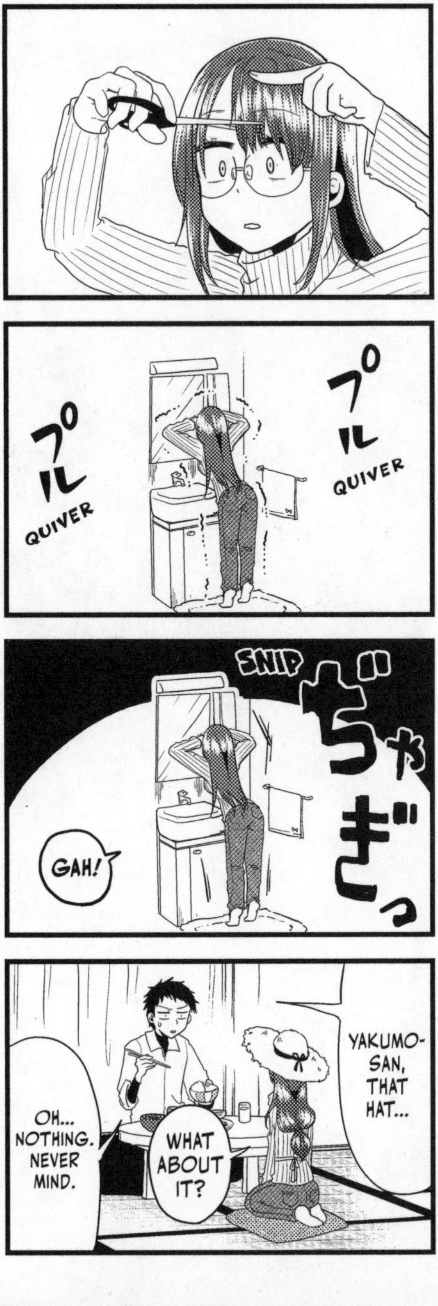
プル
QUIVER
プル
QUIVER
SNIP
ちゃぎっ
GAH!
YAKUMO-SAN, THAT HAT...
WHAT ABOUT IT?
OH... NOTHING. NEVER MIND.

A BEAUTIFUL GIRL'S TEARS

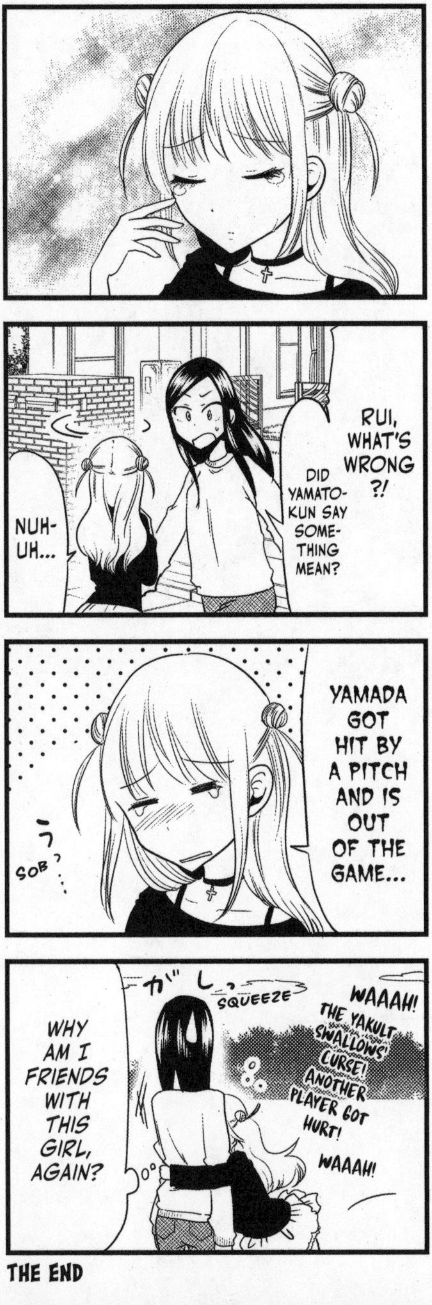
RUI, WHAT'S WRONG?!
DID YAMATO-KUN SAY SOME-THING MEAN?
NUH-UH...
YAMADA GOT HIT BY A PITCH AND IS OUT OF THE GAME...
う
SOB
がしっ
SQUEEZE
WAAAH! THE YAKULT SWALLOWS' CURSE! ANOTHER PLAYER GOT HURT!
WAAAH!
WHY AM I FRIENDS WITH THIS GIRL, AGAIN?

THE END

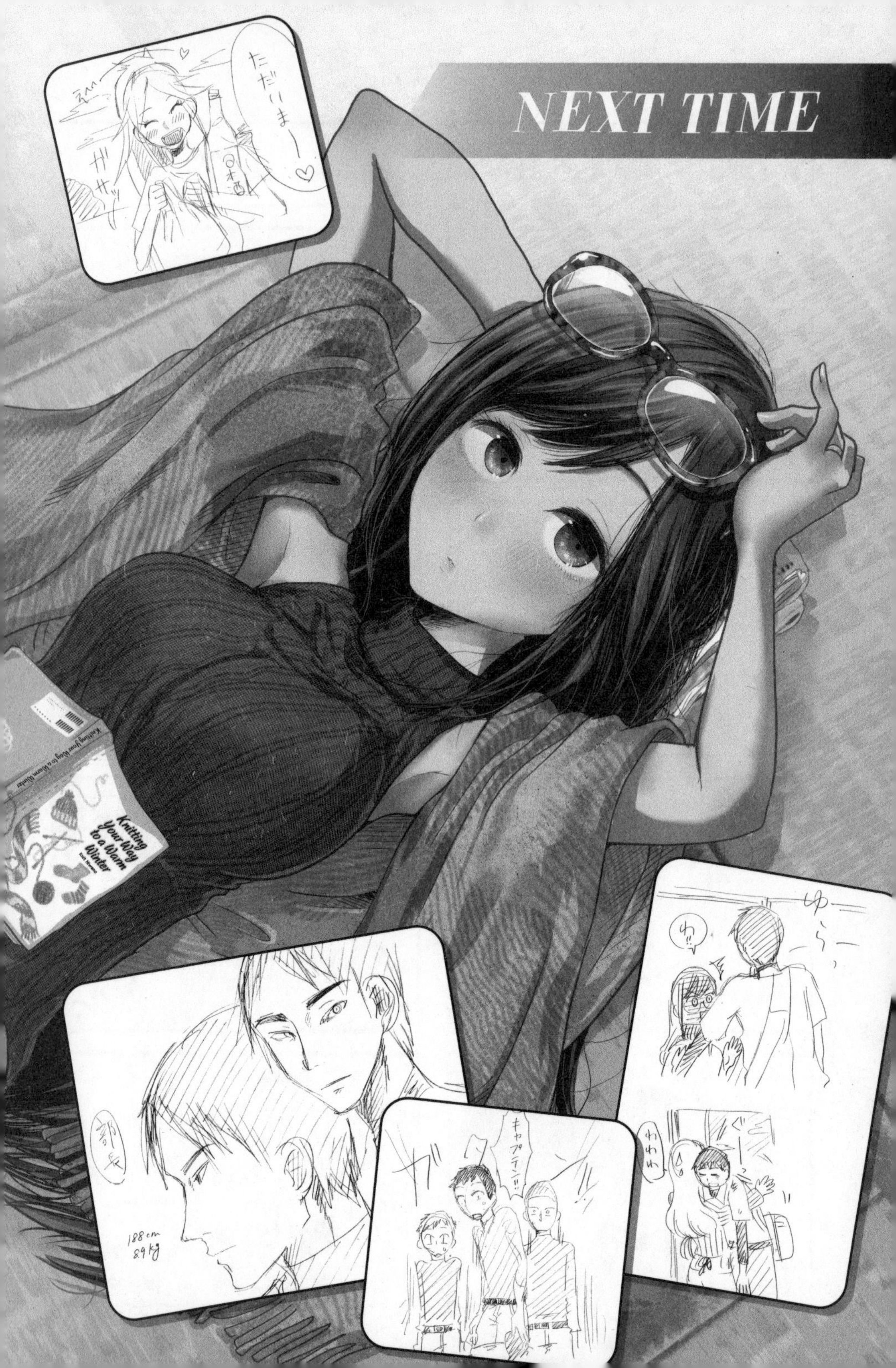
NEXT TIME
ただいまー♡
ガサッ
日本酒
Knitting Your Way to a Warm Winter
ゆらー
わ!!
わわわ
ぐー
キャプテン!!
部長
188cm
89kg

Beauty and the FEAST 3

Worried that her brother hasn't been keeping in touch, Yamato's little sister drops by his apartment, only to run into Shuko! But instead of a fight-or-flight response to being confronted with this girl who happens to look just like Yamato, Shuko's "feeding soul" goes into overdrive!!

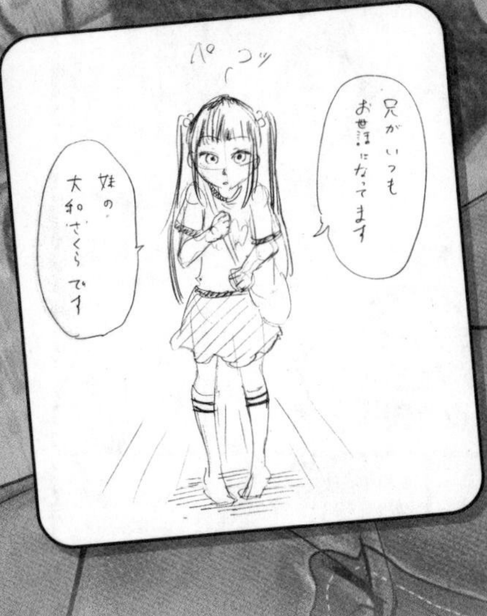
ペコッ
兄がいつも お世話になってます
妹の、大和さくら です

COMING SOON!!

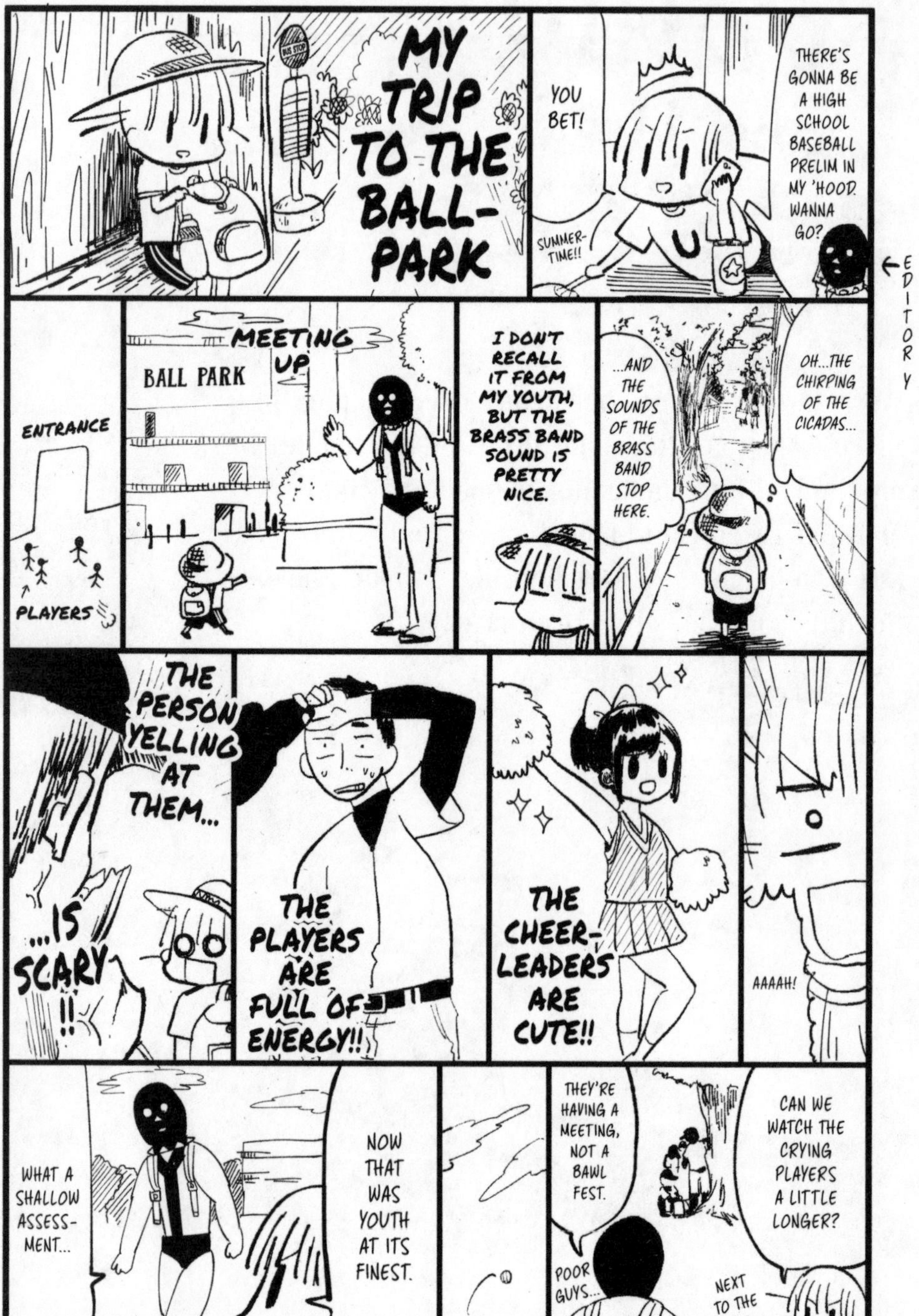
THERE'S GONNA BE A HIGH SCHOOL BASEBALL PRELIM IN MY 'HOOD. WANNA GO?
← EDITOR Y
YOU BET!
SUMMER-TIME!!
MY TRIP TO THE BALL-PARK
BUS STOP
OH...THE CHIRPING OF THE CICADAS...
...AND THE SOUNDS OF THE BRASS BAND STOP HERE.
I DON'T RECALL IT FROM MY YOUTH, BUT THE BRASS BAND SOUND IS PRETTY NICE.
MEETING UP
BALL PARK
ENTRANCE
PLAYERS
AAAAH!
THE CHEER-LEADERS ARE CUTE!!
THE PLAYERS ARE FULL OF ENERGY!!
THE PERSON YELLING AT THEM...
...IS SCARY!!
CAN WE WATCH THE CRYING PLAYERS A LITTLE LONGER?
NEXT TO THE TREE...
THEY'RE HAVING A MEETING, NOT A BAWL FEST.
POOR GUYS...
NOW THAT WAS YOUTH AT ITS FINEST.
WHAT A SHALLOW ASSESS-MENT...

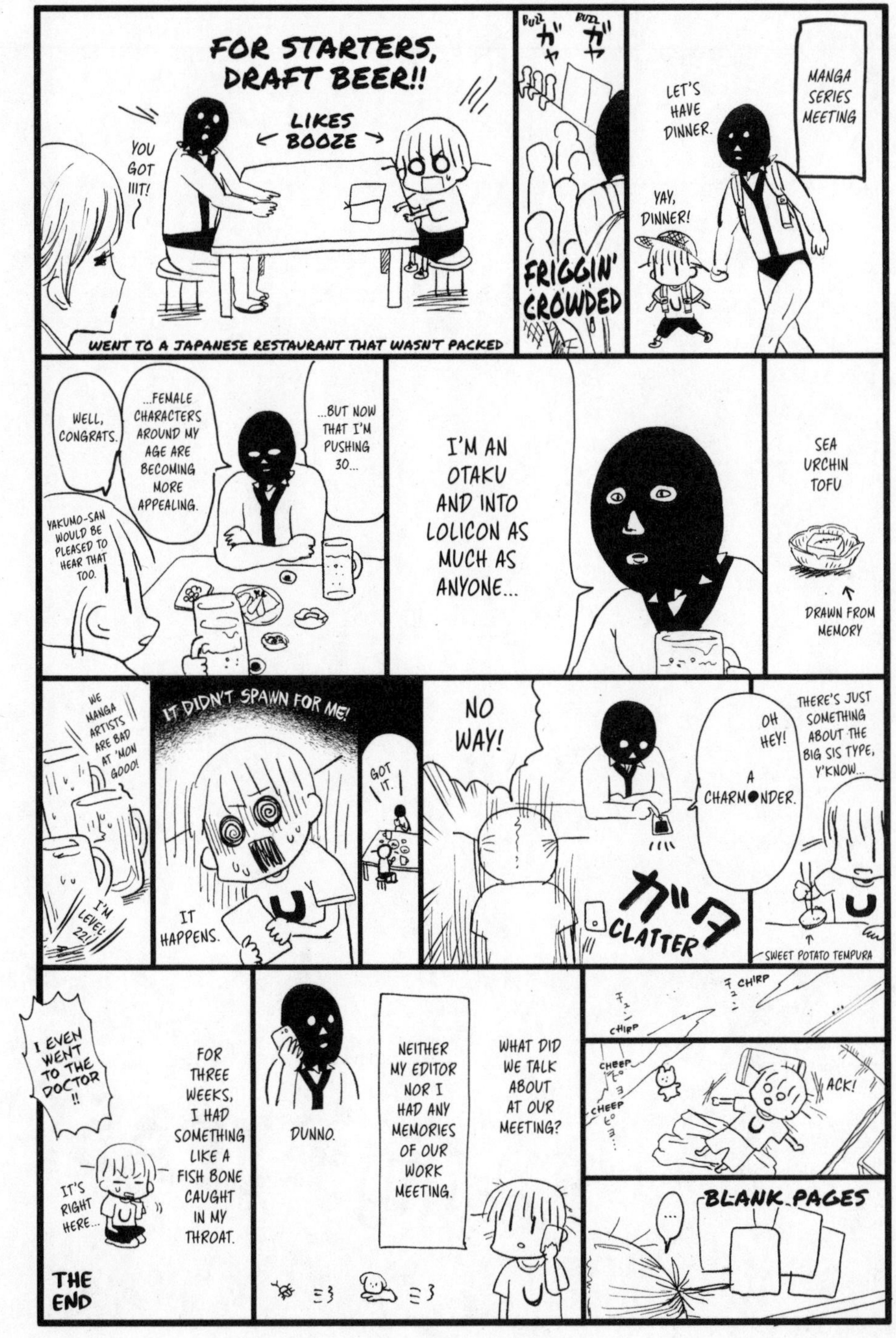
MANGA SERIES MEETING
LET'S HAVE DINNER.
YAY, DINNER!
BUZZ ガヤ
BUZZ ガヤ
FRIGGIN' CROWDED
FOR STARTERS, DRAFT BEER!!
LIKES BOOZE
YOU GOT IIIT!
WENT TO A JAPANESE RESTAURANT THAT WASN'T PACKED
SEA URCHIN TOFU
DRAWN FROM MEMORY
I'M AN OTAKU AND INTO LOLICON AS MUCH AS ANYONE...
...BUT NOW THAT I'M PUSHING 30...
...FEMALE CHARACTERS AROUND MY AGE ARE BECOMING MORE APPEALING.
WELL, CONGRATS.
YAKUMO-SAN WOULD BE PLEASED TO HEAR THAT TOO.
THERE'S JUST SOMETHING ABOUT THE BIG SIS TYPE, Y'KNOW...
SWEET POTATO TEMPURA
OH HEY!
A CHARMONDER.
NO WAY!
ガタ CLATTER
GOT IT.
IT DIDN'T SPAWN FOR ME!
IT HAPPENS.
WE MANGA ARTISTS ARE BAD AT 'MON GOOO!
I'M LEVEL 22!
チュン CHIRP
チュン CHIRP
...
CHEEP ピヨ
CHEEP ピヨ...
ACK!
BLANK PAGES
...
WHAT DID WE TALK ABOUT AT OUR MEETING?
NEITHER MY EDITOR NOR I HAD ANY MEMORIES OF OUR WORK MEETING.
DUNNO.
FOR THREE WEEKS, I HAD SOMETHING LIKE A FISH BONE CAUGHT IN MY THROAT.
I EVEN WENT TO THE DOCTOR!!
IT'S RIGHT HERE...
THE END

Beauty and the FEAST

Hamburger Steaks with Fried Eggs

Rice Balls, Fried Chicken, Salmon

Vienna Sausages, Sweet Rolled Omelets, and more!

Beauty and the FEAST

Beauty and the FEAST

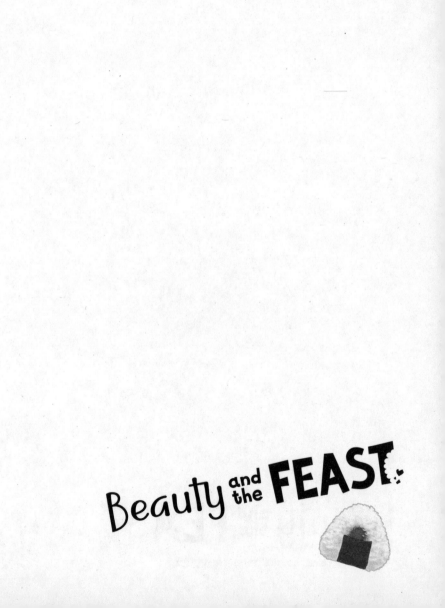